Screen Savers II

Also by John DiLeo

Tennessee Williams and Company:
His Essential Screen Actors (2010)

Screen Savers:
40 Remarkable Movies Awaiting Rediscovery (2007)

100 Great Film Performances You Should Remember—
But Probably Don't (2002)

And You Thought You Knew Classic Movies:
200 Quizzes for Golden Age Movie Lovers (1999)

Screen Savers II

My Grab Bag of Classic Movies

John DiLeo

H
P
G

HANSEN PUBLISHING GROUP

All photographs courtesy of Photofest.

Cover photograph: Katharine Hepburn and Cary Grant having some fun in *Holiday* (1938).

Hansen Publishing Group, LLC
302 Ryders Lane
East Brunswick, NJ 08816
http://hansenpublishing.com

Preface

The idea for this book came about when my publisher, Jon Hansen, suggested that I compile selected posts from my blog (screensaversmovies.com). I was very pleased about sharing this material with more readers, but the notion sparked additional thoughts. Why not add the ten never-published essays that we had decided not to include in my book *Screen Savers: 40 Remarkable Movies Awaiting Rediscovery* (2007)? And what about those 85 quizzes I had written after my movie quiz book, *And You Thought You Knew Classic Movies!* (1999), had already been published? If readers had enjoyed those books, perhaps they would be glad to know that these "lost episodes" existed. So, this book is partially a sequel to my first and third books.

John DiLeo

TABLE OF CONTENTS

Screen Savers II

Ten More Movies Awaiting Rediscovery

The ten unused *Screen Savers* essays had been excised for thematic reasons. I first conceived the book as being about fifty movies rather than forty. But, instead of devoting my final two chapters to specific genres (as in the eight preceding chapters), I decided to make the last two sections about individual artists, director Anthony Mann and actor Joel McCrea, with five films apiece representing why I held each man in such high esteem. My editor and I agreed to keep the book thematically cohesive, sticking only with the eight chapters (again, five films apiece) arranged by genres. Of course, I couldn't part completely with my Mann and McCrea material, so I found places for three of my Mann selections (*Devil's Doorway* in the "Westerns" chapter, and *Border Incident* and *The Tall Target* in the "Film Noir and Variations" chapter), while finding room for one of my McCrea picks (*Stars in My Crown* in the "Life and Times in America" chapter). This meant, of course, that four movies were deleted from those chapters, and also that six pieces about Mann or McCrea movies were left "on the cutting room floor."

Here, at last, are my essays about *Branded* (1950), which was originally intended for the "Westerns" chapter, followed by *Ivy* (1947) and *The Fallen Idol* (1948), both meant for the "Film Noir and Variations" chapter. Then come the two missing Anthony Mann films, *The Furies* (1950) and *The Far Country* (1955), both westerns. When reading about *The Furies*, you may realize that the opening and closing paragraphs did actually appear in *Screen Savers*, framing my *Devil's Doorway* offering. Here they are restored to their original placement.

The four McCrea films—*These Three* (1936), *Primrose Path* (1940), *The Palm Beach Story* (1942), and *Ride the High Country* (1962)—appear next. As presented now, the effect is very close to my original intention of taking the reader through an overview of McCrea's underappreciated career, with just one gap between *The Palm Beach Story* and *Ride the High Country* where *Stars in My Crown* would have appeared. Finally, you'll find my thoughts about *Two Family House* (2000), which would have been the most recent film included in *Screen Savers*. This was the film I cut from the "America" chapter to make room for *Stars in My Crown*.

JD

Branded (1950)
Hollywood's Little Big Man

To describe the very blond Alan Ladd as a limited screen actor is an understatement; he could be downright wooden. And yet, he was never quite a blank; *something* seems to be going on within him. His dispassionate demeanor implies depths he's concealing and loath to share, and it's rather compelling. The alertness in his seemingly sleepy blue eyes conveys not only his potential for cunning action but also allows for occasional hints of the vulnerability he guards so stalwartly. Therefore, any *open* expression by Ladd has the power to startle. If he actually goes so far as to smile, the sheer surprise of his face's mobility can strike viewers dumb. The issue of Ladd's abbreviated height (5' 4" or 5' 5") is always ignored rather than incorporated on-screen, unlike the treatment of other shortish male stars, such as James Cagney or Dustin Hoffman. You can't help wondering if Ladd is standing on a box now and then, or if all the tall actors are keeping their distance from him, but he manages to hold the screen by looking as if he doesn't care if anybody is watching him or not. That coolness made him a star when he played Raven, a sullen killer, in Paramount's *This Gun for Hire* (1942), a tight thriller that kicked off his memorable association with four-time co-star Veronica Lake. Audiences were fascinated and touched by Ladd's outcast Raven, in much the same way that Lake's character warmed up to him and tried to get beneath his hard-shelled alienation. But except for *Shane* (1953), in which director George Stevens mythologized him into an icon of heroism, Ladd didn't star in any real classics. *Branded* is a forgotten Technicolor western, released three years before *Shane* lionized him in the genre, but it's one of his more worthwhile pictures. Ladd has a role that takes advantage of the star-making anti-social stance that he brought to Raven. In the Texas-set *Branded,* Ladd's character is similarly messed up; he's a bad guy who doesn't know that there's any other way to live.

Choya (Ladd) is a gunfighter chosen by no-good Leffingwell (Robert Keith) to play a role in an elaborate scam he's concocted. Twenty-five years ago, a five-year-old boy was kidnapped from his wealthy family and never heard of again. Because of Choya's age and looks, Leffingwell is confident that he can

BRANDED: What happens when con man Alan Ladd develops feelings for his new "sister" Mona Freeman?

pass off the gunslinger as the long-lost son (and heir!) of the Lavery family. With a new tattoo identical to the lobster-shaped birthmark known to be on the boy's shoulder, Choya is ready to go. He gets work on the Lavery ranch and bides his time, waiting for the perfect moment to allow Mr. Lavery (Charles Bickford) to get a glance at his "birthmark." Lavery, his wife (Selena Royle), and their daughter, Ruth (Mona Freeman), gratefully accept Choya as Richard, Jr. Embraced by this loving family, Choya is increasingly uncomfortable, and he begins to experience self-loathing for his handiwork. (The plan was a good idea until it *worked*.) He's also falling in love with "sister" Ruth. Choya wants out, but Leffingwell isn't going to walk away from this gold mine without a fight.

Admittedly, there's an ordinariness about many of the scenes, but the movie soars on its humdinger of a plot. It could almost be a fairy tale by the Brothers Grimm, one in which a young prince is kidnapped and an impostor comes along to steal his place and assume his wealth and position. It plays stirringly as an identity-theft tale of the old West, with the ranch a mighty kingdom and Mr. Lavery Texan royalty. *Branded* is driven by the consistent emotional suspense regarding the Laverys' reactions to Choya, and, even more so, by his reactions to them. Stories of people flabbergasted by their unexpected affection

4

for their prey is a staple of the movies and, when done well, irresistible. (Think Jean Arthur in *Mr. Deeds Goes to Town,* or Charles Boyer in *Hold Back the Dawn,* or Johnny Depp in *Donnie Brasco,* to name but a few.) The moral issues raised are engrossing, and the transitions humanize the characters beyond our expectations. Ladd begins the film in his cardboard pose: the tough guy who's nobody's patsy. But then something is flung into Choya's path—confusion—and he's never the same. Unsettled by the family's love, his feelings for Ruth, and the extent of Leffingwell's evil, Choya becomes determined to move from bad guy to good guy, not an easy passage in a western (even though Ladd wears a white hat from the beginning). As this change is being effected by one of the most understated of movie stars, there's no danger of it turning sentimental or laughable; Ladd lets us come to him.

Branded begins in mid-action, providing a sense that the story being entered has been taking place all on its own, rather than waiting for the movie camera to cue it to begin. Choya, who has shot a man in self-defense, is trapped inside a store as men gather outside, on rooftops and behind wagons, to capture him. His hostage asks if he has any friends. Choya responds, "My guns." Any kinfolk? "My horse." And that's all you need to know about Choya. (The fact that "Choya" is an English spelling for the Spanish word for "cactus" is telling.) It's obvious that he's a formidable gunman by the number of men assembled to nab him. He escapes easily. In the first scenes with Leffingwell, in which the plan is broached and negotiated, Ladd exhibits the shrewd cynicism and dry delivery by which Choya operates. When two such shady characters come together, there can never be any real trust. And when a big movie star begins a film as a villain, it always helps to have a supporting character who's much *more* villainous. The star can therefore retain a certain likability by comparison. Choya doesn't know any better, whereas Leffingwell is true scum.

After trespassing onto the Lavery ranch and getting himself hired (through Ruth's infatuated intervention), Choya maintains a surly, troublemaking persona. His plan will play better if he doesn't seem to be trying to get anyone to like him. It's interesting that there's little difference between what he's acting and what he really is: Choya is an insolent loner pretending to be an insolent loner. A shirtless Choya calculatingly gets himself into a dusty brawl, first with Lavery, then with *all* the cowhands. The moment has come. When the men get hold of him, his "birthmark" is seen by Lavery. This does the trick, and Ladd punctuates the scene with victorious smirks that go unseen. Though Choya has been "acting" ornery and inaccessible, he'll soon be prone to such behavior once the Laverys envelop him with their stored-up love. After delivering his rehearsed "memory" of young Richard's rocking horse—the fact of which expunges any lingering doubt as to who he is—the first signs of his sickening discomfort with the plan's success are apparent. The Laverys' unceasing joy is hard to endure, especially for someone as unfamiliar with open, especially happy, emotion as Choya. Their love, of which he's undeserving, reminds him what a heel he is. Then there's the problem of his attraction to Ruth; the touch of her sisterly hand positively riles him.

For 25 years, Mr. Lavery has renewed the reward for his missing son; the horror of the boy's disappearance has not quelled one bit. Through Choya, the quarter-century nightmare is ended. As Lavery, Charles Bickford fills the screen with one of his granite-sturdy performances of strong men, like those in *The Song of Bernadette* (1943), *Johnny Belinda* (1948), and *The Big Country* (1958). When he speaks the lines about what it means to Lavery to know that his own flesh and blood (Choya) will take his rightful place on the ranch, it resonates with enormous pride and satisfaction. Bickford is also sensitive to Lavery's solicitous attention to his fragile wife, on whom the boy's loss took the greatest toll. The actor makes it stoically plain that it's been every bit as hard on Lavery, though he'll not let anyone see the hole in his heart. Later, when the situation is upturned once again, Bickford's unmitigated rage is balanced by palpable heartbreak.

The return of Leffingwell is unwelcome. Casting Robert Keith in this role, an actor associated with warm paternal types in films like *My Foolish Heart* (1949) and *Young at Heart* (1955), stimulates the movie. Leffingwell genuinely feels sorry for himself because none of his dastardly schemes have brought him the big pay-off. He is unaffected by the misery he's caused because he's incapable of seeing things from any perspective but his own. Tired of waiting in town, he shows up at the ranch. Choya suggests a less financially gainful compromise to their deal, one that will get Choya out of there as soon as possible. He can't stand them "staring at me every minute." The arrival of Leffingwell disturbs him further; revelations prove that Leffingwell is even more loathsome than suspected. Robert Keith gives Leffingwell an unctuous quality—when he's not feeling sorry for himself—that makes the character hard to dismiss. You keep hoping you've seen the last of him, but he keeps coming back.

The bond between Choya and Ruth is complicated. From her first glimpse of him, she's attracted to Choya. Later, she flirts with him, just another rich girl aroused by a handsome, rebellious bad-boy. Then she finds out that he's her brother. Choya, once he realizes his attraction to her, tries to steer clear of her, even though she now thinks only of him as a brother. Ladd makes more good use of his moodiness here. Since Choya's never been in love, he's ruffled. That the object of his affection thinks he's her brother, and doesn't know that he's a liar and a thief, only convolutes things further. The appearance of guilt in Choya and his desire to confess humanize him further. In Ruth, he sees both the possibility and impossibility of happiness for him. He loves her, but how can he ever deserve her after what he's done? His deepening feeling for her (and her parents) only exacerbates his self-contempt for what he's perpetrated. In El Paso, following their cattle drive, he starts to come clean with Ruth, wishing he had "someplace to crawl and hide." This thwarted love scene—love is the reason he can't tolerate another minute of this sham—is, of course, underplayed by Ladd, but even the slightest chink in his acting armor speaks volumes because it's such a rare occurrence. An ostensibly unknowable man (the character *and* the actor) comes that much closer to revealing himself. There isn't all that much chemistry between Ladd and Mona Freeman, nor are their characters' feelings for each other exactly unmistakable, but the romance still works as an effective subplot. Freeman, who had made a name for herself in *Dear Ruth* and *Mother Wore Tights,* two big hits from 1947, is spunky though a bit bland.

I'll not spoil the plot twists that occur from this point on, but an important addition to the cast is Joseph Calleia as Mateo Rubriz, a Mexican bandit. This chunk of the movie, in which Choya goes on a redemptive quest in Mexico, introduces other new characters and further complicates the issues of familial love and familial betrayal. Though these Mexican scenes are the least well-written in the film, and are an opportunity for a number of bad accents, Calleia is a dynamic and weighty presence with an eye-opening streak of vulnerability. This last portion of the movie also has the most action: a horse stampede, an extended chase, the crossing of the Rio Grande. But the film has veered from its emotional center once Choya leaves the Laverys. Sydney Boehm and Cyril Hume wrote the screenplay, based on the novel *Montana Rides!* by Evan Evans (a pseudonym for Max Brand). In the book, the Choya character, known alternately as Montana, the Kid, and El Keed, is big and black-haired rather than small and blond. Boehm later wrote the screenplay for *The Raid* (1954), another exceptional film that places a man (Van Heflin) in a struggle between his mission and his conscience. Within a plot of considerable chicanery, *Branded* surges with love and goodness. It may remind you of *The Searchers,* made six years later, another western that deals with the grief of a kidnapping and the hopes that endure.

Branded was directed by Rudolph Maté, who is primarily known as the great cinematographer of Carl Dreyer's *Passion of Joan of Arc* (1928) and Hollywood films such as *Foreign Correspondent* (1940), *Sahara* (1943), and *Gilda* (1946). As a director, where his work is far less distinguished, he's best known for the minor noir classic *D.O.A.* (1949). In *Branded* there's nothing as forward-looking, either visually or psychologically, as in the work being done by Anthony Mann in the genre at this time, and some of Maté's direction may seem a bit square, but he tells a fine story with speed, clarity, and unabashed emotion. Behind the camera for Maté was Charles B. Lang, Jr., who enhances the narrative with his eye for craggy landscapes and blue mountains.

Ladd, who, incidentally, had a bit part at the end of *Citizen Kane* (1941), later starred in *The Proud Rebel* and *The Badlanders*, two worthy post-*Shane* westerns from 1958, the latter a westernized remake of *The Asphalt Jungle*. If *Branded* was considered just another assignment on Ladd's Paramount contract at the time it was made, now it can be appreciated as one of his top vehicles rather than being branded a churned-out oater. Ladd, who died at age 50 in 1964, will always be remembered as Shane, the shining knight of the West, but his Choya deserves to share in some of that spotlight.

Ivy (1947)
Casting Against Type

Casting major stars against type is a surefire source of amusement at the movies. When this occurs in superior movies, the pleasure is twofold: there's the obvious satisfaction of seeing a good story well told, but also the surprising enhancement of the story due to the fresh, offbeat casting. When a tough guy like Edward G. Robinson, or a he-man like Gary Cooper, plays a comic nerd in, respectively, *The Whole Town's Talking* (1935) and *Ball of Fire* (1941), the fun doubles. Viewers can enjoy these winning comedies and, at the same time, share an inside joke as stars fool with their images. One of the longstanding staples of casting against type is putting beautiful women, sans makeup, into "plain" roles; think Olivia de Havilland becoming *The Heiress* (1949) and Grace Kelly *The Country Girl* (1954). Both were rewarded with the Best Actress Oscar for their deglamorized courage. Then there are the cases of light comedians exposing their dark sides: Fred MacMurray in *Double Indemnity* (1944), Dick Powell in *Murder, My Sweet* (1945), and Ray Milland in *The Lost Weekend* (1945). Of course, when daring casting backfires, then a bad movie seems even worse, as in the case of an un-macho, humorless Clark Gable playing the sickly title character in *Parnell* (1937).

But the most eye-catching kind of unexpected casting is when good girls go bad. *From Here to Eternity* (1953) cast not one but two "nice" girls to play its shady female leads: elegant Deborah Kerr as the cheating wife, and girl-next-door Donna Reed as a club's "hostess." In the decade before *Eternity*, quite a few "ladies" of the screen went in a bad-girl direction: poised Gene Tierney, fresh from being adored as *Laura* (1944), took the psycho-murderous route in *Leave Her to Heaven* (1945); saintly Jennifer Jones, blessed by Oscar for *The Song of Bernadette* (1943), couldn't control her lust for Gregory Peck in *Duel in the Sun* (1946); patrician Eleanor Parker, Warner Brothers' redheaded ingénue, became one tough cookie thanks to her prison stretch in *Caged* (1950); and little Miss Anne Baxter, the unfortunate Sophie of *The Razor's Edge* (1946), turned to steel for *All About Eve* (1950). Is anyone surprised that all these actresses garnered Oscar nominations for their bold transformations?

IVY: Joan Fontaine so exquisitely up to no good.

One of the most noteworthy, yet least known, examples of casting a good-girl actress as a villain was Universal's choice of Joan Fontaine for the title role in *Ivy*. After a promising turn as the only timid character in the all-female ensemble of *The Women* (1939), Fontaine came to deserved prominence when she starred in Alfred Hitchcock's *Rebecca* (1940). As the second Mrs. de Winter, she embodied shyness and insecurity so convincingly that she became both an Oscar nominee and a breakout star. For *Suspicion* (1941), another Hitchcock mystery, she played a similarly inexperienced young bride and this time won the year's Best Actress Oscar, though her performance was nowhere near as interesting or accomplished as her work in *Rebecca*. Fontaine was now the era's prime player of reticent, unassertive, though lovely and charming, women. Unsurprisingly, two films with time-tested roles of this sort soon came her way. In *The Constant Nymph* (1943), for which she received her third Oscar nomination in four years, she gives a warm, bewitching performance as a spirited teenager with a heart condition, but in *Jane Eyre* (1944) she's lifeless as the titular governess, sleepwalking through the entire movie.

By 1947, Fontaine was overdue to tackle something that would explode perceptions of her demure, and thus far limited, abilities. As Ivy Lexton, Fontaine plays an adventurer, an adulterer, and a murderer. She even frames an ex-lover for the murder she's committed. What's so intriguing about Fontaine's performance is that her Ivy doesn't behave all that differently—publicly any-way—from the characters that made Fontaine famous. Since Ivy feigns girl-ishness, tenderness, weakness, modesty, and fearfulness, Fontaine isn't far off the mark from her usual on-screen self. But this time those traits are a bag of tricks, a way to manipulate men and set devious plots into unsuspected mo-tion. Fontaine is so good at fooling people in *Ivy* that you may never look at *Rebecca* the same way again, perhaps wondering if the second Mrs. de Winter is *really* as sweet as she seems. Treacherous Ivy released Fontaine from the victimization of her early roles, and she gives a coolly calculating performance that helps make *Ivy* one of the more deliciously wicked films of its time.

In addition to Fontaine's casting, the other key force behind the film's quality is the teaming of producer William Cameron Menzies and director Sam Wood. Menzies, Hollywood's foremost "production designer"—having moved from the position of art director to being in charge of a film's overall look—had collaborated with Wood in that capacity on six movies, beginning in 1939 with *Gone With the Wind* (for which Wood directed some scenes). From the haunting black-and-white intensity of *Kings Row* (1942) to the open-air, Technicolor radiance of *For Whom the Bell Tolls* (1943), Wood and Menzies mounted sumptuous motion pictures. For *Ivy*, Menzies took on producing chores and Richard H. Riedel designed the sets, though Menzies' elaborate, yet refined, taste is ever present. *Ivy* is a visual feast, a film whose imagery is so unusual and unsettling that the physical production tells the story as vividly as the script and cast.

The plot of *Ivy* sounds like that of a film noir, with a femme fatale dangling three gullible men and resorting to murder and betrayal. It's noir all right, but it's *period* noir, an impeccably detailed picture set in Edwardian London, which makes its ruthless story all the more unseemly. (*So Evil My Love* [1948], starring Ray Milland and Ann Todd, is another good example of a period noir.) Gorgeous Ivy Lexton and her ineffectual husband of five years, Jervis (Richard Ney), have spent all his money and are now penniless, though they still move in high-society circles. Ivy has her avaricious eye on middle-aged millionaire Miles Rushworth (Herbert Marshall), even though she hasn't quite rid herself of Dr. Roger Gretorex (Patric Knowles), her current lover. In order to land Miles, Ivy must dispose of her husband. To this end, she steals poison from Roger's laboratory and systematically murders Jervis. When an autopsy discloses the poisoning, Ivy cleverly frames Roger for the murder. Enter Inspector Orpington (Sir Cedric Hardwicke), a shrewd crime solver in no rush to accept Roger's guilt.

Behind *Ivy*'s opening credits is a large urn; it metamorphoses into a skull just before the film begins. The tone has been set. The movie opens as Ivy, a blond white-gowned angel carrying a parasol, walks down a narrow residential lane. The sides of the street are peculiar; they are not parallel. A black cat crosses Ivy's path but she takes no notice. The strangely beautiful setting gets weirder once Ivy arrives at the home of a fortune-teller (Una O'Connor), complete with oddball male assistant at the harpsichord. There's a ravishing close-up of Fontaine, at the peak of her exceptional beauty, her face honeycombed by her hat's netting, as she sits waiting for O'Connor. From behind a curtain O'Connor appears, but only the top half of her face is visible. It's a scene of one macabre detail after another, practically black-comic in its heightened ghoulishness, yet so visually mesmerizing, who would dare giggle? The revelations that Ivy is headed for money and a new man make her impervious to her bizarre surroundings. As the close-ups alternate between Fontaine's lusciousness and O'Connor's severity, the characters never connect. Ivy is so self-absorbed, latching onto thoughts of her impending romance and good fortune, that she carelessly ignores the fortune-teller's accompanying warnings and ominous manner. O'Connor, best remembered for her dithery comic turns in *Bride of Frankenstein* (1935) and *The Adventures of Robin Hood* (1938), is formidable here, magnifying the Grand Guignol atmosphere.

Ivy sets her seductive eye on Miles at their first meeting. Fontaine displays considerable confidence in Ivy's ability to wheedle an array of men. None of her conquests can see the amoral hardness beneath her femininity because her "performance" is so smooth, so seemingly human. Yet the vulnerability in her smile is merely a mask. Husband Jervis never doubts her, lover Roger can't bear to be dumped by her, and Miles allows himself to be tempted, taking for granted his current lady, Bella (Molly Lamont). Usually in a picture like this, one of the men would be as rotten as the villainess, but here all three are predominantly decent fellows taken in by Ivy's lies. Fontaine shows no feeling for anybody, which is apt; Ivy is a user and she has no time for the used-up.

Miles invites Ivy and Jervis on a yachting party, thereby allowing Ivy to set her trap. Regarding Bella, Ivy tells Miles, "She's…charming." That slight pause is Fontaine's sly way of transmitting Ivy's contempt for her passive rival; it's also an almost subliminal way to belittle Bella for Miles' benefit. Fontaine bristles at every mention of this mild woman, merely for being what little obstacle she is. Ashore, Miles buys Ivy an expensive handbag with a cameo clasp that has a tiny secret compartment. Fontaine's smiles, as she watches him buy the bag, are privately triumphant: only material things can thrill Ivy. Later, alone aboard ship (except for the servants), they are to share dinner in his room. As a storm crashes and the lights go out, the two are silhouetted. They kiss. When he lights the lamp, the expression on Fontaine's face is victorious, and she's decidedly ready to offer him whatever he'd like. She's a seductress who somehow maintains an air of virginity. His honor gets the better of him; he'll not make love to another man's wife. Fontaine is every inch a rejected goddess as Ivy is dumbfounded by this setback. She must make herself single again.

Only in private moments can Ivy be believed; every public moment is an act. One such private scene occurs when Ivy, alone in Roger's lab, spots the bottle of poison. Trancelike, she moves toward it. In a stylized sequence, the lighting around her dims to darkness as she spoons the poison into her handbag's compartment. When she's finished, she comes out of her trance and the room's normal light returns. *Ivy* is no realistic portrait of a murderess; it's a film that uses voluptuous visuals to tell a larger-than-life melodrama. When she returns to her apartment, she speaks to Jervis, who is hidden from view; the camera faces the back of the black chair in which he sits. He's a disembodied voice, practically entombed already, until his arm and empty glass emerge when he asks for a brandy and soda. That empty glass is a chilling cue for the inevitable. Ivy obliges, of course, and the camera stays on the brandy and seltzer while, just out of sight, there's no doubt what she's doing to Jervis' drink. (In *Suspicion,* Fontaine feared poisoning from hubby Cary Grant; this time, she's fine with doling it out herself.)

Fontaine acutely clarifies that Ivy's nerves appear only when she's worried about whether or not she'll get away with something; she's never troubled by the diabolical actions themselves. She can be sorry that Jervis is dying a slow death—she bears him no malice and is even, in her way, rather fond of him—but she's certainly not sorry to see him go. Nerves kick in at the prospect of being caught. Fontaine has two effective eavesdropping scenes, both following Jervis' death. In the first, she listens to Inspector Orpington's interrogation of her maid. Fontaine moves from fear to confident pleasure as Ivy realizes how Roger's visit to Jervis' deathbed, and his incessant lovesick phone calls to her, can place a suspicion of murder upon him. In the second scene, at Roger's home, she overhears Orpington's discussion with Roger, savoring the fact that Roger has foolishly taken her damning advice about what to say, unknowingly signing his own death warrant. For all Ivy's despicability, the movie never tries to explain her. I mean that as a good thing; the character would be diminished if the film offered facile reasons for her evil. There's little motivation, aside from insatiable greed, to prompt her horrible behavior. No one has done her wrong; she's got nothing to avenge. Add to this the fact that she isn't likable, sympathetic, or redeemable. She's incapable of guilt, and she can't even be dismissed as crazy. But she surely is riveting.

In her own interview with Orpington, Ivy is, of course, the shattered widow. Fontaine plays the scene properly confused and defenseless (for Orpington's sake), but the character's moment-to-moment machinations are always readable on the actress' face. Cedric Hardwicke's Orpington is the only man who's a match for Ivy. Hardwicke, who retains his cool throughout, is an effortlessly commanding presence with a cagey intelligence. (He and Fontaine had played father and daughter in *Suspicion*.) Fontaine becomes increasingly frazzled as the film nears its end, edging closer to being the fragile creature Ivy has always pretended to be. In the bravura ending, a befittingly theatrical finish to a tale of extravagant corruption, Ivy goes to hell—if only in a metaphorical sense.

Based on the novel *The Story of Ivy* by Marie Belloc Lowndes (which is set in the 1920s), *Ivy*'s juicy screenplay was written by Charles Bennett, a frequent Hitchcock collaborator whose credits include *The 39 Steps* (1935) and *Foreign Correspondent* (1940). The duo of Wood and Menzies comes through with a picture that places opulence and gruesomeness side by side. Every awful thing that Ivy does is in the name of beauty: glittering gowns (by Orry-Kelly), enormous hats, jeweled handbags. Her accoutrements *are* the content of the film; they drive Ivy to commit reprehensible acts. Bad things happen in the name of pretty things. Russell Metty's black-and-white cinematography lavishes attention on Fontaine's bone structure in a way reminiscent of director Josef von Sternberg's worship of Marlene Dietrich. Metty also renders compositions of wondrous, breath-catching artifice, such as the first glimpse of Ivy on Miles' yacht, sitting with her feet up while reading a magazine, framed in an off-balance way by the curve of the deck and the stripes of the black-and-white canopy. There's also a striking exterior sequence in which Ivy fights off Roger's kisses at a ball as a fireworks display blazes all around them.

Miles is a smallish role, yet Herbert Marshall still manages to bring his consummate skills and grace to the part. Richard Ney, best known as Mrs. Miniver's oldest boy (and Greer Garson's real-life husband) is rightly dismissible as the forgettable Jervis, and Patric Knowles is dependable in the thankless role of Roger. The supporting actresses shine more brightly. Rosalind Ivan provides energy and humor as Ivy's maid, and Sara Allgood has reserves of good-heartedness as Roger's servant. Best of all is the august Lucile Watson as Roger's mother. Watson had played many strong, steadfast mothers, notably Norma Shearer's in *The Women* (1939), Robert Taylor's in *Waterloo Bridge* (1940), and Bette Davis' in *Watch on the Rhine* (1943). Always smart, often moving, this time she fights valiantly to save her innocent son's life.

There's even Fontaine's own mother, Lilian Fontaine, on hand as a society lady. Fontaine's sister, the more gifted Olivia de Havilland, was reportedly offered *Ivy* but turned it down. (Mom never appeared in a de Havilland film.)

Fontaine returned to glamour-conscious conniving as Christabel in Nicholas Ray's pulpy *Born to Be Bad* (1950), in which she made life miserable for, among others, Zachary Scott and Robert Ryan. Her acting in this film isn't as proficient as in *Ivy*; she can't seem to muster Christabel's imperative sexual hunger. Still, it is again perverse fun to see her behave so disgracefully, but much of the enjoyment of her casting comes from the fact that Joan Fontaine was definitely *not* born to be bad.

The Fallen Idol (1948)
The Butler Didn't Do It

D
irector Carol Reed and author-screenwriter Graham Greene were the
Englishmen behind *The Third Man* (1949), one of the screen's great
thrillers and a contender for the most beautiful black-and-white film
ever made. The film's reputation is secure, ever increasing, but a price has been
paid; it has overshadowed *The Fallen Idol*, the previous Reed-Greene collaboration, another great thriller and a once-ballyhooed work no longer as widely
known or valued as it once was. *The Third Man* dealt with such large issues as
ravaged post-war Europe and inhumanity for profit, whereas *The Fallen Idol*
tells a more intimate story primarily from the focus of an eight-year-old boy.
The film's enthralling suspense is heightened by dual and parallel realities:
what is actually happening, and what is perceived by the child to be happening, thus elevating a rudimentary domestic situation into an unusual and
insightful look into a child's mind. The boy becomes an unpredictable force
on the action because of his helpless inability to understand the adult world.

Phillipe (Bobby Henrey), the young son of the French ambassador, lives
in a palatial London embassy. When his father leaves for the weekend—to
retrieve the boy's mother after eight months of hospitalization—Phil is left in
the care of the butler, Baines (Ralph Richardson), whom he adores, and the
housekeeper, Mrs. Baines (Sonia Dresdel), whom he fears. Baines has fallen
in love with Julie (Michèle Morgan), an embassy typist, and seeks freedom
from his harsh wife. Phil can't quite put the pieces of the situation together,
while Mrs. Baines sets her trap for Baines and Julie. When an accidental death
occurs, Phil believes Baines to be guilty of murder yet tries hard to protect
him, though his help is a decided hindrance for all involved.

The Fallen Idol opens with a shot of Phillipe—familiarly called "Phil" by
Baines—crouched behind a third-floor railing, as though behind bars, looking
down on the massive embassy foyer. This geometrically varied main setting—a
mesmerizing expanse of checkerboard floor, a curving grand staircase—offers
much for a bored boy to observe. A blond moppet clad in short pants, little
Bobby Henrey evokes a storybook lad. Phil is the lonely offspring of a busy

THE FALLEN IDOL: A devoted friendship between young Bobby Henrey and butler Ralph Richardson.

father and an ailing mother, adrift in a palace without siblings or playmates. His two companions are his pet garden snake, MacGregor (whom he keeps behind a loose stone on a terrace) and Baines. Amid the activity of scurrying employees, only Baines notices Phil staring down. The film wordlessly establishes their bond as Baines slyly acknowledges Phil by performing amusing bits—notably an improvised dance step as he empties an ashtray into the fireplace—intended solely for the boy's delight. The humor, from a butler of all people, makes Ralph Richardson's Baines instantly likable and worthy of the boy's keen affection. The two have presumably come together in shared loneliness: a boy who doesn't remember his mother very well and who can't get closer than shouting distance of his father, and a husband trapped in lovelessness.

Carol Reed ingeniously devised shots from the boy's perspective throughout the film. Since the basic plot—unhappy man, shrewish wife, attractive lover—is deliberately simple, Reed can emphasize the child's viewpoint without endangering our ability to follow the action. Scenes between the adults are often played in long shot, establishing the boy's vantage point, and without the alternating close-ups that would allow subtler evaluations of the adults. Since there's never any doubt about what's happening, Reed can stress the boy's perspective freely. The story is experienced through Phil's eyes, and so the film is always clear about what the boy understands and what confuses him. Bobby Henrey is extraordinary in his yearning to master grown-up ways (especially the art of keeping secrets) and in his struggles with the complicated frustrations and pressures that result. Phil is bright, speaks English and French, but is simply too young to grasp the emotions engendered by a heated love triangle. It's fascinating to watch a film in which the main character hasn't a clue as to what's really going on. The omniscient viewer simultaneously absorbs Baines' story with Phil's distorted impressions.

Phil accurately grasps Mrs. Baines' cruelty. Reed first shows her in silhouette, establishing her as a shadowy, untrustworthy presence. Sonia Dresdel's dark, physically slight but hyper-intense Mrs. Baines is an electrifying portrayal of a woman scorned, and also a spooky-housekeeper turn to rival Judith Anderson's Mrs. Danvers of *Rebecca* (1940). Henrey, so beguiling in conveying Phil's loving warmth for Baines, is equally convincing in his terror of Mrs. Baines. After referring to MacGregor as "vermin," she locates his hiding place, then comes down the basement stairs carrying a small bundle. It is ironic that Phil apologizes to her for an earlier infraction at exactly the moment she places the concealed MacGregor into the incinerator. It's one of filmdom's more casually administered acts of senseless malice. Dresdel creates a figure of icy imperiousness, feared and loathed by her staff, severe with her husband, and physically abusive to Phil, the kind of person whose very entrance silences a room. She wears her bitterness offensively, perhaps a response to a husband who doesn't love her, perhaps because she is merely rotten. Believable in a portrait of one so unyielding, Dresdel's Mrs. Baines comes undone once her world shows signs of unraveling. Not as strong as she pretends, she becomes the film's unstable monster, stalking through the house with eyes ablaze in pursuit of vengeance. Dresdel never seems over the top because her mad rage is plausibly fueled by the character's fear, desperation, and outrage.

Phil follows Baines and locates him with Julie in a tea shop, but his experience of the moment is markedly different from theirs. For the boy, who enters shouting Baines' name, this is just another game with his treasured friend, but for the lovers it's the shock of being discovered together. Julie has decided to leave London because the relationship is hopeless, thus breaking Baines' heart. As Phil chows down on sweets, the couple speaks in whispers. Their words would be mere soap opera if played openly but, with the awkward presence of a listening child who is oblivious beyond sensing their overall gloom, it becomes a scene of coded remarks and aching restraint. The gentleness and sensitivity in Ralph Richardson's performance, in all his dealings with the boy, are admirable, even touching, and sustained throughout the film, even at such painful times for Baines. Later, Phil eavesdrops on Baines' confrontation with his wife, another scene observed entirely from the boy's view, this time from the top of the basement stairs. Baines speaks delicately of their mutual unhappiness, and his wife becomes angry, yet all Phil absorbs is a general feeling of conflict, not connecting it to Julie (whom he assumes is Baines' niece) or able to guess what it is Baines really wants. The Fallen Idol is about a boy in over his head, thrust into a situation beyond his comprehension. He's trying to master a world of secrets and lies, a world beyond his innocence.

Once Mrs. Baines stages her false exit (supposedly visiting an aunt), the film builds to its stunning centerpiece. When Phil, Baines, and Julie return from the zoo, they know the staff has the weekend off, but they don't know that Mrs. Baines is lurking within. In a tingling shot, Reed films the trio's arrival from inside the basement window, while a hand slips quickly into the frame to remove a hat and coat from the table, vanishing in an instant. They are unknowingly entering a haunted castle. After the threesome has dinner, the house becomes the setting for an uncommonly large-scale game of hide and seek. The sequence's accumulating force derives from the horror of knowing that a cheerful "scary" game is being played while an unseen madwoman is plotting real scares. The furnishings, draped in white sheets, are ghostly observers. As Phil races through the house and hides, things suddenly aren't what they appear: he confuses Mrs. Baines' skulking feet for Julie's, and Mrs. Baines' closing of a door is assumed by Baines and Julie to be Phil's action. For all his emphasis on relationships and subjectivity, Reed can also deliver a humdinger of a maniac-on-the-loose set piece, marked by the unbearable suspense of when Mrs. Baines will strike and when the others will discover just how frightening their game really is. The deranged Mrs. Baines in close-up is a terrifying sight, a moment brilliantly anticipated when a hairpin lands on Phil's pillow. Phil witnesses the showdown between husband and wife in segments, missing key parts of it whenever he scoots down the fire escape to move nearer the action (yet safely distanced from it, too). Naturally, the scene peaks at the grand staircase—Mrs. Baines definitely has a theatrical flair—and much of it is shot from Phil's far-off stance. With cunning editing, the film clarifies three separate experiences of the climax: what actually occurred; what Baines saw and assumes was the cause; and what Phil saw and misinterpreted as Baines' guilt. Neither saw what we saw or knows what we know.

In the film's showiest section outside the house, Phil, barefoot and in his pajamas, runs aimlessly into the night in response to what he saw. The sequence highlights Georges Périnal's depth-filled black-and-white photography, featuring gorgeous shafts of light from varying sources as Phil dashes across cobblestone streets and splashes through puddles before being confronted by a cop. The most telling aspect of the police-station scene is that Phil gravitates toward the streetwalker in custody (delightfully tarty Dora Bryan) and away from the kindly cops, aching for the maternal comfort long denied him.

The last part of the film shifts the suspense from the dispensing of revenge to the solving of a mystery, without getting bogged down in interrogative talk. There's a breathless moment when an incriminating telegram, turned by Phil into a paper airplane, is sent soaring above the checkerboard floor, its damaging weight belied by its leisurely buoyancy. Another choice visual occurs when the inspector (Denis O'Dea) faults Baines' testimony, while in plain view is the unsuspected location of the necessary evidence, making you want to shout at the screen. Plus there's the fact that we know Baines has a gun in a drawer. As Phil founders in his attempts to help the beloved surrogate father he believes to be guilty, Baines struggles with his own fears but never at the expense of the boy. Their relationship is the film's core, built honestly upon several tender scenes, such as one in which Baines soothingly consoles Phil after MacGregor's untimely death, or the times he enchants the boy (and provides some much-needed fantasy for himself) with his made-up tales of his life in Africa.

Reed's refined filmmaking tells this story splendidly, nurturing the Baines-Phil friendship, expanding our view of things with those shifts in points of view, dazzling the senses with bursts of cinematic invention and steadily escalating suspense. Based on his own short story, *The Basement Room* (1935), Graham Greene's screenplay combines some basic tools of thrillers—adultery, violence, death—with an imaginative, eye-opening glimpse into a child's psyche. The script is a multi-faceted reworking of the story, deepening the characters and relationships and shifting the emphasis. (In the story, Baines is guilty and Phil doesn't try to help him.) The movie's refreshing openness about Baines and Julie sleeping together reminds you that this isn't a Hollywood film. With welcome flourishes of light humor, such as Phil's mistaking the zoo's gated men's room for an animal exhibit, and final moments poignant in their cathartic gratification, *The Fallen Idol* is more than just a great thriller; it's a great movie.

Reed and Greene received Oscar nominations after *The Fallen Idol* was released in America in 1949. (Both lost to Joseph L. Mankiewicz for directing and writing *A Letter to Three Wives*.) Reed was cited as the year's best director by the New York Film Critics' Circle. Ralph Richardson was also nominated for a 1949 Oscar, but for his magnificent supporting performance in *The Heiress*, playing Olivia de Havilland's cold, resentful, and all-too-human father, a sublime contrast to his avuncular, sympathetic Baines. French Michèle Morgan, Jean Gabin's co-star in the fatalistically romantic *Port of Shadows* (1938), and also a Hollywood veteran of films like *Higher and Higher* (1943) and *Passage to Marseille* (1944), brings her lovely intelligence to Julie. French-born Bobby Henrey appeared in only one other film but his Phil ranks with the best child performances of the 1940s, a decade filled with exceptional work from kids. *The Fallen Idol's* supporting cast is rounded out by such reliable English actors as Jack Hawkins and Bernard Lee, both cast as detectives. Sonia Dresdel all but steals the show, and her character's relentless, obsessive drive is akin to the equally formidable Kathleen Byron's erotically explosive nun in *Black Narcissus* (1947).

Prior to *The Fallen Idol*, Carol Reed directed two other fine thrillers, the clever and comically inclined *Night Train to Munich* (1940), starring Rex Harrison, and the internationally acclaimed *Odd Man Out* (1947), starring James Mason. Reed, Greene, and Richardson reunited on *Our Man in Havana* (1960), a diverting comic intrigue starring Alec Guinness. Reed crowned his career with a Best Director Oscar for *Oliver!* (1968), one of the few meritorious movies among the mostly terrible 1960s screen adaptations of stage musicals. *Oliver!* may not constitute Reed's best work but, if Oscars are to be handed out, then the maker of *The Fallen Idol* and *The Third Man* should have one.

The Furies (1950)
Mann of the West

It's silver-screen serendipity when a working director seemingly stumbles upon the genre for which he was meant. Just imagine if Englishman James Whale hadn't been the director of Universal's *Frankenstein* (1931). Would he have had the opportunity to prove himself the greatest director of American horror films? (And would *Frankenstein* and *Bride of Frankenstein* have become screen classics without him?) Let's not even ponder the gaping hole in twentieth-century cinema if Alfred Hitchcock hadn't made *The Lodger* (1926) and, thereafter, dominated the suspense genre for the next fifty years. Thankfully, Howard Hawks, the man who directed *Scarface* (1932), got the chance to reveal his knockabout knack for screwball comedy with *Twentieth Century* (1934), leading to his even more delectable *Bringing Up Baby* (1938) and *His Girl Friday* (1940). And, after *Counsellor at Law* (1933), it was obvious that William Wyler was the man to see if you were going to bring a stage play to the screen, such as *The Little Foxes* (1941) and *The Heiress* (1949). Quite surprisingly, it was Hungarian-born Michael Curtiz who revitalized the adventure film when he made Errol Flynn a star in *Captain Blood* (1935). Curtiz and Flynn later collaborated on *The Adventures of Robin Hood* (1938), the adventure film of all adventure films. Perhaps the purest example of all is Anthony Mann and his singular association with the western. Mann left behind a body of work in the genre that rivals the best of John Ford. The picture that changed everything was *Winchester '73* (1950), which not only elevated Mann's art but gave moviegoers a new, edgy, more complicated James Stewart. Mann and Stewart made five westerns together and the best of them, *The Naked Spur* (1953) and *The Far Country* (1955), typify what came to be known as psychological westerns, character-driven pictures that shook up the good-guy/bad-guy genre with troubling gray areas, an alarming intensity of feeling, and percolating subtexts. Mann's westerns have more explicit emotions and disturbing undertones than most oaters, and his work, both with Stewart and others, helped make the 1950s the greatest decade for the screen western.

THE FURIES: Walter Huston caught in the middle between Judith Anderson, the new woman in his life, and Barbara Stanwyck, the daughter with whom he is un-healthily close.

Mann's second western was *The Furies*, made at Paramount and featuring an A-list cast playing some of the juiciest roles the genre had yet seen. Noted for its volatility, the suddenness of its violence, and its unmistakable strain of incest, *The Furies* is quite a show. It's a peak picture for most of its contributors, notably the best of Barbara Stanwyck's eleven westerns (not to mention her television series *The Big Valley*). *The Furies* makes short work of the genre's conventions and gives us something messier, something that truly bristles. Operatically extravagant, it's a film in which love and hate are so closely allied that they are barely distinguishable. After the opening credits, we read that what we are about to see is a "flaming page" in the history of the Southwest. Flaming is putting it mildly.

T. C. Jeffords (Walter Huston) is one of the most powerful men of the New Mexico territory of the 1870s, and his cattle ranch, The Furies, is a vast empire. A widower, T. C. has two grown children: a son, Clay (John Bromfield), who disapproves of his father, and a daughter, Vance (Stanwyck), who's every bit as shrewd and ruthless as T. C. himself. Vance is the obvious successor to T. C., but The Furies is in deep financial trouble, surviving thanks to a bank loan. Romantic entanglements create friction between Vance and T. C. She falls for gambling-joint owner Rip Darrow (Wendell Corey), the son of T. C.'s deceased—thanks to T. C.—enemy. Not long after Vance is humiliatingly dumped by Rip, T. C. brings Flo Burnett (Judith Anderson), a marriage-minded widow, to The Furies. Vance detests her instantly. (Both T. C. and Vance are able to spot their "rivals" for the scoundrels that they are.) The closeness once shared by father and daughter turns ugly (and violent), with Vance vowing to destroy T. C. and claim The Furies for herself.

In its central relationship, the one between father and daughter, *The Furies* has a *King Lear*-like grandeur, with T. C. a ruler on more fragile ground than he suspects, and Vance, in her devotion and cruelty, a composite of Lear's three daughters. She's first seen wearing one of her dead mother's old gowns, very much the lady of the house even though she's nothing like her soft, refined mother. Vance is all T. C., and no one else seems to exist for either of them. She's won his admiration by always standing up to him, and he's pleased to see himself reflected in her. But there's something creepy going on, more than just the strutting bravado of an ironfisted dynasty. Stanwyck makes it clear that Vance adores her daddy in an unhealthy way. She plays some of their scenes with a positively seductive smile, and their verbal sparring is nothing less than outright flirting. Stanwyck is alternately enticing and hard-boiled in order for Vance to sustain T. C.'s interest. She's both a stand-in for her mother (in her looks) and the fearless and headstrong son T. C. hoped for. When she kisses him, it's on the lips. She calls him "T. C." rather than "Daddy." When he wants his lower back scratched, it's she that he turns to (this is a ritual of theirs). The glittering necklace he gives her seems like a present for a lover (and they just happen to match Mama's earrings). Stanwyck glows from the beams of his favor, "turned on" if you will, and she can't be bothered to conceal it. The actress broadens Vance's strength and confidence under T. C.'s attentive, proud gaze. He, in turn, is sparked by the challenge of her smarts and toughness. The incestuous content here is suggestive (though you can't miss it), and it's played as instinct, openly and without embarrassment. There's simply nobody around who measures up to either of them. They know that they are the most exciting people in any room.

Walter Huston's T. C. is a life force of overpowering dimension. His macho exuberance permits him to envision himself an out-west Napoleon. No matter how cruelly or selfishly T. C. behaves, Huston gives him a grand, larger-than-life personality that appears to have gone a long way in excusing his worst actions. (Huston was able to play outsized characters without going over the top.) He also brings a refreshing dose of humor to the man, making him an often likable, even sympathetic, titan. Vance will have a devil of a time finding a man to compare with her daddy. Witness Huston proudly wielding T. C.'s prowess before an entranced Stanwyck. When they speak of a potential husband for Vance, it plays like a mating dance, each knowing there's no substitute for what they already share. The relationship is an odd one for the Hollywood of 1950, and it gives the film an extra kick. If T. C. and Vance are cut from the same cloth, then so are Huston and Stanwyck, both of the just-do-it, unvarnished school of acting. You can feel the mutual respect emanating from them as they play off each other.

T. C. is the only one who is man enough to stand up to Vance, so when Rip arrives and treats her like dirt she's a goner. She flaunts her interest in Rip before T. C., which only heightens the inappropriate feeling of a love triangle. It's not hard to figure out that Vance is attracted to Rip because he's as arrogant as T. C. Rip doesn't show up when he's expected; he slaps Vance around; he submerges her face in a basin of water. Vance respects anyone who can get the better of her (and, before now, who has?). Stanwyck's Vance is shaken by love, as she uncharacteristically and helplessly surrenders her upper hand. Being in love "puts a bit in my mouth," and she doesn't like it, though Rip's hard-to-get, uncaring nature only increases her ardor. When the relationship is suddenly over, Stanwyck reveals a Vance who's hardened by the experience yet forever softened by the realization of her own vulnerability.

If your widowed father brought home Judith Anderson, how would you feel? Stanwyck sensibly plays every encounter with Anderson with outright hostility. This is particularly enjoyable because Anderson's Flo won't be riled; instead, she overflows with implausibly maternal kindliness and feigned ignorance (while quietly plotting to take over). Flo is an ideal Anderson role, the prospective wicked stepmother decked out in finery, all polished charm and utterly untrustworthy. Vance and Flo have each other's number on first sight, and their casually bitchy exchanges provide an entertaining clash between Anderson's theatricality and Stanwyck's no-nonsense. The look on Stanwyck's face when Huston asks Anderson to scratch his back turns catty rivalry into all-out war. (In this movie, characters are often sideswiped, and sent reeling, by competitors they underestimated). Stanwyck's confident, superior smile all but vanishes, replaced by a mask of seething, immovable anger.

The Vance-Flo conflict explodes in the most memorable scene in the movie. Flo is drinking tea in the first Mrs. Jeffords' "preserved" room, imagining the moment when all this will be hers. Vance discovers her there, and their usual round of bitchery is halted by Flo's announcement that she's to wed T. C. (and redo this room). A stunned Vance walks to her mother's dressing table and absentmindedly picks up a pair of scissors. While speaking openly of herself as an "adventuress," Flo approaches Vance and places the scissors back on the table. T. C. interrupts, and it becomes clear that Flo has won, with Vance soon to be packed off to Europe (her consolation prize). Vance picks up the scissors from behind and, suddenly, flings them at Flo's face. Flo screams, and the bloody scissors fall to the floor after gashing her right eye. It's quite a scene for Stanwyck: she suggests a bereft little girl in the moments when she realizes she's lost T. C. *and* The Furies; she has a mad gleam in her eye when she hurls her weapon, an act of life-or-death desperation; and she exits in a daze, emotionally hollowed out. She slowly, obliviously descends the house's grand staircase, a chilling contrast to the servants rushing about in response to what she's done. Mann builds the tension of this sequence expertly (that first bit of business with the scissors is a clever tease). Because the scene begins in the combative but civilized manner of all the previous Vance-Flo scenes, there's nothing to lead you to expect the level of violence that will erupt, especially within the confines of an elegantly feminine bedroom. With sharp attention to his characters, Mann makes certain that the dramatic action, no matter how frenzied, is always grounded in recognizably human impulses. However bizarre, the scene feels nothing less than inevitable.

In retaliation, T. C. executes Juan Herrera (Gilbert Roland, in a rare good role), a squatter on the property and Vance's one true friend. After promising to let Juan and his family leave the land in peace, T. C. decides to hang him for horse-stealing because he knows it will devastate Vance. (In this movie, a genuine good guy like Juan doesn't stand a chance.) The scene unnerves because of its remarkable quiet and calm. Matter-of-factly, Huston utters, "Hang him." And you can't believe it's going to happen. (Instead of the shock of violence of the "scissors" scene, here Mann provides the sickening dread of knowing what's coming.) Juan doesn't put up a fight, and he asks Vance not to demean herself on his behalf. Set at dawn, the sequence is a fine example of Mann's evocative use of natural surroundings. With the characters silhouetted against the gray morning light, it already has the feeling of a funeral. Vance confronts T. C., each atop a horse. Spewing the character's hatred and her vow of vengeance, Stanwyck is all emotion, a thrillingly uncontained counterpoint to Gilbert Roland's dignified resignation.

The film shifts to Vance's revenge, in which she plots to buy up all of T. C.'s I.O.U.s and cause his financial ruin. Rip re-enters Vance's life at this point, but the best scene from this last part of the picture features T. C. and the now disfigured Flo. The unguarded honesty exhibited between a cunning tycoon and a fortune hunter is unexpected. Over a hotel-room supper, he confesses that he's broke and asks her for the money that he's lavished upon her. She admits how afraid she is that she might lose him now that she's irreparably scarred. Huston's sensitivity and directness are no surprise, so it's Anderson who's the revelation. (This was their third film together, following 1943's *Edge of Darkness* and 1945's *And Then There Were None*.) Restraint is not a word one usually associates with the actress who won fame as the floridly sinister Mrs. Danvers of *Rebecca* (1940), but that's exactly what she brings to this scene. To see the formidable Anderson as a creature fearing abandonment and loneliness makes for an unusually touching moment. It's a very well-written scene, allowing Flo to be sympathetic but also, justifiably, selfish and sensible. Yes, there's self-pity, but Anderson stays with you because of the candidness with which she voices Flo's realistic perceptions about her options.

Based on the novel by Niven Busch, *The Furies* has a reasonably faithful screenplay by Charles Schnee, co-writer of the beefy Howard Hawks western *Red River* (1948). Schnee later won an Oscar for his script of *The Bad and the Beautiful* (1952), which shares a flashy intensity with *The Furies*. Schnee certainly knew how to startle an audience with bursts of emotional and physical violence. (In Busch's book, the "scissors" scene is premeditated and not nearly as electrifying as in the film.) *The Furies* is a film about the lure of power, the need to maintain it, the sexual potency of those who have it, and the destructive qualities of those ruled by it. The novel, unsurprisingly, is more cold-blooded than the screenplay, which is marred by too much niceness near the end, presumably concessions so that there could be an ending with hope and redemption, but it's not exactly credible in light of all that has transpired. But there's no faulting the dark beauty of Victor Milner's Oscar-nominated black-and-white cinematography, in which every sky is a *dramatic* sky, and outdoor scenes exist in the netherworld of half-light, half-dark. There's very little brightness to be found in a story of such rottenness.

Stanwyck was past forty when she played Vance, yet she's remarkably convincing playing much younger. (Bette Davis, a year younger than Stanwyck, was playing Margo Channing in *All About Eve* that year.) Stanwyck is a blonde as Vance, and she looks far more attractive than she did when she blonded herself for *Double Indemnity* (1944). Her voice seems to get lower and lower as Vance's story gets rougher and rougher, until it's just about scraping the bottom. Whatever her Vance is feeling, it's always 100 percent. With her innate resiliency, Stanwyck excelled in hell-hath-no-*fury* roles, and *The Furies* turned out to be the last top-notch film of her extraordinary career. She shares one scene with character actress Beulah Bondi (as a banker's wife). They had been wonderful together a decade before in the exquisite *Remember the Night* (1940), the film that arguably contains Stanwyck's finest performance. *The*

Furies also furnishes Stanwyck with a brief yet unforgettable run-in, in Rip's office, with a tart who says, "I'm new in town, honey." To which Stanwyck replies, "Honey, you wouldn't be new anyplace."

This was Walter Huston's final film. He died in April of 1950, four months before *The Furies* was released. He had recently triumphed with an Oscar-winning turn as a veteran gold prospector in his son John's red-blooded adventure *The Treasure of the Sierra Madre* (1948), a performance that's not only a hoot but a multi-layered characterization. Huston's contribution to movies also endures in his superb recreation of his legendary stage performance in William Wyler's film *Dodsworth* (1936). Imagine how marvelous Huston would have been as James Tyrone in *Long Day's Journey Into Night*. Fittingly, the last line Huston spoke on the screen was T. C.'s "There'll never be another like me."

Unfortunately, Wendell Corey is miscast as Rip. Corey was a talented actor, but he was not a sexual presence, something Rip must be. And there's nothing really bad-boy about him; he doesn't have a flair for malice. Someone like Steve Cochran would have been terrific as Rip: sexy, nasty, and brash enough to stand up to Stanwyck. This was Corey's third Stanwyck picture, coming after *Sorry, Wrong Number* (1948) and *The File on Thelma Jordon* (1949). Finally, there's Blanche Yurka, in the small but pivotal role of Juan's mother. Yurka is best remembered for her volcanically terrifying Madame De Farge in *A Tale of Two Cities* (1935). She's pretty scary in *The Furies*, too, primarily spitting and shooting.

Anthony Mann was now at home in the genre that would demonstrate his immense skills as an astute director of text and actors, and a visual artist who used the American landscape for its awe-inspiring beauty and threatening turbulence. His propensity for exploring troubled psyches with probing depth and unshackled emotionality makes his film legacy very modern. How very fortunate for the western that it became Mann's medium in which to examine the human condition.

The Far Country (1955)
Mann's Reinvention of James Stewart

Y ou can't discuss director Anthony Mann's films, particularly his westerns, for very long without addressing his remarkable collaboration with James Stewart, the actor who became Mann's prime protagonist in his searching explorations of flawed humanity. Stewart had had a great success as a western star in *Destry Rides Again* (1939), a rowdy comedy that's still every bit as rip-roaringly entertaining as it was when released in that watershed movie year. It wasn't until 1950, when Stewart starred in Mann's *Winchester '73*, that he was back in an on-screen saddle. In no small part due to that film's success, westerns appeared to become Stewart's preferred form of expression thereafter. His association with Mann is as significant to his screen legacy as his partnerships with Frank Capra and Alfred Hitchcock. Stewart was simply one of Hollywood's great cowboys. At ease on horseback, and iconic in his all-American looks, he was thoroughly at home in tales of the West, as essential to the genre as John Wayne or Randolph Scott. The Stewart of Mann's westerns isn't the innocent nice-guy that the actor is usually identified as being (thanks to Capra). He was in his forties when he made these films; the characters' baggage of emotional scars and physical wear-and-tear has frayed his innocence. Mann's Stewart has a past that lingers troublingly over the present, and the results are some of the genre's most psychologically intricate characters.

After the acclaim and popularity of Universal's *Winchester '73*, which followed the titular rifle as it passed from hand to hand (sort of a *La Ronde* for the gun set), Stewart and Mann reunited on *Bend of the River* (1952), again at Universal, and *The Naked Spur* (1953) for MGM, the latter featuring Stewart's best performance in the genre in an emotionally raw, pressure cooker of a role. It's a terrific western, and so is their next one, *The Far Country*, back at Universal. These two films make a great double bill because Stewart's characters in them are so unlike each other. In *The Naked Spur*, he bares explicit feeling and vulnerability; in *The Far Country*, he keeps it all inside. Though they behave differently, both characters have been deeply bruised; both now operate cyni-

THE FAR COUNTRY: Inseparable pals James Stewart and Walter Brennan face a lawless wilderness.

cally; and both are in for a few surprises as to what the path to happiness really is. If the former film is a power struggle enacted by five wary characters in the middle of nowhere (the Colorado Rockies), the latter is an examination of an isolated individual and his resistance to the notion, and benefits, of community.

After driving his cattle from Wyoming to Seattle, Jeff Webster (Stewart) plans to sell his beef to the gold hunters of the Klondike. As he and his sidekick, Ben (Walter Brennan), get aboard the ship to Skagway, Alaska, Jeff is accused of murdering two of the men on his cattle drive but he eludes capture. In Skagway, he's jailed by Mr. Gannon (John McIntire), "the law," when Jeff's cattle interfere with a public hanging. The corrupt Gannon settles Jeff's fine by seizing the herd for himself. Hired by Ronda Castle (Ruth Roman), an attractive saloonkeeper, Jeff and Ben make their way into Canada, moving Ronda's supplies to Dawson, an up-and-coming camp of gold seekers, so that she can open a new saloon. Jeff decides to get in on the gold rush, buying a claim to share with Ben. Gannon's might spreads to Dawson as his thugs rob and kill those who try to leave with their newfound wealth. Jeff, who's more than handy with a gun, refuses the people's request to become their much-needed marshal, preferring his outsider status and lacking any interest in helping others. But things steadily worsen, and Jeff, following a personal loss, finally takes action.

Stewart's Jeff is emotionally distant right from the start. He's the kind of man you may not be comfortable approaching because everything about him says "stay away." Ready for a fight, he isn't surprised when one comes along. Stewart's even-keeled reactions when things go awry (the murder accusation; being jailed; losing his cattle) speak to Jeff's pessimistic view of the world: he expects people to wrong him, time and again. This is why Jeff has retreated from participating in any aspect of life except that from which he profits. He's a westernized version of Rhett Butler or *Casablanca*'s Rick, other self-reliant characters who state plainly that they put themselves above any cause. In situations where his help is needed and requested, Jeff's most frequent response is, "Why?" Stewart's readings of this word are chilling in their blunt, unembarrassed apathy. He seethes with anti-social bitterness whenever Jeff talks about himself or alludes to his past. In *The Naked Spur*, we learn of Stewart's character's unhappy past—while he was fighting in the Civil War, his fiancée sold his ranch and ran off with another man—but in *The Far Country* we don't discover the specific blows that have rendered Jeff so hard and unforgiving. He does make a fleeting reference to having trusted a woman, making it clear he won't ever again. Jeff intends never to be hurt or made vulnerable. Stewart arms himself against the other characters with an uncharacteristically closed-off, seemingly unreachable demeanor. He's disturbingly matter-of-fact in his selfish pursuits. He says that "thanks" is a term he seldom uses and that "nobody ever did anything for nothing." Most baldly of all, "I don't need other people. I don't need help. I can take care of me." Unapologetically, Stewart doesn't court audience sympathy, just as Jeff doesn't court the characters around him.

The exception in all of this is Ben, Jeff's old-timer sidekick. Ben embodies all the warmth and compassion that Jeff has numbed in himself. Walter Brennan, with his transparent heart and grizzled appeal, plays an old geezer who genuinely trusts and likes people. But Ben, in his wifely devotion to Jeff, is not your average business partner. He longs for the realization of his dream in which he and Jeff settle down on a ranch ("a very little house") in Utah. The tiny bell on Jeff's saddle (its ringing is his calling card) is a gift from Ben, intended for the entryway of their future home. Ben speaks of their having "been together a lot of years...it's been good, *real* good," revealing his tender attachment. He does the cooking and the washing, keeping house for Jeff and deferring to his wishes. Hardly a candidate for a tryst on Brokeback Mountain, Brennan comes off as asexual and naïve, oblivious to the idea of a gay subtext. Still, it strikes one as unusual to see a man pining for domestic bliss with another man within the confines of a 1955 western set in 1896.

(Brennan played a similar role in 1948's *Red River,* opposite John Wayne.) In any case, in their scenes together, Stewart can at least smile and feel secure in the companionship of the one earthling on whom Jeff can depend. Whenever Stewart lights Brennan's pipe, we're able to see flickers of the man Jeff used to be, someone able to connect with another person in an affectionate, relaxed manner. Otherwise, Stewart carries the tension of a man at war.

Considering the mood of the main character, it's interesting that the film develops into a love triangle between Jeff, saloon gal Ronda, and Renee (Corinne Calvet), a big-hearted French girl who's an unexpected presence here. Ronda is a beautiful, experienced woman, whereas Renee is a childlike tomboy. Ronda is a realist; Renee is an idealist. Ronda shares Jeff's world-weary attitude and selfish motivations, but Renee is perplexed by his indifferent, disengaged behavior. Though Jeff has lustful feelings for Ronda, and is friendly in a brotherly way to Renee, he never really enters the love triangle. He's too remote a presence to get close enough to either woman, while their feelings for him strengthen. Ruth Roman makes a sexy, throaty-voiced shady lady, and she raises Stewart's temperature noticeably. Their first encounter—when she hides him in her ship cabin—has them getting under her bed covers together, sharing a single bed after barely meeting. Later, she grabs and kisses him. Since she assists Gannon with his takeover of Dawson, her real feeling for Jeff is her one redeeming feature. Ronda has dimension in being both a crooked character and, ultimately, an unselfishly loving one. Calvet's Renee is another character who turns out to be more than expected. This French-accented life force is not the pest you suspect she'll be, based on her earliest scenes. Calvet is truly charming; her ingenuous presence is no fake, and she's a fresh addition to the frontier. (Renee keeps threatening to sing for Jeff, but, in a running gag, all her attempts are thwarted.) Neither Calvet nor Roman, both second-string (third-string?) Hollywood actresses of the 1950s, has ever been more effective.

As Gannon, top-hatted John McIntire (looking like a defrocked preacher) gives a masterful portrayal of an evil whose breadth is masked by his humor and slithering charm. Often smiling and joking, and always intelligent, McIntire embodies corruption with a casualness that unsettles. If Gannon wants something, he fixes the law to get it. He changes the rules to meet his appetites. But Gannon can't stomp over Jeff the way he can over everyone else. When Jeff offers him a sarcastic comeback when they first meet, Gannon laughingly replies, "I'm gonna like you." And if Jeff didn't get in his way, Gannon really would enjoy his company. However, Jeff and Ben steal their cattle back from Gannon and sell the herd to Ronda in her new Dawson digs. Soon after,

Gannon's villainy spreads across the Canadian border, taking advantage of the lawless wilderness that is Dawson. McIntire indelibly stamps the role of Gannon with a smirking depravity.

The contrast to Gannon and his henchmen is Dawson itself. Nothing more than a collection of shacks sitting in mud, Dawson is an almost-town peopled by a band of lovable eccentrics. These inhabitants give the film a welcome breeze of infectious good will. They include Hominy (Connie Gilchrist), who runs the hash house, and Grits (Kathleen Freeman), two full-figured pals. With their robust generosity and an openness similar to Ben's, Hominy and Grits are the life-affirming antithesis of Gannon's greed and Jeff's detachment. There's also a Sourdough, a Molasses, and other oddballs, all who've come to hit it rich, though some will stay to forge a town. Jeff keeps his distance from these people, but Ben becomes part of their circle. One of the more pleasurable scenes in the movie is when bedraggled Hominy, without mincing words, tells off glamour-queen Ronda as she makes her unwelcome arrival in Dawson. For Connie Gilchrist (Linda Darnell's mother in *A Letter to Three Wives* and *Auntie Mame*'s Nora Muldoon), it may be the top moment of her career. Hominy and her ragtag ensemble create a valued community, and their basic desire and need for civilization is no joke.

As Gannon kills more people and steals claims staked by others, Jeff finds it increasingly difficult to go his own way. As long as Jeff has been able to keep himself from feeling, he's been able to live his dispassionate life. He won't take sides, still believing that existing solely for himself is the only code to live by. He and Ben have unearthed a wealth of gold, and Jeff wants to depart without becoming embroiled in the local trouble. He wants no ties or responsibilities; he needs to keep *moving*. In the scene where the decent folks offer him the marshal job, he rebuffs them firmly with, "I'm not interested," and exits. His attempt at leaving Dawson (with Ben) leads to a bloody confrontation with Gannon's gunslingers, and it changes everything. With his shooting hand wounded and unusable, Jeff must wait for it to heal before he can act. As soon as he's fit, we'll get the showdown we're waiting for. The movie generates considerable suspense in simply waiting for a hand to heal. Jeff's arm is in a sling, and he stares at it impatiently. Then one day in his cabin, in a stirring moment, he removes his sling, stretches his fingers, puts on his gun belt, and then caresses his holster. The anticipation is heightened by the question of whether or not Jeff is really ready or merely can't wait another minute to confront Gannon and his men. Dramatically, it's richly satisfying to see Stewart move closer and closer to reclaiming Jeff's involvement in the world around him. Building on an already tense situation, the bell on Jeff's saddle becomes a key component in the excitingly filmed climax; it's a gentle prelude to the violence about to erupt.

Partially filmed in the Jasper National Park in Alberta, *The Far Country* doesn't look like just any western. Photographed in Technicolor by William Daniels, the outdoor sequences, particularly those on the journey from Skagway to Dawson (including an avalanche), have a majestic, awe-inspiring beauty. As the travelers make their way, the screen is just about split horizontally: the top half has blindingly white, snow-covered mountains set against a baby-blue sky; the bottom half is bathed in the warm browns and greens of the earth.

Borden Chase, the fellow who co-wrote *Winchester '73* and wrote *Bend of the River* for Mann, and co-wrote Howard Hawks' grand (though uneven) *Red River* (1948), penned *The Far Country*'s story and screenplay. His script depicts the world as a mean, brutal, stinking place, yet it's equally convincing at portraying hope and optimism. I like the way Chase lets things unfold. Events are mentioned, but the details get filled in later on—as in what really happened regarding Jeff's murder charge—and we're compelled to follow the threads and piece them together. Chase's restraint in dealing with Jeff's past is to be commended, as is his offbeat approach to a love triangle. But it's Jeff's gradual transition from isolation to community that is the percolating force that drives the screenplay.

Anthony Mann's compositions—such as the one in which Brennan speaks facing forward while, high up and in the distance, a posse on horseback sneaks into the frame and starts shooting—have a visceral yet unforced power that can be admired simultaneously for their formal beauty and rattling intensity. The West is always a realistic place in Mann's films, a place that continually challenges and tests all who inhabit it. In this authentic atmosphere, Mann probes Jeff's disquieting darkness and Dawson's painful yearning for civilization, creating a first-rate western drama whose weightiness is deceptive because its effects are achieved in such a natural fashion.

I'm not a fan of the three nonwestern Mann-Stewart collaborations *(Thunder Bay, The Glenn Miller Story,* and *Strategic Air Command)*, but their fifth and final western, *The Man from Laramie* (1955), made for Columbia, is another fine piece of work. It's the one that has Stewart memorably lassoed and dragged through a campfire, but, emotionally speaking, Stewart had been dragged through many a campfire in his Mann westerns, a quintet that stands as one of the best things ever to happen to the genre. Add *The Furies* and *Devil's Doorway* (1950) to this line-up, plus Mann's later westerns, *The Tin Star* (1957) and *Man of the West* (1958), and you've got an astonishing directorial track record out West.

Mann died at age 60 in 1967 from a heart attack during the production of *A Dandy in Aspic,* a spy picture he was directing. The film's star, Laurence Harvey, replaced Mann at the helm. Repeat watchers of popular Mann films like *Winchester '73* and *The Glenn Miller Story* may not be conscious of who directed them, but I'm hopeful that Mann's name will become steadily more familiar to those who care about movies. In the summer of 2004, the Walter Reade Theater at Lincoln Center in New York City had a 25-film retrospective devoted to Mann's work. I can only presume that there were hundreds of movie fans present who now count Anthony Mann as one of their all-time favorite filmmakers.

These Three (1936)
Triumph Over Censorship

Joel McCrea was a born film actor, not merely a natural on the screen (though few others could compete with him on that score) but someone who used his ease to reflect the human experience with depth, brains, and humor. There was nothing larger than life about McCrea, but that was okay because there was plenty for him to explore within the confines of recognizable, ordinary characters. Film actors who shared his gift at a comparable skill level, men like Henry Fonda and Spencer Tracy, became much bigger stars than McCrea. The same is true of Gary Cooper, the actor whose masculine, outdoor persona was closest to McCrea's own. (McCrea's roles often looked suspiciously like Gary Cooper's cast-offs.) It would be hard to imagine a more unselfish movie actor; McCrea always projected that he was more interested in his fellow actors and the overall movie than he was in himself, resulting in a string of understated, authentic performances in which you cannot ever catch him "acting." This lack of on-screen ego is what makes him such an attractive, unglamorized, and seemingly modern presence. Even in his most famous movies, *Dead End* (1937) and *Sullivan's Travels* (1941), he was under-appreciated. People tend to remember Humphrey Bogart and the Dead End Kids in the former and Preston Sturges' writing and direction of the latter, but McCrea's unassuming style contributes indelibly to both films; *Sullivan's Travels,* especially, wouldn't be the classic it is without him. McCrea is often mentioned in the same breath with white-bread Randolph Scott since both eventually became synonymous with westerns, but this is ridiculous. Able and likable as Scott was, he was nowhere near McCrea as an actor. McCrea distinguished himself in many genres, but his approach was always the same: give it everything you've got but never give it *too* much.

Raised in and around Hollywood, McCrea haunted movie locations as a kid. In silents, he came through the ranks as an extra and stunt man. His all-American good looks and tall build got him noticed in early talkies, such as Cecil B. DeMille's *Dynamite* (1929). He was the golden-boy hunk in adventures like *Bird of Paradise* (1932) and *The Most Dangerous Game* (1932),

THESE THREE: The titular trio: Merle Oberon, Joel McCrea, Miriam Hopkins.

and four Constance Bennett melodramas. But his instinctive way of infusing dialogue with spontaneity, his subdued sexuality, and his relaxed good humor made him stand out among the throngs of handsome, romantic-lead wannabes overpopulating Hollywood. His break came in working with director William Wyler on *These Three,* a film that significantly bolstered both their careers. Wyler was one of the all-time great directors of actors, and it makes sense that he would respond to McCrea's talent for truthfulness and economy. *These Three* stars Miriam Hopkins and Merle Oberon, both of whom are billed above the title, whereas McCrea is billed below it. But he'd be getting the star billing he deserved before too long.

These Three is an adaptation of Lillian Hellman's play *The Children's Hour,* a 1934 Broadway sensation. Hellman put lesbianism at the center of her play, meaning there was no way it could be brought to the screen intact, if at all. The playwright herself replaced the lesbian theme with a heterosexual love triangle, and the film became a critical and commercial success. Still, the film has often been shunted aside as mere bowdlerization, a casualty of censor-ridden Hollywood, and a shadow of Hellman's original intentions. Obviously, Wyler felt this way, too, to some extent, since he remade the movie, with its original title, in the more lenient sexual climate of 1961. The irony is that the remake proved nowhere near as effective as *These Three,* and the result was a shrill, ponderous drama. Even with Audrey Hepburn, Shirley MacLaine, and James Garner as "these three," *The Children's Hour* was no more than an earnest, honorable mediocrity. This only reinforced what should have been apparent in 1936: that the juice of Hellman's drama is derived from the destructive force of a lie, be it about lesbian sex or "straight" infidelity. Her play is a ferocious melodrama, and Wyler's first screen version treated it as such, rather than with the grave "serious picture" drabness that marred his remake. The play is, first and foremost, a piece of 1930s theatre, and though the 1961 film is true to its text (though Hellman did not write the screenplay), I'd argue that *These Three* is truer to its spirit by capturing the energy and drive of what compelling drama meant at that time. *These Three* is a superbly wrought, straightforward 1930s drama, rivetingly paced, highly emotional, and both moving and bracing. Its soap-opera aspects are tempered by Wyler's knack for getting his players to dig deeper than usual (a skill nowhere apparent in his remake). To give you an idea of just how frightened Hollywood was of this notorious material (even "cleaned up"), not only was the title changed (and weakened) but the credits read "Original Story and Screen Play by Lillian Hellman." Not even a mention that the film is based on a famous contemporary play.

College mates Martha Dobie (Hopkins) and Karen Wright (Oberon) graduate and decide to open a girls' boarding school in a New England farmhouse inherited by Karen. During the renovation of the property, Karen becomes romantically linked to Dr. Joe Cardin (McCrea), but Martha, too, harbors love for Joe, though she keeps her feelings secret. The school is a success until Mary Tilford (12-year-old Bonita Granville), a vicious, spoiled-rotten student, foments trouble by lying to her wealthy grandmother (formidable Alma Kruger) that Martha and Joe are carrying on inside the school, behind Karen's back. Scandal erupts, and the school closes. Not only are their reputations ruined, but the crisis puts the future of Karen and Joe in jeopardy and places Martha in the wretched position of feeling guilt-ridden over her ardent feelings for Joe, even though she never acted on them.

As Karen and Martha wander together through clusters of graduates and their families at their commencement ceremony—removed from the excitement around them—Wyler has defined them in purely visual terms. Without family ties, they are united by solitariness and the resulting freedom to chart their own courses. They have no one but each other, really, and their friendship is a joint source of strength. Proof of Wyler's incisive handling of stars is evidenced from the fine work turned in by Miriam Hopkins and Merle Oberon. Hopkins, a waning star, had an ostentatious tendency to overact, and wet-eyed Oberon, a rising star, had limited talent. (A favorite Oberon moment of mine comes in 1943's *Stage Door Canteen,* when her veddy British speech manages to make *steadfastness* sound like a one-syllable word.) Under Wyler's guidance here, rarely has either been more persuasive. Hopkins shows notable restraint throughout, delicately suggesting her private feelings for Joe, and porcelain-beauty Oberon appears to have much more going on inside her than usual, especially as her doubts about Joe and Martha taunt her. These are focused, thoughtful portrayals. But, good as they are, they are outclassed by McCrea's confidence and candor. The film works only if we can believe that both women could be smitten with this guy. In his first scene, in which the women discover him on their arrival at the ramshackle farmhouse, it's clear that he's smart, affable, and sexy. No problem accepting their infatuations. The true bond between the three of them is established in this easygoing scene.

McCrea is introduced in beekeeper netting, tending to the roof of Karen's house, a place that has become something of a hobby of Joe's when free of the hospital's demands. The women take him for insane, especially after he says he's "from the hospital." One of the key reasons this heated drama is never strident or wearisome (like the 1961 film) is that Wyler and Hellman incorporate many light scenes that provide necessary balance. Instead of diminishing the film's impact, these airy scenes deepen our identifications with the characters and allow the film's later intensity to stand in more striking contrast. McCrea was years from coming into his own as a master of light comedy, but his obvious gift is on full display in the scene in which Joe tells Karen that he loves her. He tries wooing her at an amusement park, but she's more interested in riding the merry-go-round. When he finally gets his chance, McCrea is a surprise and a delight *shouting* how much he loves her. The actor's mix of humorous anger and tender feeling makes the scene, and McCrea, irresistible. Earlier, at the side of a country road, he impulsively kissed the back of her head. He says he was just taking a splinter out of her hair, but she knows what it was, and their romance is winningly sparked.

Martha's feeling for Joe is revealed in his second scene. As he approaches the doorway, and she hears his voice, she quickly removes her eyeglasses. Hopkins never has to say a word. Martha's love for Joe is there in her face ever after, most explicit in a private scene in which she gazes down upon a sleeping Joe and gently touches him, and then sits and stares some more. When he wakes, his arm accidentally sends a glass of milk shattering to the floor, and it's a shocking mood breaker, a foreshadowing of what's to emerge from this placid world.

Martha does have one relation, her Aunt Lily (Catharine Doucet), a selfish, manipulating stage actress who raised her—if you can call it that. Every time Doucet enters a scene, watch Hopkins tighten and her face go ashen, immediately evoking the pain of Martha's unloved childhood, on the road with stock companies and waiting on her diva aunt. (She tells Joe about those years, and Hopkins delivers this speech about Martha's lonely past with a refreshing lack of self-pity.) Doucet's Lily is a toxic Auntie Mame. She's grand and colorful, but she's base and cruel and a user, relying on her whirlwind of theatrical wiles to finesse people, especially her niece, into doing as she wants. Lily is reluctantly taken on as the school's elocution teacher. Talking about her craft, Lily says, "Pity makes the actress." Luckily, Doucet doesn't follow that advice. She pulls no punches, rendering Lily in all her spotlight-hogging unpleasantness, her monstrous self-centeredness, her smoke-and-mirrors charm, and her irritating chatter. She's a useless, frivolous person, but she's also dangerous. Most disturbing is the emotional abuse she aims so skillfully at Martha, which speaks to the years of practice she's had. Once she figures out that Martha loves Joe, Lily unsympathetically rubs it in her face. Hopkins registers the sobering realization that people can actually *see* Martha's love for Joe, and it catches her touchingly off-guard. She flashes an angry, worn-thin desperation to be rid of her aunt. Through Doucet's discerning work, it's clear that Lily must keep Martha in a state of low self-esteem so that she can continue to dominate her (and have the young woman continue to take care of her financially). In a delicious switch, it was Hopkins who, 25 years later, played Lily in the remake, but she's a huge disappointment. Oh, she's annoying enough for the part, but she lacks the stylish cunning to pull off a grand dame like Lily. Playing the other half of her 1936 scenes, I wish she had remembered what the far superior Catharine Doucet had brought to the role and stolen it. Instead, she gave a distracted, colorless performance.

Wyler does amazing things with the young actresses playing the students. There's a nicely self-possessed turn by Carmencita Johnson as Evelyn, a sharp, no-baloney kid, but the two main roles are doozies: bad-seed Mary and her victim Rosalie. Bonita Granville's Mary and Marcia Mae Jones' Rosalie are two of the most fully realized child performances of the period. Mary has just been pulled from one school (the details aren't revealed), and so Karen and Martha's new school opens at an opportune moment. Mary comes to dislike both women because she cannot manipulate them. They see through her incessant lying and punish her accordingly. If you're not *with* the paranoid Mary, then you're the enemy. She functions best in the presence of her doting, soft-touch grandmother, or an easily flattered woman like Lily, or a timid classmate like Rosalie. Wyler enhances Granville's ability to scare the hell out of you by having her enter scenes half-seen: first, she's partially concealed behind her grandmother in a car's backseat; later, she peeks through the window of the class she's late for, and her face is somewhat masked by a curtain. Most memorable of all is the sight of her after a confrontation between Martha and Lily. The camera records Hopkins crying on a chair and then pans down the hall to an eavesdropping Mary (a long shot, soon followed by a close-up), tucked in an alcove, her face chillingly half-hidden. Later, Mary gets her idea to use what she saw and overheard that night to blast the school wide open, and, in a crystal-clear example of visual storytelling, Wyler conveys this by having her go back to the hall and filming her in the same long shot and close shot of the earlier scene. In recreating those visuals, there can be no doubt what she's thinking.

You can get away with a lot when playing a role like Mary because the character is always self-dramatizing, and it doesn't detract if you can see right through her. Of her lying skills, she says, "I can always do it better on the spur of the moment." She screams, throws tantrums, faints, feigns pain, and is particularly schizophrenic around her grandmother, alternating with lightning speed between hysteria, coy helplessness, and lovey-dovey girlishness. It's a maniacal display of on-off histrionics, unstoppable until she gets what she wants. Steely Granville, a real trouper, is even good enough to make you feel Mary's contempt for her victims' susceptibility. She's so horrifyingly precocious that you expect her to light a cigarette or down a whiskey. Watching emotional and physical rage emitted from a child gives the film a significant amount of its potency. Mary surpasses herself in terrorizing poor Rosalie, blackmailing her—Mary knows that Rosalie stole another girl's gold bracelet—and forcing her to take an oath that she'll do *whatever* Mary asks. As Jones cries through her taking of the oath, Wyler moves closely in on Granville's coolly triumphant face. When Rosalie confronts the scandal's victimized threesome, she, at Mary's behest, lies that she saw things between Joe and Martha, without even understanding what she's saying. Cherub-faced Jones plays this false admission with screams that are as heartbreakingly poignant as they are blood-curdling. You may recall Jones from two of Shirley Temple's prime vehicles, *Heidi* (1937) and *The Little Princess* (1939) but she was never better than as Rosalie. Granville, who would soon star in a series of Nancy Drew pictures, developed into an appalling actress, profoundly terrible as a German peasant girl in *The Mortal Storm* (1940), even unsympathetic when being tortured in *Hitler's Children* (1943). But, as Mary Tilford, no one could touch her for pint-sized evil and sadism.

Through the ordeal that follows, Hopkins and Oberon display reserves of pride and dignity, and McCrea comes through with unwavering love and sturdiness. They may stand together stalwartly but their vulnerability is increasingly visible. The tribulations harden the ladies; a toll is taken. (There's a beautiful shot of them in their sitting room, with strange, vertically moving circles of light that turn out to be—once it's clear that the camera is outside—raindrops sliding down their window.) Joe remains a rock. McCrea is incapable of being melodramatic, and he gently professes Joe's sustained love to Karen as her doubts mount. If not for McCrea's exquisitely naturalistic line readings, and his utter directness, Joe might seem too good to be true. In the play and 1961 film, he has Karen's predicament, wondering if there's any truth to the rumors (the ones about *Karen* and Martha.) In a telling through-line regarding his insight and decency, Joe sees fraud in both Lily and Mary from the first. He stuns Lily with sarcasm rather than deference, even nicknaming her "the duchess," and feigns fear of Mary by lurching back when she passes. Joe isn't impressed by theatrics, and he can spot phonies.

The climactic scene between the women—the one we've been waiting for—is, again, marked by admirable restraint. If you feel cheated by not hearing Martha confess her lesbianism, you can take refuge in the fact that she doesn't meet the same suicidal fate that she does in the play and the remake. I prefer seeing her gayness excised rather than watch her suffer through the stereotypical misery and shame that Hellman originally cooked up for her. In that regard the remake, which wallows in gay self-disgust and hopelessness, is far more dated than *These Three*. Miriam Hopkins' Martha has considerably more resolve; her final moments are more likely to engender exit applause than pity. The ending of *These Three* may strike you as too cute and romantically escapist, but I feel that after all we've been put through we've earned it. And it's in keeping with those light love scenes from earlier in the picture.

Hellman was very shrewd in reworking her play—which otherwise would not have been filmed until 1961—embellishing it with short, cinematic scenes that defy the material's stage origins. The script is particularly good at dramatizing how many small, specific events (a stolen bracelet; an arm accidentally caught in a door; a glass of milk crashing to pieces) can accumulate, resulting in devastating consequences. It's also noticeable for its absence of mothers; of the main characters only Rosalie has one and she's never seen. Everyone seems more exposed by being devoid of maternal support. Aunt Lily is a waste, and Mary's grandmother allows herself to be blind to Mary's failings and so gullible to the child's calculated protestations of love.

Wyler's uncanny aptitude for turning stage plays into photoplays is at its best here. You never feel you're watching a filmed play, or that the camera is weighed down by talk. The play is opened up without strain, and the final result holds up phenomenally well. Wyler's series of smart, unbound play adaptations are noted for their savvy positioning of the camera, visual depths, and full-scale characterizations. Preceding this film were his renderings of *Counsellor at Law* (1933) and *The Good Fairy* (1935), and among those that came after were *Jezebel* (1938) and *The Letter* (1940). He directed another Hellman play, *The Little Foxes* (1941), with the same *These Three* team: producer Samuel Goldwyn and cinematographer Gregg Toland. It's an impressive film despite an inflexible performance from Bette Davis, who was truly awful (and twitchy) in another Hellman play adaptation (not directed by Wyler): the smug, outdated *Watch on the Rhine* (1943). Even so, Davis would have been sensational as Martha.

Mention must be given to Margaret Hamilton, as the Tilford maid, for delivering the cathartic, cheer-inducing slap to Granville. Hamilton is instantly treasured because her character doesn't hide the fact that she loathes little Mary. *These Three* also benefits from a gorgeous, transporting score by Alfred Newman that augments the movie's emotional values.

These Three surprisingly received only one Oscar nomination, for Granville's supporting performance (in the first year that supporting roles were honored). Wyler did have a big nomination-getter that year with his *Dodsworth,* another sterling stage adaptation, which nabbed him his first directing nomination. (It was also a Best Picture nominee.) Merle Oberon worked with Wyler again on *Wuthering Heights* (1939), but the role of Cathy proved beyond her depths; she wasn't able to turn the character's inconstant desires into a cohesive characterization. Wyler was very loyal to Miriam Hopkins, employing her as a character actress not only in *The Children's Hour* but in *The Heiress* (1949) and *Carrie* (1952). Hopkins and McCrea made five films together, but *These Three* is by far the best. And Wyler and McCrea would work together on *Come and Get It* (1936), when Wyler replaced Howard Hawks near the end of filming (the two directors share screen credit). The third and final McCrea-Wyler collaboration was *Dead End* (1937), a first-class adaptation of Sidney Kingsley's play (with a screenplay by Hellman) that further highlighted the director's faith in the actor's abilities. Let's not forget that launching Joel McCrea as a major leading man ranks among William Wyler's finest achievements.

Primrose Path (1940)
Ginger Rogers and the Oldest Profession

After proving to be a top-flight leading man opposite both Merle Oberon and Miriam Hopkins in *These Three* (1936), Joel McCrea had found the means to advance his career. As a "name," though not a first-rank star, he became an ideal co-star to the screen's main female stars in *their* vehicles. In McCrea, they got an actor who brought out the best in his leading ladies, but one who wasn't a big enough star to share their spotlight equally. McCrea's unmannered skills supplied earthly balance to the showier facets of screen goddesses, creating a series of winning partnerships. These actresses appear to know how lucky they are to be on the receiving end of McCrea's attentive on-screen support and nurturing concentration. (Witness his lovely rapport with Sylvia Sidney in 1937's *Dead End*.) Over a 23-year period, Barbara Stanwyck—no fool, she—worked with him six times, their most famous teaming being the Cecil B. DeMille epic *Union Pacific* (1939). McCrea's choicest match-up to date came when director Gregory La Cava's *Primrose Path* paired him with Ginger Rogers at a pivotal moment in her already glittering career. After becoming America's best-loved female dancer via nine RKO musicals with Fred Astaire, and now on a roll with some swell zinger-laden comedies that established her as a brilliant comedienne, primarily La Cava's appetizingly hard-boiled (yet soft-centered) *Stage Door* (1937) and Garson Kanin's beguiling *Bachelor Mother* (1939), Rogers was ready to test her dramatic mettle. Not only is *Primrose Path* her first full-scale dramatic vehicle, but it was also the first time she appeared as a brunette since her early days in film. It's a very interesting picture, boldly seesawing between grim drama and romantic comedy. Flawed though it is, it has a host of valuable performances and a clear-eyed take on some raw subject matter. It's a standout film from a golden year.

Before the Production Code was enforced in 1934, it wasn't uncommon for major stars to play hookers. Ladies of the evening had a banner year in 1932 with Joan Crawford in *Rain*, Marlene Dietrich in *Shanghai Express,* Jean Harlow in *Red Dust,* Carole Lombard in *Virtue,* and Tallulah Bankhead in

PRIMROSE PATH: Joel McCrea and Ginger Rogers on the rocky path to happiness.

Faithless. Though movies were sanitized in 1934, you could still figure out what *Dead End*'s Claire Trevor, and others, did for a living. But in 1940 there appeared two grade-A films that dealt with prostitution in surprisingly bare terms: RKO's *Primrose Path* and MGM's *Waterloo Bridge*, the latter starring Vivien Leigh as a dancer who becomes a streetwalker after she's led to believe that her fiancé (Robert Taylor) has been killed in action in World War I. In *Primrose Path*, it's Marjorie Rambeau (as Rogers' mother) who takes on the oldest profession. Though both films afford these women heartfelt sympathy, the censors made certain that their fates were doomed (as if anyone might be inspired to follow in their woeful footsteps otherwise). Despite the concessions to "decency," *Primrose Path* brought a noteworthy ugliness to 1940 screens. The melodrama may sometimes be coarse, and some of the comedy less than organic, but the movie is tonally rich and diverse, and the feelings beneath the contrivances ring true.

Ellie May Adams (Rogers) lives on Primrose Hill, a poor neighborhood near a cannery town on the California coast, with her alcoholic father, Homer (Miles Mander), a broken-down intellectual; her mother, Mamie (Rambeau), who supports the family by taking trips with companion-seeking gentlemen; her cruel grandmother (Queenie Vassar); and her little sister, Honeybell (Joan

Carroll). When Ellie May falls for gas-pumping Ed Wallace (McCrea), she marries him without telling the truth about her background. Their bliss is shattered when a family reunion backfires and causes the couple to separate. A family tragedy leads Ellie May to consider the family business.

Rogers enters the film in pigtails, dressed like a tomboy, playing down Ellie May's womanliness. Ellie May plays roles throughout the film in her painful path to a *real* life, charting a trail from perennial teen to lovestruck ingénue to sassy wife to brassy "tomato." Her first pose—the ageless youngster—is a direct avoidance of her feminine appeal, a protection against the world in which Mamie thrives. In this endless adolescence, Ellie May ignores her encroaching sexuality. She knows how her mother supports them but it's best not to dwell on it. One of the more rewarding elements of the movie is Ellie May's attachment to both of her hard-luck parents. Rogers makes it intimately clear that, though the world sees a whore and a lush, Ellie May sees the loving, bruised people she treasures. When Marjorie Rambeau's Mamie enters, she brings a shot of excitement and glamour into the Adams' shabby house. Back from one of her days-long trips, she returns with gifts for all, a Santa Claus in fox fur. Mamie has made her bargain with life, making the best of what she's been dealt. She's the breadwinner and doesn't have the time or the inclination to feel sorry for herself. Rambeau gives a classic whore-with-a-heart-of-gold performance, and her bountiful capacity for love and commendable lack of self-pity make it a wise, no-bull characterization. She also conveys that Mamie's lifestyle, while no picnic, at least affords her a welcome respite from her miserable home life. Inebriated Homer is as useless as Mamie is dependable. Miles Mander's heartbreakingly exposed drunkard is a doddering contrast to Rambeau's survivor. Sobriety is psychically unbearable for him. Rogers is so sweet and gentle with Mander, basking in Ellie May's pride in Homer's college degree and his knowledge of "them Greeks," while patiently nursing him through the crippling effects of his addiction.

This Adams family is a model of dysfunction: Homer can keep himself in gin thanks to Mamie's "business"; Honeybell doesn't attend school; Granny is a vile person who speaks cruelly of son-in-law Homer in front of his daughters; they appear to live on a diet of Chinese take-out. As Mander's Homer, rail-thin and vibrating with thirst, and Rambeau's Mamie, with her soft, soothing nature, play together you can almost see the couple they once were, and how the faint memory of that happiness makes bearable their present despair. They both have their share of shame and disgrace, but Mamie does what she must without undue drama, while Homer makes pathetic pronouncements meant to reclaim some of his dignity. These are good people living unfortunate lives with little chance of betterment. And the film's look offers no softening of the squalor. The house is unrelentingly depressing, marked with few brightening touches.

Ellie May meets Ed in the hamburger joint/gas station run by his Gramp (Henry Travers). She's unamused by the waitering Ed and his attempts at charming the customers with jokes about the crummy food. McCrea has some fun in playing a small-town heartthrob, a guy who takes for granted his appeal with the ladies. He cockily snaps his elastic bow tie when he asks for her order, but she's *so* hard-boiled that he can't get a rise out of her. She tops his punch lines, ruffling his feathers, and after she leaves he says, "Say, she ain't so bad on the comeback." He follows her to the beach and tells her how necessary his lunch-counter "repart*ee*" (long "e") is for business. As characters, and as actors, this duo's natural affinity for repartee connects them securely. Rogers puts on a little-girl voice for the early scenes outside the house—warming up for her 1942 role in *The Major and the Minor* as a woman posing as a 12-year-old—part of Ellie May's armor. Once she acknowledges her love for Ed, the little-girl voice slips away with all the other vestiges of her prolonged childhood. There's a nice arc of a romance: first he's chasing after her because she won't give him a tumble; then, after his kiss renders her helpless, it's she who can't let go. (The reckless motorcycle-sidecar ride, in which the kiss takes place, is the worst scene, a broad attempt at giving a delicate film some trumped-up "action.")

Ellie May's decision to get dolled up and locate Ed leads to one of the movie's more affecting scenes. Having pieced together a grown-up outfit, Ellie May is delighted when Mamie tops it off with her prized fox fur (the hideous kind with the head still on). The two women have a heart-to-heart on the porch, probably their first adult conversation. As Ellie May speaks about the no-going-back effects of that kiss, Mamie is open and encouraging, sharing thoughts about her own first love (not Homer). Rambeau plays the scene warmly, more like a big sister than a mother, passing on the stuff Mamie knows (such as how to walk seductively). Perhaps Rambeau's triumph is that there's nothing cynical or bitter about her Mamie, though there's no doubt that she's been around. (It's that irresistible, restrained heart-of-gold thing, again.) Add to this Rogers' tenderness as a girl about to embark on womanhood, and you have an uncommonly believable portrait of familial closeness.

The scene that puts Ellie May and Ed into each other's arms begins at a waterfront dive and then moves out on the pier. It's fun to watch Rogers, the epitome of an Art Deco film star, founder awkwardly in attracting the man she craves. When Ed spots her—her "sexy" walk has caused her to trip—he's appalled at seeing her glamorized beyond recognition. As these characters come together, it becomes plain that they are equally innocent. She's a novice in matters of the heart, telling too many lies about how she's run away from strict parents, and he's utterly gullible, perhaps a big man with bar gals but of no experience with relationships. No longer playing the toughie tomboy, Rogers is now swept away by lovesickness; Ellie May won't leave the pier until the boy is hers. It doesn't hurt that the Rogers-McCrea kisses carry a palpable charge.

Rogers and McCrea are quite a couple, romantically, dramatically, and comedically. They spar beautifully, their aim is dead-on, and, like the best screen couples, you feel lucky to share their company. The idyllic married life of Ellie May and Ed is apparent once they're both working behind the counter. They revel in repartee, putting on quite a show for their eager customers, mocking the food, kidding their union. You could say it feels self-conscious, and it does, but in the right way. For Ellie May and Ed, their happiness is so large that it spills over into their public life. They don't require outside attention; they're just so elated that they can't be contained. The characters appear to be starring in their own romantic comedy, savoring their shtick and their "roles" (she's the wisecracking hash-house waitress; he's the man-about-town boxed-in by marriage). The two stars are so loose with each other, and so loosely funny, that the characters' mad-dash union seems reasonable. Sparked by the pleasures of verbal give and take, in public and in private, the actors convey delirious romantic satisfaction without the slightest bit of strain. A neat touch is McCrea's endowing Ed with a mock irritability that is highly appealing because it's merely a humorously low-key expression of his ecstatic joy.

When Mamie, her pal Thelma (Vivienne Osborne), and two gentlemen pull into the gas station, the fantasy ends. (Ellie May has had no contact with her family since she set out to snare Ed.) Mamie attracts attention by making mischief with a water hose, prompting a customer inside to say, "The old gal's feeling pretty high." Before turning her head to look, Rogers registers instantly not only that Ellie May knows who is out there but that her dream life is over. She turns slowly, and her reaction is made more complex by her genuine gladness at the sight of her beloved mother. A male customer identifies Mamie and, after he makes a suggestive remark, Ellie May tells him off and starts to cry, confusing everyone. Henry Travers, best known as wings-seeking Clarence in It's a Wonderful Life (1946), makes Gramp the film's grounding force, the antidote to all the dysfunction. The character's protectiveness of Ed and Ellie May, and his even-keeled manner, make him an unobtrusive guardian angel (more relaxed than Clarence). Travers' benevolent, levelheaded tone does for the coastal scenes what Rambeau does for the hilltop scenes.

But the commotion over Mamie—no one down here knows that Ellie May is her daughter—bewilders Ed and he'll not drop it.

The scene in which Ellie May bravely brings Ed home for a family dinner is the centerpiece of the movie, the chilling flip side to a similar scene in the comedy *You Can't Take It With You* (1938). The nervous anticipation brought to the scene by Rambeau is offset by the snarling negativity of Queenie Vassar's Grandma, who would love to see the night a flop. Grandma is a fascinating creature, noted not just for her blatant rancor, but for the kind of insecurity dramatized by her not being able to abide situations that make her feel inferior (such as Ed's visit). She delights in mercilessly demeaning Homer, never having forgiven him for his lofty education. Old-timer Vassar is shockingly cold and selfish as Grandma, a stark contrast to Travers' Gramp. There's a stunning moment when Ed meets Mamie and tells her that he's seen her before. Rambeau stops dead in her tracks, making it evident that a woman in Mamie's line could conceivably have *known* Ed and not remembered him. Ellie May's explanation (the gas-station episode) allows Mamie to release her discomfort and resume her breezy welcome. When the front door opens and a soused, wraithlike Homer enters, McCrea's reaction is to grip his chair's armrests instinctively as if he's seen a ghost. In the movie's most painfully humiliating moment, Homer, assuming that Ed is one of Mamie's tricks, confronts the young man until Mamie makes him understand who Ed is. Ellie May and Mamie put Homer to bed, leading Ed to ask Grandma the million-dollar question: "Who works in this family?"

Following Ed's abrupt exit, Ellie May tracks him down at his old waterfront haunt. Rogers plays the scene with great care, reaching out to him achingly while taking all his sarcasm as her punishment for past lies. For McCrea, it's a plum drunk scene, played understatedly yet exposing Ed's wounded pride, stinging distrust, and self-loathing at having been a chump. Key to the scene is McCrea's acidic ease with Ed's vindictive nature, mocking Ellie May in front of his friends, even kissing another woman before her eyes. McCrea doesn't get sidetracked overindulging an outward show of drunkenness. He slurs his speech and loosens his body just enough to free Ed to say what he wants and bare his potential for unkindness. Rogers takes it all in, and it's a touching, one-sided showdown. Out on the pier now, Ed busts up their relationship. As she hurries away, he makes a crack and laughs at his own cleverness, but the laugh drains from McCrea's face and he suddenly looks empty.

After Homer shoots Mamie during a drunken episode, Rambeau and Rogers share a second beautiful scene. Enhanced by convincing physical intimacy between mother and daughter, it's a scene about seeing things as they are. From her sickbed, Mamie asks Ellie May to take care of the family (if necessary). As she faces the prospect of being released from her responsibilities, Rambeau endows her character with a kind of serenity. As the worn-out Mamie speaks candidly about her difficult life, Rambeau plays the scene with grace and dignity and also offers glimpses of the darkness and pain that Mamie usually conceals. Yet she has no resentments, no apologies, and she has never punished anyone else for her woes. (Rambeau's supporting performance received *Primrose Path*'s only Oscar nomination.) The melodrama then takes a necessary (yet excruciating) turn, wielded by Grandma's meal-ticket desperation and delaying the couple's reconciliation. I say necessary because it gets the movie to the place it has been heading from the first: Will Ginger Rogers go down the primrose path or not?

The discovery of Rogers tarted up is a guilty pleasure. (Don't you at least want to see what Ginger would look like *if* she went through with it?) The picture doesn't trivialize the situation; the misery in the Adams household is transparent and their options limited. To Rogers' credit, she looks as though she could handle Mamie's racket. Scared, yes, but flinty, too. The climax of the picture is her parading her new self in front of Ed at the bar, her turn for a public display of revenge. Now *she's* got the zingy wisecracks, but, again, the subtext is their mutual, unextinguishable love. The romantic resolution is a bit silly and elaborate but it provides the essential catharsis. Is it a cop-out? No, because this is a movie about two kids who belong together, and also because we've witnessed, and shared in, their thorny passage to adulthood. It's interesting that in a Ginger Rogers picture, it's McCrea who gets most of the dialogue in the final scene. And if it all looks a little too neatly wrapped, in walks Homer for a last jolt of discord, a perfect finish to a film that maneuvered comedy and drama so deftly.

Despite the considerable comic flourishes and the escapist romance, *Primrose Path* is Gregory La Cava's best drama. Like most films of its time dealing with unpleasant issues, it's anchored by a love story, a way to pull audiences in. La Cava's sensitive direction results in a disarming movie made all the more memorable for its kitchen-sink wretchedness and complicated emotional ties. He also makes tangy use of some vibrant coastal locations, giving the film a distinct ambiance. La Cava co-wrote the screenplay with Allan Scott (who co-wrote six of the Astaire-Rogers musicals), based on the play by Robert L. Buckner and Walter Hart, which itself was based on the novel *February Hill* by Victoria Lincoln. (Lincoln's book is set in New England and features a larger central family. Rogers' character has a weakness for shoplifting, and McCrea's character is a rum runner.) In addition to *Stage Door,*

La Cava had also directed Rogers in the comedy *Fifth Avenue Girl* (1939), a charm-free misfire, and he had directed McCrea in the cheeky, pre-Code *Bed of Roses* (1933) and the admirable psychiatry drama *Private Worlds* (1935). McCrea and Rogers had previously co-starred in the negligible soap opera *Chance at Heaven* (1933).

Rogers won the 1940 Best Actress Oscar, but for the drearily ordinary "woman's picture" *Kitty Foyle* rather than for the far superior *Primrose Path*. Rogers' Ellie May is her finest dramatic performance, with its compelling growth from girl to woman, much more alive and individualized than the blandly soap-operatic Ms. Foyle. As for McCrea—who also starred in Alfred Hitchcock's highly enjoyable thriller *Foreign Correspondent* that same year—he took the regular-guy role of Ed and imbued it with substantial dimension, making *Primrose Path* just as much his film as Rogers'.

The Palm Beach Story (1942)
The Deadpan Among the Zanies

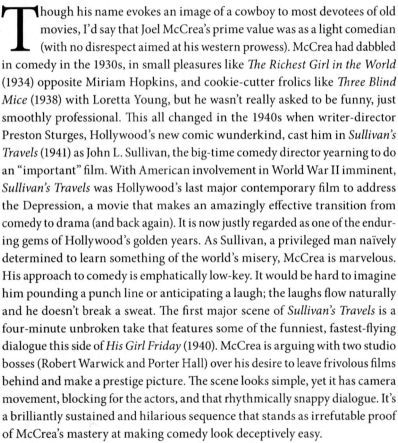

Though his name evokes an image of a cowboy to most devotees of old movies, I'd say that Joel McCrea's prime value was as a light comedian (with no disrespect aimed at his western prowess). McCrea had dabbled in comedy in the 1930s, in small pleasures like *The Richest Girl in the World* (1934) opposite Miriam Hopkins, and cookie-cutter frolics like *Three Blind Mice* (1938) with Loretta Young, but he wasn't really asked to be funny, just smoothly professional. This all changed in the 1940s when writer-director Preston Sturges, Hollywood's new comic wunderkind, cast him in *Sullivan's Travels* (1941) as John L. Sullivan, the big-time comedy director yearning to do an "important" film. With American involvement in World War II imminent, *Sullivan's Travels* was Hollywood's last major contemporary film to address the Depression, a movie that makes an amazingly effective transition from comedy to drama (and back again). It is now justly regarded as one of the enduring gems of Hollywood's golden years. As Sullivan, a privileged man naïvely determined to learn something of the world's misery, McCrea is marvelous. His approach to comedy is emphatically low-key. It would be hard to imagine him pounding a punch line or anticipating a laugh; the laughs flow naturally and he doesn't break a sweat. The first major scene of *Sullivan's Travels* is a four-minute unbroken take that features some of the funniest, fastest-flying dialogue this side of *His Girl Friday* (1940). McCrea is arguing with two studio bosses (Robert Warwick and Porter Hall) over his desire to leave frivolous films behind and make a prestige picture. The scene looks simple, yet it has camera movement, blocking for the actors, and that rhythmically snappy dialogue. It's a brilliantly sustained and hilarious sequence that stands as irrefutable proof of McCrea's mastery at making comedy look deceptively easy.

Sturges and McCrea were soon at it again, this time on *The Palm Beach Story*, a flat-out screwball comedy, a companion piece to Sturges' classic *The Lady Eve* (1941) in terms of combining sex and slapstick, and cynicism and romance into a gleeful package. These two films—in which love defeats all other impulses—received top-of-the-line Paramount productions that still shimmer. (Victor

THE PALM BEACH STORY: Claudette Colbert pleasurably torn between husband Joel McCrea and millionaire Rudy Vallee.

Milner photographed both.) And with their joint refusal to tame their female protagonists, and their up-front (for the time) acknowledgment of sexuality, they are among the least dated and most bewitching comedies of their era. Claudette Colbert is *The Palm Beach Story*'s star and she sails through it with the dreamy aplomb that made her one of the screen's more sophisticated comediennes. Her character drives the film, and Colbert's finesse—her line readings, physical agility, and sheer glamour—is impeccable. With her providing the comic razzle-dazzle, McCrea is on hand as her dry and deadpan counterpart. He never had the energized charisma that Cary Grant brought to romantic comedy, which means that people often can't remember who plays "the guy" in *Sullivan's Travels* or *The Palm Beach Story*, though no one ever forgets who "the guy" is in *The Awful Truth* (1937) or *Bringing Up Baby* (1938). That's not McCrea's fault; he was a different breed from Grant, more the understated wisecracker than a magnetic comic personality. McCrea was a tall and handsome leading man with an acerbic edge, subtle sexiness, and innate warmth. He's the lean beef that complements the flavor of Colbert's creamy Béarnaise.

After five years of marriage, Geraldine ("Gerry") Jeffers (Colbert) decides to leave husband Tom (McCrea) because their union has been a financial flop.

Tom is against the break-up but Gerry is only being practical, and she soon heads for Palm Beach to secure her divorce "while we're still young enough to make other connections." Imagining wealthy suitors at her disposal, she's sure she can help Tom secure the $99,000 he needs to build a working model of his invention: an airport suspended above the city with a steel mesh bottom ("stretched like a tennis racket"). On the train south, Gerry meets John D. Hackensacker III (Rudy Vallee), one of the world's richest men, and he's quickly entranced by her. When Tom catches up with her in Florida, Gerry introduces him to Hackensacker as her brother, determined to follow through with her plan for financial stability though she's now distracted by Tom's hard-to-resist presence.

The opening-credits sequence is one of the screen's screwiest. There's no way to make sense of what we're seeing: silent snippets of scenes accompanied by the *William Tell* overture, including a maid screaming and fainting three times; two Colberts, one in a wedding gown and the other (in a satiny slip) bound and gagged in a closet and trying to bust out; an anxious minister alone at the altar; and McCrea dressing in a cab. It's a whirlwind mini-spoof of film clichés—everything but the heroine tied to the railroad tracks—thrusting us into the frenetic climax of a silent-film melodrama and setting an anything-can-happen tone for whatever is to come. What's particularly amusing are the freeze-frames whenever a new credit appears on-screen, such as when the maid is suspended in mid-faint for "Claudette Colbert and Joel McCrea in," followed by McCrea caught with his mouth wide open for "The Palm Beach Story." The sequence is mesmerizing lunacy, ending with the wedding of Gerry and Tom. In Sturges' most daring move, not a bit of what we've just seen is even mentioned until the film's deliriously satisfying final minutes, and most of it is mischievously never explained. This nutty opening ends with the title "and they lived happily ever after," followed by "or did they?"

The action picks up five years later, with the Jeffers' Park Avenue duplex up for rent because of their delinquency in payment. Colbert appears on the upper floor, clad in a lustrous robe, looking down as prospective tenants peruse her home. Pushing forty—potential career suicide for this era's leading ladies—Colbert never looked more radiantly lovely than she does here. With longer hair than her usual short-cropped style and a lighter tint to her brunette, plus a swell array of Irene fashions, she looks smashing. This isn't just window dressing, because the plot hinges on Gerry's ability to attract men at will. Continuing his tweaking of melodramatic conventions, Sturges begins with a variation on an old chestnut of a plot: "I can't pay the rent," "You must pay the rent," "*I'll* pay the rent." The male half of the apartment-seeking couple, an old and deaf cowboy-hatted Texan (Robert Dudley), takes a shine to Gerry after he discovers her hiding behind her bathtub curtain: "I don't suppose you go with the flat." It turns out that this coot is the Wienie King ("Lay off of 'em, you'll live longer"), and he eagerly offers her $700 to pay her debts. *The Palm Beach Story* is about being young and good-looking and wanting to take advantage of those attributes before it's too late. Time is always ticking, and this farce merely accelerates the clock's hands.

When Tom arrives home and learns of their windfall, all he wants to know is what Gerry had to do to get the money. McCrea makes it insinuatingly plain that Tom can't enjoy being debt-free—he can't smile or show relief—until he knows what shenanigans got him there. Though he's far off the mark, this sets up Tom as someone increasingly threatened and emasculated by his failure as a provider. McCrea's choice sarcasm is a direct reflection of Tom's low-earning shame and wounded pride; he's stubbornly joyless at their lucky fate. As a guy in love who is resisting the upturning of his world, McCrea makes surly agitation touching and charming. How could Tom's male ego not be diminished when his wife has been rescued by someone known as the Wienie King?

Like *The Awful Truth, His Girl Friday,* and *The Philadelphia Story* (1940), *The Palm Beach Story* is one of those hallowed movies about putting a split couple back together—where they obviously belong. Suddenly out of the red, Gerry thinks it's a good time to separate, impatiently putting her logic ahead of her feelings. She's sure they'll fare better financially on their own. Out to dinner (courtesy of the Wienie King's dough), in which they get quietly plastered, she explains that she'll always be like a sister to him and emphasizes her inadequacies as a wife, such as her cooking. McCrea mutters under his breath, "I remember that pot roast you tried." By giving Tom his suspended-airport dream, Sturges stresses the contrast between Tom's romantic view of things with Gerry's more earthbound outlook. When he asks where all her supposed wealthy wooers will come from, Colbert, with breezy assurance, replies, "They're always there, and they make new ones every year."

Three scenes—the dinner scene and the two apartment scenes that sandwich it—form the foundation for the farce that's about to be ignited. Despite their monetary woes, Gerry and Tom still have a powerful sexual bond. In Sturges' comedies, no one ever pretends, as in countless other romantic comedies, that sex doesn't exist. When they return home from dinner, her inability to unzip the back of her gown leads her to ask for his assistance, which lands her eventually onto his lap. With a straight face, McCrea cracks, "You don't think this is a little intimate, do you?" In one of the sexier of comic couplings, he kisses her spine twice, allowing Colbert to have some fun playing Gerry's intense arousal while struggling against it. He then wraps his arms tightly around her, knowing full well that all her ranting about their dead relationship is absurd. When he sprawls her across the sofa and kisses her passionately, you understand the full force of what Gerry is up against in sticking to her plan. She is carried off to the bedroom, clinging to him as she continues mumbling that their union is just "a bad habit." Colbert is playing a woman with her mind made up, though she's lying to herself in thinking she can run from her emotions, while McCrea, in the injured-party role, is a heartbroken fellow so sure that he and his wife belong together that he'll do whatever it takes to bring her to her senses. Both stars enrich the humor with their coexisting strength and vulnerability, playing people muddling through the best they can.

Morning returns her to sobriety and clearheadedness, all packed and ready to go while he lies sleeping. In a swell bit, she pins her Dear John note to his blanket but fastens it too deeply and stabs him in the ass; he wakes with a shriek. Her quiet getaway is suddenly a sprint with a frantic husband in pursuit. The film rarely catches its breath from this point, but it's always grounded in the fact that Tom and Gerry (always good names for a comic duo) love each other and belong together. The chase may be daffy but what's at stake is very real; his determination to get her back matches hers to get away. Amid the giddy abandon, *The Palm Beach Story* ponders the difficulties of sustaining marital bliss once life starts getting in the way.

Sturges enjoys the notion that a pretty woman can travel from New York to Palm Beach without a cent. From cabbies to millionaires, men can't wait to come to Gerry's aid. Enter the Ale and Quail Club, a group of older millionaires she encounters at Penn Station. Colbert's helpless charm—her sly sympathetic-waif act—does the trick; the club members offer her a stateroom in their private car. The Ale and Quail Club makes an indelible contribution to the film, if only in giving Sturges' extraordinary stable of character actors a chance to be part of this movie. Aside from the peerlessly crabby William Demarest, the actors' names aren't well-known—portly Robert Greig, miniature Jimmy Conlin, ever-drunk Jack Norton—though their faces elicit smiles from die-hard old-movie fans. Some of them barely speak here; the effect is like being at a Hollywood party and happily watching recognizable faces go by. With this band of idiosyncratic actors on board (literally), cast as a crew of rich eccentrics devoted to drinking and shooting, they naturally hijack the picture for the short time they inhabit it. Imbibing leads to gunplay, as a mock shooting contest gets out of hand; real shells are suddenly blasting through windows and light fixtures. The conductor will eventually disconnect their car, and that's the last we'll see of these mostly cuddly, yet lethal, grandpas. You have to be grateful to Sturges for finding room for them, however briefly.

The Palm Beach Story will remind you of *Some Like It Hot* (1959), with its Florida-bound train and its scenes set in a sleeper car. Colbert, having run from the shotgun mayhem (and clad in the oversized striped pajamas borrowed from one of her hosts), locates an empty upper berth, thus awakening the occupant of the lower one. It's Vallee's Hackensacker, who sticks his head out only to have Colbert's dangling foot land on his face and crunch his pince-nez. He's so mild-mannered that his response to her apology is, "Oh, that's quite all right, just pick off any little pieces you see, will you?" so that he can open his glass-sprinkled eyelids. Vallee, the popular crooner of the 1920s, masterfully underplays this benign, nerdy millionaire who prefers lower berths to state-rooms. There's a good in-joke when Vallee later warbles "Isn't It Romantic?" and Colbert patronizingly compliments him: "Oh, you have a *nice* little voice." Vallee is a childlike delight, guileless and big-hearted. (Here again the film anticipates *Some Like It Hot* with its oddball, yacht-owning zillionaire.) In the morning, Gerry learns that her clothes and handbag were left behind in the disconnected car. The patchwork outfit she pieces together—including a blanket skirt that brands "Pullman" on her rear end—is a witty respite from Colbert's high-fashion parade. Gerry doesn't know who Hackensacker is, but his offer to buy her new clothes in Jacksonville and then take her to Palm Beach by boat is too good to pass up. Vallee is often seen writing in a little black book, taking immense pleasure in jotting down all his expenses (even though he admits he never tallies the numbers). He has a ball spending money on Gerry, in what amounts to an extensive wardrobe. It's Cinderella time again for Colbert, who was the recipient of John Barrymore's unexpected largess—a trunkful of new clothes—in *Midnight* (1939).

Gerry eventually learns who Hackensacker is, once they're aboard his yacht! Colbert wheedles him beautifully, not that he's much of a challenge. She arouses his sympathy with tales of her brutish, large husband, to which he bemoans, "That's one of the tragedies of this life, that the men who are most in need of a beating up are always enormous." On their arrival in Palm Beach, two things kick the movie into higher gear: a fuming Tom is waiting at the pier, and Hackensacker's sister, Maude (Mary Astor), a thrice-divorced, twice-annulled man-eater currently known as the Princess Centimillia, meets their yacht by speedboat. The Princess is accompanied by her latest plaything, Toto (Sig Arno), a foreign refugee with a flair for pratfalls who speaks no known tongue (perhaps Baluchistan, the Princess opines). Their conversations consist mostly of "Yeetz" and "Neetz." Cast against type, Astor is all saucy merriment as the Princess. An ingénue in silents, the beautiful, dark-haired Astor did outstanding supporting work in the 1930s in dramatic parts in films like *Red Dust* (1932), *Dodsworth* (1936), and *The Hurricane* (1937), plus bitchy roles in the comedies *Holiday* (1930) and *Midnight* (1939), the latter featuring her sparring with Colbert. Astor hit her peak in 1941, winning the supporting-actress Oscar for her catty fireworks in *The Great Lie,* and starring opposite Humphrey Bogart in *The Maltese Falcon* in which she gave an iconic shady-lady performance. Coming off those meaty roles, Astor is genuinely surprising as the dippy Princess; it's the lightest, most playful work of her career. The blond wig she sports seems to free her to indulge in some high-style naughtiness. She talks fast and incessantly ("Nothing is permanent in this world except Roosevelt, dear"), and she adores sex: one look at McCrea and he becomes her new project. That doesn't seem to be a problem because he's introduced as Gerry's unattached brother, one Captain McGloo.

The four performers, each so different, are a wonderful quartet (now all sharing the Princess' mansion). Colbert has ever more lies to juggle elegantly, while McCrea stews, unhappily cast in her charade; Vallee is sweetly transported by newfound love, while Astor is a perfumed barracuda, titillated by her new prey's cool inattention. McCrea finally tells her, "You never think of anything but Topic A, do you?" "*Is* there anything else?" she retorts. McCrea doesn't play Tom as cowed by her outrageous advances; he's there for one reason—to get Gerry back—and the Princess is nothing he can't handle. With his plain-toned speech and relaxed demeanor, McCrea is an excellent foil for both of his scintillating female co-stars. (Astor and Vallee were robbed of supporting Oscar nominations.) Though Gerry has easily snagged Hackensacker for herself, Tom's proximity wears her down. Colbert enacts a delectable struggle, trying hard not to succumb to Gerry's old pattern of falling into Tom's arms yet powerless to control herself. Getting out of one of those Irene-designed creations will be her undoing once again, back on his lap, in position for another one of their smoldering clinches.

In *The Palm Beach Story,* a real romantic predicament is hilariously amplified by the extravagant lengths to which Colbert's Gerry goes in seeking remedy. Along with *The Lady Eve,* Sturges made two divine comedies about sex and money, both of which end up being about incontrovertible love, without getting sugary. For all Sturges' celebrated skill at comic frenzy, his great works are rooted in the humanity of his characters, their recognizable problems, and the intimacy of their relationships. Long takes were essential to his directorial style, allowing the actors (and the audience) to settle into the rhythm of his dialogue and savor the shape and momentum of his scenes.

Without unnecessary edits, we can watch the actors truly play off each other. Colbert, who had already displayed on-screen compatibility with McCrea in the drama *Private Worlds* (1935), never again had a comic vehicle this good but, along with *It Happened One Night* (1934) and *Midnight*, it's eternal proof of her stature in screen comedy. Seeing how glamorous she is here, it's a bit shocking that just two years later she played full-grown Jennifer Jones' tasteful mother in *Since You Went Away* (in which naval officer Joseph Cotten periodically shows up to flirt with Colbert, assuring the audience, and the star herself, that she's still desirable). Similarly, Astor, in those same two years, went from blond bombshell to Judy Garland's matronly mother in *Meet Me in St. Louis*.

The Great Moment, the third and final Sturges-McCrea picture, might best be described as a bizarrely slapstick drama. Made in 1942, it was recut by Paramount against Sturges' wishes and finally released in 1944 when it expectedly and deservedly bombed. The movie is an honest botch in which Sturges failed to mix comedy and drama as deftly as he had in *Sullivan's Travels*. It is a biopic about the dentist who discovered ether anesthesia in the nineteenth century. (Putting people to sleep is never a good idea at the movies.) McCrea's brief comedy-star reign continued with one more film, George Stevens' tasty wartime romp *The More the Merrier* (1943), which cast him opposite the wondrous Jean Arthur and an Oscar-winning Charles Coburn. McCrea exhibits the same expert comic ease that he did in his first two Sturges pictures. He would never make another comedy, becoming increasingly devoted to the western genre until it became his *only* genre. This was a loss for romantic comedy, even though the quality of the genre's output dropped significantly after World War II. But too bad he couldn't have squeezed in comic match-ups with Myrna Loy or Carole Lombard or Irene Dunne before the era vanished forever.

Ride the High Country (1962)
Sunset for Two Western Legends

No survey of Joel McCrea's screen career would be complete without a look at his association with the western, the genre he increasingly favored; he didn't appear in anything but westerns after 1953. McCrea is probably best remembered as a cowboy star, and he came by that persona naturally. A grandson of a stagecoach driver, McCrea was a real-life horseman and silent-film wrangler who became a successful cattle rancher while, incidentally, a movie star. In the late 1930s and early 1940s, his westerns were lively but fairly undistinguished—*Wells Fargo* (1937), *Union Pacific* (1939), *The Great Man's Lady* (1942), and *Buffalo Bill* (1944)—particularly when compared to his comedies and dramas of the same period. After World War II, his focus tightened on westerns, but films higher in quality than his previous forays in the genre. *Four Faces West* (1948), co-starring his lovely wife, Frances Dee, is supposedly the only western in which a shot is never fired. It's an unusually humane western, if a bit corny, and it highlights McCrea's decency of character (as a sympathetic bank robber) while showcasing his outdoor skills. Even better is the gorgeous and compelling *Colorado Territory* (1949), Raoul Walsh's westernized remake of his own *High Sierra* (1941), in which McCrea was again cast as a sympathetic outlaw. It isn't quite a 1950s-style psychological western, but it appears to be heading in that direction. Among McCrea's better '50s westerns are *The Outriders* (1950), *Wichita* (1955), and *Trooper Hook* (1957), though in none of his western fare thus far had he registered as an actor in the distinctive way he had in his William Wyler dramas or his Preston Sturges comedies. He was reliably honest, comfortable, and diligent, but his roles were certainly not the challenges that director Anthony Mann had been flinging James Stewart's way.

Rarely does a film-star's career resolve with the perfect closure that MGM's *Ride the High Country* afforded McCrea's: it's easily his best western; it contains one of his all-time top performances; and it united him with Randolph Scott, another genre icon ready for a classy exit. Both men—Scott is top-billed— give crowning performances in this elegy not only to the Old West but to

RIDE THE HIGH COUNTRY: It ain't like the old days for Randolph Scott and Joel McCrea.

the classic Hollywood western. McCrea's work is a culmination of the direct, unvarnished, restrained acting style that he had been honing for thirty years. Scott, of late, had been making better westerns than McCrea, coming off his series of seven fine Budd Boetticher-directed oaters (1956-60), yet Scott was never the actor that McCrea was and there's little worth recalling from his filmography aside from his late-career westerns. *Ride the High Country* was the second feature directed by Sam Peckinpah, the man who would go on to make the bloody, convention-crushing western classic *The Wild Bunch* (1969). So, with seasoned McCrea and Scott directed by forward-looking Peckinpah, *Ride the High Country* is a fusion of old and new, an ageless film that benefits immeasurably from the authenticity of its stalwart western stars. It's the last great "old" movie *and* a modern-feeling contemplation of aging, self-esteem, moral ambiguity, redemption, and making the best of one's choices. That same year, John Ford made his end-of-an-era western, *The Man Who Shot Liberty Valance,* with two other genre legends, John Wayne and James Stewart, but it's an artificial, slow-going, and heavy-handed film, lacking the grace, beauty, and subtlety of Peckinpah's movie. Ford's film ludicrously ignores the advanced ages of its stars, in roles obviously meant for younger men, whereas *Ride the High Country* embraces its longtime stars' ages as an essential component.

The plot of *Ride the High Country* provides a seemingly simple framework for its thematic richness, featuring four main characters who make significant growth within themselves and in relation to each other. Old-timer Steve Judd (McCrea), a former federal marshal, gratefully accepts a job transporting gold dust from Coarse Gold, a California mining camp, to a bank. After accidentally meeting up with Gil Westrum (Scott), his old pal and colleague, Steve hires Gil and his young sidekick, Heck Longtree (Ron Starr), to assist him. Steve doesn't know that Gil and Heck are planning to steal the gold. On the way to Coarse Gold, they spend a night at a ranch, meeting Elsa Knudsen (Mariette Hartley), a young woman who accompanies them so she can escape her rigid father (R. G. Armstrong) and join her fiancé, Billy Hammond (James Drury), at the camp. In Coarse Gold, the trio collects the gold and winds up rescuing Elsa from her hasty marriage to brutal Billy. As they make their way back, Gil plots his getaway and Elsa and Heck grow closer. Meanwhile, Billy and his brothers seek Elsa's return. All Steve wants is pride in a job well done.

Ride the High Country is about getting old and living with the choices that have shaped your life. Steve and Gil represent two different philosophies: Steve craves the peace of a life lived honorably and proudly; Gil wants the overdue rewards he feels he has coming. The central struggle in the story is that only one of them can get what he wants on this journey. Steve long ago sacrificed personal happiness to law enforcement, so he needs to know that it's been worth it. He doesn't have money or a family, and he's clearly past his prime, so how does he assess his life's value? McCrea is gray and not as trim as he once was, but still cuts an attractive figure. The film opens with him on horseback, stumbling upon some public event whose excited crowd he misinterprets as tribute to his once-renowned exploits as marshal. Lifted by the attention, he smiles and tips his hat, only to discover dishearteningly that he's in the way, interfering near the finish line of a race. Called "old man" by a cop and nearly run down by an early motorcar, Steve is a dinosaur soon to be extinct but wanting one more chance to prove his mettle, mostly to himself. McCrea carries Steve's disappointments and loneliness inwardly and without self-pity. Steve is cerebral yet a man of action, an ideal combination for an actor as thoughtful yet uncomplicated as McCrea. When his bank employer tells him that he was expecting a much younger man, McCrea says plainly, "Well, I used to be…we all used to be," retaining Steve's fragile dignity. In a flash of his former confidence, he negotiates a good deal, then asks to read his contract in private. Alone, in the bathroom, he can wipe the nervous sweat from his brow and put on his reading glasses. McCrea is authoritative and sure in public scenes, and his exposing of Steve's vulnerabilities is offhandedly touching because it's handled without any actorly vanity or self-consciousness.

The reunion of Steve and Gil is good for their souls, a reminder of their glory days. However, it also emphasizes how little they have to show for those years, with Steve more recently employed as a bouncer and bartender and Gil now working in a sideshow. Randolph Scott, too, is gray but lean as ever, and has never been more charming or so casually funny. Despite his underhanded plan, Gil is comic relief for much of the film, the easygoing contrast to serious, record-keeping Steve. Gil tries to use psychology to win Steve over to his way of thinking, mentioning the lacks—especially cash and love—in their old age. The clash between resolute McCrea and charismatic bad-boy Scott builds in suspense, heading toward an inevitable showdown between two stubborn men. Even so, the bond between them is real. You believe they share a history and understand each other, and that they are warmed by the presence of an old friend, teasing each other about their ages and laughing over old times. Sometimes the reminiscing is painful. When they're about to go to sleep in a barn, in their long johns, Gil mentions Sara, the woman Steve almost married but who opted instead for someone in a less dangerous profession. McCrea makes it apparent that Steve doesn't want to talk about her, ignoring his rambling partner. When Scott mentions her children, McCrea abruptly interrupts, "Grandchildren, now…three of 'em," and it's clear that not only has Steve been listening but that Sara is still in his heart, kept track of to this day. McCrea's reaction, denoting Steve's concealed pain, has a firmness designed to end the conversation. When asked if he thinks she's happy, McCrea, after a long pause, says, "If my sleeping bothers you, don't you bother to let me know." His humorous way of deflecting the question almost breaks your heart. McCrea's humor and understatement prevent Steve from ever possibly coming off as a righteous stiff.

You expect the two young people at the center of the film to be of minor interest and only present to give the film some youthful appeal at the box office. Instead, these two spirited characters add greatly to the film's overall impact. Heck begins as one of the genre's typically cocky hotshots. He's unimpressed by Steve, merely stomaching him and his integrity until it's time to steal the gold. What's wonderful about the role, and never-seen-again Ron Starr's performance, is the way Heck subtly switches allegiances from Gil to Steve. Heck is a man-boy caught between two father figures, and it's a sign of his maturity and self-awareness that he increasingly looks to Steve as his example, slowly disillusioned by Gil's sarcasm and selfishness. This transition is believable and affecting because it happens without exclamation points and isn't rushed. Elsa is a sheltered farmgirl, a tomboy yearning to be a woman. Mariette Hartley, billed with "Introducing…," is no Hollywood starlet. She's radiantly fresh, without the usual glamorization that could wreck an actress' credibility in this part. Hartley's Elsa is feisty, sexually curious, and desperate to break free from her violent, Bible-obsessed (and presumably incestuously inclined) father. She's no victim, yet she is an innocent about to have her eyes opened wide. The love that buds between Elsa and Heck is appealing because the duo connects through their conversations, including their squabbles. Elsa recognizes the tenderness beneath his bravado, and Heck is confused to learn that he can feel something more for a girl than lust.

Coarse Gold is a grubby, muddy, tent-filled camp in which a whorehouse is the only evidence of civilization. Billy Hammond and his four brothers seem at first like the Pontipees in *Seven Brides for Seven Brothers*, a filthy, ignorant, brawling clan (though free of balletic skills). What emerges is more like something from *Deliverance,* with the mangy brothers expecting to share Elsa. It's difficult to watch the recklessly naïve Elsa in a situation in which she doesn't stand a chance. Peckinpah stages a beauty of a wedding in a brothel, the film's nightmarish centerpiece. With the fat, torpedo-bosomed, and boa-clad madam as bridesmaid, four whores as flower girls, drunken patrons as well-wishers, and a soused judge officiating, it's a spectacle of such vulgarity and tawdriness that it must be set somewhere near hell. Hartley's Elsa doesn't cry or make a scene; she goes through the motions in stupefied awe, as if it were happening to someone else, lost in an encircling swirl of color and movement. Edgar Buchanan's performance as the judge is an adroitly sustained drunk scene. His sermon is funny (marriage should be entered into "soberly"), yet oddly lucid and wise, painting the judge as a man who has fallen far. Peckinpah presents the scene from Elsa's perspective, confronting her with some of the things about which her father warned. The ante is raised when her new brothers-in-law start with their inappropriate kisses, and a drunken Billy leads her to a whore's room for their wedding night. When he slaps her, it's a bracing moment; she has traded an abusive father for an abusive husband. Then she must fend off a Hammond-family gang rape. It's horrifying to witness this strong young woman's vulnerability.

On their way back, with the gold and Elsa in tow, McCrea's performance deepens as Steve opens up to Gil. Speaking of regained self-respect, McCrea quietly beams, exhibiting a Steve who feels like his old self. When he says, "All I want is to enter my house justified," it's a rich, full moment, infused with both intimate feeling and staunch belief. Whatever happens to Steve hereafter, he's already got what he came for. He's reclaimed the satisfaction of a life well lived. So, when Gil and a now reluctant Heck make their move, it's a betrayal of staggering proportions, not just ethically but personally. But Steve anticipates their actions, catches them in the act, and makes them his prisoners. After the bare simplicity of scenes in which he conveyed Steve's inner life, McCrea brings his performance to a boil, a rare chance for him to play a big, raised-voice emotional moment. His controlled, yet command-ing, fury is fueled by the hurt beneath it. He may fume, but it's the personal wounds he can't help but expose that make his hardening so poignant. Scott, too, impresses; never had he been so cagily intelligent or multi-faceted as he is as Gil. Or as unguarded, as when he later asks McCrea to untie his hands at bedtime "because I don't sleep so good anymore."

There are two superlative action sequences, both shoot-outs with the Hammonds, one in the mountains and one at Elsa's farm. Peckinpah displays his flair for death scenes, warming up for *The Wild Bunch,* when a slow-dying Hammond brother has his rifle snatched from his arms as he watches in helpless disbelief, then crumples and rolls to clumsy death. The second shoot-out leads to the most moving ending in any western, and that includes *The Searchers* (1956). Aided by the rapturous beauty of Lucien Ballard's CinemaScope color photography, the final stand-off has a majesty and poetry that the film has earned. After this rousing, brief climax, the movie ends with the dignity and justification longed for by Steve Judd and so eloquently rendered by Joel McCrea.

Partially shot in California's Inyo National Forest, *Ride the High Country* is one of the most outdoors of westerns, and in addition to the marvels of Ballard's wide-screen compositions is the film's striking use of yellow, grace-fully augmenting the autumnal theme. Ballard would go on to photograph four other Peckinpah films, including *The Wild Bunch,* and he also shot three other films in *Screen Savers: The Raid, The Killing,* and *Hour of the Gun.* Peckinpah's direction of *Ride the High Country* never falters in its exquisite sensitivity to the themes of innocence and maturity, friendship and betrayal, and aging and death. Perfectly judged at every turn, this movie feels utterly spontaneous, always perceptively human and truly suspenseful in both character and story. (It received not a single Oscar nomination.) Written by N. B. Stone, Jr., the screenplay offers original characters and a plot that flows without contrivance. Elsa's plotline intersects with the main plot in an unpredictable yet true-to-life fashion, allowing the two story threads to combine and enhance each other. *Ride the High Country* is one of the great western films, prized by many yet still not as widely known as it deserves to be. The film's only flaw is George Bassman's score—the one aspect of the film that feels remotely dated—which overdoes the pounding of its main theme.

Steve Judd's yearning for a fitting resolution provided the occasion for McCrea's career to achieve the same. Though he appeared in two obscure 1970s westerns, *Ride the High Country* was McCrea's true swan song as a star, an actor, and a cowboy. He died in 1990 on his and Frances Dee's 57th wedding anniversary, a few weeks shy of his 85th birthday. (Scott retired after this movie and died in 1987.) McCrea may have played Buffalo Bill, Wyatt Earp, Sam Houston, and Bat Masterson, but his Steve Judd is his most memorable western character and one of the best performances in any western. He was never a chameleon, never an actor with a showy range, never an Oscar nominee, but I hope I've convinced you that Joel McCrea was one helluva movie actor.

Two Family House (2000)
Myth of the Melting Pot

As a proud Italian-American, I'm very interested in, and sensitive to, the screen portraits of "my people." I was sixteen when *Saturday Night Fever* (1977) came out and, though I loved the movie (and even wore a John Travolta-style white suit at my high-school graduation), I can remember cringing at its depiction of Travolta's Italian family as a stupid, crass, smack-you-around lot. Even worse, the picture mean-spiritedly used them for laughs, grotesque caricatures to laugh *at*. I wonder how many Italian-Americans were ruffled by *Two Family House*, a little-seen, independent sleeper from writer-director Raymond De Felitta. The overall portrayal of the film's Italian-American community is decidedly critical, but it isn't cruel, shallow, or thoughtless. De Felitta has a real point to make, and it transcends specific ethnicities. *Two Family House* is about the ways in which the insular, protective nature of single-ethnicity neighborhoods can be a severe detriment to those who want to venture beyond the imposed boundaries and forge a unique path. The film recognizes that much of an ethnic neighborhood's security and solidarity comes from agreed-upon enmity for those that are "other." The story is universal; it could be about any group, in any city (you would just have to adjust the particular prejudices and taboos). I assume it was easiest for a man named De Felitta to make his central character an Italian. This isn't the urban fairy-tale world of the lovably overdramatizing characters in the affectionately over-the-top *Moonstruck* (1987), but, in its way, *Two Family House*, too, is an urban fairy tale, one in which a man discovers that he may have to ditch the world that created him to become the most authentic person he can be. It's a rewarding film, operating as social critique, American Dream quest, and offbeat love story. These three elements are very well-integrated and strengthen each other, creating a feel-good film balanced with appropriate doses of feel-bad.

It's 1956, and Buddy Visalo (Michael Rispoli), an ordinary Joe in a working-class Italian neighborhood on Staten Island, New York, buys his first house (on the outskirts of Italian turf). He and Estelle (Katherine Narducci), his

TWO FAMILY HOUSE: Michael Rispoli getting in touch with his inner Sinatra.

wife of eleven years, will live upstairs, and the downstairs will be turned into a tavern, fulfilling Buddy's dream of having his own business. But it isn't going to be easy. Estelle is against the idea (as she is all of Buddy's ambitions), and then there's the problem of the upstairs tenants—an Irish couple, Jim O'Neary (Kevin Conway), a broken-down lush, and his much younger and very pregnant wife, Mary (Kelly Macdonald)—who refuse the new owner's request that they depart. The birth of Mary's baby boy changes everything: it's clearly half-black. Jim walks out on Mary, then, at Buddy's insistence (egged on by Estelle), Mary and her baby leave. Buddy, feeling guilty and worried, secretly rescues Mary from misery. He finds her a decent apartment, pays her rent, and soon realizes that this angry, proud Irish girl may understand him better than anyone has before.

Buddy's first big dream was to be the next Sinatra. In a 1945 flashback, there he is crooning at a Special Services show during his Air Force days. Radio celebrity Arthur Godfrey spots him and offers him an audition on his return to civilian life, an opportunity Buddy lets go by when fiancée Estelle nixes the idea, fearing his public failure (not to mention a life off Staten Island). In the ensuing years, Buddy has continually struggled with the ramifications of his thrown-away chance for success. (The Godfrey anecdote is both his proudest achievement and his deepest shame.) This is rich material for an actor to mine, and Michael Rispoli proves an ideal Buddy. He may be a good-natured, easygoing guy, but he's also determined to do something big, aching to find an outlet that will show the world (and himself) that he's special. He's been kicking himself all these years for caving in to Estelle's wishes and sacrificing possible stardom, feeling as though he has cursed himself by turning down Godfrey's opportunity and is now powerless to turn the tide. Rispoli carries the toil of Buddy's eleven years of failed business schemes in a sad-sack demeanor and slightly pudgy figure. (Buddy is a machine operator in a baked-goods factory; he and Estelle have been living with her parents all their married years.) But there's also the never-far-off twinkle in Rispoli's boyish face, signifying Buddy's latest brainstorm for bettering his life. Rispoli makes it evident that Buddy is driven to have his second chance at success (and fulfill the potential Godfrey once noticed in him). With a bar, Buddy can be his own boss *and* his own, free vocal entertainment. The downside of Buddy's initiative is the lack of support and encouragement it meets in the form of Estelle. Buddy has adjusted to the fact that Estelle assumes everything he touches turns to failure, but that doesn't mean it doesn't sting every time she cuts him down, or that his resentment isn't building. He's been tainted by her lack of belief in him, shackled by her pessimism. His failures constitute eleven years of self-fulfilling prophecy.

It's easy to dislike Estelle, but you have to hand it to writer-director De Felitta and actress Narducci for not making her a dismissible villain. She says horrible things—such as Buddy is "pregnant with failure"—she's selfish and vindictive, ignorant and closed-minded, but it isn't difficult to detect her motives, even if they aren't readily apparent to her. For all her tough talk and abrasive manner, Estelle is terrified and insecure. Her world is small and unexciting but she knows she can count on it, and she does her best to preserve it from change and embarrassment. This makes her a terrible match for Buddy, a man with dreams. Estelle is content to stay at her parents' house, have Buddy continue at his menial job, and never risk anything. She has mastered the little world into which she's been born. Anything else is a threat, such as Buddy's business ventures and singing-star fantasy. (Isn't she scared that a successful Buddy might leave her? She can hold on to him if she keeps him in place.) In her quest to tame Buddy, Estelle belittles him at every turn, even humiliating him in front of their friends. She likes to call him "big shot," ironically. It's fascinating when a brassy character like Estelle is increasingly exposed as weak and fearful, whereas seemingly soft Buddy proves to have guts of epic proportions. Though there's nothing to like or admire about Estelle, that doesn't mean you can't understand why she makes such poor, pitiable choices.

Who could have guessed that the catalyst for Buddy's rejuvenation would be Mary, a feisty, positively scandalous girl (and Irish to boot)? Similarly to the way Narducci won't let us categorize Estelle as inhumanly shrewish, Kelly Macdonald doesn't make her woeful Mary a fragile waif. Who isn't ready to feel compassion for a lovely young thing married to an abusive drunk, then cast off by the world for a sexual indiscretion? You'll want to like Mary long before Macdonald will permit you to, which only makes her thawing more satisfying. Sensibly, the actress plays Mary with all the rage and distrust and spine that a maltreated girl would possess and defensively wield. Her pronunciation of "Eye-talian" carries quite a sting. She's suspicious of everyone, worn down by her life, but defiantly proud. Macdonald begins her transformation once Mary is able to trust in Buddy's warmth and kindness. The pacing is right; the actress and the movie itself give the thorny Mary the time she needs.

Although Buddy gets along with everyone in the neighborhood, he seems to be the only one dissatisfied with the status quo. Rispoli talks the rough talk with the fellas, but Buddy seems to be playing a role that doesn't fit. He has trouble being as tough as he'd like to be with the Irish tenants. He's a decent guy, uncomfortable with ugly confrontation. Innately sympathetic, he can't forget Mary once she leaves his house, and he certainly can't engage in the jokes at her expense once word gets out about her "Black Irish" baby. Rispoli looks sickened as Buddy hears these jokes, and this signals Buddy's escalating detachment from his community. Buddy's pals and Mary's husband get satisfaction taking out their anger and disappointment on others, but not Buddy. Who else among his cronies would have the gumption to aid an outcast Irish mother and her black baby and be able to see them as equal to himself? Despite the Italian-American fortress behind which he has lived, Buddy, unlike Estelle and their gang, seeks to be his own person, a free agent.

The coming together of Buddy and Mary is heartwarming without ever being sloppy, implausibly engineered, or too easy. She's been cast off by society, whereas he's been smothering inside it. He moves her, in secret, from a fleabag hotel into a nice apartment, yet she's unable to show gratitude. Rispoli intuitively plays this section as if Buddy is being carried away by unseen forces, not questioning his surprising actions and unconcerned with trying to explain them to himself. When Mary is finally able to say thank you, Macdonald says the line without looking at Rispoli, stressing just how huge a step this is for the walled-off Mary. And as she learns to trust in him, they really start to talk. The breakthrough comes after she misinterprets his visit and slams the door in his face, and, in depressed frustration, he breaks one of her windows with a toy gun (an inappropriate baby gift), then cries, "I just want to talk to someone." Rispoli, in an emotionally stark expression of Buddy's loneliness and bruised self-esteem, crumbles to the ground in tears. Up in her apartment, his thoughts and feelings come pouring out, especially those about Estelle; it's a great release, eleven years' worth. He says that his plan to be a success hasn't worked out, and she tells him, "It hasn't *yet*." Those three words, said calmly, change everything. An encouraging voice! His kindness to her, and her support of his dreams, have linked them in a significant, never-before kind of way. And as Mary becomes part of his life, Buddy is less patient with Estelle's demeaning cracks. In one confrontation with her, he responds to her comment that his ideas don't work by saying, "They haven't *yet*." It's an illuminating moment when Rispoli lets us see that Buddy realizes he has just quoted Mary, a moment that solidifies his connection to her but also unsettles him; it's now clear just how important she is to him.

Then again, Buddy strangely admired her from the first, this mad-at-the-world renegade determined to keep her "disgrace." She was an inspiration to him in her not caring what anyone thought of her. Although it's highly pleasing to see Macdonald's Mary smiling at last (and especially at the sight of Buddy), the Buddy-Mary bond isn't yet on firm ground. She makes a derisive, ego-wounding comment—just the kind of thing he can get at home—and he gets mad. Weary of being laughed at, he tells her off. As Rispoli fires up, it's a tribute to his performance that what comes through is Buddy's vulnerability more than his fury; he's more hurt than incensed, and firing back at her brings no satisfaction. When she explains her comment as a defensive reaction ("I'm not used to people doing good by me"), it reveals the legitimate fears of a discarded person. It's a naked admission, allowing Macdonald to reveal more of Mary's inner life and, when Buddy softens, Rispoli affectingly puts his character's compassion ahead of his injured pride. Not only are they communicating, but they finally seem to be *relaxing* (even though Mary continues to call Buddy "Mr. Visalo"). Buddy can talk about his feelings without being shot down, and Mary no longer sees the world as inextricably heartless. Her unforced enthusiasm for his ideas brightens him, and his steadfast support of her and her baby gives her faith. But what does it mean when you've never been so alive and it may come at the expense of everything you've ever known?

Two Family House has a male narrator (Frank Whaley) who tells the story from a 2000 vantage point. The voice is that of Mary's baby, now, of course, an adult. This is a very beneficial effect, taking us through the unusual proceedings in a lighthearted manner. His presence ensures that things will work out well enough for the baby so that he will have a story to tell, yet there's no way of knowing how it's going to play out until we see for ourselves. So, the narration provides both reassurance and suspense. Another key contribution comes from Kevin Conway, as Mary's repellent husband, a grizzled sot.

Yet, for all the vileness Conway brings to the early part of the picture, he also provides some malicious laughs, notably his character's inability to pronounce Buddy's last name (Visalo) the same way twice, partly out of confusion, partly out of Italian-hating spite. Conway is as creepy here as he was in *Rambling Rose* (1991), though this time he wears his ugliness on his sleeve rather than furtively concealing it.

The musical moments cast a nostalgic, escapist wave across the film. Whenever Buddy sings, the movie is suffused with his past and present dreams. But it's not only the music that turns the clock back so convincingly. Physically, *Two Family House* replicates the 1950s persuasively. One moment stands out for me as emblematic of how well this film puts you back in time. As Buddy and Estelle go from her parents' house to the new place, there's no moving van, or even a car. What we see is the two of them and a bunch of their friends *carrying* their things (suitcases, a lamp, their bed), strolling through the middle of the street. The comfort and familial spirit of the neighborhood come through resoundingly in this one dense, yet utterly natural, image.

With fresh subject matter, believable yet unpredictable characters, and an equally credible social framework, Raymond De Felitta has made one of those out-of-nowhere films that is instantly identifiable as one of its year's best. It's about so many sizable things: the cost of breaking the rules; the wages of prejudice on those who exert it; the drawbacks of tribal separatism; the fact that the melting pot rarely melts; and that people are happier when surrounded by people who believe in them. De Felitta sees ethnic neighborhoods as safety nets and protective barricades, but also as prisons. And the hostility between the Irish and the Italians heightens our sense of just how far Buddy reaches out of his world in associating with Mary. *Two Family House* is a winning celebration of individualism, and a reminder that rose-colored looks at the good old days don't tell the whole story. An intensely appealing Michael Rispoli is the film's core, an Italian-American everyman who finds himself in a situation that brings out the worst in his family and friends but the best in himself. Buddy is a movie character to root for, and he may remind you of Ernest Borgnine in *Marty*, 1955's dubious Best Picture Oscar winner, another film about a likable, NYC-borough Italian in the 1950s trying to get his life together. Kelly Macdonald was seen the following year in Robert Altman's late-career masterwork *Gosford Park* and was just as splendid there, as the incomparable Maggie Smith's maid, as she is here. Much of *Two Family House*'s cast will be familiar to watchers of *The Sopranos*, including Rispoli, Narducci, and several others. Like *The Sopranos*, *Two Family House* offers a less than flattering portrait of Italian-Americans but I don't think you can label it as dishonest or unfair. Besides, it's a period piece and times have changed. The writing is sincere, probing, and three-dimensional; you know you're in worthy hands. Anyway, De Felitta balances his social criticism with his positive principal portrait: Buddy is the film's main Italian-American, and he's quite a guy.

I. Another 32 Remarkable Movies Awaiting Rediscovery
screensaversmovies.com

Café Metropole (1937)
October 11th, 2008

The recent DVD box set of ten Tyrone Power movies, billed the Matinee Idol Collection, doesn't feature any well-known titles. Power's classic films have already been released on DVD (notably *Nightmare Alley,* my personal favorite), so it's nice to see some overlooked films find their way to audiences after many decades of obscurity. Of the ten titles in the box, there's one I recommend above the others: *Café Metropole* (1937). Power had been a star for only a year when this picture came out, and it's one of five films he made with Loretta Young between 1936 and 1938. No one thinks of this duo as a team because only their final film together, *Suez* (1938), is at all remembered.

Set in Paris, *Café Metropole* is among the countless romantic comedies of the '30s and '40s revolving around a mistaken-identity plot. Power plays an American posing as a Russian prince; Young plays an American heiress. One of the elements that makes this comedy such a refreshing delight is that Young knows Power is a fake from the start (yet she still can't resist him). So, gone are all those potentially tiresome scenes of her finding out the truth. This unsung gem sustains its charms right up to the end, with little surprises along the way to keep it buoyant. Breezily directed by Edward H. Griffith, who had scored with film versions of two Philip Barry plays, *Holiday* (1930) and *The Animal Kingdom* (1932), *Café Metropole* is exquisitely mounted, solidly constructed, and graced with consistently funny dialogue. The film's "original story" was written by cast member Gregory Ratoff, who plays a waiter. Ratoff was later immortalized for his performance as producer Max Fabian in *All About Eve* (1950).

Miss Young is radiant and winsome, while Mr. Power is dashing and appealing. And both are staggeringly beautiful, making it obvious why Fox paired them together so many times. In the supporting cast you'll find a cynical

Adolphe Menjou (the café owner), Charles Winninger (Young's father), and Helen Westley (Young's aunt). Winninger and Westley, who had just played Irene Dunne's parents in *Show Boat* (1936), are both hilarious here. The movie puts a smile on your face immediately and keeps it there throughout. It's no masterwork, but it's one of many bright and worthwhile second-tier romantic comedies that deserve to be discovered.

Road House (1948)
October 17th, 2008

Another recent DVD release that warrants celebration is Fox's *Road House* (1948), a wonderfully tawdry melodrama enlivened by first-rate quips. It's the quintessential film of the great Ida Lupino. To some, Lupino was the poor man's Bette Davis, but not to those of us who love and admire her talent, guts, and surprising versatility. My favorite Lupino performance is in *Deep Valley* (1947), in which she was cast against type as a stuttering farm girl awakened by first love. Her director on that underrated drama, Jean Negulesco, also directed *Road House,* which put Ida back on familiar turf, a milieu in which she could chain-smoke, drink, and toss off sarcastic one-liners. With her throaty voice, Lupino is cast (somewhat hilariously) as a lounge singer. And not even in some seedy nightclub…she croaks out tunes in the bar of a bowling alley!

Beautifully photographed and designed, *Road House* is an A production of B material. It's divine rubbish. The second half veers off track, once the power shifts from Ida to a typically loony Richard Widmark (still in his psychotic *Kiss of Death* mode, laughing maniacally), and the plot becomes less restrained. But Ida is terrific throughout, absolutely at her hard-boiled, no-nonsense best. Cornel Wilde, Widmark's good-guy rival for Ida's love, gets to show off his shirtless torso, while classy Celeste Holm, the era's epitome of feminine wit and sophistication, is somehow stranded here as the bowling alley's cashier, pining for Wilde. How in the world did Holm end up here? Did she accidentally report to the wrong set?

The film's highlights are Ida's irresistibly husky renditions of standards, such as "Again" and "One for My Baby." She accompanies herself on the piano and leaves her lit cigarettes atop it when she must interrupt a smoke in order to sing. She knocks 'em dead through the sheer force of her personality, daring listeners not to like her while clearly not giving a hoot. Ida was "unsung" in many ways, and she deserves recognition as one of the Golden Age's supreme actresses.

The Man with Nine Lives (1940)
October 30th, 2008

That's the title of a Boris Karloff mad-scientist movie, but it's a tag that might also be hung on Mr. Karloff himself. After all, his film career lasted five decades! He may not have had a thousand faces like Lon Chaney, but didn't he come awfully close? So, for Halloween, here's a mini-tribute to the screen's greatest horror star and a marvelous, underrated actor who never got the acclaim he deserved because of the genre to which he was attached. He was brilliant, both terrifying and moving, as the Monster in the *Frankenstein* series, and no one elevated more dreck (not just B pictures but C and D pictures, too) than Karloff.

I've written about Karloff in my two most recent books. In *100 Great Film Performances You Should Remember But Probably Don't,* I included Karloff's terrific work in *The Black Room* (1935), in which he stunningly delineated twin brothers, one good, and, naturally, one evil. In *Screen Savers,* I write about *Isle of the Dead* (1945), one of the great Val Lewton-produced horror pictures. In *Isle,* Karloff is a cold, unyielding general whose world is shaken when a plague strikes and his skills are of little use. But let me get back to *The Man with Nine Lives,* a good example of one of those quickie fantasy pictures that Karloff churned out between his *Frankenstein* and Val Lewton years.

The title is an exaggeration, but *The Man with Nine Lives* (available on DVD) is a better-than-average mad-scientist melodrama despite some lame dialogue and a bland supporting cast. The plot is an entertaining grabber and Karloff, yet again, gives a B picture some class and heft. It's all about "frozen therapy," the 1940 version of cryogenics, with the ingenious Dr. Karloff making this disease-fighting research his life's work. He disappeared ten years ago, while working on Crater Island, but he's found frozen and is promptly thawed. Of course, Karloff's mad scientist gets madder as the film proceeds, needing to continue his work at all costs. He's a good man with a noble cause, but he eventually resorts to murder to keep his work going. More sci-fi than horror, the film's most memorable visual is its ice chamber, a magical (if inexpensive) movie set. When you made as many B movies as Karloff did, every once in a while one of them turned out better than expected. I guess the title makes sense because Karloff and this little picture are still with us all these years later.

Man's Castle (1933)
February 4th, 2009

This weekend, Manhattan's Film Forum is screening the rarely shown Frank Borzage gem *Man's Castle* (1933), starring Spencer Tracy and Loretta Young. It's a gentle and touching Depression love story suffused with romanticism, reminiscent of Borzage's silent treasure *Seventh Heaven* (1927). Tracy and Young, both so effortlessly natural, play together beautifully, each offering a tender and richly felt performance. Tracy conceals his softer feelings beneath a tough-guy pose, while Young is positively radiant and impossibly pretty. Because it's a pre-Code drama, it includes a discreet skinny-dipping sequence for the stars, followed by their moving in together in a Hooverville in New York City. They find heaven in hell. Pregnancy leads to marriage. The movie veers off course with a slide into melodrama involving Tracy's foray into crime, but it finds its way back for a haunting fade-out. It's a delicate, gorgeous black-and-white picture. Along with *Seventh Heaven*, as well as *Street Angel* (1928), *A Farewell to Arms* (1932), and *Desire* (1936), *Man's Castle* is a high point in Borzage's career and certainly a harbinger of all the good things to come from Tracy and Young.

Gentle Annie (1944)
March 13th, 2009

This past week, Turner Classic Movies showed one of my favorite B pictures of the 1940s, *Gentle Annie*, a western set in 1901 Oklahoma. You expect a churned-out programmer, but the results have a surprising depth of feeling despite the familiar goings-on. The film might be described as a heartwarmer about train robbers, and it utilizes the old infiltration plot, with U.S. marshal James Craig posing as a drifter. He befriends robbers Harry Morgan and Paul Langton, brothers whose ma is none other than Marjorie Main, the title character. This was three years before she became known as Ma Kettle in *The Egg and I*. A feisty, bruised Donna Reed also comes under the wing of the family. *Gentle Annie* is emotionally layered, dealing with essentially good people who rob; attachments form and secrets fester. No one becomes a caricature. Director Andrew Marton (best known for co-directing the 1950 *King Solomon's Mines*) is to be commended for discovering so many textures in what easily could have played as routine fare.

Main is in her usual warm and blustery mode, even getting to indulge some sentimental strokes, such as when she becomes speechless at the gifts of a new hat and a gramophone. James Craig is seen in his brief star period. He was a low-wattage Clark Gable stand-in while Gable was off to war. Craig does a solid job but you never confuse him with a "star." Donna Reed shows early signs of the fine actress she would become in *It's a Wonderful Life* and *From Here to Eternity*. Morgan and Langton, in the best roles, are hold-up artists with consciences. *Gentle Annie* is a fine example of MGM's taste for Americana during the war years. Make a note to catch it the next time it airs on TCM.

The Girl in White (1952)
March 28th, 2009

Here's another sleeper to be on the lookout for as you peruse upcoming TCM guides. *The Girl in White* stars June Allyson as Emily Dunning, the first woman doctor to practice in a New York hospital. I realize how dismal that sounds, but this biopic is surprisingly effective, and it unexpectedly stays true to its feminist impulses, all the way to the end. (No need to roll your eyes at the fade-out.) Ms. Allyson is little more than adequate, and she's done up as Judy Garland in *Meet Me in St. Louis* for a while, yet she's good enough not to get in the way of the picture's overall impact. This is a handsome MGM production with a fine turn-of-the-last-century period look and flavor.

It is quite a winning and absorbing movie as we root for Emily, who breaks down barriers one person at a time. Interesting relationships develop, including a good female support system at the hospital and a believable love triangle between Allyson, Arthur Kennedy, and Gary Merrill. Best of all is Allyson's friendship with her inspiration and mentor, an older female doctor played by Mildred Dunnock in one of her best roles. John Sturges, best known for manly-man pictures, did an exceptionally good job of directing this worthy and rewarding movie.

Ever in My Heart (1933)
April 14th, 2009

It is easy to forget what a big star Barbara Stanwyck was in the early 1930s, mostly because her films from this period are not the ones for which she is best remembered. But ever since Frank Capra's *Ladies of Leisure* (1930), Stanwyck had been a major Hollywood player. One of her finest films from this era, and one to be on the lookout for in TCM listings, is *Ever in My Heart*, a striking and unusual love story that begins in 1909 New England. Stanwyck plays a rich girl who falls in love with, and then marries, Otto Kruger, a German who becomes a science professor at a U.S. college. Everything is idyllic: love at first sight, the wedding, a baby boy, Kruger's U.S. citizenship. But then comes World War I.

Anti-German sentiment whips through the U.S. and Kruger loses his job. The situation goes from bad to worse, including a family tragedy, and Stanwyck returns to her family while Kruger heads back to Germany. They divorce. The melodrama truly kicks in when Stanwyck, now a canteen girl in France, suddenly meets up with Kruger, a German spy. They are still deeply in love but on opposite sides. In only 68 minutes, director Archie Mayo weaves a delicate love story with a fast but unhurried pace. The climax is positively operatic.

Ever in My Heart is a poignant look at love versus country, but it even more strongly shows the devastating impact of bigotry on a happy home. It is about love in an unkind world. Stanwyck is a bit miscast at the start, not exactly anyone's idea of a girl with breeding and position. (It is more of a Margaret Sullavan role.) But she improves as the story proceeds and is ultimately rather touching, making this one of her loveliest early performances. Kruger, hardly a leading man, lacks the romantic appeal required, but he responds well to Stanwyck. He is best remembered as a character man in later films such as *Cover Girl* (1944) and *Magnificent Obsession* (1954).

Everybody Sing (1938)
April 24th, 2009

This snappy, unpretentious black-and-white musical is my favorite pre-*Wizard of Oz* Judy Garland picture. It's a "B," and the plot is the usual backstage-showbiz silliness, but it's a high-spirited, genuinely "screwball" musical that occasionally reaches hilarious heights. Of its kind, it's a dilly, despite, it must be said, a mediocre score and forgettable "big" numbers.

What's best about *Everybody Sing*? The cast! Well, two cast members in particular. Yes, Judy, whose vocals gleam. Here, in her in-between phase, she tries to appear younger than she really is, though her voice is gloriously mature. She's a brassy swing singer, expelled from school for rocking the joint in music class. ("When I hear music, it *does* something to me.") Despite the indignities of a hideous milkmaid/pantaloon get-up in the ugly finale, and an audition in black face ("Swing Low..."), Garland is enchanting, clearly bound for greatness.

But the movie is stolen by Billie Burke, doing one of her scatterbrained matrons. But this time she is also a star stage actress. Burke gives a model high-comedy performance of an extravagantly self-conscious woman who can't stop acting and is *always* acting. She is about to star in something called *Hidden Destiny*. When Burke is on-screen, *Everybody Sing* is as funny as *My Man Godfrey*. (Garland and Burke were just one year away from *Oz*.) Burke was Oscar-nominated that year for another supporting comic turn, in *Merrily We Live*, but she's seen to better advantage in *Everybody Sing*.

Fanny Brice plays the family's Russian maid. Here is Ziegfeld-star Brice playing opposite Burke, Mrs. Ziegfeld herself. Brice is likable and goofy, and good with the wisecracks, but oh-so broad. As Brice mugs, Burke glides by and effortlessly reaps the biggest laughs. And top-billed Allan Jones, still riding high from *Show Boat* (1936), is totally bland (as a singing chef) and completely swallowed up by the competition. His presence simply evaporates.

Everybody Sing is a minor musical with some major pleasures, one of those forgotten pictures worth singing about.

Men Must Fight (1933)
May 5th, 2009

MGM's *Men Must Fight* is one of the great curiosities in the Turner Classic Movies library. Like most war movies made in the early 1930s, it is fervently anti-war, but this one has the twist of being set in 1940, predicting World War II. In just 72 minutes, it manages to tackle an astonishing amount of content: the knee-jerk flag-waving that arises in wartime; the home-grown violence spawned from "patriotism"; the difficulty in standing firm against a war's mounting popularity; and an acknowledgement that it's the young who must die in war. But those are the most conventional elements of this unknown movie. Though it is too short to develop any of its themes, *Men Must Fight* even gives the other side its due, theoretically addressing how the peace movement made us vulnerable as we lagged behind in the arms race, with thousands of Americans dead as a result. Mostly, the movie is about women's powerlessness in stopping men from eventually succumbing to calls of honor and duty and their fears of being tagged as cowards. And so, men must fight. The movie is appropriately hopeless.

In true pre-Code fashion, *Men Must Fight* begins with an unmarried couple, a flier and a nurse, getting dressed after a sexual encounter. The setting is WWI France; the flier is Robert Young; the nurse is Diana Wynyard. After Young's death in the air, Wynyard, a firm pacifist, marries loyal friend Lewis Stone (dull as ever). He accepts her pregnancy and agrees to raise the child as his own. In 1940, Stone is America's peace-promoting Secretary of State, while Wynyard's grown-up love child, Phillips Holmes, is another idealistic pacifist. Stone and Wynyard are happily married until an assassination brings a new threat of war. Though sympathetic to his wife's views, Stone is soon in favor of the war (with "Eurasia"), while Wynyard staunchly opposes it. Imagine a movie in which the wife of the Secretary of State leads an anti-war rally in Manhattan, making appeals to the mothers of the world to stop the killing of the "other sons of other mothers." Young Holmes eventually enlists and the picture ends with him flying over Manhattan and headed for our enemies. The most jaw-dropping sequence is the bombing of New York, with the special-effects team destroying the Brooklyn Bridge and the Empire State Building! The movie shows a future of television and picture phones, and features much talk about chemical warfare as the way of the future.

Men Must Fight is no undiscovered classic, barely even a good movie, but it is consistently fascinating. British Diana Wynyard, a bit too cross-eyed for major stardom, had her big year in 1933, also starring in the Best Picture Oscar winner *Cavalcade,* one of the worst of all victors in that category. Wynyard was up for Best Actress for *Cavalcade;* also competing was her *Men Must Fight* co-player May Robson (for *Lady for a Day*). Robson is the comic relief here, as Holmes' feisty grandmother. She believes the world ought to be run by women. Both Wynyard and Robson lost the Oscar to Katharine Hepburn *(Morning Glory).*

A final chilling note. Phillips Holmes ended up dying in a plane crash in World War II at age 35, having enlisted in the Royal Canadian Air Force. What a stinging coda to the film's timeless message.

A Letter for Evie (1945)
May 27th, 2009

A romantic-comedy sleeper, MGM's *A Letter for Evie* is a charming wartime reworking of the basic *Cyrano de Bergerac* plot. (Interestingly, 1945 also produced a dramatic update of *Cyrano,* the Joseph Cotten-Jennifer Jones "woman's picture" *Love Letters.*) The most refreshing element of *Evie* is its casting, moving two worthy supporting players up to lead status. Marsha Hunt, who is still with us at 91, was one of the more enchanting and intelligent of MGM's contract players in the '40s, notably in *The Human Comedy* (1943) and several of the major Greer Garson vehicles. Here she is a radiant leading lady, warm and delightful. Though her career was sidelined by the '50s blacklist, TCM makes it possible for film lovers to discover Hunt during her heyday at MGM, plus brawling with Susan Hayward in the powder room in the non-MGM *Smash-Up: The Story of a Woman* (1947).

The other charmer here is Hume Cronyn, coming off his excellent Oscar-nominated performance in the WWII drama *The Seventh Cross* (1944), one of the forty films discussed at length in my book *Screen Savers*. Cronyn was in his brief tenure at Metro and, like Hunt, he is immensely appealing. *Evie's* hunk is John Carroll, at the end of his brief period of almost-fame as one of MGM's Clark Gable stand-ins while Gable was off at war. No one could mistake Carroll for Gable, despite the dark hair and the mustache, and he drifted away once Gable returned.

Evie's director, Jules Dassin, another short-term resident on the MGM campus, did a nice job, though the film is marred by a few comic sequences that go on much too long and aren't ever very funny. But the overall film is a neat little comedy and a sweet romance. Dassin hit his stride in film noir, with a string of notable works, such as *Brute Force* (1947), again with Cronyn, *The Naked City* (1948), and then his two best, *Thieves' Highway* (1949) and *Night and the City* (1950). He, like Hunt, was a victim of the blacklist, but he found great success abroad with the admired caper *Rififi* (1955) and then a series of pictures with eventual wife Melina Mercouri, including *Never on Sunday* (1960) and *Topkapi* (1964), two famous pictures that can't compare with his best work.

None Shall Escape (1944)
June 6th, 2009

*N*one Shall Escape is a remarkable WWII movie made and released during the war but set *after* it, at the international war-crime tribunal of a Nazi (Alexander Knox). It also deals more explicitly with the Holocaust than any other Hollywood film made during the war. And in attempting to make a Nazi a three-dimensional lead character, and chart his evolution, the film, again, feels years ahead of its time. It also connects the aftermath of WWI to the inevitability of WWII. Essentially a B movie, this exceptional war picture is the best film ever made by director Andre de Toth *(House of Wax)*. Efficiently and cleverly plotted, the film utilizes a flashback format via the testimonies of three witnesses.

Alexander Knox, nominated for a Best Actor Oscar that year for *Wilson*, is far more impressive here (as the central Nazi) than he was as Woodrow Wilson. Knox plays a German WWI veteran who returns to a Polish village to resume his teaching job. He lost a leg in the war and walks with a cane. Marsha Hunt, in one of her typically fresh and honest performances, is his love interest, but she rejects him once she learns his post-war political views. After raping and impregnating a student, Knox returns to Germany and by 1933 is an S.S. leader. In 1939, the Polish village is Nazi-occupied, with Knox returning in glory to punish his former friends and associates, even organizing a whorehouse using local girls. This is not your average war movie, and, even more so, not your average '40s picture.

Knox's performance seethes with resentment for every former slight, creating a portrait of a man filled with self-pity and insecurity, which is expressed through cruelty. As Knox moves from spurned lover to vengeance wielder, losing a little more of his humanity each step of the way, the character becomes increasingly twisted, soulless, and ultimately irredeemable.

The film's railway massacre of Jews seems a direct anticipation of Steven Spielberg's black-and-white *Schindler's List*. As the Jews are about to be taken away by train, a rabbi urges them to fight back. They are gunned down. The movie ends by telling us that it's now up to us to dole out punishment and get justice. This overlooked film packs a wallop, making it one of the very best films about the war, especially among those that came out *during* the war.

Angel Face (1952)
June 11th, 2009

This exceptional and beautifully shot L.A. film noir was inventively crafted by Otto Preminger, making it one of the director's finest achievements. Fascinating for its flawed relationships, unsympathetic characters, and shocking violence, *Angel Face* stars a just-right Robert Mitchum as an ambulance driver with a blond girlfriend (Mona Freeman) and a dream of opening his own garage for race cars. Then he meets Jean Simmons, and before you can say "double indemnity" he's a goner. His yearning to feel free makes him vacillate between the well-planned life set before him and the thrills of being with the rich, strange, and beautiful Simmons. In true noir fashion, the corruptible male is vulnerable to the machinations of a femme fatale. She's a manipulator; he's a chump. They're both louses and they belong together. Simmons makes Mitchum the family chauffeur.

The marvelous Simmons is at her best here, this time playing a cool and delicate conniver. Like Gene Tierney in *Leave Her to Heaven* (1945), she is obsessed with her father (Herbert Marshall) and amoral about murder, a kitten made of steel. Simmons is remarkably assured and complex, so concentrated that her performance quickly becomes mesmerizing. Unlike Tierney's hyper-intense and somewhat campy performance, Simmons is disturbed and obsessive in a believable way, not coming off as a villainess though she surely is scary. She also comes to feel guilt over her actions, even aches to confess. This all leads to one of the more jaw-dropping climaxes in all of film noir.

As a slick lawyer, Leon Ames plays just about the same role he played in *The Postman Always Rings Twice* (1946). Though Mitchum is one of my favorite actors, this cynical and unusually credible noir belongs to Simmons. (She likes him from the moment he slaps her.) Hers is a masterly portrait of self-absorption. Now 80, Simmons was one of the brightest lights of 1950s Hollywood, leaving behind a string of superb performances, including those in *The Actress* (1953), *The Big Country* (1958), and *Elmer Gantry* (1960). I've written about *The Actress* in my second book and about *The Big Country* in *Screen Savers*, and I hope someday to write at length about the psychologically turbulent *Angel Face*.

The Sundowners (1960)
July 6th, 2009

For me, there are only two candidates for the best English-language film of 1960, Alfred Hitchcock's *Psycho* (no surprise there) and Fred Zinnemann's *The Sundowners*, a film lauded in its day but shamefully overlooked ever since. Zinnemann is best remembered as the man who made *High Noon* (1952) and *From Here to Eternity* (1953), but he also made the underrated WWII drama *The Seventh Cross* (1944), featured in my book *Screen Savers*, as well as the overrated prestige picture known as *A Man for All Seasons* (1966). Zinnemann's two finest films are the exquisite drama *The Nun's Story* (1959), which has Audrey Hepburn's greatest performance, and *The Sundowners*, a film that defies easy classification.

Reteamed after their big success in *Heaven Knows, Mr. Allison* (1957), Robert Mitchum and Deborah Kerr surpassed themselves in *The Sundowners*.

This tale of Australian sheep drovers takes us into its world with impeccable detail and enormous affection for its characters, all so effortlessly. This is a movie that really breathes. Mitchum and Kerr are married and have a teenage son; their sheep-droving life keeps them on the move. (Sundowners are people without homes.) Zinnemann's filmmaking is so graceful and vibrant, never hitting a false or pushed note.

This wonderful movie is about "home," the yearning to have one, but it's also about what the term "home" truly means. This is an honest family entertainment that sustains an easy comic tone. Episodic in nature, the film is consistently warm, funny, and textured. It is also one of the great films about marriage, with Mitchum and Kerr not just believably in love but believably living together through good times and bad, big events and small. Kerr and Mitchum are a sexy couple in a realistic rather than "Hollywood" way. Not many on-screen marriages have generated this kind of natural heat.

The great Kerr is superb, and different than she is in any other film. She's no elegant lady here (nor is she a "tart," as she was in Zinnemann's *Eternity*), creating a full-bodied portrait of an earthy, hearty woman, tough and sarcastic but also wise and loyal. And she brims with love for Mitchum. He, too, is at his best, utterly credible with his Aussie accent and infectious zest for living. No sleepy-eyed Mitchum this time around.

The film offers the further delights of Peter Ustinov and Glynis Johns, plus gorgeous color cinematography from Jack Hildyard and stunning Australian locales. Among its many spontaneous and awe-inspiring moments, *The Sundowners* offers a forest fire, a dingo chase, a horse race, and a hilarious sheep-shearing contest.

The Sundowners received five Oscar nominations, for picture, director, screenplay, actress, and supporting actress. The big winner that year was *The Apartment,* a solid choice, but Deborah Kerr and Glynis Johns had the indignity of losing their Oscars to undeserving picks, for this was the year of Elizabeth Taylor in *Butterfield 8* and Shirley Jones in *Elmer Gantry.* Taylor did a fine job in a crappy movie but hardly merited an Oscar, while Jones was hopelessly amateurish in her attempt to convince us that she was a prostitute. Kerr and Johns would have been winners that Oscar could have looked back on with pride. Best Picture would have been nice, too.

In Name Only (1939)
July 17th, 2009

Though merely a minor effort from Hollywood's greatest year, the soap *In Name Only* has a lot going for it, particularly its star power of an unusually high wattage. This triangle stars Cary Grant (on his way up), Carole Lombard (at her peak), and Kay Francis (on her way down, but not without a fight). It's a quality "woman's picture" that overcomes its more contrived elements through John Cromwell's smooth direction.

Beautiful Lombard, a witty and radiant comedienne, here gives what is probably her finest dramatic performance, so natural and effortlessly affecting, positively timeless. She's a widowed commercial artist and fashion designer who falls for rich-boy Grant, who is miserably married to viper Francis (who married him for his dough and won't grant him a divorce). Grant is charming and loving, but he's playing a weakling, allowing the two actresses to dominate. Francis was never a great actress, but she surely was a star, and here she has a high old time as an all-out bitch and phony. It becomes a battle of the wardrobes for the two actresses (each with her own designer), and I have to declare Lombard the winner.

Though the film is a drama, thank goodness Lombard and Grant are allowed to have some comic interplay, taking advantage of this golden opportunity and proving that they have chemistry in spades. The more melodramatic writing can be thin and foolish, leading to Grant in an oxygen tent, but at last we get a decisive and satisfying confrontation between the ladies. As '30s soaps go, this baby really delivers, reveling in its trio of stars.

Interesting footnote. Charles Coburn plays Grant's father. In 1943, Coburn won an Oscar for *The More the Merrier*. When that comedy was remade in 1966 as *Walk, Don't Run*, Grant, in his final film, played Coburn's role.

Apartment for Peggy (1948)
July 23rd, 2009

This thoughtful, sensitive comedy is unusual for tackling two hardly hilarious subjects: suicide and miscarried pregnancy. It is also a timely post-war film, dealing with the G.I. Bill and the era's overall mix of optimism and gloom. Fresh from his Oscar-winning Kris Kringle in *Miracle on 34th Street* (1947), and again directed by *Miracle*'s George Seaton, Edmund Gwenn stars as a retired professor, bent on suicide, who re-engages with life thanks to the young married couple, William Holden and Jeanne Crain, who moves into his attic and changes his life. The professor might have been played by Clifton Webb, but Gwenn's casting automatically makes him warmer. Ultimately, it is Gwenn who is the film's magic ingredient. *Apartment for Peggy* is in color, an unexpected choice for a contemporary comedy of the 1940s.

The film is marred by Crain (what film in which she appeared wasn't?). Her part required a comedienne with a natural vitality, a young Jean Arthur, but Crain is her usual plasticized self, forced and a bit tiring to watch. But a dark-haired Holden brings glimmers of his 1950s (post-*Sunset Blvd.*) darkness to the film's post-war mood. He is excellent, as usual, as natural and connected as Crain is effortful and phony. (This was Holden's first of four films with Seaton.)

It's now shocking to watch Holden smoking around the pregnant Crain, but it's far more shocking when Crain miscarries, in a comedy! Despite the eventual uplift, *Apartment for Peggy* feels risky, genuinely trying to be something somewhat offbeat and probing. If you can forgive Crain (and the movie is intelligent and touching enough so that you should be able to), this sleeper is most pleasing and thought-provoking. Another triumph for Santa Claus.

Saddle the Wind (1958)
August 10th, 2009

Though Robert Taylor's finest western is Anthony Mann's extraordinary *Devil's Doorway* (1950), one of the forty films featured in my book *Screen Savers*, Taylor made several other quality oaters in the 1950s, among them *Westward the Women* (1951) and *Saddle the Wind*. Unlike *Devil's Doorway*, in which Taylor played a Shoshone Indian (and was astoundingly good), *Saddle the Wind* is blessedly available on DVD. Directed by Robert Parrish, the Oscar-winning editor of *Body and Soul* (1947), it is one of the last outstanding westerns of the genre's greatest decade.

Taylor was an actor of limited talent, as often disappointing (as in 1946's *Undercurrent*) as he was exceptional (as in 1940's *Waterloo Bridge*), but he's in fine form in *Saddle the Wind*, with a lot more going on inside him than was usually the case. He had by this point been under contract to MGM for over 20 years, and this was one of his better efforts from his twilight years at the studio. The crux of the story involves his painful relationship with his beloved but troublesome younger brother, played excitingly (if a bit over the top) by a remarkably young John Cassavetes. The female lead is Julie London, in the same year she graced another top western, the Anthony Mann-directed

Man of the West, opposite Gary Cooper. London always needed to kick up her energy in her film roles (and never quite did). She is a rather unnecessary love interest here, a dance-hall gal involved with both brothers. Her finest screen work was as Tom Ewell's hallucination in *The Girl Can't Help It* (1956), taunting him with her fabulous rendition of "Cry Me a River."

Old reliable Donald Crisp, so good in Mann's *The Man from Laramie* (1955), gives a strong performance as the most powerful man in town. But the best work comes from Royal Dano as a squatter. He walks off with the movie, giving an impassioned performance, climaxed by his impressive death scene.

Saddle the Wind is a thoughtful, probing western with smart dialogue, interesting relationships, and honest feeling. It is well made, good-looking, and should be better known than it is. Ultimately, it is a powerful essay on violence and its legacy.

Wild River (1960)
August 16th, 2009

One of Elia Kazan's best (and most overlooked and underrated) films, *Wild River* is a beautifully made drama set during the Depression, dealing specifically with the Tennessee Valley Authority. TVA man Montgomery Clift must remove old Jo Van Fleet from the tiny island her family has owned and lived upon for generations. A new dam is coming through, harnessing the river, and the island is in its path. Clift's attempts to get Van Fleet to sell to the government constitute the framework of this multi-layered and textured drama about loss and progress and racism, as well as love once Clift begins an affair with Lee Remick, Van Fleet's widowed granddaughter.

Paul Osborn's screenplay is superb, filled with marvelous dialogue and deeply emotional passages. (Kazan, Osborn, and Van Fleet had all worked together on 1955's *East of Eden.*) But everything about the film is impeccably handled, from its outstanding color photography and evocative period flavor to its blue-grassy score and terrific performances. Kazan's film is leisurely in the best sense, then bursts forth with startling power. And the sexual heat is palpable, even though Clift is essentially doing one of his weakling types, however strong-willed. Fine as Clift is here, and he is indeed fine, this film belongs to the women. Remick is wonderful as the single mother of two, conveying deep loneliness and then surprising sensuality and maturity as her relationship with Clift turns serious. Her character is never predictable, and Remick offers a remarkably intelligent and poignant performance.

At 46, Van Fleet is playing 80! And she's utterly convincing and altogether astounding. She may have won her Oscar for *East of Eden* but her un-nominated work here is her finest hour. She is, as they say, a force of nature (but in a believably worn-out body), as well as a hillbilly grand-dame. The character (Ella Garth) is very much of the 19th century, untouched by the modern world, yet she's as shrewd as any city slicker and as indomitable as any power-wielding matriarch. Van Fleet gives Ella real stature and dignity, while Kazan handles the end-of-an-era content with affecting restraint.

Whirlpool (1934)
September 13th, 2009

I recently caught a 1934 programmer from Columbia titled *Whirlpool* on TCM. I watched it only because it's a Jean Arthur movie I had never seen before, assuming it would be forgettable nonsense that wasted her, unaware of her special gifts. Though she would burst into major stardom in 1936 in Frank Capra's *Mr. Deeds Goes to Town,* it is generally acknowledged that the Jean Arthur persona, smart and cynical but warm and vulnerable, and deeply funny, emerged in John Ford's *The Whole Town's Talking* in 1935. Well, if you love Arthur as I do, don't miss *Whirlpool* when it rolls around again. Not because it's a forgotten gem (it isn't) but because *here* you will find the first appearance of the fully formed Jean Arthur, already radiant and wise and humorous, and, of course, working as a newspaper reporter.

A good little melodrama, *Whirlpool* moves from carnival picture to love story to prison flick in its first ten minutes, and then later becomes a mobster movie and a newspaper yarn. Arthur doesn't show up until the story moves twenty years ahead. She believes that her father (Jack Holt) died in prison, but he actually escaped and became a big-time racketeer. She tracks him down while investigating a story and recognizes him from her mother's photograph. This leads to what is probably the first great scene in Arthur's career. After pretending to be a stenographer, she reveals the truth of her identity to Holt, and the scene is an unexpectedly moving moment in a picture that doesn't quite deserve it. The depth of her feelings, the warmth that emanates from her, and her ageless naturalness make it a sequence to treasure. She brings a genuine glow to a film that would just be plot, plot, plot without her.

She is obviously on the verge of stardom, poised to become the queen of Columbia and the quintessential Capra female of the 1930s, forever to be remembered for her distinctively gurgling voice. The 1940s saw her in two George Stevens winners, *The Talk of the Town* (1942) and *The More the Merrier* (1943), and she would make her swan song in Stevens' *Shane* (1953). What a treat to discover yet another wonderful performance from one of the Golden Age's brightest stars. And without Arthur's comic prototype we may never have had Shirley MacLaine or Diane Keaton or Renee Zellweger, all of whom owe a debt to the savvy wit and charming befuddlement of Arthur's characters. She was, after all, the Annie Hall of her day.

Vacation from Marriage (1945)
October 5th, 2009

Vacation from Marriage (1945) has a fresh, delightful story idea that was given a charming execution. A dowdy British married couple (star Robert Donat and newcomer Deborah Kerr) is separated in 1940 when the husband joins the navy. (Kerr is homely enough at the outset to foreshadow her 1958 performance in *Separate Tables*.) Then the wife joins the "wrens" (like the WACS). During their wartime duty, each blossoms beyond recognition, performing bravely in action and discovering a sense of individuality and accomplishment, which just happens to improve their looks as well. About to be reunited after three years apart, they're both fearful of a return to their domestic rut and dull partner. They've outgrown their old lives and their old selves. How satisfying when they finally get a good look at each other, two attractive and confident people.

Donat and Kerr are well cast and marvelous. He, of course, was already the Academy Award-winning actor from *Goodbye, Mr. Chips* (1939), not to mention the star of *The Count of Monte Cristo* (1934), *The 39 Steps* (1935), and *The Citadel* (1938). Kerr was on the brink of major stardom with *Black Narcissus* only two years away, followed by her being whisked away to Hollywood and appearing opposite Clark Gable in *The Hucksters* (1947), thus posing a threat to MGM's Greer Garson in the great-British-lady department. (Kerr actually mentions Gable in *Vacation from Marriage*.) In a decade, she'd be one of the top actresses in American movies.

The supporting cast includes the delicious Glynis Johns as Kerr's fellow wren. The two actresses would later appear together in the great Fred Zinnemann film *The Sundowners* (1960). The direction of Alexander Korda is dullish (was it ever anything but dullish?), and the film is noticeably cheap, but the plot is kind of a realistic version of *The Enchanted Cottage*. This very winning tale of love and war was diverting enough to win an Oscar in the

Best Original Story category, and it remains a transporting light comedy and romance.

Miss Tatlock's Millions (1948)
November 4th, 2009

Though the sub-genre of screwball comedy was essentially over after Preston Sturges' inspired 1944 pair of wartime Americana, *The Miracle of Morgan's Creek* and the even better *Hail the Conquering Hero* (featured in my book *Screen Savers*), there was a delightful screwball holdover in 1948, *Miss Tatlock's Millions,* an underrated charmer that's clever and involving and completely "screwy." It probably would have been a smash, and possibly a classic, had it been made in 1938 instead of 1948. Its director, Richard Haydn, better known as a character actor (Max in *The Sound of Music*), was no Sturges, but he did a fine full-out job. The picture's star is John Lund, a barely remembered leading man, tall and blond and handsome, best known as the male lead in the female-dominated *To Each His Own* (starring Olivia de Havilland) and *A Foreign Affair* (starring Jean Arthur and Marlene Dietrich). In the best role he ever got, Lund walks away with *Miss Tatlock's Millions.*

He plays a Hollywood stunt man (and Ray Milland's stunt double) hired by Barry Fitzgerald to impersonate a rich, crazy fellow for whom he is a look-alike. Fitzgerald knows that the actual guy is dead but the family hasn't received this news, nor have they seen their relative in ten years. The two men arrive just in time for the reading of the grandparents' wills. The family is full of awful, greedy characters, including Monty Woolley, Robert Stack, and Ilka Chase. The exception is sweet Wanda Hendrix, Lund's new "sister." Playing insane, Lund evokes Jerry Lewis (one year before Lewis' screen debut in *My Friend Irma,* which starred Lund!). He may also remind you of Steve Martin's Ruprecht in *Dirty Rotten Scoundrels.* With eyeglasses, a high-pitched voice, spastic body language, and a mad grin, Lund is a joy. It's a completely unexpected performance, a wacky delight.

An "accident," a fall, leads to Lund's cured insanity and emergence as a strong, likable, and studly fellow. In a daring twist, not only does Lund fall for his "sister" but she starts to fall for him, and she really thinks he is her brother, bringing a naughty undercurrent of incest to a slapstick comedy. There's a sexy scene of Hendrix innocently writing the alphabet on Lund's bare chest, teaching the newly "sane" Lund to read and write but driving him crazy, a forerunner to Jack Lemmon and Marilyn Monroe's train-berth scene in *Some Like It Hot.*

Miss Tatlock's Millions is an offbeat, appealing post-screwball find, one that deserves far greater attention and at the very least a DVD release!

Angel (1937)
November 15th, 2009

During her box-office poison period, Marlene Dietrich starred in *Angel*, a sadly underrated Ernst Lubitsch picture that combines high comedy and romantic melodrama in its depiction of a love triangle. An impossibly chic and elegant movie, the kind in which everyone can play the piano, *Angel* gave Dietrich two expert leading man, Herbert Marshall and Melvyn Douglas, tip-top light comedians and effortless charmers. However, the movie belongs to Dietrich. She is radiantly soft and tenderly vulnerable, and so subtly seductive, all the while devastatingly attired in a Travis Banton wardrobe. She actually says, "I really need some new clothes," leaving your jaw to drop. Rarely did Dietrich look as lovely as she does in *Angel*.

Angel is an adult look at a woman's needs. As the neglected wife of statesman Marshall, Dietrich craves attention. Enter Douglas (who went on to have a much bigger Lubitsch success in *Ninotchka* in 1939). This swoony film is suffused with glamorous longing, making it the type of European-set Hollywood romance that vanished with the start of World War II. And it contains several textbook examples of the Lubitsch touch, scenes defined by what Lubitsch *doesn't* show, the delicate and unexpected ways in which he transmits essential information.

Also on hand are Edward Everett Horton as Marshall's valet (and an opera queen), and Laura Hope Crews (Aunt Pittypat, two years before *GWTW*) as a woman who runs a Parisian "salon" for assignations. Like *Desire* (1936), an even better and also underappreciated Dietrich vehicle (co-starring Gary Cooper), *Angel* is just about all you could want from a sophisticated black-and-white entertainment of the 1930s.

Remember the Night (1940)
November 26th, 2009

One of my favorite movies, *Remember the Night*, became available on DVD this week, thanks to the TCM Vault Collection. It is a film with an impressive pedigree: an original screenplay by Preston Sturges; direction by Mitchell Leisen; and a cast led by Barbara Stanwyck and Fred MacMurray. A bittersweet love story with romantic-comedy flourishes, it's one of those rare films to blend dramatic and comedic elements quite easily and naturally.

Stanwyck plays a hardboiled shoplifter arrested in New York. MacMurray is the prosecuting attorney. Feeling guilty about locking her up over the Christmas holiday, he arranges her bail. Because of their shared Indiana roots, he offers to drive her home and then pick her up on his way back to the city. After her disastrous family reunion, MacMurray takes her to his family for the holiday. Stanwyck is bowled over by the family's hospitality, and she and MacMurray soon fall in love despite the likelihood of her incarceration.

I'd go so far as to hail Stanwyck's performance as her finest, combining some of the best elements of her most famous performances: the unsentimental approach to sentiment that she brought to *Stella Dallas* (1937); the tough-gal wit with which she endowed *Ball of Fire* and *The Lady Eve*, both from 1941; and the calculating smarts of her femme fatale in *Double Indemnity* (1944). The success of *Remember the Night* rests on her ability to make a believable and moving transition from a brassy cynic to a woman transformed by the love and kindness that come unexpectedly into her life. As Stanwyck thaws, her characterization deepens, exposing the sensitive and vulnerable young woman who resides underneath her outer display of bitterness and mistrust. Her defenses crumble, along with the years of pain and regret and the lack of any love in her life. What might have been hokey is beautiful to behold because there's a richness and depth of feeling in this performance (and in the overall film) that is unexpected, heightened by the possibly temporary nature of the character's newfound good fortune. Neither a martyr nor a masochist, she transcends melodrama thanks to Stanwyck's timeless honesty and innate dignity. Beulah Bondi (as MacMurray's mother) and Elizabeth Patterson (as his aunt) are also pretty wonderful.

Remember the Night is one of the major directorial works of the underrated Leisen, and it remains one of the best romantic pictures of its golden age. MacMurray is in top leading-man form, in the first of his four pictures with Stanwyck, followed by *Double Indemnity* (their most famous teaming and a film-noir high point), *The Moonlighter* (1953), and the Douglas Sirk melodrama *There's Always Tomorrow* (1956). Sturges, who began directing his own scripts after *Remember the Night*, worked with Stanwyck on her very next film, *The Lady Eve,* which contains another reasonable candidate for "greatest Stanwyck performance," though it is inarguably her funniest.

If you're looking for a fresh Christmas movie this season, you're unlikely to find better company than Stanwyck and MacMurray and Sturges and Leisen.

Wichita (1955)
April 6th, 2010

Though my face always goes blank whenever anyone asks me what my favorite movie is, I never pause when asked to name my favorite old-time movie actor. Joel McCrea certainly wasn't the greatest actor of the first three decades of talking pictures, but he was possibly the most underrated, the most taken for granted, often looked upon as the guy you got when Gary Cooper was busy.

One of my favorite of McCrea's pictures is *Wichita* (1955), one of three films he made with director Jacques Tourneur, the man who gave us *Cat People* (1942) and *Out of the Past* (1947). Tourneur's three McCrea films are not noir-ish pictures like those two 1940s classics, but, rather, two westerns and one semi-western. The semi-western, *Stars in My Crown* (1950), in which McCrea beautifully plays a small-town parson, is the best of the trio, and it is one of the films featured in my book *Screen Savers*. *Stranger on Horseback* (1955) is easily the least of the three McCrea-Tourneur collaborations. Let's look at the final one they made together, a very special low-budget western, a real sleeper.

Though *Wichita* is one of countless westerns about Wyatt Earp, it has fresh content, a mature subject, and a fascinating conflict. Known as a "trail town," Wichita makes its money off of thrill-seeking cowboys looking for liquor and whores after all their hard work handling cattle. The town's slogan is "Everything Goes in Wichita," which unsurprisingly leads to considerable danger and violence for the local citizens. Recognized as a "natural-born lawman" after stopping a bank robbery, McCrea is pursued by the town's big shots to become their new marshal. Though he first resists, he changes his mind after a five-year-old boy (named "Michael Jackson") is killed by a stray bullet. McCrea becomes tough on crime, so much so—and here's where the story gets really interesting—that the town fathers soon regret his success, which is affecting the economy. When McCrea institutes a ban on guns and has certain cowboys expelled from Wichita, the question for the community becomes whether or not Wichita can remain safe without destroying its prosperity.

McCrea's Earp is a man of blacks and whites in a world of grays. He refuses to change his methods, nor will he step down. Most of Wichita doesn't deserve him, though the mayor (Carl Benton Reid) and young Bat Masterson (Keith Larsen) stand beside him. Also adding to the colorful mix are Vera Miles as McCrea's love interest, Peter Graves as one of the Earp brothers, and Lloyd Bridges as one of those vile cowboys.

Wichita is a compact, intelligent western, well shot and with fine dialogue. The overriding theme of morals versus economics will never get old. What's especially intriguing about *Wichita* is that it's scary in an everyday fashion, presenting a realistic West with believable dangers, not some backlot recreation driven by tired genre conventions. But it would be far less than it is, ultimately, without McCrea, who is so unassailably firm and sure. Who is more at ease and secure on a movie screen than McCrea? And who more solidly projects dependability and unadorned goodness? And he's never a pain about his virtues, wearing them so effortlessly, so simply.

Before he devoted himself exclusively to the western genre, McCrea had been an accomplished light comedian (*Sullivan's Travels* and *The Palm Beach Story*), a strong dramatic actor (*These Three* and *Dead End*), an action star *(Foreign Correspondent)*, exemplary at whatever he attempted. The never-nominated McCrea gave at least two Oscar-caliber performances, in *Sullivan's Travels* and *Ride the High Country* (1962), his greatest western, but in *Wichita* he is at his quintessential best, thoroughly at home and lived-in in the genre he liked most of all.

Wichita recently became available on DVD through the TCM Archive.

Five Graves to Cairo (1943)
April 12th, 2010

In 1942, Billy Wilder directed his first Hollywood movie, the comedy hit *The Major and the Minor,* starring Ginger Rogers and Ray Milland (who later starred in *The Lost Weekend,* Wilder's big Oscar winner of 1945). In 1944, Wilder made the classic film noir *Double Indemnity,* with Barbara Stanwyck and Fred MacMurray (who later appeared in *The Apartment,* Wilder's *other* big Oscar winner, from 1960). Between directing Ginger's comedy and Barbara's noir, Wilder directed *Five Graves to Cairo* (which he co-wrote with Charles Brackett), a forgotten but highly enjoyable WWII picture, the kind of comic-book adventure version of the war that inspired last year's *Inglourious Basterds.* Shot and designed in superb black and white, the film is escapist intrigue of a high order, stylishly and inventively fashioned by Wilder, who ensured that the film would be enormous fun, not just clever and suspenseful and beautifully paced but also touching.

Set in Northern Egypt, out in the desert, the film's main location is a remote hotel run by an amusingly timid Akim Tamiroff. As a British corporal stranded from his tank regiment, Franchot Tone is the film's star. When the

Germans arrive at the hotel, Tone poses as Tamiroff's waiter (who died), not knowing that the waiter had been a German spy. Anne Baxter is the French maid whose brother is in a concentration camp back in Germany. And Erich von Stroheim—seven years before appearing in Wilder's masterpiece *Sunset Boulevard*—makes a grand Rommel.

Merely adequate, Tone has the feeling of being a second choice for his role, but Baxter is excellent, fresh from her lovely work in Orson Welles' extraordinary drama *The Magnificent Ambersons*. Cool and smart, charming and poignant, Baxter is also sexually mature, keeping eager males at bay while also ready to offer herself to a German in exchange for her brother's safety. Despite the script's expected (and forgivable) propaganda speeches, this is an exceptionally well-done entertainment, another early feather in Wilder's directorial cap, yet a film rarely mentioned when people are writing about or just talking about Wilder's illustrious career. It seems he made too many good movies, thus pushing at least one of them out of the spotlight.

My Reputation (1946)
May 20th, 2010

Though I'm firmly on record proclaiming *Remember the Night* (1940) as the film that contains my all-time favorite Barbara Stanwyck performance, I must say that *My Reputation* (1946) has *another* of my fave Stanwyck turns. Yes, there are many Stanwyck jewels to choose from, starting with her sublime screwball work in *The Lady Eve* (1941) and her definitive femme fatale of *Double Indemnity* (1944), not to mention her heartbreaking restraint in the final minutes of *Stella Dallas* (1937). Oh, and the pure fun of *Ball of Fire* (1941), too! Then there's a slew of lesser-known Stanwyck pictures with so much to savor: *The Miracle Woman* (1931), *Ever in My Heart* (1933), and *Baby Face* (1933) from her early years, and *East Side, West Side* (1949), *The Furies* (1950), and *All I Desire* (1953) from the later years. From her middle years (her peak), *My Reputation* is a standout among unsung Stanwyck pictures. It is one classy soap.

Handsomely directed by Curtis Bernhardt, *My Reputation* is a well-paced and absorbing drama of a newly widowed woman (Stanwyck), a 33-year-old with sons ages 12 and 14. She finds her way to independence, away from the control of her domineering mother (formidable Lucile Watson), and is reborn through the love of a dashing major (George Brent). With Stanwyck's shades of timidity, and that nightmare mother, the film recalls *Now, Voyager* (1942), which is probably no accident considering the former film's popularity and the fact that they both came out of Warner Brothers. Like Bette Davis in 1942, Stanwyck makes a very satisfying emergence from fear, intensified by the exposed vulnerability she exhibits earlier in the picture. Stanwyck is terrific: warm and likable and poignant, imbuing the film with her innate honesty and professional integrity.

My Reputation takes a strong subject—widowhood—and treats it with dignity, while also using it as ideal fodder for a juicy "woman's picture" of the day. After all, it's got gossipy friends, mother-daughter melodrama, and burgeoning romance. Imagine how many wartime widows found comfort in such an emotional yet hopeful look at the issues confronting women who suddenly found themselves alone. As in most women's pictures, the actual man is almost beside the point, and George Brent would have known this, having played dozens of them. (Brent made five pictures with Stanwyck, *eleven* with Davis, with all three of them appearing together in 1932's *So Big*.) The one to watch, aside from Stanwyck, is Eve Arden, surprisingly cast as Stanwyck's *married* friend, as opposed to one of her usual single-sidekick, gal-Friday roles. Despite a horrifying Max Steiner score, which is brain-numbingly cheerful, *My Reputation* is an all-around winner.

One film that *My Reputation* may remind you of is Douglas Sirk's 1955 *All That Heaven Allows* (considered a classic by many), since both films have starting-over widows at their centers. In the Stanwyck slot is Jane Wyman, with Rock Hudson the new man in her life. As overrated as *My Reputation* is underrated, *All That Heaven Allows* is heavy-handed, obvious, and bloodless. It also contains an accidental wink at Hudson's real-life sexuality: when he tells Wyman to hang tough, she says, "And you want me to be a man."

Crime Wave (1954)
June 11th, 2010

Just when I thought I had seen every major film noir (many times over), along comes *Crime Wave*. I first became aware of this cops-and-robbers flick when Martin Scorsese featured it in his documentary on American film. And I've had it in my Netflix queue for months and months. I guess I wasn't really expecting all that much, or why else wouldn't I have seen it sooner? For any film lover who feels he has seen just about everything, it's such a joy to discover a genuine sleeper like Andre de Toth's *Crime Wave*. Though de Toth was the man who made the 3-D smash hit *House of Wax* (1953), he left behind two bona fide gems: *None Shall Escape* (1944), his WWII masterwork and one of the finest of war movies made *during* the war; and, yes, *Crime Wave*, a pure, quintessential L.A. noir.

The plot of *Crime Wave* is often routine, standard stuff, but the execution is a marvel. This is one of those inventive black-and-white movies that is a nonstop visual pleasure, superbly shot by *Stagecoach*'s Bert Glennon in both stylishly "black" scenes and starkly "white" ones. Three escaped convicts (Ted de Corsia, Nedrick Young, and a young Charles Bronson), on a spree, seek protection from an unwilling ex-con (Gene Nelson) who has since gone straight. The movie opens with the trio holding up a gas station and killing a cop, with the marvelous contrast of Doris Day's " 'S Wonderful" cheerily ringing out from a radio.

In 1954, Gene Nelson was one of the screen's top dancers, tapping his way through a string of musicals at Warner Brothers, and he is best remembered today for his Will Parker of *Oklahoma!* (1955). In a dramatic role, he acquits himself rather well, never suggesting the possibility that he may have accidentally stumbled into the wrong genre. Sterling Hayden, as the police lieutenant, is more typically cast, very much at home in all things noir. His role has an interesting duality: he may be a cop but he's the scariest guy in the movie, particularly hard on Nelson, whom he continues to look upon as a criminal. Unfortunately, Hayden's hardboiled role and performance are filled with cliches, bordering on parody. One nice touch is his penchant for chewing on toothpicks as a way to avoid smoking (following doctor's orders), giving him some much-needed human dimension and likable humor. Hayden, de Corsia, and Timothy Carey (another baddie) were all reunited in Stanley Kubrick's film noir *The Killing* (1956), one of the films I write about in my book *Screen Savers*.

Crime Wave also has good performances from Phyllis Kirk *(House of Wax)*, as Nelson's loyal and attractive wife, and the usually comic Jay Novello in a serious role as an ex-con doctor. With gritty locales, a snappy pace, and an interesting emerging theme (the tough fate of parolees like Nelson, who strive to make good), *Crime Wave* peaks with a bank robbery both exciting and surprising. Don't wait as long as I did to catch up with *Crime Wave*.

Three Hours to Kill (1954)
June 17th, 2010

For my money, the 1950s was the greatest decade for the Hollywood western, the period that produced *The Gunfighter* (1950), *Devil's Doorway* (1950), *The Furies* (1950), *Rio Grande* (1950), *High Noon* (1952), *The Naked Spur* (1953), *Shane* (1953), *Johnny Guitar* (1954), *Wichita*

(1955), *The Searchers* (1956), *Seven Men from Now* (1956), and *The Big Country* (1958). But beyond those titles, and so many other well-regarded examples, there are seemingly countless (and virtually unknown) quality westerns, pictures that might have stood out had the decade not been so top-heavy with exemplary work.

A good example of a top-notch "B" western is *Three Hours to Kill*, starring Dana Andrews and Donna Reed and directed by Alfred Werker. Tensely rendered and briskly paced, this compact movie tells an instantly compelling tale. Andrews returns to his hometown after three years away, following an incident in which his friends tried to lynch him for the murder of his lover's brother. (Wasn't getting hanged in 1943's *The Ox-Bow Incident* enough punishment for Andrews?) Innocent of the murder, Andrews has returned to find the real killer and reconnect with Reed, who married someone else while he was gone (but gave birth to his son). The hook of the plot is the three hours given to Andrews (by the sheriff) to unmask the villain.

The flashback to the murder and near-lynching is violently intense, as is the escape and chase that follow. (Andrews has a scar on his neck from that day.) As the film explores betrayal, revenge, and mob violence, it also becomes a neat murder mystery, with the main suspects a barber, a saloonkeeper, a gambler, and a romantic rival. The film also takes an adult look at love, specifically in the premarital sexuality between Andrews and Reed, with Reed, commenting later on their bad luck, saying, "Maybe because of what we did." And there's also more than a whiff of incestuous feeling for Reed by her soon-to-be dead brother. The film's modest budget is obvious, but the picture is brightly colorful and consistently absorbing (though its ending is too abruptly resolved). It's got a surprise twist, a likable floozie (Dianne Foster), and a nice balance between action and personal drama.

Andrews' career as a leading man was certainly in decline by 1954, but Donna Reed, at the time of the picture's fall release, was the reigning Best Supporting Actress Oscar winner for *From Here to Eternity* (1953). Opportunities on the big screen soon diminished for her as well, but sitcom stardom awaited her in 1958.

If you've got 77 minutes to kill, you won't regret spending them with Dana, Donna, and company.

The War Against Mrs. Hadley (1942)
July 16th, 2010

In the same year that MGM released *Mrs. Miniver* (1942), its enormously popular and Oscar-laden tribute to the British home front, the studio delivered another morale booster for the war effort, more a B picture than an A, and with a much pricklier title character than Greer Garson's impossibly "wonderful" Mrs. M. *The War Against Mrs. Hadley*, released two months after *Mrs. Miniver*, stars Oscar winner Fay Bainter *(Jezebel)* in a rare leading screen role.

Mrs. Hadley is a selfish, wealthy matron who finds the war a nuisance, an inconvenience, until she (and you know it's coming) finally accepts responsibility, embraces unselfishness, and does her part. Which means of course that it's not too late for those of us in the audience to pitch in, those of us who may not be quite as naturally inspiring as Greer Garson. The picture is a feel-good booster of the times, saying that there's hope for all of us, and *good* in all of us. Its effectiveness is in no small part due to Bainter's excellent acting and the skill with which she believably charts her transition.

George Oppenheimer's screenplay (which lost the Best Original Screenplay Oscar to *Woman of the Year*, also featuring Bainter) is shameless in its manipulations, which is part of the fun of these wartime propaganda pictures. Mrs. Hadley's son, played by Richard Ney (who was also a son to Mrs. Miniver, and then married Garson in real life), moves from rich-brat drunk to decorated war hero, the message being that war is the best thing that can happen to a troubled young man. When Mrs. Hadley receives a congratulatory letter from F.D.R. (whom she loathes because she is a Republican), the lesson is to put politics aside and support our leader at this crucial moment. Yes, it's a fantasy of unification, but darn if the thing doesn't actually make you feel good. Though pure B-movie hokum of the wartime variety, it works very well on these terms.

The Animal Kingdom (1932)
July 23rd, 2010

Though sorely underrated in her day, the great (and never Oscar-nominated) Myrna Loy gave at least a handful of magnificent performances, starting with the sophisticated comic artistry that she brought to *The Thin Man* (1934), opposite her favorite leading man, the equally witty William Powell. Who can ever forget Loy's moving understatement in the superb post-war drama *The Best Years of Our Lives* (1946), particularly her exquisitely rendered homecoming sequence with husband Fredric March? I also happen to adore her in two other dramas: *Test Pilot* (1938), in which both Clark Gable and Spencer Tracy are at their best, too; and *The Rains Came* (1939), in which she falls in love with Tyrone Power. And what epitomizes effortless comic precision better than Loy's monologue to the house painter in *Mr. Blandings Builds His Dream House* (1948)?

Perhaps the first great Loy performance came in *The Animal Kingdom*, based on Philip Barry's stage hit, a pre-Code talkie that now feels both terribly modern and hopelessly dated. Though the content is adult, bohemian, and overtly sexual, the ideals are simplistic, the writing melodramatic, and the filmmaking (by Edward H. Griffith) static and stagy. But it's still compelling fun to watch characters in an old movie wrestle with art versus commerce, freedom versus convention, integrity versus selling out. It's all very lofty and high-minded, just like top-billed Ann Harding as a fashion magazine artist turned painter. In her past, she lived with rich boy Leslie Howard, a book publisher. Not merely sex partners, they were soulmates. Yet they had no claims on each other, no responsibilities. (Harding calls herself a foolish virgin, "well, foolish, anyway.") Howard decides to marry Myrna Loy at just about the time that Harding is ready for marriage herself.

Harding was fresh from her Oscar-nominated role in the 1930 film version of Barry's *Holiday* (in which she's surprisingly good in what would become the Katharine Hepburn role in 1938), but she's the third wheel here. The plot revolves around the women's struggle for Howard's soul. Loy, in the larger and better female role, walks off with the movie. She plays a sly manipulator, an icy goddess who uses sex to get what she wants. But she's never obvious or a cliche; she's always a real person. She has a masterful negligee-seduction scene that keeps husband Howard from attending Harding's art opening. Being with Loy compromises Howard, keeping him from Harding, who serves as his artistic conscience.

Harding can be smug, with hands on hips, but she's also smart and romantic, while Howard is his usual elegant self (repeating the role he played on Broadway). What Loy possesses that obliterates her co-stars is her subtlety, her believable cunning and potent unforced sensuality. Loy is a tactful schemer, a quietly ruthless woman, a poised and relaxed seductress, and she's altogether devastating. Good as Harding and Howard are here, they are clearly from an old-time era in screen acting, while Loy's work feels ageless, as natural and plausible today as it was 78 years ago.

The Big Clock (1948)
December 2nd, 2010

Reuniting the cast of *Payment Deferred* (1932)—Charles Laughton, Maureen O'Sullivan, and Ray Milland—*The Big Clock* is a nifty, clever thriller with a glamorous publishing-world setting. Milland operates *Crimeways* magazine, one of several publications owned by Laughton, an imperious, feared, and hands-on kind of boss. When Milland foolishly goes out drinking with Laughton's mistress (Rita Johnson), missing the West Virginia-bound train carrying his wife (O'Sullivan) and their little boy, the plot moves from urban workplace drama to a tale of murder. Laughton bashes Johnson's head with a metal sun dial, but, naturally, he has no intention of taking the blame, instead pinning it on the unknown fellow who had been seen out with Johnson all evening. When Laughton asks Milland to locate this fellow, under the guise of an unrelated news story, Milland quickly realizes that he's being asked to track down himself. The drama heats up as Milland tries to avoid all the many witnesses who can identify him.

Milland, still in the glow of his Oscar win for *The Lost Weekend* (1945), is at the peak of his stardom, delivering a solid and confident performance. Ms. O'Sullivan, wife of the film's director, John Farrow, is stuck in the dreary role of Milland's wife, perhaps for the pleasure of spending all those days on the set with her husband. Laughton, with an unattractive mustache, manages to do what very few actors can, simultaneously underplaying and overacting. He gives the character the kind of "subtle" tics that are so eye-catching that they quickly become actorly mannerisms. When he throws a line away, he does so *so* self-consciously that he's still hammy. You don't believe he's this character for a second, yet he's so entertaining and delightfully self-amused that he gives the film a pleasurable kick.

With Laughton at the center, his real-life wife Elsa Lanchester can't be too far behind. Here she shows up as an eccentric, much-married painter, bringing some delicious comic relief as only she could. (Laughton and Lanchester appear together only near the end.) Despite Farrow's stylish direction, the film suffers from a few silly touches in the writing and a disappointingly brisk and abrupt finish. It's nonetheless a tricky little effort, one of those old movies that begins at a climax and then flashes backward (36 hours), later to return to the scene that opened the picture, when we now know exactly what's going on. (*Mildred Pierce* memorably used this storytelling device in 1945.) Milland's extended drunk scene cannot rival his Oscar-winning lost weekend, but the picture is one of his more satisfying vehicles. *The Big Clock*'s chief asset is the black-and-white cinematography of John Seitz, who continually roves his way through offices and apartments and bars with a fluidity that is most impressive.

Also on hand is Dan Tobin, an actor who played coded gay characters, notably in *Woman of the Year* (1942). Here he's the bow-tied employee who speaks about his seeing a psychiatrist. You may also remember that Laughton and O'Sullivan had appeared together as father and daughter in *The Barretts of Wimpole Street* (1934). If the plot of *The Big Clock* sounds familiar, it's because it later became *No Way Out* (1987), starring Kevin Costner in the Milland slot. It just wasn't the same without the black and white, though.

The Romance of Rosy Ridge (1947)
July 9th, 2011

Here's a movie I had avoiding seeing ever since Turner Classic Movies started showing it. Doesn't the title make it sound awful? Don't you expect some forced hillbilly comedy with Ma and Pa Kettle living "down the road apiece"? *The Romance of Rosy Ridge* turns out to be a surprisingly good drama about an interesting moment in American history, the immediate months after the Civil War, when the nation's hostilities were still raw. Set in Missouri, a place in which dwelled sympathizers of both sides, the film manages to be a richly felt and unexpectedly sensitive piece, despite its flaws.

The film's only claim to fame has been as the movie that "introduced" Janet Leigh to moviegoers, beginning her tenure as an MGM contract player, which resulted in just a few movies as good or better than this one (*Act of Violence*, *Scaramouche*, and *The Naked Spur*). She is certainly seen to advantage, making a charming debut as a farmgirl. She's fresh, pretty, natural, and, yes, already costumed to highlight her generous female attributes. Her parents are Thomas Mitchell (as die-hard a Southerner as he was in *Gone With the Wind*) and Selena Royle, and her little brother is Dean Stockwell. Actually, *Rosy Ridge* is a Van Johnson vehicle, with Johnson billed solo above the title. He plays the stranger who mysteriously shows up one night and stays to help the family with their many chores. But did he favor the North or the South? And has he arrived here deliberately? The usually terrific Mr. Mitchell overacts here (especially in his country accent), and Mr. Johnson seems out of place in a period setting (and his singing and harmonica-playing don't help much). Of course, Johnson and Leigh fall in love.

Even more striking than Leigh's radiant simplicity is Ms. Royle's performance, the film's best. Royle was part of the MGM stock company in the

1940s (before being blacklisted in the '50s), and you may recall her from *The Harvey Girls* (1946) or *The Green Years* (1946), among others. But MGM never gave Her a role as rich as the quietly strong country woman of *Rosy Ridge*, a part similar to all those mothers Anne Revere played to acclaim in the '40s. Royle acts with dignity and intelligence, as well as unvarnished honesty and directness; she unobtrusively walks away with the movie.

Directed with care by Roy Rowland, and beautifully photographed in black and white, *Rosy Ridge* is a fine effort at an offbeat family drama. There are memorable passages: a stirring opening when the family, racing to each other from their separate chores, mistakenly believes that the oldest son has returned from the war; Royle giving Leigh a brush-up lesson in square dancing; the square dance itself (called a "play party"), which uneasily reunites enemies created by the war; and, best of all, a thrilling visual sequence in which the family and Van work tirelessly to get all the bundled hay into the barn before a raging storm descends. I don't recall a single mention of Rosy Ridge, which only adds to the inanity of the title. Mr. Johnson gets some climactic he-man heroics, but the film is stronger at bringing people together than in tearing them apart. Its understated message of hope and peace and community is lovingly rendered. And, don't worry, neither Ma and Pa Kettle nor the cast of *Tobacco Road* ever show up.

H.M. Pulham, Esq. (1941)
July 25th, 2011

Austrian-born Hedy Lamarr, one of the Golden Age's standout beauties, made an auspicious American screen debut opposite Charles Boyer in *Algiers* (1938), cast as a poor but now jewel-laden Parisian about to sell herself in marriage to portly, much-older Robert Greig. But in the casbah she clicks with Boyer, perfectly matched in their nonchalance and devastating glamour, soon smoldering together quite exquisitely. In the next two decades, Lamarr made mostly lousy movies, with even her most famous films fairly terrible. In *Ziegfeld Girl* (1941), a '40s version of *Valley of the Dolls*, she gives a sleepwalking performance. You wouldn't be surprised if the film had a late-breaking revelation that showgirl Hedy was actually a vampire; she's, at the very least, *some* kind of zombie. In *White Cargo* (1942), no better than a lesser Tarzan movie, she announces, "I am Tondelayo," then primarily speaks of herself in the third person thereafter. As vehicles go, it was worthy of Maria Montez.

Samson and Delilah (1949) remains Lamarr's best remembered movie, despite being a clumsy, slow, and dramatically anemic spectacle. It took five costume designers to clothe her Delilah, and yet she and co-star Victor Mature have similar hairstyles (and zero chemistry). This is a laughable love/hate soap opera, and, despite her stunning face and reasonable vitality, Lamarr gives an obvious and amateurish performance that is perfectly in sync with Cecil B. DeMille's cardboard direction. And in what universe could Lamarr and Angela Lansbury be sisters?

Lamarr did get one exceptional role, as the independent career woman of MGM's *H. M. Pulham, Esq.* (1941). She came through with an outstanding performance, proof that she was, after all, an actress as well as a goddess. Directed by King Vidor, this is a very fine and unusually mature drama, a modern-feeling and quite intelligent look at life's choices. How many other Golden Age pictures penetratingly deal with self-fulfillment and mid-life crises? Not a soap or a melodrama, it's a surprisingly probing examination of two lives, the title character (Robert Young) and the female lead, Marvin Myles (Lamarr). Does anyone on the planet look less like a Marvin than Hedy?

Young, from a privileged Boston family, meets Lamarr when they are co-workers at a New York ad agency. They fall in love. Freed from being cast solely because of her looks, Lamarr delivers a smart, strong piece of acting that is consistently interesting and nuanced. Though she loves Young, she refuses to compromise herself to fit into Boston society. Young, too, was never better, honestly struggling with his character's conventional and unconventional inclinations. He and Lamarr create a believably romantic yet complicated connection.

Handsomely mounted and sensitively written, *H. M. Pulham, Esq.* is a movie with genuine integrity without being full of itself. It never feels pretentious in its tackling of life's big questions. Yes, it's one of Vidor's more underrated movies, but I think it's most important as the film in which the ravishing Hedy Lamarr gave her one and only superb performance.

II. They Can't All Be Gems
screensaversmovies.com

You Can (and Should) Run Away From It
October 2nd, 2008

TCM recently aired *You Can't Run Away from It* (1956), the rarely seen musical version of the classic Frank Capra romantic comedy *It Happened One Night* (1934). Most people are surprised to learn that there exists this written-for-the-screen musical of the beloved, multi-Oscar-winning charmer. That's because it sank without a trace, deservedly so. Imagine taking one of the screen's sexiest comedies and remaking it, but leaving out the erotic component. In place of the original film's brilliant stars, Clark Gable and Claudette Colbert, a couple smoldering with chemistry and brimming with charm, we get mechanical June Allyson and asexual Jack Lemmon. Instead of '30s sexiness, we get '50s coyness.

When Gable played the reporter, he had a rakish appeal. As Gable finds himself reluctantly falling for runaway heiress Colbert, he becomes more disagreeable because he thinks there could never be a future for them. Lemmon doesn't comprehend that the character's ornery moods come from sexual frustration. Gone, in 1956, is Gable's scene in which he teaches Colbert how a man undresses. What was slyly steamy coming from Gable would have been ludicrous from the juvenile Lemmon. Gable's climactic scene with Walter Connolly (Colbert's dad) is truly hilarious and altogether irresistible, enough to merit Gable the Oscar he ended up winning. Lemmon's version of the scene doesn't register at all (not one laugh to be had). Lemmon seems too naive to be in a romantic comedy, almost as if he doesn't understand what's at stake emotionally or sexually. Colbert made her realization of love a transformative experience for the inexperienced society girl, but Allyson is never less than a hardened trouper, manufacturing every response and lacking a requisite light touch. Colbert had such elegance and refinement (you believed she was rich and spoiled), whereas Allyson seems a bargain-basement knock-off.

The 1956 version is also a film without a context. Capra's film was a Depression-era film in which contemporary America was this road picture's background. Common folks, as represented by Gable, know how to function in this world, while the rich, meaning Colbert, are useless and helpless, a flattering notion for Depression audiences. Among the film's most memorable sequences are Gable teaching Colbert how to do things that people should know how to do *properly*, such as dunk a donut. By 1956, the plot had no connection to the here and now, and, therefore, seemed dated and pointless.

I recently hosted a screening of *It Happened One Night*, which was especially gratifying because many in the audience had never seen the whole movie. (Everyone had seen the famous hitch-hiking sequence excerpted everywhere.) Of course, everyone loved it. How could they not? It's absolutely ageless, feeling as fresh and spontaneous as it did 74 years ago. It is one of the screen's most influential movies, the granddaddy of several decades' worth of romantic comedies. Hundreds of pictures have stolen from it freely, sometimes quite blatantly as in *There Goes My Heart* (1938). Most romantic comedies owe something to it; it's the yardstick by which all the others continue to be measured, the one with the kind of emotional pull to which every romantic comedy aspires.

The musical's songs were written by Gene de Paul and Johnny Mercer, who were coming off the phenomenal success of their *Seven Brides for Seven Brothers*, one of the all-time great musicals written for the movies. You'd never guess that the two films have scores by the same team. Lemmon sings well enough, while Allyson's voice is utterly ragged, but that's not where the fault lies. How could anyone turn the iconic hitch-hiking scene into a witless upbeat ditty called "Thumbin' a Ride"? Shouldn't Allyson be paying attention to cars going by, rather than launching into a frenzied number? The equally famed "Walls of Jericho" scene becomes the musical number "Temporarily," about how virginal Allyson is playing wife to the even more virginal Lemmon for one night only. Allyson also has an athletic "Scarecrow" ballet in the haystack scene (when she's supposedly starving). The songs are poor and poorly staged, simply reminders of people coming together to butcher one of the most glorious films of Hollywood's Golden Age.

Some trivia to leave you with: Gable and Colbert travel from Florida to New York, while Lemmon and Allyson go from California to Texas. Near the end, Gable asks Colbert's dad for the $39.60 he spent on Colbert; Lemmon asks Allyson's dad (Charles Bickford) for $37.75. Why did it cost Lemmon less, 22 years after Gable?

White Woman (1933)
November 26th, 2008

Last night I went to a double feature at NYC's Film Forum. The occasion was the twelve-day tribute to Carole Lombard in honor of the 100th anniversary of her birth. The two pictures that drew me there were rarities I've always wanted to see, both from the period before Lombard was Lombard, before she established an identifiable and original persona and found her calling as the queen of screwball comedy.

Stuart Walker's *White Woman* (1933) is a feverish bit of nonsense, one of those exotic "island" movies. No one ever comes out and says, "The natives are getting restless," but it's frequently on the tips of the characters' tongues. Lombard looks lovely and is breathtakingly photographed and sumptuously clothed. Yes, she's the "white woman," and she's top-billed, but she's no competition (who is?) for co-star Charles Laughton.

Lombard plays a scandalous chanteuse who marries wealthy Laughton as a way out of her nowhere existence. She goes with him to his lavish houseboat on his rubber plantation. Lombard and Laughton fared better in 1940 in *They Knew What They Wanted,* but, ironically, *White Woman*'s plot plays like a quickie jungle version of their 1940 picture. This means that there's a handsome fellow (Kent Taylor) who arrives on the scene to turn it into a triangle. Laughton may lose the girl but he walks away with the movie. It seems clear that Laughton, recognizing that he was making a turkey, decided to amuse himself by giving an outrageous performance. Oh, boy, does he! He injects the movie with a crazy vitality and a strangely humorous streak. Clad in almost foppish costumes and sporting an over-the-top mustache, Laughton holds one's attention because he's so unpredictable: alternately funny, queeny, cruel, and cunning, sometimes all at once. Mostly he's a joyously theatrical actor having a lark. *White Woman* is an oddity, and it did nothing for either of its stars, but Laughton makes certain that you can't dismiss it as forgettable. Bad, yes, but not forgettable.

The Model and the Mechanic
November 30th, 2008

Continuing my report on the Carole Lombard series at NYC's Film Forum, I now address *Sinners in the Sun* (1932), a hilariously extravagant title for a picture about a model and a mechanic, poor but in love, who take a melodramatic and improbable (though not unenjoyable) journey, only to learn that money doesn't bring happiness. Be careful what you wish for! This is one of those movies that wants to have it both ways. It intends to reassure Depression audiences that love far outweighs the pleasures of material goods, but does so only after the stars have overindulged themselves in luxury. Audience members get to feel that their own lives aren't so bad, while vicariously swimming in a lavish lifestyle (before it's rejected by the stars). This brand of movie manipulation has never really gone away. *The Devil Wears Prada* did a variation on this old chestnut just two years ago.

Luscious Lombard is the fashion model, and Chester Morris is the mechanic who wants to marry her *now*! It's Lombard who wants *more*, and it's almost comical how quickly both stars find wealthy lovers. Morris marries the woman who hires him as her chauffeur, and Lombard becomes mistress to a married (separated) man. Oh, the cars, clothes, travel, jewels, and all that unfulfillment, all that numbing dissatisfaction. Wouldn't it have been more fun, just once, to see a happy couple split over financial issues and find greater happiness with partners of real means? If only for the novelty of it! Lombard and Morris take an elaborate path back to square one. But, since this is a pre-Code drama, at least Lombard doesn't have to be punished for being sexually adventurous.

A very young Cary Grant has two scenes here as a dapper smoothie interested in Lombard. They starred together in *In Name Only* (1939), a good soap opera, but here, in 1932, they are both unformed. She isn't Lombard yet, and he isn't Cary Grant, but they are on their way to finding their on-screen selves. They may or may not be sinners but they're clearly headed for careers in the sun.

Cold-War Bette
March 24th, 2009

The rarely seen Bette Davis drama *Storm Center* (1956) has its heart in the right place, so it's unfortunate that it becomes such a heavy and graceless movie. It's a drab '50s drama, directed in a lumbering yet overwrought fashion by co-screenwriter Daniel Taradash. The story is cautionary but unconvincing. The great Bette is hopelessly phony and self-conscious here, managing to be both subdued and mannered. Her chirpy, clipped line readings don't help; she speaks to everyone like she's their kindergarten teacher. Actually, she's a librarian extraordinaire, as well as a WWI widow. Her city council wants to ban *The Communist Dream* from her shelves and she refuses on principle. Fired, she becomes a pariah. It's a witch-hunt drama, a left-leaning problem picture. None of it is helped by one of the worst child performances you'll ever see, in the other central role. I'll leave him nameless, but, boy, does he have a whopper of a big bad scene in which he denounces Bette publicly, leading to her slapping and shaking him. Trying to slap and shake a performance out of him?

It's all rather feeble, but it was nonetheless a treat when TCM screened it at the end of last year. After all, it was something of a lost Bette Davis movie. I don't recall it ever being on TV before. The picture now has a time capsule feeling for those feverish times. Bette was long past the point of being cast as ordinary people, women who could blend into a room, or even a town. She fared no better that same year as the Bronx housewife in *The Catered Affair*. *Storm Center* was originally set to be a comeback vehicle for Mary Pickford. From Mary Pickford to Bette Davis! Not really such a leap when you consider how much Bette resembled the Pickford look when she played Baby Jane Hudson six years later.

Earthbound "Starlift" (1951)
April 6th, 2009

The new 5-disc Doris Day DVD collection that debuts on April 7th doesn't offer a particularly enticing quintet, but the inclusion of the rarely seen *Starlift* is of great interest. Well, until you see it, that is. Warner Brothers obviously thought that it could do for the Korean War what it had done for WWII, without taking into account the passage of time, or the fact that this was a different kind of war. WB had given us *Thank Your Lucky Stars* (1943) and *Hollywood Canteen* (1944), two big entertain-the-troops musicals filled with major stars playing themselves and doing their bit for the war effort. *Starlift* is the 1950s version of that formula and it's a dud.

Starlift's brand of romanticized corn feels more like 1944 than 1951, with Janice Rule (as a fictional star) and Ron Hagerthy (as a corporal who looks twelve) falling for each other. Their happy ending is clinched when she proves that she knows how to make a chocolate malt just the way he likes it. This isn't charming and sweet; it's coy and sickening. But who remembers that Rule could dance? There she is kicking up her legs in two big dance numbers opposite the terrific Gene Nelson.

Doris Day and Gordon MacRae share a bland duet, but Day does better with standards like "You Do Something to Me." She is sporting that dreadful early 1950s haircut of hers, too. Day also has a brief scene with Jimmy Cagney, making this their second of three film appearances together, after *The West Point Story* (1950) but before *Love Me or Leave Me* (1955). MacRae and Nelson share the screen briefly as well, a reminder of their big success together in the forthcoming *Oklahoma!* (1955).

Perhaps the oddest musical number is a western spoof set in a saloon, sung by an unfunny Phil Harris and with a speaking role for Gary Cooper! But the picture is mostly about Hollywood stars telling us how selfless they are. In a roomful of bedridden soldiers, Ruth Roman deigns to drop her mink coat to give a soldier a shave. What a gal!

Wake Up and Dream (1946)
May 12th, 2009

For every undiscovered treasure of Hollywood's Golden Age, there's an undiscovered piece of dreck. An example of the latter is this oddball bit of whimsy, a charmless post-war semi-musical set during the war. Hick farmer John Payne goes off to the navy, enlisting despite his deferment and leaving behind a waitress girlfriend (June Haver) and a kid sister (Connie Marshall). After the news arrives that Payne is missing in action, young Marshall is possessed by the irrational notion that she will find him on an island. So, she and Haver hook up with old man Clem Bevans and set off on his sailboat. (Though no one ever says so, they appear to be going from Maine to Florida.) This bizarre and unmagical film strains to be about "believing" and "a child's faith." The result is lame-brained slop.

Handsome Payne, miscast as a hick, is sorely missed for most of the picture (though he must have been glad about having little to do here). Haver, so manufactured and artificial, actually had a whole career at Fox based on her usefulness as a threat to Betty Grable, the studio's superstar, just in case Grable got out of line. Both ladies were blond singer-dancers, but who could confuse the easy and likable Grable with the robotic Haver? (They starred together in the 1946 musical *The Dolly Sisters,* memorable for the campy and outrageous items-in-your-makeup-bag production number.) Haver makes Grable seem as complicated as Barbara Stanwyck. Yet, there was Haver in every Technicolor musical that wasn't good enough for Grable, and considering how bad most of Grable's musicals are, that really says something.

Haver must be hiding hair and makeup people on that sailboat because she always looks flawless, even when the boat makes it to the swamps. Connie

Marshall is in Margaret O'Brien mode: moody, emotional, irritating. The oft-repeated song is "Give Me the Simple Life," sung in the credits, then sung by Payne, by Haver, and heard on a jukebox. The picture's most startling and inadvertently memorable element is its use of "We're Off to See the Wizard." In a non-MGM movie, no less! It is first heard as underscoring, leaving you to doubt what you are hearing, but it continues when an off-screen chorus sings the words. Surprising, yes, not least for making absolutely no sense. This is a garishly colorful Fox picture, struggling to turn itself into a sentimental favorite. Marshall does get to "find" Payne, because he comes home and then has to go out and search for her and Haver! By then, who cares? Whimsy and magic cannot be spun from something this stupid. It was based on a story by Robert Nathan, author *Portrait of Jennie*, which became a sublime work of film fantasy (and one of the forty movies profiled in my book *Screen Savers*). Here, despite all that singing about "the simple life," what we get is convoluted claptrap.

Elvis and the Divas
May 20th, 2009

I admit to not being a fan of the Elvis Presley films, and further admit that I have seen only about half of them, still waiting for the accidentally good one, if such a one exists. I do like the black-and-white numbers in *Jailhouse Rock* (1957), but that's as far as I can go in giving any of the films a positive response. What does stand out for me, though, is the presence, amid all those forgettable ingenues and the occasional big-star co-player (such as Ann Margret in *Viva Las Vegas*), of two big-name divas supporting Elvis: Angela Lansbury and Barbara Stanwyck.

Lansbury, one year away from her greatest screen performance, as Laurence Harvey's mother in *The Manchurian Candidate* (1962), played Elvis' mom in *Blue Hawaii* (1961), one of the worst and flimsiest of the Presley musicals, though Hawaii comes off rather well. Lansbury, apparently approaching the role with a what-the-heck-it's-only-an-Elvis-movie attitude, goes way over the top, seemingly for her own amusement, in a very broad caricature of a Southern matron. Elvis, back from the army, doesn't want to go into his family's pineapple business, a troubling matter for his snobby mother. It's a rare dimwit role for Lansbury, and it's obvious that she's too smart to fool anyone, so she just hoots and mugs her way through, as if appearing in a variety-show sketch. If you want to see a great actress in an unfunny cartoon performance, check out *Blue Hawaii*, which features "gems" such as "Rock-a-Hula Baby."

In 1964, moviegoers could see Bette Davis in *Dead Ringer,* Joan Crawford in *Strait-Jacket,* and Barbara Stanwyck opposite Elvis in *Roustabout.* (You can decide who got the worst deal.) The pickings were few for the legendary ladies of Hollywood's past. Here Stanwyck owns a carnival and Elvis becomes an employee, eventually saving the financially strapped operation with his groovy tunes and screaming fans. White-haired Stanwyck is in butch mode, very trim in her jeans, tough-talking but kind-hearted. It would be nice to report that the film is elevated by her distinguished presence, but that's not the case. Like *Blue Hawaii,* it's square as can be, with Elvis learning to be a team player. In both movies, he comes alive only in the musical numbers, and only in the songs in which he can gyrate and hip-swivel. ("Hard Knocks" is the highlight here.) Otherwise, he's a dead weight.

Both movies have lots of songs, most of them awful. If these films are low points for Lansbury and Stanwyck, at least both actresses make you sit up and notice whenever they come on-screen. I wish Elvis had paid more attention to the master classes they were offering while slumming in his pictures.

Broadway Rhythm (1944)
April 26th, 2010

The rare MGM musical that went directly into oblivion, *Broadway Rhythm* is a fascinating oddity, a predominantly terrible movie photographed in the most rapturous Technicolor, a B musical trapped in an A production. Unofficially, this was the fifth and final picture in the *Broadway Melody* series, and the only one in color. The title comes from the hit tune of *Broadway Melody of 1936,* even though that song is never sung or heard anywhere in this picture. I saw *Broadway Rhythm* for the first time in the 1980s at a revival house in New York, and I can remember being stunned by the sight of so many lavish and deservedly long-forgotten production numbers, none of which had made it into the first two *That's Entertainment!* movies. Even MGM could put considerable hard work and craft into something mediocre and instantly disposable. They had gone one *Broadway Melody* too many.

Directed by Roy Del Ruth, *Broadway Rhythm* plays more like a vaudeville program than a musical. It runs amok with the idea of specialty numbers, turning into a seemingly endless vaudeville nightmare, especially toward its end when it seems unable to stop cramming numbers into its already over-inflated running time. The plot is no different from hundreds of backstage musicals, just as forgettable, just as cliche-ridden, just as hokey. It is supposedly based on Jerome Kern's 1939 Broadway musical *Very Warm for May*, but Kern is pretty much tossed aside. George Murphy, playing Broadway's latest boy wonder, sits at a piano and thumbs through the *Very Warm for May* songbook, playing tiny bits of tunes. Then Ginny Simms, as a Hollywood star in search of a Broadway vehicle, sings Kern's great "All the Things You Are," which just happens to be my favorite song. She reprises it in the finale, and that's that for Mr. Kern! Instead, we get a boatload of non-Kern songs, a mix of standards, novelty songs, "hep" numbers, Latin tunes, etc. Eclectic, exhausting, desperate.

Murphy, a bland song and dance man, and Simms, a female crooner, are not really movie stars, neither capable of carrying or charming their way through a ten-ton color extravaganza. (He's no Gene Kelly; she isn't even Kathryn Grayson.) They fade into the woodwork as the supporting cast grasps for attention. Charles Winninger, as Murphy's retired-comic dad, yearning to get back on the boards, is his usual old-trouper self and at his quintessential worst when singing "I Love Corny Music." Auburn-haired Gloria DeHaven, as Murphy's stagestruck kid sister, fares better, especially in her circus duet with Kenny Bowers, but she's stuck playing the forties cliche of the self-dramatizing teen, or, rather, a lame satire of a teenage girl as conceived witlessly by adult writers (as was the case in every Andy Hardy movie).

Also showcased in this expensive kitsch is Lena Horne as Fernway de la Fer, a character with two songs yet not a single line of dialogue. Her first number is the tacky "Brazilian Boogie," complete with a dancing chorus. Thank heaven she returns for a straightforward and lovely rendition of "Somebody Loves Me," one of the movie's few scenes that offers nothing to complain about. The great Nancy Walker, here the 1940s version of Patsy Kelly (the screen's mannish wisecracker of the 1930s), gets only one number, as a swing-shifter complaining about her milkman's noisy bottles. This is disappointing material for a talent as big as Walker's (which was soon to be better served on Broadway in 1944's *On the Town*).

Broadway Rhythm has the distinction of having the freakiest number in any MGM musical, the Ross Sisters' "Solid Potato Salad," a jive tune to which the girls perform a horror show of contortionist tricks, which may very well have you spitting up your not-so-solid potato salad. On the more positive side, the film presents two young juveniles with potential, not just Kenny Bowers but also tap-happy Walter B. Long, both of whom quickly vanished from the screen. Another welcome sight is pianist Hazel Scott, the film's black and female answer to José Iturbi. She delivers a jazzy, knockout "Minute Waltz."

There's a spectacular nightclub set with red walls, costumes by both Irene *and* Sharaff, and yet it's all for naught. Even though the hideous sets probably outnumber the attractive ones, the Technicolor is never less than transfixing. The finale has a seated Simms descending from on high, in an orange satin gown, joining an all pink and sky-blue production number, looking as if she were taking her place in movie-musical immortality, not knowing that what she's really becoming part of is an abominable footnote in a glorious musical era, proving that even MGM could spoil its own recipes, this time not only putting an end to a franchise but possibly turning you off potato salad for good.

Athena (1954)
May 6th, 2010

Last week I wrote about *Broadway Rhythm* (1944) as an example of a botched MGM musical of the 1940s. Ten years later, *Athena* is a good example of a lousy MGM musical 1950s-style. Things were tougher for *Athena* because it was made when the demise of the genre (that of "original" movie musicals) was imminent, even though 1954 also saw the release of *Seven Brides for Seven Brothers*, one of the finest and most popular of Hollywood's written-for-the-screen musicals. Yet *Seven Brides* did little to turn the tide, a tide that included: the end of the studio system; the rise in television variety shows; a general cost-cutting; and the prominence of film musicals adapted from Broadway (which would keep movie musicals thriving, at least in terms of ticket sales, for another 15 years).

Produced by Joe Pasternak and directed by studio stalwart Richard Thorpe, *Athena* is decidedly a B picture, a forgettable and dimwitted musical comedy. It "boasts" a score by Hugh Martin and Ralph Blane, the men who wrote the songs for *Meet Me in St. Louis* (1944), another of the finer musicals ever conceived within Hollywood. However, the *Athena* score is mostly mediocre and tirelessly dependent on reprises of songs you won't want to hear the first time. It even dares to resurrect a *St. Louis* classic, "The Boy Next Door," changing "boy" to "girl" and handing it to Vic Damone, who opens the picture with it. *Athena* stars Jane Powell, the recent female lead of *Seven Brides*, at the peak of her popularity after a decade in movie musicals. Her performance in *Seven Brides* was superb, worthy of an Oscar nomination, and she's one of the reasons I included that film in my book *Screen Savers*. Perhaps *Athena* looked promising on the page, with its offbeat family of health nuts committed to exercise and vegetarianism, shunning any alcohol and cigarettes.

As the eldest of seven sisters (a nod to *Seven Brides*?), Powell is a numerologist, a perky pest who stalks uptight Edmund Purdom *(The Egyptian)*, a stiff lawyer about to embark on a political career *and* about to marry luscious, redheaded Linda Christian (then Mrs. Tyrone Power, later Mrs. Edmund Purdom!). Though we are obviously supposed to be delighted by Athena, she is, after all, a gal bent on breaking up an engaged couple (all because she likes his "numbers"). After one meeting, she arrives at Purdom's estate with a mad desire to mulch his five dying peach trees. Boy, can that girl mulch! And, in the process, she sings "Vocalize," a pretty melody with lyrics capable of leading to dangerously high blood-sugar levels. Later, she and her sisters redecorate Purdom's house without asking his permission. Such fun!

While Powell pursues Purdom, she encourages sister Debbie Reynolds to go after Damone, who plays a celebrity crooner. In secondary non-roles, Reynolds and Damone share the screen simply because they have been forced to do so, not having any real purpose in the movie (which they seem to figure out as it lumbers along). Damone's "Venezia," sung in his nightclub show, is a lavish yet lackluster production number that has Damone uncomfortably clad in a red tuxedo. Linda Christian may be playing a stock bitch but at least she wears all the best clothes. (Powell, oddly, is seen only in whites and pale shades of blue and gray and lavender; shouldn't she be a walking celebration of nature's colors?) Some zip is provided by reliable old-timers Louis Calhern and Evelyn Varden as the girls' grandparents; he's a fitness guru and she's some kind of spiritualist. Plus there's a whole fraternity of musclemen living with them in their paradisical commune. (To make money, the family runs a health-food store.)

Trivia: Calhern played father to Powell and Reynolds in *Two Weeks with Love* (1950); four years later, he leaped ahead to grandfather status. And two of the other sisters, Virginia Gibson and Nancy Kilgas, had been among the actual *Seven Brides*. In her autobiography, Esther Williams grumbles about having this film taken away from her and refashioned for Powell. Williams would have made more sense in a film about health and fitness, but she can't really believe she lost out on some jewel, which hardly would have been any better with Williams instead of Powell.

Powell tries to inject this stinker with her innate charm and infectious energy, and she does have one good ballad ("Love Can Change the Stars"), but there's only so much she can do with such uninspired material. Just in case you forgot this was a Joe Pasternak production, Powell, for no reason whatsoever, sings an aria from *Daughter of the Regiment* while attending a party with Purdom.

The film climaxes at the Mr. Universe pageant, in which the body build-ers, including eventual winner Steve Reeves, curiously make their poses to the melody of "Jealousy." Powell gets Purdom, Reynolds gets Damone, and everyone sings "Vocalize" yet again. Apparently those peanut burgers are causing serious damage to those who swear by them. However, *Athena* provides one great moment from the always-glorious Kathleen Freeman, here as Purdom's chocolate-eating secretary. When Purdom begins his own health kick, there's his loyal secretary, without a word, walking across the screen chomping on a carrot.

Natalie Wood: Rebel in Peril
July 2nd, 2010

Natalie Wood salvaged her career as a child actress when she made the enviable transition into teen stardom opposite James Dean and Sal Mineo in Nicholas Ray's instant classic *Rebel without a Cause* (1955). She even nabbed an Oscar nomination for supporting actress (compensation for not getting a juvenile Oscar for *Miracle on 34th Street* back in 1947). Wood achieved full-fledged adult stardom with the back-to-back *Splendor in the Grass* and *West Side Story*, both from 1961. *Splendor* put her in another Oscar race, this time as Best Actress. But the six years between 1955 and 1961 were not promising, particularly those first two years after *Rebel* and her newfound Oscar recognition. Yes, she went from *Rebel* directly into another classic, John Ford's *The Searchers* (1956), but her role was small and her performance didn't contribute much to that film's stature as a western landmark.

Wood made four other films in 1956 and 1957, all of which I've just seen for the first time thanks to TCM's tribute to Wood last month. Here's a rundown.

A Cry in the Night (1956)—The 18-year-old Wood is kidnapped by deranged mama's boy Raymond Burr (whose role looks ahead to both *Psycho* and *The Collector*). The actual inspiration appears to be Lennie from *Of Mice and Men*, another pathetic, childlike, sometimes sweet, sometimes brutal lug. Wood is completely wasted as the pretty victim, while her policeman dad, Edmond O'Brien (overacting shamelessly), and his superior, Brian Donlevy (underacting shamelessly), lead the manhunt. The film mixes painfully thin psychology, lame dialogue, and slack direction (by Frank Tuttle). My only tingle of pleasure came from identifying Alan Ladd as the uncredited speaker of the opening narration.

The Burning Hills (1956)—Who knew that five years before *West Side Story*, Wood had already played a Spanish-accented Latina named Maria? That's the only surprise in this ordinary western from director Stuart Heisler (who had directed Wood in 1952 as Bette Davis' daughter in *The Star*). Wood plays a half-Mexican, half-Yankee young woman living on a sheep ranch with her uncle and younger brother. She finds love with Tab Hunter, since they share a desire for revenge against villain Ray Teal and his crazed son Skip Homeier, the family responsible for the deaths of Wood's father and Hunter's brother. Wood shows more life than Hunter does. She may not be all that convincing in her role but she has presence and energy, and at least the role was a challenge and not just a decorative accessory.

The Girl He Left Behind (1956)—Another teaming with Tab Hunter, but this one makes *The Burning Hills* look like *The Searchers*. A comedy-drama about a spoiled rich boy (Hunter) "growing up" in the army, the film returned Wood to window-dressing status as his girlfriend, prompting her to vanish for long stretches. Beyond forgettable, this one features deadly direction from David Butler, plus a script that allows much too much time for Hunter's inevitable conversion. Wood is simply appearing in a Hunter vehicle, whose comedy isn't funny and whose drama is a snore. What to watch for? Well, newcomer James Garner appears as one of Hunter's fellow soldiers. But the most memorable sequence is Hunter's physical. Photographed shirtless and above the waist, he is asked by the doctor to turn his head and cough, and then to turn his head the other way and cough again. Was this a movie first? Topping that moment, the next scene has another doctor asking Hunter, "Do you like girls?" He says that he does, this being years before he came out of the closet.

Bombers B-52 (1957)—It's just a cardboard melodrama attached to a lot of hardware, a Cold War picture as square as can be, all about our being "combat ready" and how the titular planes are being manufactured "to prevent wars." Top-billed Wood is relegated to the sidelines as the daughter of Karl Malden, the air force's maintenance "line chief." Trouble brews when Wood falls for Efrem Zimbalist, Jr., Malden's superior (whom he detests). Zimbalist is a lifeless dud, while a twinkling supporting player, Stuart Whitman, should be playing Wood's love interest. The only two interesting things about this movie have nothing to do with the plot: Wood has one scene with Ann Doran, James Dean's mother from *Rebel;* and the film informs us that Wood and Malden appeared together five years before they made the more attention-grabbing *Gypsy.*

In conclusion, I feel as if I've seen these four movies so you won't have to. To Wood's credit, she survived them and went on to do some very good work in the 1960s, especially her underrated performance in *This Property Is Condemned* (1966), her finest hour.

An American Dream (1966)
July 10th, 2010

Right before everything changed in the late 1960s, in terms of the screen's new permissiveness and the emergence of the ratings system, there were a number of sex-driven trash spectaculars released, films that anticipated the imminent new era while still being mired in glossy artificiality. Among these films are some of the most memorably awful motion pictures ever made, such as *The Carpetbaggers* (1964), *The Oscar* (1966), and *Valley of the Dolls* (1967), each one compulsively watchable, each immersing itself extravagantly into the quicksand of bad taste and flamboyant ineptitude.

Though it is nowhere near as well-known as the aforementioned atrocities, *An American Dream* belongs right alongside them, further tainted by the fact that it was released into instant oblivion. It is not about film or theatre stars (like the above trio), but it does center on a popular TV commentator, a crime-busting crusader who has taken on the mob and police corruption. (Nowadays, he would have a show on Fox News or MSNBC.) Stuart Whitman plays this role, an ex-war hero as well, and he gives an astonishingly bad performance. He has two gears only, acting either in a comatose fashion *or* working himself into monumentally unconvincing frenzies of emotion. I have often liked Whitman's work, finding him most attractive and intelligent, but he's embarrassing here, whether dealing with the histrionics of his boozy, nymphomaniac wife Eleanor Parker (who was also in *The Oscar*) or his former flame Janet Leigh. How can you make a juicy piece of crap with a stiff at its center?

The first half hour is the film's liveliest section, the portion featuring Ms. Parker in a self-consciously showy role, naked in her bed with a studly pickup while watching her hubby on television. Parker gives you an idea of what her Alexandra Del Lago might have been like had she played that role in *Sweet Bird of Youth*. When Whitman later shows up to ask for a divorce, he and Parker engage in *two* separate brawls, the latter ending with Parker falling off her penthouse balcony, but not before hilariously throwing a large rock at Whitman's head. He doesn't push her off, but he does let her fall, choosing not to save her, then regretting it instantly. After going splat, she's run over by a car containing the mob boss that Whitman has been taunting on the air, who just happens to be riding around with moll Janet Leigh, the girl Whitman once impregnated and hasn't seen in a decade. Parker may be over the top but the film becomes a tedious drag without her.

I haven't read the Norman Mailer novel on which this film is based, but I'd venture to guess that the distance between the book and the film is about as vast as the distance between the book and film versions of *Myra Breckinridge*. Lamely directed by actor Robert Gist, *An American Dream* qualifies as camp, especially when floozie Janet Leigh (dubbed) is singing for mobsters in a nightclub, suddenly channeling Gladys George! Leigh tries to be bruised and hardboiled, but how can she be taken seriously with all that white eye makeup? Speaking of camp, how about the film's final line, Leigh's to Whitman's corpse after she has ratted him out: "What did you expect from a whore?"

There's much yelling in this movie, much of it confused with acting. Some of the worst offenders include Barry Sullivan and J.D. Cannon as policemen hoping to nab Whitman for murder. Director Gist also allows a red neon light to flash continually into Leigh's apartment, yet when the sign is seen in exterior shots it doesn't flash. I guess that's called "style."

Though Parker and Leigh never appear together here, they had been the two leading ladies in another film, a wonderful one, 1952's *Scaramouche*. That's the one to see them in!

The Viking (1928)
November 23rd, 2010

D
id anyone out there catch TCM's showing of the rarely seen and utterly forgotten MGM epic *The Viking* (1928)? It isn't a good movie, but it surely is a fascinating artifact, making strides in both sound (with its synchronized music and effects) and, more strikingly, in its use of two-strip Technicolor. The restoration of the film's color is rather breathtaking, even though "two-strip" is basically red and blue, with all kinds of browns and beiges as well. Though you're aching for green and yellow to show up, it's easy to become hypnotized by all those saturated reds and ocean blues.

Directed by Roy William Neill, who directed *The Black Room* (1935), one of my favorite Boris Karloff movies, *The Viking* tells a stale, two-dimensional action tale centered on Leif Ericsson, played by Donald Crisp (in a long auburn wig and mustache). Crisp is a far cry from his Oscar-winning role in John Ford's *How Green Was My Valley* (1941) and none too comfortable-looking. He, and every other guy in the movie, is in love with Viking gal Pauline Starke, a pretty and feisty blonde. After lots of swashbuckling, and fear of falling off the end of the world, it ends with the discovery of Rhode Island!

In Our Time (1944)
January 14th, 2011

One of countless war propaganda movies churned out by Hollywood during WWII, Warner Brothers' *In Our Time* isn't close to being one of the best. Like many in the European-set sub-genre of these movies, *In Our Time* pays tribute to a particular country's valiant fight against Nazi aggression, in this case Poland, a nation that had recently received another screen tribute but in a comic and satiric vein in Ernst Lubitsch's *To Be or Not to Be* (1942). Other countries got the gallant, gutsy treatment in *Edge of Darkness* (Norway), *Hangmen Also Die!* (Czechoslovakia), *The Pied Piper* (France), *The North Star* (Russia) and on and on. *In Our Time* is among the least convincing, being both slow-paced and heavy-handed. Call it a failed prestige picture, succumbing to preachiness, hokiness, and an overall simple-minded approach, all of it blandly directed by Vincent Sherman while Chopin melodies soar throughout. However, it's still worth a look for film buffs.

In Our Time is one of so many movies, everything from *Dragonwyck* (1946) to *Elephant Walk* (1954), that stole shamelessly from Hitchcock's *Rebecca* (1940). Traveling abroad (from England), Ida Lupino is the mousy paid companion/secretary to Mary Boland, a gaudy and crass well-off woman, unmistakably evoking Joan Fontaine and Florence Bates in *Rebecca*'s opening section. Paul Henreid shows up (in the Laurence Olivier slot) as a wealthy count who lives on a great estate and is inexplicably entranced by the unassuming Lupino. They marry, Boland vanishes, and Lupino finds her bearings in her new and mostly unwelcoming world. Yep, that's *Rebecca*.

No one loves Ida Lupino's work more than I do, but she is surely off her mark here. It's truly bizarre that the British Lupino seems far less at home playing English here than she does when she's playing one of her brassy all-American dames, as in *The Man I Love* (1946) or *Road House* (1948). Forced to rein herself in, she seems surprisingly dull and increasingly arch as her virtuousness gains traction. Lacking excitement and complexity, the character is undone by her all-out wonderfulness, leaving Lupino high and dry. Henreid finds her inspiring for some reason, and they begin a boringly resourceful journey to making their own way, free from Henreid's uncle (excellent Victor Francen), who holds the family purse strings and is trying to make nice with the Nazis. It would help if Henreid and Lupino had any chemistry, but they clearly don't. Henreid was best on the periphery, as in *Casablanca* and *Now, Voyager*, but when center stage he just doesn't seem *enough* to sustain our attention.

The film offers the chance to see two legendary actors from the Moscow Art Theatre cast as brother and sister. Nazimova plays Henreid's fragile, emotional mother, while Michael Chekhov (Anton's nephew) plays Henreid's warm, lovable uncle. Nazimova overacts here, but Chekhov all but steals the film (as he would *Spellbound* the next year), genuinely funny and forging a tender bond with Lupino. Then there's *Kings Row*'s Nancy Coleman as Henreid's cold, tight, stiff-backed sister. We keep waiting to find out what's going on with her but we never do. Of course, the fabulous Mary Boland never disappoints, and, along with Chekhov, she gives the film what humor and vitality it has.

Lupino and Henreid become devoted to their "peasants," sharing the harvest with them, teaching them how to ride a tractor, even inviting them up to the mansion for a party! So, the film gives us a portrait of "happy peasants" not too far removed from your garden-variety operetta. The aristocracy (aside from the stars) is useless. Lupino gets a Scarlett O'Hara moment when she comes in from harvesting the fields (after the men go off to fight Hitler), all muddy and exhausted but glowing. The picture ends with Lupino, Henreid, and Chekhov remaining while the other family members flee. The two stars burn down their Tara (and then their fields), but it all seems a bit premature. Couldn't they wait till the Nazis got a bit closer? Well, it makes them feel fearless. And we're supposed to gaze admiringly at these stick figures.

Coleman, Henreid, and Lupino were also seen together in *Devotion*, the Brontë family biopic filmed in 1943 but not released until 1946. Though the film is a disappointment, Lupino is quite moving as Emily. See, I can't write about Lupino without giving her a rave somewhere in this post.

III. Revisiting the Classics
screensaversmovies.com

Bing and Ingrid and Meryl and Philip
February 1st, 2009

I was just thinking that *The Bells of St. Mary's* (1945) and *Doubt* (2008) would make a swell double feature. After all, both films depict a tense relationship between a nun (a principal of a Catholic school) and a priest (her superior). Though, of course, the notion of a child's molestation by a priest would have been impossible screen fare back in 1945, Bing Crosby's Father O'Malley does have an inappropriate knack for sticking his nose into other people's business, reconfiguring their lives to an outcome that he deems best. Naturally, the movie tells us that he's always right, but he certainly makes assumptions about people, followed by meddling actions (such as tracking down a woman's runaway husband) that could easily end in disaster. Apparently, forced happy endings justify any means. Crosby tends to play God, but we're supposed to find him charming and lovable. Many of his choices are appalling, notably his decision to make Ingrid Bergman think she's being transferred as a punishment when it's actually for her health. Crosby thinks that letting her know she has tuberculosis will weaken her will. Huh? It's a lot of movie manipulation, on-screen masochism, and questionable behavior. A sequel to *Going My Way*, 1944's Oscar winner, *Bells* is a letdown (and *Going My Way* is quite far from being a great movie). At least the earlier picture had irascible Barry Fitzgerald to cut through much of the slop. Without Fitzgerald, *Bells* is too cute and so darn sure of itself. Crosby coasts along in a smugly passive-aggressive manner and finds far too many excuses to sing.

Bergman would probably have loved lashing into Crosby the way Meryl Streep lashes into Philip Seymour Hoffman in *Doubt*. Streep's Bronx accent trumps Bergman's Swedish lilt in the art of intimidation. In both films, the leads are at odds on most issues pertaining to the school's methods. Crosby and Bergman argue about the grading system, while Streep and Hoffman's discussions would make their predecessors blush. *Bells of St. Mary's* romanticizes a religious culture, while *Doubt* seeks to expose the behind-the-scenes drama. Some of the things done in the 1945 picture, particularly the church's improper actions in getting an old man to donate his building to them, can be nearly as eyebrow-raising as the things Hoffman is accused of doing. The most interesting connection between the films is that the women are powerless in both movies (*Doubt* is set in 1964). The episodic *Bells of St. Mary's* is an overlong and forced movie that grossed a fortune, while *Doubt* is a good adaptation of a very good play. See them together someday to compare and contrast their portraits of the men and women of the Catholic Church. One thing is certain: *The Bells of St. Mary's* could use a lot more "doubt."

Charles the Great
June 1st, 2009

The recent DVD release of the British classic *The Private Life of Henry VIII* (1933) is a reminder that Charles Laughton, in the title role, gave a truly magnificent performance. He won the 1933 Best Actor Oscar, and his is one of the rare Oscar-winning turns every bit as good as the award implies. The picture, too, holds up surprisingly well, mostly because it isn't a heavy biopic, but, rather, a film with a light winking tone, some saucy sexuality, and the good sense to have a very limited focus, specifically Henry's love life. Its refreshing humor (still funny and charming) serves to heighten the startling impact of its shifts into drama. Everything Laughton does is executed (no pun intended) with supreme artistry.

Laughton is a dazzling visual, a portly and commanding presence who carries his elaborate costumes with effortless panache. No one can tear into a capon and fling its bones as he does, belching all the way. Laughton has a marvelously theatrical collapse on a grand staircase, making a full spin before falling! Another unforgettable scene is his dry announcement, just before he thinks he is going to bed Anne of Cleves (Elsa Lanchester): "The things I've done for England." Laughton and Lanchester (Mr. and Mrs. Laughton) are a hoot together, playing cards in bed. Though his is a large performance, it has illuminating moments of unexpected quiet and subtlety. There is no moment better than when he learns of Katherine Howard's infidelity; his initial anger turns to grief. Bringing his hands to his eyes, he cries like a baby. A witty comic turn has become a superb dramatic performance. Every subsequent Henry owes something to Laughton's definitive portrayal.

As Katherine, Binnie Barnes is the nominal female lead, though Lanchester is the wife who steals the picture. Merle Oberon is seen briefly (and beautifully) as Anne Boleyn, but it's Laughton's show, whether he's hilarious or touching, crafty or childish, vocally booming or in private pain. Alexander Korda was not a great director but here he shows a light touch. Korda's film has the feeling of authenticity, a fast pace, and more than a dash of pre-Code bawdiness. It is now a film more than 75 years old and yet no screen Henry in all that time can unseat Laughton from his throne.

The Crowd (1928)
July 12th, 2009

T his masterpiece, one of the last of the great silent pictures, is one of the finest achievements of director King Vidor, the man who gave us *The Big Parade* (1925), *Stella Dallas* (1937), and *The Fountainhead* (1949), among so many varied movies. *The Crowd* is a moving and powerful work, honest and timeless, and Vidor's direction excels in both the smallest character details and the expansive expression of his themes. Superbly photographed on location in Manhattan, *The Crowd* provides an astonishing record of the pre-crash NYC. The film is about how, no matter how special or destined for greatness we think we are, most of us are merely part of the crowd, Everymen and Everywomen carrying big dreams through ordinary lives, sometimes weighed down by the pressures of the American Dream.

James Murray stars as a 21-year-old who comes to the big city primed for success but with no specific aspirations. He meets and marries Eleanor Boardman (Vidor's real-life wife) and they, named John and Mary, become the Everycouple. The film charts the usual rituals of work, marriage, and leisure. John is a faceless bookkeeper at a big insurance company, lost in a sea of desks, aching for the upward mobility that isn't forthcoming, waiting for his luck to kick in and so sure that it will.

Nothing about John and Mary is unique, from their honeymoon in Niagara Falls to their financial worries and in-law troubles, even their having one son and one daughter. Murray and Boardman, in their portrayal of what is essentially a love story, both give fresh and natural performances that are ultimately very touching and emotionally transparent. (Boardman's looks and her all-around radiance may remind you of Meryl Streep.) The film's portrait of a marriage is more realistic than most cinematic depictions of that institution. *The Crowd* makes one major misstep, when the drama moves from the mundane to the melodramatic, which feels like a betrayal of the theme, moving the couple from being ordinary to being marked by tragedy.

The ending, which may remind you of the finale of *Sullivan's Travels* (1941), is a stunning visual as well as the perfect expression of all that the film has to say. Further poignancy, as well as irony, is added by the knowledge of the real-life suicide of star Murray, eight years later, when his career was unable to sustain the high of *The Crowd*. Though the overall content of this classic might classify it as a downer, nothing this artistically thrilling is likely to bring you down.

Gay Rabbit
August 4th, 2009

Did you read this week that Steven Spielberg is going to do a remake of *Harvey*, the 1950 semi-classic starring James Stewart? I'm not a particular fan of the film, so I don't hold out much hope for a new version, even if it ends up starring Tom Hanks, the man most often called this generation's Stewart. Based on Mary Chase's 1944 Pulitzer Prize-winning play, the 1950 *Harvey* was directed by Henry Koster, a solid studio man capable of good work (*It Started with Eve, My Cousin Rachel*) and bad (*The Robe, The Singing Nun*), with this film somewhere in the middle.

Harvey pushes for laughs, growing increasingly silly and contrived, though Stewart never succumbs to the heavy-handed proceedings around him. He remains easy and affable, with impeccable comic timing and enviable grace. He plays Elwood P. Dowd, the rich, 42-year-old bachelor whose best friend is an invisible 6' 3" white rabbit named Harvey. Stewart's Elwood is a friendly, oblivious fellow who owns the house that he shares with his older sister (Josephine Hull, in an Oscar-winning performance). The short and chubby Hull is charmingly flustered and lovable, running about, though her supporting Oscar seems unwarranted in the year of Thelma Ritter and Celeste Holm in *All About Eve*. (In a reverse of her other famed role, in 1944's *Arsenic and Old Lace,* Hull is now trying to put a family member in the nut house, whereas in *Arsenic* it was Cary Grant trying to institutionalize her!) It is when the action shifts to the hospital that the film falls to pieces, mired in stupidity.

Harvey is a pooka, a "fairy spirit" in animal form. The movie makes a major misstep when Harvey is revealed to be *real,* when we see doors open by themselves, instantly removing the genuine magic and mystery from the piece. But the most interesting element of *Harvey* today, and the reason a remake might be worthwhile (but don't hold your breath), is that the script works as a gay metaphor, with Harvey and Elwood as a male couple of a closeted age. Consider the following: they are constant companions, yet their partnership is "invisible" to the world of 1950; Elwood is an unmarried, middle-aged man, with Harvey as his only strong non-familial attachment; though Elwood is perfectly happy, his family wants him "cured"; the Elwood-Harvey relationship is the family secret, even its shame. Then there are the amusing details of how Elwood and Harvey met (which is described as a pick-up at a lamppost) and how they spend their time (in bars). Near the end, Elwood has some competition for Harvey's attention, in the form of doctor Cecil Kellaway (closet case?), briefly turning the movie into a triangle. But, of course, Elwood and Harvey end up together. Even though we can't see Harvey, the film finishes with them walking off together into the distance. What other movie of that time ends with a male couple wandering toward their future bliss?

If Spielberg wants to explore some of the issues hinted at in 1950, then that might make a remake reasonable. But why do I have a horrible feeling it's going to be about how much better our special effects are than they were sixty years ago?

The African Queen (1951)
March 21st, 2010

This week marks the long-awaited DVD release of *The African Queen* (1951), the justly beloved John Huston movie starring Humphrey Bogart and Katharine Hepburn. Set in German East Africa in 1914, the film is an irresistible combination of genres—comedy, romance, war, and adventure—with Bogart a boozing riverboat operator and Hepburn a strait-laced Methodist missionary. (He's Canadian; she's British.) The outbreak of WWI leads to their sharing Bogie's titular boat, turning an unlikely duo into one of the more delightful, touching, and believable couplings in film history.

Rarely has such deeply felt love developed so convincingly between two on-screen characters, and the effect is heightened by their initially comic mismatching. Love turns likably mangy Bogart into a man of tenderness, and it puts rigidly proper Hepburn in touch with the physical world. Her love makes him feel brave, and his love makes her feel beautiful, intensifying characteristics they didn't know they already possessed. It's the screen's greatest ugly-duckling romance. The characters form an effortlessly equal partnership, admirably sharing all of their onboard labors and hardships. Their dangerous, invigorating journey, which includes leeches and the rapids, feels simultaneously like a fairy-tale odyssey and an unconventional honeymoon.

Bogart and Hepburn were rarely better than they are here. Each makes a glorious transformation, strengthened by the other's presence. Marvelous separately, they achieve something extraordinary together, enhanced by their offbeat chemistry. Bogart won his only Academy Award for this film, and, despite competition from Marlon Brando in *A Streetcar Named Desire* and Montgomery Clift in *A Place in the Sun*, he richly deserved the honor, with a performance unlike any other he ever gave, filled with comic invention, roguish charm, and disarming reserves of feeling. As for Hepburn, well, she would have joined Bogie at the Oscar podium (had she been inclined to attend such affairs) if only she hadn't been up against Vivien Leigh in *Streetcar*, one of the rare performances that could have plausibly snatched the prize away from the Great Kate, which is exactly what happened.

The African Queen was the fifth of the six teamings of Bogart with director John Huston, following *The Maltese Falcon* (1941), *Across the Pacific* (1942), *The Treasure of the Sierra Madre* (1948), and *Key Largo* (1948), and preceding *Beat the Devil* (1954). This was an actor-director collaboration rarely rivaled in Hollywood history, with *The African Queen* a major work in both their careers. It is a movie that I loved as a child, a teen, and an adult, and never more than when I saw it again in middle age.

The Night of the Hunter (1955)
December 30th, 2010

One of my Christmas presents was the Criterion Collection DVD of *The Night of the Hunter,* one of my all-time favorite movies. It'll be quite a while before I actually watch the movie, so consumed am I with all the extras. Though I haven't even gotten to the second disc, there are plenty of jewels on Disc One. *Night of the Hunter* is one of those films sorely overlooked in its day, which makes me wonder about what possible treasure we all ignored in 2010. Because its greatness is so apparent now, it seems inexplicable that it was brushed aside, especially in a year in which the Academy thought *Marty* was a great movie. The film's so-called failure resulted in Charles Laughton never directing another movie, making *The Night of the Hunter* his one and only effort, a masterpiece his first time out.

I've written about this movie before, when I included Robert Mitchum's astonishing performance as a psycho preacher among my selections in my book *100 Great Film Performances You Should Remember But Probably Don't* (2002). With his virile beauty, down-home charm, and twangy verbal finesse, Mitchum revels in the role's audacious fakery. But he can also turn into a wild animal and is frequently as imposing and relentless as Frankenstein's Monster. It's a consistently risky, fearless, and innovative piece of acting. Then there's Lillian Gish's radiance and strength as the film's contrasting representation of good, with the already legendary Gish giving the non-silent performance of her life. Plus there's a remarkably soft and fragile Shelley Winters as Mitchum's foolish and doomed wife, and a performance from little Billy Chapin that ranks among the more unaffected and moving by a child.

The film is great on many levels, as an evocative portrait of the Depression, as an unbearably suspenseful thriller, as a poignant and heartbreaking look at childhood, and as a formidable battle between good and evil. After murdering their mother (Winters), Mitchum pursues Chapin and his little sister (Sally Jane Bruce) across the Midwest to snatch away from them the money stolen by their now-dead father (Peter Graves). With its God-invoking maniac, frank sexuality, and black-comic overtones, it was, as they say, way ahead of its time. Cinematographer Stanley Cortez's breathtakingly inventive black and white made this a film that doesn't quite look like any other.

I'm not the first to write about the Coen Brothers' homage to this classic in their very satisfying new version of *True Grit*. Their use of the hymn "Leaning on the Everlasting Arms" will evoke *Hunter* to anyone familiar with the earlier movie, in which Mitchum's soothingly beautiful rendition belies his true intentions, enhancing the film's disturbing theme of our inability to see cunningly concealed evil. But the Coen Brothers also appear to have been inspired by *Hunter*'s exquisite nightscape journey, in which the two children travel by boat down the Ohio River in a sequence that is quite magical, otherworldly, and strangely haunting. At *True Grit*'s climax, Jeff Bridges, on horseback with the snake-bitten Hailee Steinfeld, rides ruthlessly to get Steinfeld to a doctor. As they race through the night, the imagery is mysterious, stunning, and non-realistic, evoking the same balance of beauty and danger, the same feeling of wonder in the nocturnal world, and the same overwhelming mixture of visual splendor and emotional depth in the *Hunter* sequence.

So far, the most fascinating extra on the DVD is a clip from *The Ed Sullivan Show* around the time of the film's release. Winters and Graves perform a scene as their characters, Willa and Ben Harper. Interesting, right? Well, what makes it of even greater value is the fact that they perform a scene *not* in the movie, a prison visit in which Winters shares some precious time with Graves not too long before his execution (by hanging). Winters and Graves perform this snippet quite beautifully, inhabiting their roles as fully as in the film itself. It's a priceless artifact, a lovely grace note to the finished film.

On Holiday with Lew Ayres
January 7, 2011

In the nine years since I wrote *100 Great Film Performances You Should Remember But Probably Don't*, I occasionally see a screen performance that I wish I had included in the book. Not that I'd want to delete any of my choices, just make room for a few more. I'm sorry there was no space for Henry Fonda in *Young Mr. Lincoln* (1939), Joan Fontaine in *Ivy* (1947), Billie Burke in *Everybody Sing* (1938), to name a few, and I was just reminded of another, having just rewatched *Holiday* (1938). No, not the performances of Katharine Hepburn or Cary Grant, but that of supporting-player Lew Ayres, who gives the standout performance.

Philip Barry's play, *Holiday*, was a great success on Broadway in 1928 and holds up surprisingly well in its early-talkie version of 1930, with memorable performances from Ann Harding and Mary Astor as the central sisters. Hepburn had understudied Broadway's Hope Williams in the role of Linda (played by Harding on film) and finally got to play it in George Cukor's 1938 remake at Columbia. It was the third Hepburn-Grant picture following two box-office misses: Cukor's gender-bending curiosity *Sylvia Scarlett* (1936) and Howard Hawks' utterly brilliant *Bringing Up Baby*, with its ingeniously funny performances from both Hepburn and Grant. After *Holiday*, they would make *The Philadelphia Story* (1940), a huge hit based on another Philip Barry play (which had starred Hepburn in 1939), again directed by Cukor. The Hepburn-Grant *Holiday* does not rank among the finest romantic comedies of the 1930s, yet it's still literate and charming, never better than when Ayres takes focus.

Ayres made his mark as the naive young soldier of *All Quiet on the Western Front* (1930) and in the first and best version of *State Fair* (1933) in what became the Dana Andrews role in 1945. After *Holiday*, he immediately became the star of MGM's *Dr. Kildare* series, churning out picture after picture with time for few other roles. His career was almost destroyed during WWII when he declared himself a conscientious objector, yet he served honorably with the Army Medical Corps and as an assistant chaplain. After the war, he got an Oscar nomination for his warm, gentle turn opposite Jane Wyman in the moving and delicate *Johnny Belinda*, the only Ayres performance that ranks alongside his work in *Holiday*.

Holiday is one of those 1930s comedies set among the super-rich, with Hepburn the oldest child of wealthy banker Henry Kolker, followed by sister Doris Nolan and baby brother Ayres. They are "one of America's 60 families." Nolan has become impetuously engaged to Grant, after knowing him only ten days in Lake Placid. Grant is doing well financially, at a big New York firm, but he yearns for freedom, ready to break with convention and "retire young, work old," uninterested in piling up money for its own sake. It's obvious after a few minutes that Grant is with the wrong sister, utterly mismatched with cold, humorless Nolan and perfect for frustrated, dreamy Hepburn. The whole thing feels tricked from the start and there's very little surprise as it sorts itself out properly. Grant seems a bit less than usual, lacking the sharp self-awareness of his most irresistible performances, while Hepburn sometimes seems too self-consciously aglow, too calculating in her "radiant" effects. They're both splendid when compared with normal earthlings but they're not up to their especially high standards, in no small part because of the roles themselves.

I have no comparable reservations about Ayres as Ned, the alcoholic brother too weak and pessimistic to defy his father, thus going to his bank office and putting in the time as if it were a prison sentence. Ned gets little attention here, no real delving into his problems. We know that his music ambitions as a musician and composer were thwarted by daddy and that Ned hasn't the courage to stand up to him. And so he drinks and drinks. *Holiday* is a comedy and so it would have been quite easy for Ayres to go for easy drunken laughs, yet he keeps things remarkably subtle, offering a quiet and darkly shaded portrait of a man suffering silently. And yet he is still very funny, but funny in a realistic way, exposing his wit and smarts under his breath, often for his own amusement. His drunkenness is real, too, nicely sustained, believably embarrassing, never theatrical.

It's an aching, mysterious performance, one that allows for the possibility that Ned is a closeted gay man. After all, Ned has no girlfriend or any dates, and he seems to be living in a private hell that cannot be shared, even with Linda, the sister with whom he's closest. When Hepburn reveals to him her burgeoning love for Grant, and Ayres understands perfectly, it appears as though Ned knows a thing or two about unrequited love and about a love that dares not reveal itself. The affection that Ayres displays with Hepburn shows us some of the depth in Ned, a man too scared to face the world, perhaps always to be lavishly sheltered from becoming the person he was meant to be. If there isn't enough real conflict and ambiguity in *Holiday*, there surely is in Ayres. Without love, without music, he immerses himself in alcohol and may never emerge from his trap as Linda will from hers. As Hepburn and Grant go off to start their "holiday," what stays with you is the lingering image of Ned, for whom holidays may never be anything more than days off from the bank.

It's remarkable that Ayres didn't get a supporting Oscar nomination for this performance, especially in the year that the great Walter Brennan was cited for one of his worst performances, in *Kentucky*, the first in-color performance to win an Oscar. Now no one remembers Brennan's cantankerous overacting (like an all-steamed-up Colonel Sanders) in *Kentucky*, but *Holiday* viewers will never forget sad and funny Lew Ayres unable to leave his ivory tower.

IV. Movie Musings
screensaversmovies.com

The AFI Is at It Again
June 23rd, 2008

Last week, the American Film Institute aired their annual countdown program. This year's topic was the top ten films in ten different genres. Most of it was fairly predictable and decidedly tame, but a few of the choices demand to be ridiculed. Take their "Westerns" line-up. Who in his right mind thinks that the mildly amusing spoof *Cat Ballou* (1965) is among the top ten of Hollywood westerns? The list managed to ignore at least three of the genre's masterworks, *My Darling Clementine* (1946), *The Gunfighter* (1950), and *Ride the High Country* (1962), rendering the results a joke. I mean, really, *Butch Cassidy and the Sundance Kid* (1969) is one of the top ten westerns? Have you seen it lately? And what about *Dial M for Murder* (1954) as one of the all-time best mysteries? It's not even anywhere near the top ten of Hitchcock movies! I realize that I'm only taking the AFI's bait and ranting about a meaningless and disposable event, but, with all the wonderful movies in our past, it's disappointing to see most of the same movies getting all the attention.

Shirley's Little Brother
July 11th, 2008

Did you happen to catch the AFI salute to Warren Beatty this past week? These life-achievement specials used to be shown on the major networks but have recently been airing on USA. Imagine the Big Three giving up a night of "reality" stupidity to honor one of American film's most impressive forces of the last forty years. But that's another story.

The Beatty tribute was especially fine because it was the kind of event that convinced you that its subject was indeed deserving. After hitting it big in

1961, in both *Splendor in the Grass* and *The Roman Spring of Mrs. Stone,* Beatty made offbeat choices that proved to be interesting failures (*All Fall Down, Lilith, Mickey One*). This was preferable to going "Hollywood" and ending up like George Hamilton (OK, that's an exaggeration). With *Bonnie and Clyde* (1967), he found his niche, making films that were artistically daring but had considerable box-office allure.

Films he made (and remember that he—at various times and in different combinations—acted, wrote, directed, and produced) will live on: *McCabe and Mrs. Miller, Shampoo, Bugsy,* plus the lesser but beloved *Heaven Can Wait.* I suspect that *Bulworth* will receive greater appreciation as the years go by. And then there's *Reds* from 1981. The fact that *Reds* exists at all is astonishing, a film about a real-life American Communist who went to Russia. Who else but Beatty could have gotten such a film greenlighted? (Today, I imagine that only George Clooney, the Warren Beatty of the 21st century, could get such a film made and do as good a job of it.)

Perhaps the most exquisite element of *Reds* is the ferociously intelligent and impassioned performance from Diane Keaton. Keaton spoke at the AFI tribute and rarely have I heard anyone speak so intimately and personally at one of these affairs. She talked specifically about the filming of the great train-station reunion scene and of what that experience meant to her. I'll not diminish her words by trying to paraphrase them, but Keaton spoke so genuinely that it was yet another confirmation of why she has been such an extraordinary screen actress for 35 years. There's never anything phony or put-on with Keaton. I've loved her work since I saw *Play It Again, Sam* when I was eleven.

I'll leave you with one bit of trivia. Warren's big sister, Shirley MacLaine, was famously discovered by producer Hal Wallis when she, an unknown understudy, went on for Carol Haney in *The Pajama Game* on Broadway. The rest, as they say, is history. A half-decade later, Warren's career makes a leap when he stars on Broadway in William Inge's *A Loss of Roses*...opposite Carol Haney! How bizarre that Haney was a key element in the career advancement of both sister and brother. Inge went on to write *Splendor in the Grass* and, again, the rest is...you know.

We're Not in Oz Anymore
October 25th, 2008

Moviegoers, specifically fans (and who isn't one?) of *The Wizard of Oz* (1939), may get a special tingle when they come upon a post-*Oz* movie that reunites two of *Oz*'s iconic players. Though the stars are playing other roles, you somehow still feel that, deep down, they are forever their *Oz* identities. Here are three such occurrences.

The most famous example would be when Judy Garland and Ray Bolger, Dorothy and the Scarecrow, appeared in *The Harvey Girls* (1946). It's an MGM musical that I have a special affinity for (it's one of five musicals I write about in my book *Screen Savers*), a film whose many pleasures include this Garland-Bolger reunion. Despite the fact that they are now out West, and playing different characters, we still get a unique shiver of joy when they make eye contact. We know, as do they, that on some level it's Dorothy and the Scarecrow together again at last. When Judy takes his arm in the famed "Atchison, Topeka" number, or when they later waltz together at a party, it's a magical meeting of the now-adult Dorothy and the newly humanized Scarecrow.

Another post-*Oz* reteaming came in *George White's Scandals* (1945), when Tin Man Jack Haley and Wicked Witch of the West Margaret Hamilton played brother and sister. They are both cast to type here: he's nervous and unthreatening; she's severe and strait-laced. He plays a musical-comedy star and she is the spinster sibling who wants to keep him from marrying Joan Davis (or anyone else). Hamilton pushes Haley around, as she did in *Oz,* though less theatrically and without special effects. It's an inane B musical, in black and white, but you can't quite believe that Hamilton and Haley are again side by side, even without, respectively, a witch hat and silver face-paint.

The Wizard himself (Frank Morgan) and Glinda (Billie Burke) were brought together romantically for *The Wild Man of Borneo* (1941), a terrible and misleading title for a mildly charming tale of a con man (Morgan) living in a theatrical boardinghouse in New York, circa 1900. Morgan is a lovable grifter, and Burke is her adorable, radiant self. Why shouldn't the Wizard and Glinda start dating? They're both single, right?

Next up, perhaps later this week, I'll look at some of the pre-*Oz* teamings of *Oz* players. In these situations, the stars have no idea that they are headed for joint immortality.

We're Off to See the Wizard
(But We Don't Know It Yet)
October 29th, 2008

H ere's Part Two of my look at *Wizard of Oz* cast members and their pre- and post-*Oz* interactions. Below are some of the pre-*Oz* match-ups. Frank Morgan (the Wizard) and Ray Bolger (the Scarecrow) were both in two Nelson Eddy musicals: *Rosalie* (1937), starring Eleanor Powell, and *Sweethearts* (1938), starring Jeanette MacDonald. Morgan, who romanced Billie Burke (Glinda) in the aforementioned post-*Oz* *Wild Man of Borneo* (1941), had already been amorously linked to her in the pre-*Oz* *Piccadilly Jim* (1936), in which he plays Robert Montgomery's never-employed Shakespearean-actor father, which, unfortunately, never proves to be as fun as it sounds. These three films are disappointments, despite their intermittent pleasures.

Better is *Party Wire* (1935), a comedy-drama sleeper starring the fresh and sparkling Jean Arthur on the brink of superstardom (which came with the following year's *Mr. Deeds Goes to Town*). It's a small-town tale set in Rock Ridge (a different Rock Ridge than the one in *Blazing Saddles*), all about the damaging power of idle gossip. Not only is Clara Blandick (Auntie Em) featured in the supporting cast (as the vicious-tongued banker's wife) but you'll also find Charley Grapewin (Uncle Henry) as Jean Arthur's apple-jack-loving father. Blandick and Grapewin would get along better once they moved to Kansas. Grapewin had already appeared with Frank Morgan in *The Kiss Before the Mirror* (1933), a souped-up and implausible melodrama in which Morgan had a starring role as a lawyer and Grapewin was his law clerk.

The best pre-*Oz* teaming of *Oz* castmates has to be *Everybody Sing* (1938), an unpretentious black-and-white musical that also happens to be a spirited screwball comedy. It's about a showbiz family, in all their theatricality, and it's fast, merry, and occasionally hilarious. A pre-Dorothy Judy Garland sings and swings sensationally. As Judy's hammy star-actress mother, there's Glinda herself, Billie Burke, in what may be her greatest performance. Whenever Billie can't stop acting or Judy can't stop swinging, it's wonderful. And off to Oz they went.

City Secrets: Books
October 26th, 2009

Earlier this year, an essay of mine appeared in *City Secrets: Movies*, a book of film recommendations, the "secrets" being overlooked movies. My choice, the period thriller *The Tall Target* (1951), is one of the movies featured in my own book *Screen Savers*. A new addition to the series (which includes many travel books), *City Secrets: Books* features recommendations of under-read books, described in short essays by people like John Guare, Oscar Hijuelos, Calvin Trillin, Buck Henry, and, oh yeah, me. Naturally, I picked a film book to tout.

My choice is the 1973 *Hollywood Director* by David Chierichetti, a tribute to Mitchell Leisen. Not only is the book underrated and forgotten but so is its subject. Leisen, a former art director and costume designer, became a leading filmmaker of the '30s and '40s, and one of the few gay men to have risen to the top of what was considered a macho profession. Excelling in romantic comedy, he directed three of the era's brightest lights in major comic turns: Carole Lombard in *Hands Across the Table* (1935), Jean Arthur in *Easy Living* (1937), and Claudette Colbert in *Midnight* (1939). His flair for sets and costumes made him a natural for visually detailed and expensive-looking period pictures such as *Frenchman's Creek* (1944), starring Joan Fontaine, and *Kitty* (1946), with Paulette Goddard.

Leisen was a master with actors, coaxing superb performances from Charles Boyer in the excellent immigration drama *Hold Back the Dawn* (1941) and Olivia de Havilland in the expert soap *To Each His Own* (1946), the film for which she won her first Oscar. And I feel he directed the greatest performance of one of the screen's greatest stars, Barbara Stanwyck's in the comedy-drama *Remember the Night* (1940).

Leisen directed scripts by Preston Sturges *(Easy Living, Remember the Night)* and Billy Wilder *(Midnight, Hold Back the Dawn)* before those fellows began directing their own screenplays. Without Leisen making such superior films of their works, it might have taken them a good deal longer to emerge as star writer-directors. Leisen is very much someone to remember and admire, as is Chierichetti's treasured book about him.

When Basil Met Nigel
February 9th, 2010

I have nothing good to say about the new *Sherlock Holmes*, the box-office juggernaut. Director Guy Ritchie shows a talent for loudness, and that's all. The movie is heavy on endless, tiring action scenes, and the overall impact is that of a period-piece James Bond rip-off. The main plot feels like a warmed-over retread of *The Da Vinci Code*, while the more personal story is a reworking of *The Front Page*, with Holmes trying to prevent Dr. Watson from getting married and subsequently dissolving their partnership. Though I think the movie would have been improved if Jude Law had played Holmes instead of Watson, such a switch would not have changed things *enough*.

There was some talk, mostly before the picture was released, about the supposed homoerotic undercurrent between Robert Downey, Jr.'s Holmes and Law's Watson, but I couldn't detect anything of that nature in their relationship, and not just because each fellow has a female love interest. There simply isn't enough chemistry between the stars, on any level. You can get much more of a gay subtext in the old Holmes pictures starring Basil Rathbone, with Nigel Bruce his comic-relief Watson. I recently caught up with five pictures in this series and found them, minor as they are, to be quite enjoyable. It surely was a more innocent time at the movies (in the late '30s to the mid '40s) when Holmes and Watson could be so inseparable without raising an eyebrow, particularly since they are both unmarried and apparently not even dating women.

The Spider Woman (1944) begins with Rathbone and Bruce on vacation together, on a fishing trip in Scotland. Are these guys ever apart? They even vacation together? The "gayest" film in the series has to be *The House of Fear* (1945), not just because of the usual Holmes-Watson chumminess or the fact that they resemble an old married couple. (Rathbone tells Bruce, "You snored like a pig!") The plot hinges on seven older-men bachelors all staying at a Scottish mansion overhanging a cliff. They call themselves "The Good Comrades" (I guess "Boys in the Band" was taken). They are the beneficiaries of each others' insurance policies. Aubrey Mather, as the owner of the mansion and also a member of the club, gives one of the nellier performances of the era. In true *Ten Little Indians* fashion, the fellows are picked off one by one, with Holmes and Watson moving in to solve the case. Of course, the gay overtones are primarily accidental and unintentional (except in Mather's case), what with everyone seeming so clueless on that score, not to mention sexless. Rathbone calls Bruce "my dear friend and colleague," but Holmes may have fainted if anyone had told him that maybe his and

Watson's devotion to each other meant that they were partners of a kind we now call life partners.

Lena Horne and Julie LaVerne
May 13th, 2010

I f the late Lena Horne was born to play one role, then that one role was Julie LaVerne, the light-skinned black actress in *Show Boat*, the legendary Broadway musical written by Jerome Kern and Oscar Hammerstein, based on Edna Ferber's novel. The third of its three screen versions was MGM's 1951 blockbuster, the version for which Horne seemed destined. She had practically screen-tested for it publicly when she played Julie in a lavish excerpt that opened MGM's *Till the Clouds Roll By* (1946), the musical biopic about Jerome Kern. Looking ravishingly beautiful, Horne sings "Can't Help Lovin' Dat Man" in a rendition so sublime that a full film version should have gone into production immediately. That was not the case.

Though Horne had played Georgia Brown in Vincente Minnelli's *Cabin in the Sky* (1942) at MGM, the studio was mostly skittish about using Horne in speaking roles. She was a gorgeous and gifted black artist at a time when there was little contact between the races on-screen, aside from the casting of African-Americans in subordinate roles such as servants. *Cabin in the Sky*, after all, was a musical with an all-black cast. And so most of Horne's career at MGM consisted of "specialty" numbers unconnected to her films' plots, songs set in nightclubs that were performed for the entertainment of the white characters. Thus we have some glorious vocal sequences by Horne: "Just One of Those Things" in *Panama Hattie* (1942); "Honeysuckle Rose" in *Thousands Cheer* (1943); "Love" in *Ziegfeld Follies* (1946); "Where or When" in *Words and Music* (1948). But these numbers also act as teases; they are hints of what might have been if Horne had been allowed to carry an MGM musical or two (or ten).

When the 1951 *Show Boat* was being readied, among those considered for Julie were Judy Garland and Dinah Shore. Huh? The eventual choice, Ava Gardner, turned out surprisingly well. She was physically believable and ultimately became the best thing in the picture, bringing a beating heart to an often overly glossy and artificial production. MGM even found a way to betray Gardner, dubbing her voice (with Annette Warren's) after she had proven she could sing Julie's songs more than satisfactorily. One of the pleasures of *That's Entertainment III* (1994) is the restoration of Ava's vocal track onto her "Can't Help Lovin' Dat Man" footage.

Good as Ava turned out to be, this doesn't excuse MGM's bypassing of Horne. The film's plotline deals sympathetically with the unfairness of Julie's treatment as a black woman, yet there was MGM guilty of the same crime, too timid to have an actual black woman play a black woman in love with a white man (who happens to love her back). After the box-office success of Jeanne Crain as an incredibly light-skinned African-American in *Pinky* (1949), MGM wasn't going to rock the show boat. We may have lost out on Horne's Julie, but at least we have those exquisite five minutes from *Till the Clouds Roll By*, in which she can't help lovin' dat man for all time.

She Had Bette Davis Eyes
August 20th, 2010

Carolyn Jones, who died much too young at 53 in 1983, got her share of pop-culture immortality for only two television seasons as Morticia on *The Addams Family* (1964-66). Prior to the series, she had been in movies for a little over a decade, mostly paying dues, but gaining some real recognition by the end of the 1950s. She moved into the 1960s primed for a screen career that never quite panned out.

In the early-to-middle '50s, Jones had supporting roles in many famous movies, including *House of Wax* (1953), *The Big Heat* (1953), *The Tender Trap* (1955), *The Seven Year Itch* (1955), *The Man Who Knew Too Much* (1956), and, perhaps most memorably, in the original *Invasion of the Body Snatchers* (1956). Watching Jones in these movies is like watching Bette Davis in her pre-*Of Human Bondage* performances. Both actresses had a striking, unconventional beauty, yet, more importantly, they also had striking, unconventional on-screen personalities. Call it nerve or flash or sparkle, but Davis and Jones had the kind of magnetism that forces you to look only at them if they're in a scene. And their physical resemblance can be astonishing because, yes, Jones had Bette Davis eyes. Filmmakers of the '50s really missed a bet by never finding an occasion for Davis and Jones to play mother and daughter, which would have been simply ideal (and possibly revelatory).

Jones never got a *Jezebel* or a *Dark Victory* to move her to out-and-out Davis-sized stardom and appreciation, but her opportunities improved when she got a supporting Oscar nomination for a six-minute role in the Paddy Chayefsky-scripted drama *The Bachelor Party* (1957). As a Greenwich Village "kook," a chatty and sexy bohemian, she gives this serviceable, earnest movie a jolt of life and humor, par for the course for Jones by now. She was back in kook mode for *A Hole in the Head* (1959), again with Frank Sinatra (after *Tender Trap*) and prickly good fun as Sinatra's bedmate, while steering clear of the film's more sentimental flourishes.

Jones got a Davis-type bad-girl role as Alan Ladd's unstable, slutty, blackmailing, and alcoholic wife in *The Man in the Net* (1959). Though the film is a dud as a mystery-thriller, and Ladd looks puffy and glued together, it allows Jones a juicy and neurotic showcase, stealing this negligible film with her dazzling fire. Unfortunately, she's not long for this movie, which hinges on her murder. In Michael Curtiz, Jones had even gotten herself a bona fide Davis director.

John Sturges' *Last Train from Gun Hill* (1959) is yet another great unsung '50s western. Filled with rich and penetrating moral dilemmas, the film pits marshal Kirk Douglas against powerful Anthony Quinn, former best friends. Quinn's son, Earl Holliman, is responsible for the rape and murder of Douglas' Indian wife. Jones is Quinn's mistress, torn between her brutal lover and her sympathy for Douglas. Compelling, gorgeously photographed, tightly focused, and intensely sustained, the picture's chief acting honors once again go to Jones. In a variation of the whore with a heart of gold, Jones is smart and sarcastic, a bruised no-nonsense woman who is likable, amusing, and deeply human. *Last Train from Gun Hill* deserves serious reappraisal, as does Jones, an actress who had enough time to show us her talent but not enough time to give that talent its due.

Clark & Viv & Leslie & Olivia pre-GWTW
October 17th, 2010

While writing my Vivien Leigh chapter for *Tennessee Williams and Company: His Essential Screen Actors*, I rewatched *A Yank at Oxford* (1938), Leigh's first American film (though it was filmed in England). In it she plays a frisky (and married) flirt, subordinate to leading lady Maureen O'Sullivan though both actresses play second fiddle to Robert Taylor; this formulaic comedy-drama is *his* vehicle. *Gone With the Wind* (1939) wasn't Leigh's at this point, but there's a standout moment in *Yank at Oxford* when student Taylor tells his tutor, "I'm still reading *Gone With the Wind* but I'm only halfway through." Two minutes later, Leigh makes her first entrance. Talk about destiny tipping its hand!

There's a more blatant and wonderfully inexplicable nod to the cast of *GWTW* in the not-bad screwball comedy *It's Love I'm After* (1937), which is all about theatre people, including Bette Davis (warming up for Margo Channing). Here you find Leslie Howard, the future Ashley Wilkes, as a womanizing stage actor who is being chased by a young and overdramatizing rich girl played by Olivia de Havilland, the future Melanie Hamilton. You get a shiver of pleasure watching them together because you know what they don't know: that they'll soon be joined in screen immortality. But things go a bit further at the end of the movie, once Olivia realizes that her mad crush on Leslie has subsided. Here's their exchange:

OLIVIA: "I was in love with Clark Gable last year and if I could get over him it's a cinch I could get over you!

LESLIE: "Who's Clark Gable?"

OLIVIA (to boyfriend Patric Knowles): "He doesn't know who Clark Gable is!"

Well, he would know soon enough.

Opening Credits vs. Closing Credits
April 28th, 2011

Nowadays a movie instantly gets points with me if it has opening credits. I've never liked the trend, more popular now than ever, in which movies deny us any credits until the end, usually starting off with the title and nothing else. Somehow it has come to pass that some movies are too "serious" to begin with the self-consciousness of announcing their contributing artists, which, so the thinking goes, prevents a viewer's complete immersion into the start of a film. I couldn't disagree more.

On artistic terms, I find the absence of opening credits to be utterly pretentious, but, thinking more practically, I simply find it annoying. I like those opening five minutes, or those five minutes after a prologue, in which I can ease into a movie during its credits. I also like knowing which actors I'm about to see, which cinematographer was involved, and, of course, which writers and director are responsible. I hate being driven mad during a film when an actor's name escapes me and I spend precious movie time trying to jog my memory. This doesn't happen when the credits are at the beginning.

I know we're long past the days of the old studio names meaning anything, but lovers of old movies can tell you the different feelings they get when they see the MGM lion or the Columbia lady or the Warner Brothers shield before an oldie begins. Film-company logos are meaningless today and yet now we ironically get to see so many more of them. Since movies get financing from so many places and have so many producers, movies now often begin with several introductory logos, one after the other. By the third or fourth one, I'm convinced the movie has started, but, no, it's just another logo. Then all the names of these individual organizations appear on the screen together and I'm almost ready to go home. Everybody wants their moment, I understand, but I don't have to enjoy it.

So, we finally get to the credits at the end of the movie, and they last a minimum of five minutes. I stay to see the cast and then I leave. I know this is considered a sacrilege, especially coming from someone who writes film criticism, and I also know that I probably miss all kinds of jokes and tags (and bad songs hoping for an Oscar nomination), but I can't help myself. I was listed in the end credits of *The Jerky Boys* (1995) for my few lines as a reporter in the opening scene (even though you can't really see me). Seeing my name was fun for me, and maybe for the people who know me, but no one else cared. Everyone deserves a pat on the back, no question, but why do I have to be present for it? Again, I look back to the old days of "The End," often followed by the cast list but that's it. Makes total sense to me.

Though I like easing into a movie via credits, I don't need to ease out of one. I'll never forget seeing *Vertigo* for the first time. When it ended, in all its stunning abruptness, I was floored. The lights came up. I was spared today's films' five more minutes in the dark and I loved the contrast, loved being shocked back into real life, which made the experience even more powerful. I like taking a movie out the door with me, rather than being "over it" after five to eight minutes of endless names.

I know, I know, I'm a dinosaur whining about how old movies are better than new ones, just a reactionary moviegoer trying to reach back into the past and not move forward. But to me it just looks like common sense, and if it wasn't broke why did they fix it?

THE END

Cowboys "Courageous"
June 24th, 2011

Do all you classic-film lovers out there know that there are some old movies available to Netflix users *only* on "Instant Play" and not on DVD? Recently, I've watched a group of movies that I can't recall having been on television in ages, such as Mitchell Leisen's *Bride of Vengeance* (1949), a trio of colorful Arlene Dahl costume pictures, and the as-bad-as-you've-heard biopic *The Buster Keaton Story* (1957). This week I watched *Cattle Drive* (1951) for the simple reason that Joel McCrea is my favorite male movie star. There are still films of his that I haven't seen; there are a few other McCrea westerns for which I cannot wait to hit "Play" in the next few weeks.

Cattle Drive was a reunion for McCrea with child actor Dean Stockwell one year after they made *Stars in My Crown*, one of my favorite McCrea films, one that I wrote about extensively in my book *Screen Savers*. *Cattle Drive* is no *Stars in My Crown* but it's not bad at all. The reason I bring it up is because it's one of those movies that stops you early on with "Hey, wait a second, I know this plot!" For anyone familiar with the '30s classic *Captains Courageous*, it won't take you long to realize that what you are watching is an unofficial (yet blatant) westernized remake of MGM's 1937 tearjerking adventure, a movie for which I've always had great affection.

It was not uncommon for successful dramas to be remade as westerns: *High Sierra* (1941) became the McCrea western *Colorado Territory* (1949), with both films directed by Raoul Walsh; *House of Strangers* (1949) returned as *Broken Lance* (1954); *The Asphalt Jungle* (1950) was reworked into *The Badlanders* (1958). And doesn't *Red River* (1948) always evoke *Mutiny on the Bounty* (1935) for you? Even *Rashomon* (1950) came back as *The Outrage* (1964).

Stockwell has the Freddie Bartholomew role from 1937, the spoiled, rich, motherless brat with the neglecting daddy (here played by Leon Ames). Instead of falling overboard, this time the kid gets off one of his dad's trains and finds himself stranded in the middle of nowhere, soon to be rescued by cowboy McCrea who brings the child into his all-male world. So, gone are the previous film's fishermen and in their place are men leading a cattle drive to Santa Fe. Forced to travel with them, Stockwell, like Bartholomew before him, makes the transition from unbearably rude and selfish monster to hardworking and well-liked member of the gang, with McCrea a true father figure. McCrea has the Oscar-winning Spencer Tracy role (without the Portuguese accent, mercifully). As much as I've always been so moved by *Captains Courageous*, I acknowledge that the film's power comes almost entirely from the wonder of young Bartholomew's acting rather than the work of Tracy, who actually gives one of his worst, least convincing performances. McCrea is untaxed by his less showy version of the role, giving it his signature easygoing, naturalistic quality.

Cattle Drive lacks the earlier film's delicate, unhurried transitions, making them far less satisfying and believable. The results feel like a thinning of the original material, therefore depriving viewers of the expected emotional wallop. Instead of recreating the 1937 ending, in which a devastating death brings Bartholomew closer to his real father (Melvyn Douglas), *Cattle Drive* provides a ridiculously happy ending, which makes it seem much more like a kids' movie than *Captains Courageous* ever did. Aside from the revised ending, *Cattle Drive* lifts whole episodes from the earlier film, making it clear beyond doubt that somebody watched *Captains Courageous* while furiously taking notes.

There's an amusing in-joke for McCrea fans. When he pulls out his wallet to show Stockwell a photo of his lady love, it's a picture of actress Frances Dee, McCrea's real-life wife.

Shangri-La, or Brigadoon, or Madara?
July 2nd, 2011

In the last few weeks, completely by coincidence, I watched (yet again) *Lost Horizon* (1937) and *Brigadoon* (1954), and, for the first time, *Desert Legion* (1953). Perhaps if I hadn't watched them so closely together, it wouldn't have been as blatantly obvious that they are three versions of the same plot, each focused on a Utopian society, a refuge from the real world and all its materialism and violence. These secret havens can be stumbled upon anywhere: *Lost Horizon*'s Shangri-La is somewhere in the Himalayas; *Desert Legion*'s Madara is not far from Algiers; *Brigadoon*'s titular village is in the Scottish Highlands. But the thing about Utopia, no matter where it is, is that after a while (a few months, perhaps, maybe even a few hours) it's really boring, not to mention stifling and so limited. In each of these films, the main character (Ronald Colman in '37, Alan Ladd in '53, and Gene Kelly in '54) discovers true love within his new paradise. Colman and Kelly both reconsider their options and decide to leave, regretting their decisions soon after and spending the rest of their movies dreaming of going back and finally, miraculously, getting back!

Both Shangri-La and Brigadoon have sensibly miserable characters, someone raining on everyone else's conformist parade. In *Lost Horizon*, it's Margo who's going nuts in all that peace and quiet, and in *Brigadoon* it's Hugh Laing (as Harry Beaton) who would like to get an education outside of 18th-century nowhere, plus a girlfriend to replace his now-married love. It ends badly for these characters, both of whom are treated as ungrateful and unable to recognize the good set-up they've got. Shangri-La may be a fountain of youth, and Brigadoon's one-day-a-century lifestyle may protect its inhabitants from many things, but all you see are theme parks whose pleasures look as though they might be used up after a long weekend.

Desert Legion's Madara does not have magical powers; it's also the tackiest of these Utopias. Like Colman and his Shangri-La, Alan Ladd has been brought to Madara deliberately, as the logical person to take over when Madara's old-timer founder (like *Lost Horizon*'s High Lama) finally expires. What all three films do not dare to show us is how things work out as time goes on (and on and on). Yes, Colman returns to Jane Wyatt, Ladd wins luscious Arlene Dahl, and Kelly can dance through the centuries with Cyd Charisse, but how long before the boys want to, say, travel, or go out for a night on the town, or simply connect in *any* way with the outer world? This isn't a cure for disillusionment; it's more an evasion, a dropping out. Each of these fantasies ends with the even bigger fantasies that happily doing mostly nothing is going to make (and keep) everybody happy. Gene Kelly leaves behind pal Van Johnson, an alcoholic cynic who never quite embraces Brigadoon. He is apparently doomed to be miserable in swanky New York nightclubs while Kelly herds sheep or makes ale or finds unconventional uses for all that heather on the hill.

Shangri-La, Brigadoon, and Madara are fantasies that sound enticing until you really start thinking about them. Maybe a trip to Epcot was all these three fellows really needed. Happy Hour with Van Johnson doesn't sound so bad to me.

V. Centenary Celebrations
screensaversmovies.com

Jezebel is 100!
June 28th, 2008

Bette Davis, one of filmdom's incontestably great actresses, would have turned 100 on April 5th. Instead of honoring her with the usual run-down of her classic performances, let's look at her early career, her dues-paying period (1931-1937).

Of her first six films, only the original *Waterloo Bridge* (1931) is memorable, though BD has minimal screen time as the leading man's kid sister. She made a leap with *The Man Who Played God* (1932), signing a Warner Brothers contract and appearing with the esteemed George Arliss. BD is lovely as Arliss' fiancee, but the plot is ludicrous: a deaf Arliss looks down from his apartment onto a Central Park bench and, using binoculars, lip-reads people's problems and solves them anonymously. She continued playing subordinate parts, unable to show her potential (while looking fetching as a blonde). There was a minor role in *So Big* (1932), a Barbara Stanwyck vehicle, and she was confined to secretary-girlfriend status in the political comedy *The Dark Horse* (1932).

The first sighting of "Bette Davis" came with *The Cabin in the Cotton* (1932), a failed mix of social concern and old-timey melodrama almost saved by BD's flashy turn as a rich Southern flirt ("I'd lak to kiss ya, but ah jes washed mah hay-eh"). But she wasn't in the foreground of *20,000 Years in Sing Sing* (1933), supporting Spencer Tracy while dolled up like Jean Harlow, or *Parachute Jumper* (1933), cast as Southern again and on hand merely to bolster Douglas Fairbanks, Jr.

Hooray for *The Working Man* (1933), an enchanting fairy-godfather comedy with BD alongside George Arliss again. He's a shoe-company owner who, incognito, sorts out the lives of the grown son and daughter (BD) of his dead rival. BD shines brightly, augmented by winning material. *Ex-Lady* (1933) was a decent attempt at a racy Norma Shearer-style photoplay, but then it was back to junk: *Bureau of Missing Persons* (1933), which plays like a whole season of *Without a Trace* crammed into 73 minutes; and *Fashions of 1934*, which underused BD while suffocating her with overglamorization. *Jimmy the Gent* (1934) proved to be her second comedy gem and, though on the periphery, she effortlessly held her own against James Cagney's colorful fireworks.

After *Fog over Frisco* (1934), an underworld drama that gave her a smallish but juicy role, she went to RKO to play the cold, cruel Cockney waitress in *Of Human Bondage* (1934), a still haunting film because of BD's uncompromising, provocative performance. Though she has a ferocious "big" scene, berating sensitive Leslie Howard, her acting is strongest in its calculating cool and vain indifference, making no attempt to soften the character or gain our sympathy (even when dying). She was unforgivably ignored at Oscar time, and her "reward" back at Warners was a career-gal service role in *Housewife* (1934), not even the title role! *Bordertown* (1935) gave her a witness-stand mad scene, and *The Girl from 10th Avenue* (1935) placed her at a Waldorf luncheon that anticipates *All About Eve*'s bitchery, but it was inexcusable to waste her gifts in dreck like *Special Agent* (1935).

BD's Oscar for *Dangerous* (1935) was a consolation prize for being stiffed the previous year. As a has-been stage actress, she brought vitality and shrewdness to a contrived script. *The Petrified Forest* (1936) was a prestige production (that hasn't aged well) with BD again opposite Leslie Howard, who pontificates unbearably while BD is stuck listening as "the girl." Prestige was certainly absent from both *The Golden Arrow* (1936), the kind of romantic comedy in which everyone ends up with a black eye, and *Satan Met a Lady* (1936), a C version of *The Maltese Falcon*.

BD fought for roles in pictures like *Marked Woman* (1937), a tough, if cliched, yarn about prostitutes ("hostesses") battling their pimp in court. Seemingly freed by no longer being a blonde, BD flaunted her electricity. But the next three did little for her: *Kid Galahad* (1937), first and foremost an Edward G. Robinson picture; *That Certain Woman* (1937), a limp remake of the 1929 Gloria Swanson soap *The Trespasser*; and *It's Love I'm After* (1937), her third with Leslie Howard and the kind of slapstick farce, like *The Bride Came C.O.D.* (1941), for which she had no natural flair.

Everything changed, at last, with *Jezebel* (1938). BD won her second Oscar, and this time she deserved it! Set in 1852 New Orleans, *Jezebel*'s plot is mostly moth-eaten, but BD infuses it with steely will and brazen passions. Her transition from a cunning, spoiled Southern belle to a woman redeemed by unselfish love has startling depth. Like many of her finest performances, its impact is enhanced by her capacity to project the vulnerabilities lurking beneath shows of confidence or arrogance. The BD of *Jezebel* is a dazzling screen presence and a mature, refined actress. It made her the superstar she is to this day.

Dame Celia
December 30th, 2008

Before we say farewell to 2008, there's one more 100th anniversary worth mentioning. December 18th marked a century since the birth of the great British actress Celia Johnson (1908-1982), best remembered as the star of the David Lean classic *Brief Encounter* (1945). One of the great love stories of the screen, *Brief Encounter* is blessed with a beautiful script from Noel Coward, Lean's delicate direction, and the two marvelous central performances from Johnson and co-star Trevor Howard. The whole thing should play as a spoof at this late date, but it has such depth of feeling that it's still a moving and irresistible romantic movie. Johnson is superb in her portrayal of an ordinary married woman who falls in love with a married doctor (Howard). Their chaste affair consists of exactly four kisses and an unconsummated tryst. Johnson's acting is honest and piercingly affecting throughout. She uncovers the pain, guilt, and desire beneath her perfect facade. Yes, it's very well-mannered as tales of adultery go, but it's touching in its portrait of two lives upturned by an unexpected, inopportune attraction. Howard is remarkably appealing in his gentleness and easy charm, but it remains Johnson's film. It takes an extraordinary talent to illuminate an average person so completely.

Amazing Maisie
January 21st, 2009

January 22nd marks the 100th anniversary of the birth of the delicious Ann Sothern (1909-2001), one of the big (and small) screen's most beloved blond comediennes. Often cast in musicals in the 1930s, notably opposite Maurice Chevalier in *Folies Bergère* (1935), she spent most of the '40s wisecracking her way through the likable *Maisie* series at MGM. Sothern's best film is *A Letter to Three Wives* (1949), Joseph L. Mankiewicz's sharp, Oscar-winning adult comedy. Yes, Sothern is one of the three wives, each of whom suspects that her husband has run off with the unseen Addie (voiced by elegant Celeste Holm).

Married to schoolteacher Kirk Douglas, Sothern plays a radio writer whose success is causing trouble in her marriage. Sothern is at her wittiest, and it's nice to see Douglas cast as a brainy, rather than brawny, fellow. Add wonderful performances from Linda Darnell, Paul Douglas, and, of course, Thelma Ritter, and you have a high spot in American screen comedy of the period.

Boom-Chick-a-Boom
February 8th, 2009

February 9th marks the 100th anniversary of the birth of Carmen Miranda, the Brazilian Bombshell, one of the authentic delights of the Hollywood musical of the 1940s, a period in the genre when all things Latin were the rage. Miranda's musicals usually had "Rio" or "Havana" or "Argentine" in their titles, even though they were filmed in mythically colorful, studio-bound imaginings of those exotic locales. Miranda quickly became beloved for her boisterous personality and joyous abandon, her charming skewering of the English language, and her outrageous costumes, specifically her perilously high platform shoes and fruit-basket hats. Fantasy was her stock in trade. For World War II audiences, was anything more escapist than the sight of Miranda?

The quintessential Miranda production number, a Busby Berkeley extravaganza, is "The Lady in the Tutti-Frutti Hat" from *The Gang's All Here* (1943). With its chorus of giant phallic bananas, it's the gayest number this side of Jane Russell's poolside romp ("Ain't There Anyone Here for Love?") with all those uninterested male athletes in *Gentlemen Prefer Blondes* (1953).

In *A Date with Judy* (1948), Miranda gives Wallace Beery rumba lessons, which is not easy. She tells him, "With you, I'm starting from behind scratch."

Miranda died in 1955 at the age of 46 when she suffered a heart attack. She's been gone a long time, but if I ever spend a night in Rio or a weekend in Havana, won't I be wondering where, oh where, is Carmen Miranda?

All About Joe
February 10, 2009

Hot on the heels (and I do mean heels) of Carmen Miranda's centenary on February 9th, comes the 100th anniversary of the birth of the great writer-director-producer Joseph L. Mankiewicz (1909-1993) on February 11th. Mankiewicz will forever be remembered as the man who made *All About Eve* (1950), his masterpiece, and he unfortunately will probably also be remembered for his famed debacle *Cleopatra* (1963). But between *Eve* and *Cleo*, there were some fine, lesser-known films, including two favorites of mine: *5 Fingers* (1952) and *The Quiet American* (1958). Both movies are featured in my second book, *100 Great Film Performances You Should Remember But Probably Don't.*

One of the great spy movies, *5 Fingers* features a magnificent performance from James Mason as the valet to the British ambassador in Turkey during World War II. It's a spellbinding true story of a discontented nobody, a man whose burning resentments find a venue for cool revenge. He becomes a traitor. Mason's acting has thrilling dimension as he portrays both the robotically efficient valet, who cunningly suppresses his personality, and the spitefully ambitious opportunist, who becomes a successful spy. The film is further fueled by its aching one-sided love story, in which Mason pursues Danielle Darrieux, a penniless countess who was once his employer. It's a film of riveting suspense, urbane humor, and romantic anguish.

Though it was remade in 2002 in a version more faithful to Graham Greene's novel, I still prefer the Mankiewicz adaptation of *The Quiet American,* primarily because it features a phenomenally fine performance from Michael Redgrave as a British news correspondent covering the battle for Indo-Chinese dominance between the Chinese communists and the French colonialists. Co-starring Audie Murphy in the title role, *The Quiet American* is a haunting film of love and betrayal set against international strife. It's a smart, pessimistic movie grounded by the depth of feeling that lies beneath Redgrave's cynicism and detachment.

An "Odd Man" and a "Good Fairy"
May 15th, 2009

This weekend marks what would have been the 100th birthdays of two great twentieth-century film actors, James Mason (May 15) and Margaret Sullavan (May 16). Though beloved by devout film fans, both stars are not as well remembered as they deserve to be, particularly Sullavan, who didn't make nearly as many films as Mason. She committed suicide in 1960 at the age of 50; Mason died at 75 in 1984.

After receiving worldwide acclaim as the star of Carol Reed's British thriller *Odd Man Out* (1947), Mason arrived in Hollywood and promptly became one of the more versatile male stars of the 1950s. His three greatest performances—and they are indisputably great—are in *5 Fingers* (1952), *A Star Is Born* (1954), and *Lolita* (1962). If you haven't seen this trio, you must do so immediately. Mason was one of those actors who was always getting better, always challenging himself (despite the many clinkers that litter his filmography).

For an example of great late-career Mason, check him out in Sidney Lumet's fine courtroom drama *The Verdict* (1982), in which he plays what first appears to be a stock character, the evil lawyer. Known as "the Prince of Darkness," his character is the masterful defense attorney up against underdog Paul Newman, an ambulance-chaser seeking redemption. Mason goes beneath the stereotype, giving a fascinating and subtle portrayal of smugly controlled arrogance and cold-blooded surety, while still allowing for glimmers of vulnerability visible to us though not to the other characters. His best moment comes in the courtroom, when he suddenly realizes that he may lose the case. In a few seconds he is shaken, momentarily unraveling, but then he recovers just as swiftly, again imperceptibly to those around him. This is superb on-screen thinking, the kind of acting it takes decades to perfect.

Margaret Sullavan is best remembered for appearing opposite James Stewart (a four-time co-star) in the Ernst Lubitsch comic treasure *The Shop Around the Corner* (1940), but my favorite Sullavan performance is in the William Wyler romantic comedy *The Good Fairy* (1935), a radiantly winning film whose magic derives primarily from Sullavan's abundant charm, comic know-how, and her delicately husky voice. It is one of the great 1930s comedies, yet it's still far too underappreciated.

Another one to watch for is Sullavan's final film, *No Sad Songs for Me* (1950), very much an old-style "woman's picture." Without an actress as restrained and intelligent in the lead role, the movie could easily have become maudlin and laughable. Sullavan plays an upper-middle-class housewife who learns that she has terminal cancer but keeps it secret, even from her husband (Wendell Corey). (Like any great star, she doesn't let her diagnosis interfere with her smoking like a chimney.) She is adored by everyone, including daughter Natalie Wood, and decides to tie up all her loose ends in the months she has left, even setting about securing her wifely replacement in the form of Viveca Lindfors. Everyone is so well-behaved, and Sullavan is so brave, with even her illness never appearing to be anything more than just plain tiring. Within the soapy world in which the plot exists, Sullavan avoids the crushing weight of martyrdom and nobility, turning in a graceful and dignified performance more moving than the material deserves. Sullavan expired in most of her dramatic pictures, and this film, a genuine multi-hankie affair, stands as a final tribute to her rare and beautiful artistry.

The One and Only Robin Hood
June 21st, 2009

This weekend (June 20th) marked the 100th anniversary of the birth of Errol Flynn, the sound era's master swashbuckler and the definitive Robin Hood in the 1938 classic *The Adventures of Robin Hood*, a wondrous and ageless film, the quintessential Hollywood adventure. Flynn, irresistibly dashing and handsome, was perfectly matched to the role, an ideal showcase for his ease and humor and charming light touch. And who looked better in green tights than Flynn? No wonder Olivia de Havilland's Maid Marian couldn't resist him. Their on-screen romance is one of the more affecting of Hollywood's Golden Age, gentle and intimate, especially in their glowing scene in her room and at her window (their "balcony" scene). It is especially nice to have an actress as wonderful as de Havilland as Marian, instead of some vacant starlet. Her talent brings out the best in Flynn, and she also makes a deeply felt transition to Robin's side, against villains Claude Rains and Basil Rathbone, two legendary and sophisticated bad guys for the price of one!

The movie, in rapturous Technicolor, is a storybook come to life, a glorious pageant, and studio-system craftsmanship at its peak. With its prankish, playful tone, there is nothing dated or campy here. Funny, touching, and rousing, it is blessed with an amazing supporting cast of beloved character actors like Eugene Pallette, Una O'Connor, and Alan Hale. Has fighting evil ever been this much fun? Or set so thrillingly to an Erich Wolfgang Korngold score?

A far less well-known Flynn film to be on the lookout for is the 1944 WWII picture *Uncertain Glory*, briskly directed by Raoul Walsh and co-starring Paul Lukas (fresh from his Oscar-winning work in *Watch on the Rhine*). Set in France, this is a tense and absorbing drama of redemption and sacrifice but not too shameless in its wartime uplift. The two leads have a "Les Miserables" sort of relationship, with Lukas the relentless inspector and Flynn the wanted man on the run. Beginning in his appealing bad-boy mode, Flynn eventually forms an unexpected bond with the upright Lukas.

Flynn died at 50, fifty years ago, though hard living made him look so much older. But at least he gets to be Robin Hood forever.

"Klaatu Barada Nikto"
August 21st, 2009

August 25th marks what would have been the 100th birthday of British film actor Michael Rennie, who died at age 61 in 1971. Though Rennie appeared in many high-profile Hollywood pictures of the 1950s, including *The Robe* (1953) and *The Rains of Ranchipur* (1955), plus the great spy movie *5 Fingers* (1952), he is best known for his elegant alien in the black-and-white sci-fi classic *The Day the Earth Stood Still* (1951), which is still the best flying-saucer movie ever made.

Rennie's Klaatu is an attractive, dignified, and intelligent creature, far superior to humans, and he's come to Earth to warn us. He and his union of planets are concerned about our WMD and our possible misuse of them, thus endangering the universe. If we don't stop our arms race, *they* will stop us. To get our attention, Klaatu shuts down the world's electricity for a half hour. Though the film's anti-nuke message hasn't aged a day, this is very much a film of the Cold War, with all the expected fear and paranoia about the end of the world.

Director Robert Wise (yes, the Robert Wise who would go on to direct *The Sound of Music*) handles the plot with a sure hand, keeping the film lean, understated, and more realistic in tone than just about any other sci-fi flick. This is a smart, thoughtful, and restrained drama every bit as powerful and resonant as it was back in 1951. The picture's chief asset is Rennie, though, who manages to be convincingly otherworldly without effort, embodying a supernatural composure. For movie thrills, Klaatu has brought along the handy Gort, a robot who can destroy weaponry with his vision rays.

Patricia Neal is far too gifted an actress for her role here, a secretary who lives with her son in the boardinghouse into which Rennie (as "Mr. Carpenter") comes to live. Naturally, Neal's presence elevates a standard role, making an already exceptional picture even better. Handsome Klaatu is actually 78 and has a life expectancy of 130 Earth years, which means he would probably be dead by 2009, yet Rennie found immortality by playing him.

Oh, and "Klaatu Barada Nikto" is the phrase that stops Gort from going on a rampage. You never know when you might need it.

Early Elia
September 7th, 2009

Director Elia Kazan, who died in 2003, would have turned 100 on
September 7th. His great decade on the screen was the 1950s, leaving behind such classics as *A Streetcar Named Desire* (1951), *On the
Waterfront* (1954), *East of Eden* (1955), and *Baby Doll* (1956). So, instead of
revisiting the obvious high points, let's take a brief look at his work of the 1940s,
specifically his two best films from that decade. *Gentleman's Agreement* (1947),
his first Oscar-winning Best Picture, is definitely not one of those films. Far
better are his first and last films of the '40s, *A Tree Grows in Brooklyn* (1945)
and *Pinky* (1949).

A Tree Grows in Brooklyn is a lovely, atmospheric adaptation of the novel
set "a few decades ago." The film's depiction of tenement life is nicely detailed,
and the emotions are never forced. While Kazan had far to go as a visual in-
terpreter of stories, he was already a great director of actors, a skill honed in
the New York theatre. Child actress Peggy Ann Garner is tenderly affecting as
wide-eyed and sensitive young Francie, and, through her, the film resonates
as a child's perception of her contrasting parents. As her pipe-dreaming alcoholic father, James Dunn won the supporting-actor Oscar that year, and it
remains one of the finest performances ever to be so honored. Charismatic and
beguiling when in blarney-spilling mode, he masks his pain artfully, but when
more exposed, in moments of unvarnished honesty, he is indeed heartbreaking. Dorothy McGuire is his realist wife, hardening by the minute. Another
wonder of the film is glorious Joan Blondell as Aunt Sissy, much-married and
flashy but warm and likable, a goodhearted dame. (How did this performance
miss out on an Oscar nomination?) The simplicity and restraint of this film
auspiciously declared Kazan's arrival in the movies.

Pinky was part of Fox's run of post-war social-issue pictures, but it holds up
far better than *Gentleman's Agreement*, though both films feature characters
posing as something they are not. In *Gentleman's Agreement*, Gregory Peck
pretends to be a Jew so he can write a story about anti-Semitism; in *Pinky*,
a light-skinned black woman passes for white. Pinky is so light-skinned, in
fact, that she's Jeanne Crain, about as white bread as you can get. Though
her casting is unfortunate (it almost always was), there was no way at that
time that the role could have gone to a black actress. But wouldn't other Fox
actresses, particularly Linda Darnell, maybe Anne Baxter, have been better
choices than Crain? She got an Oscar nomination for her effort, more for the
role than her acting. Aside from this gripe, and another about the tame fairy-

tale trajectory of the plot, *Pinky* is a compelling drama set in a very evocative Deep South. Kazan's work is far more visually expressive than it had been in his previous films, soaking up the hot, fertile surroundings and the swampy decay. A standout scene is the "headlights" sequence, a frightening almost-rape as Pinky is stalked by a menacing car at night.

Pinky has returned south after her nursing training in Boston, escaping from telling her white-doctor boyfriend (the even blander William Lundigan) that she's black. The great Ethel Waters is Crain's grandmother, and another great Ethel, Ethel Barrymore, is a bedridden dowager (just as she was in *The Spiral Staircase*). Both received Oscar nominations, but the best supporting performance comes from viperous Evelyn Varden, who has a ferociously mean and racist outburst in a store. The film backs off from a happy romantic ending because of the racial mixing, even though both actors are white. Despite everything it was up against, *Pinky* continues to play very well. You can feel Kazan making strides, getting closer to where he'd be in his peak years.

Doug Jr. and Kate, Bette, and Joan
December 10th, 2009

December 9th marked what would have been the 100th birthday of Douglas Fairbanks, Jr., who died at age 90 in 2000. As the son of the great swashbuckling star of the silent era, Douglas Jr. was truly Hollywood royalty and one of the first major second-generation movie stars. He may not be the icon that his father will always be, but he was certainly a more accomplished actor than his daddy ever was. My hands-down favorite of all his performances is his dashing and devious Rupert of Hentzau in *The Prisoner of Zenda* (1937), a scene-stealing villain of enormous wit and charm.

In 1933, already divorced from Joan Crawford, Fairbanks appeared opposite Katharine Hepburn in *Morning Glory* and Bette Davis in *Parachute Jumper*. Not bad, eh? In *Morning Glory*, Fairbanks has a thankless role as a playwright in what is clearly a vehicle for Hepburn, one that would win her the first of her four Oscars. It's a wildly uneven movie, but Hepburn is often extraordinary, notably in the opening casting-office scene in which she manages to be quite funny, heartbreaking, deliciously affected, and all-around radiant. She speaks impossibly fast and has an eccentric comic sparkle. But it is all downhill from there, becoming soapy cliches about the "thea-tuh." As handsome Fairbanks pines for her, she foolishly prefers producer Adolphe Menjou!

Parachute Jumper placed Fairbanks in the main role, with a blond Bette Davis in the thankless position as a Southern gal named Alabama. The film is fast-paced Depression-era nonsense, a melodrama with flying action, sex, drugs, and guns, in which Fairbanks is a marine, a chauffeur, a bodyguard, a smuggler, and, of course, the title role. His actorly assurance carries the movie, and Bette's spirited brightness helps, but it's a negligible movie.

Two early Fairbanks movies to watch out for on TCM are *Scarlet Dawn* (1932) and *The Life of Jimmy Dolan* (1933). The former is a surprisingly lavish Russian Revolution melodrama with an intriguing plot: Fairbanks is a an aristocrat who escapes with his servant (Nancy Carroll). Flavorful and romantic, and with genuine suspense and adventure, *Scarlet Dawn*, at a mere 58 minutes, simply goes by too quickly. Fairbanks is at his most charismatic, and the underrated Ms. Carroll is lovely and delicate. In this sexy pre-Coder, Fairbanks says, "Morals never bothered me so much, but taste is so important."

The Life of Jimmy Dolan is a real movie-movie, a satisfying and enjoyable drama in which Fairbanks stars as a cynical boxing champ who redeems himself with a new identity (once he's on the run from a possible murder rap). He stumbles upon Loretta Young's farm and eventually risks his new safety, boxing again to earn money for Loretta, her aunt, four orphans, and the farm. Though his role feels more suited to Cagney, Fairbanks is certainly superior to Cagney in the romance department. He and Loretta Young make an astoundingly beautiful couple. This film, which features Mickey Rooney and John Wayne in small roles, was remade as *They Made Me a Criminal* (1939) and starred John Garfield.

Any time you see Fairbanks' name in a cast list, I recommend checking out the movie, especially his early '30s quickies in which he is at the peak of his beauty and leading-man stature. Or just keep watching *The Prisoner of Zenda* over and over and watch him walk away with a Ronald Colman vehicle. Even though Colman has a dual role, he's no match for one Doug, Jr.

Mother of the Bride
February 15th, 2010

February 27 marks what would have been the 100th birthday of screen actress Joan Bennett, who died at age 80 in 1990. When she first caught attention, as a blond and beautiful (but rather awkward) ingenue in major early talkies such as *Disraeli* and *Bulldog Drummond*, both from 1929, she was best known as the daughter of stage star Richard Bennett and the younger sister of Constance Bennett (whose movie-star shadow she would be in for most of the 1930s). Neither of the Bennett actresses were first-rate talents, but Joan managed to have a very long career, continuing well after most of the public had forgotten Constance or their daddy. Joan was good at reinventing herself, a necessary talent for anyone who wants to last decades in the movie industry.

She was a lovely blond leading lady of the 1930s, then the raven-haired beauty of four Fritz Lang melodramas of the 1940s, making her a key femme fatale of film noir, with *The Woman in the Window* (1944), opposite Edward G. Robinson, the best of her films for Lang. At 40, she moved into the 1950s as the epitome of the upper-middle-class American housewife in *Father of the Bride* (1950) and its 1951 sequel *Father's Little Dividend*. And in the 1960s, she thrived on the small screen in the one-of-a-kind horror soap *Dark Shadows*.

Bennett had first shown glimmers of talent in Raoul Walsh's snappy, wise-cracking comedy *Me and My Gal* (1932), opposite Spencer Tracy, her future *Father of the Bride* husband. She showed a likably deadpan approach to comedy. In *Little Women* (1933), a massive hit and an instant classic, she was Amy, and director George Cukor got some charming moments from her, though hers is the least accomplished performance among the "women." A breakthrough for Bennett came in *Private Worlds* (1935), a rarely seen drama I was lucky enough to catch a few years ago at a screening at New York's Museum of Modern Art. Released a decade and a half before *The Snake Pit* (1948), it has been called the first major Hollywood film set in a mental institution. Starring Claudette Colbert and Charles Boyer and directed by the estimable Gregory La Cava, *Private Worlds* is an admirable drama remarkably free of easy answers, and it's further striking for its feminist streak, with Colbert as a great psychiatrist, the equal of her male colleagues. (The film never resorts to putting her in her "place.") Boyer plays the new boss, and he has a low opinion of female doctors. He eventually comes around. The film is unfortunately loaded with soapy plot turns, including the arrival of Boyer's murderous sister Helen Vinson, who begins an affair with doctor Joel McCrea, who is married to a fragile Bennett.

Colbert received an Oscar nomination, a year after winning the award for *It Happened One Night*, again displaying her characteristic ease, warmth, and intelligence. Boyer fares less well in a sketchier role, but McCrea is as wonderfully natural as always, even though the script undermines him by turning him into a heel. (Colbert and McCrea, cast as pals and peers here, would take their obvious rapport and turn it into pure gold when they starred in Preston Sturges' comic wonder *The Palm Beach Story* seven years later.) The surprise here is Bennett, in one of her best performances, tender and sympathetic, showing new confidence in her acting ability and making a strong and touching impression. She plays a woman who feels she is nothing without her husband, and she handles this aspect of the character with restraint and delicacy.

La Cava uses overlapping dialogue and spontaneous-feeling injections of humor, just as he would so famously in his *Stage Door* two years later. The most memorable and startling sequence is Bennett's breakdown while a storm rages outside. The visual and aural elements put you inside her mind as she mentally disintegrates and falls down a staircase.

Despite its flaws, *Private Worlds* is ambitious and affecting and made with great care. It may be uneven and abbreviated, but it's a movie that keeps you rooting for it. I hope there will be more opportunities for it to be seen. Its invisibility is a crime, especially considering the major artists involved. And it contains what is probably the best performance ever given by the blond Joan Bennett, long before she became a dark temptress or raised Elizabeth Taylor or trafficked in vampires.

Dapper David
February 28th, 2010

On March 1st, Oscar-winning Englishman David Niven would have turned 100 years old. (He died at 73 in 1983.) Beloved for his charm, wit, and elegance, Niven had an impressively long movie career filled with lasting favorites: *Wuthering Heights* (1939), *A Matter of Life and Death* (1946), *The Bishop's Wife* (1947), *Around the World in Eighty Days* (1956), *The Guns of Navarone* (1961), and *The Pink Panther* (1964). He received the Academy Award on his first (and only) nomination, winning Best Actor for *Separate Tables* (1958), in the role of a military major who had been arrested for lewd behavior as a movie-theatre masher, someone who can handle sexual matters only with strangers in the dark. In a role that was a far cry from his usually light and sophisticated parts, Niven acquitted himself most admirably.

Based on Terence Rattigan's stage play, the acclaimed *Separate Tables* hasn't aged very well; it now looks like a wildly overrated snob hit. A *Grand Hotel*-style ensemble piece, *Separate Tables* (also set in a hotel) feels obvious and worn, but Niven's performance holds up extremely well, a poignant rendering of a man with a dark secret who masks his pain and terror behind a puffed-up pose and an arsenal of military mannerisms. It is unlike any other Niven performance, and it retains a freshness mostly lacking elsewhere in the film. His character's friendship with a mousy Deborah Kerr (with whom Niven made five films) is central to the movie. Though its cast includes Burt Lancaster, Rita Hayworth, and several other "names," most of this stiff-upper-lip drama is thinly conceived and short on illumination, with only Niven handily surpassing the material, especially when his major has nothing left to hide.

If I had to pick my favorite Niven film, I'd go with *Bachelor Mother* (1939), one of the comic gems of the great screwball-comedy era. Directed by Garson Kanin and starring Ginger Rogers (with whom Niven made three films), *Bachelor Mother* is a modestly mounted romantic comedy yet a worthy member of Hollywood's classic output of 1939. Rogers is at the peak of her stardom, truly one of the Golden Age's top comediennes, and Niven partnered her delightfully. It appears to be a case of Niven getting a role only after Cary Grant had proved unavailable, but who cares? Niven makes the most of his Grant-like chance and he is irresistibly winning and deftly amusing. His debonair persona is the perfect counterpoint to Rogers' working-girl appeal, creating a bond similar to the one she had developed with Fred Astaire.

Rogers works in the toy department of a store owned by Niven's father (Charles Coburn, great as usual). When she comes to the aid of a doorstep foundling, everyone believes that the baby is hers, no matter how hard she tries to explain the truth, eventually leading to suspicions that Niven, the boss' son, is the father. The film is one of the more beguiling of dream-factory Cinderella comedies, made with an unforced charm and sustained cleverness, containing at least one major and quite hilarious comic sequence of the period, the nightclub scene in which the two stars successfully pass Rogers off as Niven's non-English-speaking Swedish date. This sparkling comedy was horridly remade for Debbie Reynolds and Eddie Fisher in 1956 as *Bundle of Joy*. Imagine Eddie Fisher stepping in for David Niven!

Trevor and Kurosawa and Conte
March 29th, 2010

With March almost behind us, I see that I missed a few 100th birthdays while I was writing about other things. Oscar-winning actress Claire Trevor would have turned 100 on March 8, Japanese director Akira Kurosawa would have done the same on March 23, and unjustly overlooked actor Richard Conte would have hit the big one on the 24th. Here are three mini-tributes.

Trevor, who died at age 90 in 2000, got her Oscar for her sensationally entertaining performance as Edward G. Robinson's alcoholic moll in *Key Largo*

(1948). Goodhearted tramps were Trevor's specialty, but this time she outdid herself, embracing the flashiness of the part and running with it. As a nightclub singer on the skids, Trevor has a classic scene of croaking her way through "Moanin' Low" in order to get a promised drink. The role had Oscar written all over it, but Trevor took it further, richly deserving the award, matching Robinson every step of the way, with both of them stealing the picture from Humphrey Bogart and Lauren Bacall in the more well-behaved roles. Trevor had actually gotten her big break opposite Bogart in a tiny one-scene role in *Dead End* (1937), playing a hooker and winning her first Oscar nomination. Her third and final nomination came for *The High and the Mighty* (1954), playing, you guessed it, a boisterous tramp in this John Wayne disaster movie, the model for *Airplane!* (1980) and almost as funny. She and Wayne had appeared together in *Stagecoach* (1939), the film that made him a star and the one in which Trevor gave the quintessential performance of the whore with a heart of gold.

Though Kurosawa, who died at 88 in 1998, made many international masterworks, including *Rashomon* (1950) and *The Seven Samurai* (1954), my favorite of his films is *Ikiru* (1952), simply because it is so moving, actually one of the more moving films I've ever seen. A simple story of an anonymous civil servant (Takashi Shimura) in contemporary Japan, *Ikiru* unexpectedly becomes an emotionally overwhelming movie about doing something with your life that is truly *worth* doing. Though long and leisurely, the film really pays off. Shimura has six months to live, and he realizes how worthless his life has been up to now. To call this film a Japanese *It's a Wonderful Life* isn't quite accurate, but it leaves you with that same kind of feeling about ordinary people and their extraordinary lives. A rewarding, unforgettable climax tops an eloquent, honestly uplifting film.

As for Richard Conte, who died at 65 in 1975, here's an excerpt from my book *Screen Savers*, with regard to his performance in *They Came to Cordura* (1959): Conte, one of Hollywood's most underrated actors, is cast exactly to type, making Trubee another of his smoothly calculating, expertly slimy characters. How could anyone have ever trusted him again after he brandished his flair for sadism on Susan Hayward in *I'll Cry Tomorrow* (1955)? He's also slickly "rotten" in the polished noirs *Cry of the City* (1948) and *The Big Combo* (1955), the one in which he says, "First is first and second is nobody." And he certainly adds to the overall verisimilitude of *The Godfather* (1972). Conte also excelled at good guys, as in the hardy *Thieves' Highway* (1949); his streetwise savvy made him the Italian John Garfield.

"Cat" Lady
April 19, 2010

Apsil 23rd marks what would have been the 100th birthday of French screen actress Simone Simon (who died in 2005). Simon got her piece of Hollywood immortality when she starred in producer Val Lewton's classic *Cat People* (1942), directed by Jacques Tourneur, the film that kicked off Lewton's great series of suggestive low-budget horror movies at RKO. With her pouty mouth and little-girl voice, Simon was ideally cast as the strange Serbian girl with a secret. As her gentle husband (Kent Smith) waits patiently for sex, the film transcends its supernatural mix of the human and the feline, becoming just as concerned with Simon's sexual fears, including her fear of her sexual power. (Will intimacy literally turn her into an animal?) *Cat People* is ultimately a sad love story marked by unavoidable violence. (Trivia: Smith's character is named Oliver Reed.)

Simone Simon had made her American screen debut six years earlier in *Girls' Dormitory* (1936), in which Fox gave her a big build-up. As a senior at an all-girls school in Central Europe, Simon has a crush on bachelor professor Herbert Marshall, while fellow teacher Ruth Chatterton also pines for him. (The ensuing triangle may remind you of *The Prime of Miss Jean Brodie*.) Shot in ethereal close-ups, Simon holds the screen easily, even if the picture launching her is strictly a "B," despite the two established stars in support of her. Why both women want Marshall is something of a mystery, and it's especially dispiriting to see the great Chatterton (the "Bette Davis" of the early-talkie years) behaving with such self-sacrifice. A young Tyrone Power shows up near the end as Simon's cousin, displaying unmistakable star quality that's just about ready to cut loose. Simon's debut is certainly striking but the movie is a little bit of nothing.

Though she would appear in other memorable films, such as *La Bete Humaine* (1938), *All That Money Can Buy* (1941) and *La Ronde* (1950), Simone Simon will forever be Irena of *Cat People*, the young woman whose entrance into a pet store drives the animals wild. Simon herself will be driving horror-movie fans wild for all eternity.

Almost Scarlett O'Hara
May 27th, 2010

June 3rd marks what would have been the 100th birthday of Paulette Goddard, one of the top female stars at Paramount during the 1940s. True, we can't ever really know the truth about the birthdates of the great ladies of the silver screen, but I'm willing to accept 1910 as her birth year if only to take advantage of the occasion to write about her fascinating career. Goddard was not a great actress, more a likable personality with an uncommonly pretty face and figure, yet she parlayed her attributes into a list of credits unlike any other female star of her time. After all, no one but Goddard managed to do all of the following: she starred opposite Charlie Chaplin in two of his greatest films, *Modern Times* (1936) and *The Great Dictator* (1940); she was nearly cast as Scarlett O'Hara until Vivien Leigh arrived out of nowhere; she had a classic brawl with Rosalind Russell in George Cukor's *The Women* (1939); she danced (rather well) with Fred Astaire in *Second Chorus* (1940), though it was probably Astaire's worst film; she made three hit comedies with Bob Hope, *The Cat and the Canary* (1939), *The Ghost Breakers* (1940), and *Nothing But the Truth* (1941); she got a supporting-actress Oscar nomination for the female-driven wartime drama *So Proudly We Hail!* (1943), opposite Claudette Colbert and Veronica Lake; she starred in three Technicolor Cecil B. DeMille extravaganzas, *North West Mounted Police* (1940), *Reap the Wild Wind* (1942), and *Unconquered* (1947); she starred in Jean Renoir's *The Diary of a Chambermaid* (1946), one of the great French director's few American films. Not bad, eh?

Goddard gave two of her best performances in films directed by the neglected Mitchell Leisen. In *Hold Back the Dawn* (1941), alongside a superb Charles Boyer and an Oscar-nominated Olivia de Havilland, Goddard is smart, sexy, and sassy as Boyer's ex-dancing partner, an Australian-Polish gold digger in a Mexican border town. She has a lovely moment when she uses champagne to seal an envelope. And naturally there's a juicy good girl-bad girl confrontation scene between the two female stars. This is a marvelous immigration drama with a script by Billy Wilder and Charles Brackett, one of those unjustly unknown treasures of the forties.

Not as good, but still worthy, is Leisen's *Kitty*, a lavish eighteenth-century reworking of *Pygmalion* with Goddard the guttersnipe who rises in the English court. Though she has a shaky Cockney accent, Goddard revels in her fashion parade against spectacular sets. She is her likable, attractive self, elevated by the wit and charm in Leisen's direction, assisted by a first-rate cast (Ray Milland is her Henry Higgins; divine Constance Collier is her Pickering). As in *Hold Back the Dawn*, Goddard is in gold-digging mode, but with a much bigger budget.

Goddard would have made a disappointing, tedious, and unnuanced Scarlett O'Hara, but when cast in less demanding roles, like the no-nonsense dames of *The Women* and *Hold Back the Dawn*, she was a true movie star and she acquitted herself beautifully, with sparkle, brains, and pin-up loveliness.

Also Known as Just Plain "Bob"
June 3rd, 2010

Just a week after what would have been the 100th birthday of Paulette Goddard comes another Hollywood centenary, that of light comedian Robert Cummings, who would have turned 100 on June 10 and who died in 1990 at age 80. Before becoming a sitcom star of the 1950s, Cummings had been a boyishly young screen actor of the 1930s, and then an all-grown-up star of the 1940s, even if most of his roles seemed to be the hand-me-downs of more virile leading men such as Fred MacMurray, Joel McCrea, and Ray Milland. Cummings still managed to co-star opposite most of the brightest comic females of the forties, including Rosalind Russell, Jean Arthur, and Barbara Stanwyck, yet he was never exactly a threat to Cary Grant. Even so, he was polished, skillful, and dependable, with boy-next-door good looks and an energized personality.

Cummings may be best remembered for his appearances in two Alfred Hitchcock thrillers, even though he was far more at home in romantic comedies. In *Saboteur* (1942), Cummings is one of Hitchcock's typical innocent men on the run, getting all tangled up with spies during WWII. Too asexual and juvenile to be playing a Hitchcock lead, Cummings nonetheless has the stamina and vigor to keep up with the plot, which is a comic book of espionage. Despite the nonstop suspense, the result is minor Hitchcock, which can also be said of Cummings' other Hitchcock feature, the 3-D *Dial M for Murder* (1954), in which Cummings isn't even the male lead (Ray Milland) opposite Grace Kelly. It was definitely time to go to television. *The Bob Cummings Show* (1955-59) brought Cummings four Emmy Award nominations. He had already won an Emmy for the original production of *Twelve Angry Men* in 1954.

I have two favorite Cummings movies. The first is *It Started with Eve* (1941), an underrated comedy directed by Henry Koster and starring Charles Laughton (as Cummings' dying father) and Deanna Durbin (destined to wind up with Cummings). It's one of those cleverly plotted mistaken-identity affairs, a complete delight, and one of five comedies that I write about in my book *Screen Savers*. A high point for all three of its stars, *It Started with Eve* is satisfying and consistently good fun.

I've also written about my other favorite Cummings movie, *Kings Row* (1942), in my book *100 Great Film Performances You Should Remember*, in which I focus specifically on the marvelous work done by Ann Sheridan, who appears not only with Cummings but also a never-better Ronald Reagan, not to mention an amazing supporting cast, including Claude Rains, Judith Anderson, and Charles Coburn. A turn-of-the-century *Peyton Place*, *Kings Row* is a beautifully mounted and intensely compelling melodrama, unusual fare for Cummings who isn't at his best, somewhat overearnest and a bit drippy as a young psychiatrist who returns to his hometown after studying in Vienna. Despite its flaws, *Kings Row* is a mesmerizing and potent soap opera.

I would also like to point out two neglected Cummings films that could use a boost, both from 1949. *The Accused* finds Loretta Young in the most fertile period of her career, in the few years after her Oscar-winning turn in *The Farmer's Daughter* (1947). Young plays a repressed college professor who kills a handsome student (Douglas Dick) in self-defense (he, wearing only a swimsuit, tries to rape her). She then conceals her actions. Cummings seems miscast as Young's love interest, as well as her victim's guardian, a bit too lightweight yet again. But it's a neat thriller, if you can overlook the hilarious psychobabble, and Young is at her best, helped by her obvious enjoyment of her transition from plain schoolteacher to Edith Head glamour girl.

Finally, there's *Reign of Terror* (also known as *The Black Book*), directed by the great Anthony Mann, who put a singular noir spin and visual palette on a tale of the French Revolution. The film is a fascinating oddity that works, even though Cummings once again feels out of place. (He was really only at home in the light comedies that made the most of his genial and animated spirit.) Here he has a heroic action role, a man of intrigue trying to secure the black book (a death list) of Robespierre (Richard Basehart). Underappreciated actress Arlene Dahl is the beauty from Cummings' past, and they argue while saving France together. A breathtakingly beautiful black-and-white movie with a plot that is enjoyably implausible, *Reign of Terror* is a one-of-a-kind sleeper.

It would seem that Cummings' best movies were the fine dramas in which he survived miscasting and coasted on his professionalism, rather than the string of romantic comedies that cast him well but were admittedly of the cookie-cutter variety. So, I guess that makes *It Started with Eve* the perfect Cummings movie, the rare case of an exceptional Cummings movie that actually used him ideally.

Loesser Was More
June 25th, 2010

June 29th marks what would have been the 100th birthday of Frank Loesser, one of Broadway's greatest songwriters (as both composer and lyricist), the man who gave us *Guys and Dolls* (1950), an enduring masterpiece of the American musical theatre, not to mention his Pulitzer Prize-winning *How to Succeed in Business without Really Trying* (1961). The movie versions of both shows have their intermittent pleasures, yet each was an artistic disappointment despite (or because of) obvious attempts to simulate the stage experiences as much as possible.

Loesser, who died of cancer in 1969 at just 59, had spent considerable time in Hollywood before taking New York by storm. He wrote the lyrics for Marlene Dietrich's "See What the Boys in the Back Room Will Have" in *Destry Rides Again* (1939), as well as creating many specialty numbers for Betty Hutton during her Paramount heyday, and he got an Oscar for "Baby It's Cold Outside" from the Esther Williams swim-sical *Neptune's Daughter* (1949).

Loesser's first big film after his phenomenal Broadway success with *Guys and Dolls* was *Hans Christian Andersen* (1952), a Samuel Goldwyn-produced vehicle for Danny Kaye, who was one of Goldwyn's biggest box-office draws. A popular hit, the film became a holiday television perennial during my childhood in the 1970s. I loved the film then, and I still loved it as a young adult, but soon after I was able to detect its flaws, primarily its very contrived screenplay by Moss Hart. But the film has two lingering assets: Kaye, at his most engaging and relaxed, and Loesser's score, which surpasses Kaye as the film's most impressive ingredient.

It was a charming idea to treat Andersen's story not as a standard biopic, but, rather, as something of a fairy tale itself. This concept might have laid an egg without those witty and endlessly melodic tunes by Loesser. The songs fall into two categories: those that musicalize actual Andersen tales, such as "Thumbelina" and "The Ugly Duckling"; and those integrated into the plot, such as "No Two People" and "Anywhere I Wander." The score is remarkably varied within what might seem some severe limitations, and every single song elevates the scene in which it appears. "Anywhere I Wander" is one of the more poignant introspective ballads to come out of Hollywood, tenderly sung by Kaye, and it seems a crime that it never became better known. It was the catchy "Thumbelina" that snagged an Oscar nomination for Best Song, losing to "High Noon" ("Do Not Forsake Me…").

Loesser and Kaye clicked beautifully, but many of the other elements fell far below their standard. The exception is Jeanmaire, the French dancer who radiantly plays the temperamental ballerina, proving to be a delightful actress as well as an exquisite dancer. Moss Hart's script takes a bad turn when Kaye's infatuation with Jeanmaire turns masochistic. And poor Farley Granger is miscast as Jeanmaire's equally tempestuous husband and choreographer, stuck playing an all-around jerk. Another unfortunate cast member is young Joey Walsh, cast as Kaye's Brooklyn-sounding apprentice. They appear to be a couple, though this could hardly have been intentional in a kids' musical of the 1950s. They "break up" over Kaye's obsession with Jeanmaire. The character of Hans becomes a bore once the plot morphs into an imagined love triangle between Kaye, Jeanmaire, and Granger. Bring back Thumbelina!

Though the film is colorful and fast-moving, it is uninspiredly directed by Charles Vidor, a man I admire for such gems as *Cover Girl* (1944), *Gilda* (1946), *Love Me or Leave Me* (1955), and *The Swan* (1956). His work here is stodgy and unimaginative, as heavy as the obviously fake sets of the storybook setting. It falls to Kaye and Loesser, countless times, to elevate the proceedings and temporarily make the picture soar. Yes, the ballet of *The Little Mermaid* is a blatant attempt to give audiences what they apparently liked in *The Red Shoes* and *An American in Paris*, but it does have its moments, notably the red, black, and white ball sequence. The film ends with a "no place like home" resolution, with Hans back from the big bad city ("Wonderful, Wonderful Copenhagen") that he never quite understood, and back with Joey Walsh, too.

I can forgive most of my complaints whenever I hear the first lines of Loesser's "No two people have ever been so in love…"

Queen of the Tenements
August 6th, 2010

August 8th marks what would have been the 100th birthday of actress Sylvia Sidney, who died in 1999 at 88. And what a career she had, beginning with stardom in the pre-Code Hollywood of the early 1930s and ending with a late-life resurgence in the sci-fi comedies of Tim Burton (*Beetlejuice*—1988, *Mars Attacks!*—1996, her final film). Plus she had a distinguished career on the Broadway stage and on television.

Sidney's screen career blossomed with the 1-2-3 punch of three 1931 dramas directed by three of the top moviemakers in the biz: Rouben Mamoulian's *City Streets* (with Gary Cooper), Josef von Sternberg's *An American Tragedy*, and King Vidor's *Street Scene*. In the von Sternberg picture, she plays the role later made famous by Shelley Winters in *A Place in the Sun* (1951). *Street Scene* would appear to be the picture that solidified Bronx-born Sidney's persona as the ultimate tenement girl. In all three pictures, Sidney is a fresh and natural actress, delicate and soulful and lovely. It seems remarkable that Sidney didn't get an Oscar nomination for one of these films, after having a year like that!

I'm very fond of her in the 1934 Preston Sturges-scripted comedy *Thirty-Day Princess* (1934), opposite a young Cary Grant and completely captivating in her dual role. But she is far more remembered for her dramatic roles, notably as the lead in William Wyler's fine screen adaptation of *Dead End* (1937), which contains Sidney's quintessential tenement role, representing all of the "depressed" working class.

Her late-'30s career was marked by her association with director Fritz Lang, with whom she made three movies: *Fury* (1936), the best remembered of the trio, is more a Spencer Tracy vehicle than a Sidney picture; *You Only Live Once* (1937), now regarded as the best of the three, is overrated, but she and Henry Fonda play beautifully together, though again she is secondary to her leading man; and *You and Me* (1938), a dud then as now.

Her other '30s picture of note is Hitchcock's *Sabotage* (1936), a British picture, skillfully done though not one of Hitch's great English films. Sidney is the American wife of saboteur Oscar Homolka, whom she finally stabs to death. Later Sidney roles of note include playing opposite Jimmy Cagney in *Blood on the Sun* (1945), as Fantine in the 1952 *Les Miserables*, and as Joanne Woodward's mother in *Summer Wishes, Winter Dreams* (1973), for which Sidney received her only Oscar nomination, losing to Tatum O'Neal! It's a dreary movie in which Sidney, as an upper-class NYC matron, dies in the first twenty minutes. You're very sorry to see her go, as you are whenever Sylvia Sidney makes an exit in one of her movies.

Van Heflin, Actor's Actor
December 11th, 2010

It's hard to write about classic movies without continually stumbling upon Van Heflin, one of the best things to happen to movies from the mid-thirties to the early seventies (but especially in the fifties). December 13 marks the 100th anniversary of his birth, though Heflin has been gone a long time, dying at only 60 in 1971. He made his film debut in *A Woman Rebels* (1936), one of the movies that famously turned Katharine Hepburn into box-office poison. But it was an association that paid off for the young actor when he co-starred with Hepburn on Broadway in the original 1939 production of *The Philadelphia Story*, with Heflin in the role that would eventually win Jimmy Stewart an Oscar.

Heflin didn't have to wait long for an Oscar of his own, nabbing the Best Supporting Actor prize of 1942 for *Johnny Eager*, an MGM attempt at making a Warner Brothers kind of gangster picture (even getting *Little Caesar's* Mervyn LeRoy to direct it). Robert Taylor is the racketeering star of this popular but corny (nearly laughable) melodrama, and a luscious young Lana Turner is the rich girl who loves him. Equally gorgeous, and equally limited as actors here, Taylor and Turner (promoted as "TNT") watch as the film is stolen by Heflin as Taylor's alcoholic buddy, a poetry-spouting lush, a role that amounts to a nearly feature-length drunk scene. Heflin serves as Taylor's conscience, and a case could be made for the character as a latent homosexual. (This superficial movie could use all the hidden subtexts that any of us can unearth within it!) The drinking could quite easily be because of unrequited love for Taylor. Heflin brings the only subtle strokes to a sentimentalized tough-guy movie, yet he gave far more impressive performances in the years to come.

Writing about *The Raid* (1954), one of my favorite Civil War movies, in my book *Screen Savers*, I say that Heflin was never better, "brimming with smarts, scruples, and shame, and helping to make the Civil War live on-screen in a unique and unforgettable way." As a Confederate major who escapes a Union prison and then infiltrates a Vermont town as a Canadian business-man (putting into motion a plot to rob the town and burn it to the ground), Heflin is allowed a remarkable character transformation as he struggles with his growing attachment to the community he has been dispatched to destroy. The personal war between his desire for revenge and his inherent humanity is beautifully delineated by Heflin, endowing the film with both moral heft and character complexity. This still-underrated gem owes much of its force to Heflin.

Perhaps *Shane* (1953) is the film for which Heflin is best remembered, even though his ordinary-guy decency in the film is often overlooked in favor of Alan Ladd, Brandon de Wilde, and Jack Palance whenever this classic western is recalled. However, I would venture to say, with apologies to Jean Arthur as well, that it's Heflin who gives the film its best—both fullest and deepest—per-formance. In *Screen Savers*, I go on to say that other Heflin highlights include "being shot by Joan Crawford in *Possessed* (1947), chased by Robert Ryan in *Act of Violence* (1948), and abused by Jennifer Jones in *Madame Bovary* (1949)." He was cast against type in *They Came to Cordura* (1959), another (along with

The Raid) of the five war movies that I focus on within *Screen Savers*. He plays a "grubby, vicious lout" and clearly relishes the opportunity.

Even in my new book, *Tennessee Williams and Company*, Heflin manages to show up, even though he never appeared in a Williams movie. Joanne Woodward is one of my subjects, though, and she made her screen debut opposite Heflin in *Count Three and Pray* (1955), a modest yet likable semi-western in which Heflin is a wannabe preacher and Woodward is an orphaned tomboy.

You may also have fond memories of Heflin well-matched opposite Barbara Stanwyck (three times), or throwing out bad-girl wife Arlene Dahl in *Woman's World* (1954), or as the star of the original *3:10 to Yuma* (1957). And, of course, there were the boffo box-office smashes *The Three Musketeers* (1948), *Battle Cry* (1955), and *Airport* (1970), his final big-screen appearance.

You might say that Heflin was the poor man's Spencer Tracy, never a star on Tracy's level but they were certainly similar in style, both capable of extraordinary intelligence and enviable economy, making it look so damned easy, making us feel so much without visible effort on their parts. Do yourself a favor and spend some time with a Heflin movie on his very big birthday.

Reagan and Lund: Two "Yanks" Turn 100
February 5th, 2011

There is certainly enough press about this February 6th being what would have been the 100th birthday of Ronald Reagan. Far less will be written about 02-06-11 also being the occasion of John Lund's hundredth b-day. While considering what to blog about, I thought, "Do I devote a post to Reagan and perhaps talk about my love of *Kings Row* (1942), even though he's hardly among the major reasons for my admiration of the movie, *or* do I give some blog space to the virtually forgotten Lund, whose leading-man years began in the late '40s and were over by the middle '50s?" In a remarkable coincidence, these guys are joined not only by their shared birthdates. Both men played the role of Yank in *The Hasty Heart*: Lund on Broadway in 1945; Reagan on film in 1949. The play's success led to Lund's Hollywood career, and the film version is one of the peaks of Reagan's career.

If you know *The Hasty Heart*, then you know that Yank, while a leading role, is subservient to the role of "Lachie" (pronounced "Lackey"), played on Broadway by Richard Basehart and on-screen by Richard Todd (in a deservedly Oscar-nominated performance). Written by John Patrick, the piece is a moving, honestly heartwarming drama of post-war 1945, set in a Burmese army hospital.

In the film, Todd, a Scottish corporal, is wounded on the war's final day. Left with one kidney, his days are numbered. He has a difficult, alienating personality and won't let anyone get close, including the five other soldiers with whom he shares quarters. Everyone knows the truth about Lachie's situation except Lachie himself. The men try their best to be Lachie's friend, including Yank, an ambulance driver getting over malaria. Patricia Neal plays the men's beautiful Canadian nurse.

The Yank role is fairly thankless, while Lachie gets to make enormous transitions, from fierce unpleasantness to openhearted joy, then back to bitterness and finally to love and friendship. But Reagan (and presumably Lund before him) provides the necessary and easygoing American charm and spirit, the likable contrast to Lachie's rigidity and mistrust. Yank is easy to overlook but the piece would be so much less without his humor, solidity, and decency. It's a stagy movie that plays like a P.O.W. drama, with its war-themed enclosed space. Vincent Sherman directed it unimaginatively but without getting in the way of the play's strengths.

From the Broadway run, Lund made his Hollywood debut opposite Olivia de Havilland in her first Oscar-winning performance in Mitchell Leisen's *To Each His Own* (1946). Lund nabbed the dual role of Olivia's lover (who dies in WWI) and (much later) her grown son. His best movie year was 1948, when he starred in Billy Wilder's *A Foreign Affair*, holding his own opposite two legendary ladies, Jean Arthur and Marlene Dietrich, and *Miss Tatlock's Millions*, an underrated screwball comedy from a post-screwball era, in which Lund gives his best performance, an unexpectedly hilarious and wacky turn from a clean-cut, all-American, tall-blond-and-handsome leading man.

Lund died in 1992 at 81, and Reagan died in 2004 at 93. Both men's careers owed so very much to the fact that they once excelled as "Yanks."

Red-Hot Blonde
March 6th, 2011

March 3rd marked the 100th anniversary of the birth of Jean Harlow, the original blond bombshell. She has been dead for 74 years, dying at the age of just 26, meaning that her life was a full decade shorter than Marilyn Monroe's. Since Harlow was the epitome of a pre-Code star, one can only wonder what her career might have been like had she lived into the 1940s and beyond. Her Code-era films (of the last three years of her life) yielded only one gem, *Libeled Lady* (1936), but even there Harlow is somewhat a shadow of her former self, no longer the brazenly sexual and daringly funny broad of the early '30s. She was still tough-talking and altogether delightful in *Libeled Lady*, but you could feel MGM muting her power, softening her image. How long before Harlow would just seem like a figure from another time, cast aside for MGM's less bold and less brassy versions of herself, such as, say, Lana Turner? But there actually wasn't a later version of Harlow because her persona was potently of its time, a short-lived but wonderfully risque and lowdown era, with Harlow its quintessential poster gal.

In 1932, the year she emerged as a superstar, Harlow played in two "Red" vehicles, *Red-Headed Woman*, opposite Chester Morris (with his beautiful profile), and *Red Dust*, the best of her six teamings with Clark Gable. *Red-Headed Woman* is a fine piece of trash all about Topic A. It's Harlow's first thoroughly self-assured star turn, as a social-climbing, home-wrecking seductress you can't help but like. She may be a conniving tramp but she's also luscious-looking (in her satins), hilariously wisecracking, and so damn fun. The picture and its star are "immorally" entertaining: Harlow chooses a dress *because* it's see-through; she lustily asks Morris to "do it again" after he slaps her; she even shoots him later on. And writer Anita Loos keeps the crackerjack lines coming: pal Una Merkel, at the sight of Harlow's silver-fox fur, asks, "Couldn't you get a gold one?"; a bit player says of Harlow that she's "strictly on the level, like a flight of stairs." After preying on Morris, and then rich old geezer Henry Stephenson, she starts playing around with chauffeur Charles Boyer. And, in true pre-Code fashion, there's no price to pay for her shenanigans. No moral lesson learned. Just racy fun. Harlow was the sex goddess with the smart mouth, and she was every bit as devastating as a redhead as she was as a platinum blonde.

Red Dust is zesty escapism, a snappy jungle melodrama with lots of sex and laughs. It's irresistibly cheap and tawdry, set on a piece of soundstage exotica (a Southeast Asian rubber plantation). You don't get any more macho than the young Gable, handsome and smart and no-nonsense while running the plantation. His wry humor and flair for self-mockery make him an ideal match for Harlow, here playing a lovably sassy and sarcastic prostitute. The arrival of "lady" Mary Astor, married to weak Gene Raymond (as Gable's new surveyor), turns the picture into a good girl/bad girl love triangle, with the so-called bad girl so honest and open, and the good girl a cheating wife. But, darn, Gable prefers the lady! (Astor is quite beautiful and such an intelligent actress.) Regarding Astor's relations with Gable, Harlow tells her, "I didn't hear any cries for help." But the whore gets him in the end! This is the movie in which a nude Harlow memorably bobs around in a water barrel. When the Chinese houseboy prances around with Astor's silk underwear, Harlow quips,

"Goodness, you even find them in the jungle." Now we'd call that a gay slur, but at least in pre-Code Hollywood there were acknowledgments that gay people existed! It was also a place in which Jean Harlow could emerge vibrantly and come to exemplify one of the juiciest periods in Hollywood history. We didn't have her for very long, and yet immortality is beyond measure.

The Prime of Mr. Ronald Neame
April 21st, 2011

Usually when I do these 100th birthday tributes, the star or director in question has been dead for a few decades. Not this time. British director Ronald Neame would have turned 100 this April 23, but he left us only ten months ago, passing away at 99 last June. This was nearly a case of celebrating a centenary with the subject around to blow out the candles. Neame was hardly a household name in America, though U.S. audiences certainly saw a number of his movies, with *The Poseidon Adventure* the disaster movie that we all went to see back in 1972. He also directed Judy Garland's screen swan song, *I Could Go On Singing* (1963), and Maggie Smith's Oscar-winning performance in *The Prime of Miss Jean Brodie* (1969).

Neame first came to prominence as a cinematographer in England, shooting David Lean's first three movies, each a collaboration with Noel Coward: *In Which We Serve* (1942), *This Happy Breed* (1944), and *Blithe Spirit* (1945). These films certainly secured Neame's place as a major cameraman of the decade.

My favorite of the films he directed is *The Horse's Mouth* (1958), adapted from Joyce Cary's novel. Incidentally, the screenplay was written by the film's star, Alec Guinness, who received an Oscar nomination for his efforts (losing to Alan Jay Lerner for *Gigi*). Guinness also should have gotten Oscar attention for his performance, one of his finest comic turns (and that's really saying something!). Guinness plays the wonderfully named Gulley Jimson, an eccentric painter with white hair and a growl of a voice. He's marvelously theatrical and offbeat and simply hilarious. It's a portrait of the artist as a charming rascal, a schemer, also practically starving. But certainly some kind of genius, a visionary unto himself, passionately and selfishly committed to his art and a bit insane. The movie celebrates his eccentricity, and Guinness' performance manages to be touching as well as delightfully inventive. For all its merriment, Neame's film shows considerable feeling for the otherworldliness of the artist, set apart from regular folks. The film also boasts extraordinary color and sublime use of music by Prokofiev.

In addition to Guinness, the cast includes a host of reliables: Robert Coote, Ernest Thesiger, Kay Walsh, Michael Gough. Two moments stay with me: Guinness' faux karate moves in his escape from Thesiger's house, and Coote (along with his wife and secretary) stepping onto a rug that is covering a large hole in the floor; slowly, rug and all, they disappear to the floor below. It's a far more wondrous effect than anything in *The Poseidon Adventure*.

Tarzan's Mate and Mia's Mother
May 15th, 2011

Irish-born actress Maureen O'Sullivan died in 1998 at age 87 and would have turned 100 this May 17th. Though MGM put in her just about every kind of movie during the 1930s, there was, of course, one role in which she clicked most indelibly with the public, as Jane in six films opposite Johnny Weissmuller's Tarzan, beginning with *Tarzan the Ape Man* (1932) and finishing off with *Tarzan's New York Adventure* (1942), her final film before a six-year retirement, which was mostly spent having babies with her film-director husband John Farrow. (Their little girl Mia was born in 1945.) Dark-haired O'Sullivan, a great beauty even when not in jungle garb, had seven children and was married to Farrow until his death in 1963.

In addition to the Tarzan films, O'Sullivan appeared in her share of beloved movies, though most often in support of bigger female stars, such as Myrna Loy in *The Thin Man* (1934), Norma Shearer in *The Barretts of Wimpole Street* (1934), Greta Garbo in *Anna Karenina* (1935), and Greer Garson in *Pride and Prejudice* (1940). O'Sullivan's youth, prettiness, and often demure manner made her a perfect ingenue, with rarely a shot at a juicy role. She did show up in the horror goodie *The Devil-Doll* (1936) and then got to have some fun with the Marx Brothers in *A Day at the Races* (1937). One interesting element of the *Tarzan* films is the way they handled the enforcement of the Production Code, which arrived mid-series. What began with proper English Jane giving herself over to the natural world, embracing her more animal side with a loinclothed hunk, then became the ongoing tale of Jane's domestication of Tarzan, including their spotless tree house, as close to "civilization" as possible.

When she returned to the screen in 1948, there were some good opportunities: *The Big Clock* (1948), a film noir co-starring Ray Milland and directed by Farrow; Douglas Sirk's melodrama *All I Desire* (1953) with Barbara Stanwyck; and Budd Boetticher's western *The Tall T* (1957) with Randolph Scott. Much later, she would appear with daughter Mia in Woody Allen's *Hannah and Her Sisters* (1986).

I saw O'Sullivan on Broadway in 1980 in *Morning's at Seven* and remember her as being utterly captivating, completely effortless at casting her radiance to the balcony. She previously had an enormous stage success on Broadway opposite Paul Ford in the 1962 play *Never Too Late*, a situation comedy in which the "situation" is O'Sullivan's late-life pregnancy (while her married daughter tries hopelessly to conceive). Like many hit stage comedies of the '60s, including *Mary, Mary* and *Any Wednesday*, *Never Too Late* became an awful movie, despite the casting of Ford and O'Sullivan in their original roles. This kind of synthetic, tee-hee sex comedy would soon become extinct in Hollywood, once the ratings system kicked in and the New Hollywood, with its newfound permissiveness, arrived. After decades of providing more "adult" sexuality than could be seen on-screen, Broadway comedies, in their transfers to the movies, suddenly seemed outdated, smirking, and puerile. Hollywood passed them by.

The 1965 film version of *Never Too Late* may be worthless but it is interesting as a piece of trivia. Consider the following: it was produced by Norman Lear and directed by Bud Yorkin; it centers on a grouchy, conservative father and his docile, homemaking wife named Edith; also living in the house are their blond, married daughter and son-in-law (who constantly bickers with the dad). Sound familiar? Can you say *All in the Family*? The classic series made its debut on television six years later.

In *Never Too Late*, O'Sullivan retains her grace and dignity, looking lovely with honey-colored hair and never pushing for a laugh (unlike most everyone around her, including the usually impeccable Ford, plus daughter Connie Stevens and son-in-law Jim Hutton). O'Sullivan's natural warmth is the picture's chief asset. The sustained "joke" is Ford's embarrassment regarding his wife's surprising pregnancy; he shows no pride in his mid-life virility. It's all so "cute" and sentimental and witless (with plenty of visual gags concerning an uninstalled toilet). It ends before the baby's birth but with Ford finally happy about the situation.

Also in the cast is Lloyd Nolan as the mayor. Two decades later, Nolan and O'Sullivan played opposite each other in *Hannah and Her Sisters*.

For someone who never became a star of the first rank, O'Sullivan certainly had longevity and staying power, from those glorious black-and-white costume pictures to her reign as the jungle's perfect wife, followed by her return to the screen in more grown-up roles and then her unexpected success as an over-fifty theatre star, crowned by her supporting turn as the boozy, flirty mother of

Hannah and those sisters. A full and varied career for anyone, but especially impressive coming from a mother of seven. There's nothing like swinging on jungle vines to build up your stamina.

Priceless Vincent Price
May 23rd, 2011

Halloween may have to come a bit early this year, in celebration of the 100th birthday of horror-movie icon Vincent Price, born on May 27, 1911. (He died at 82 in 1993.) Price appeared in a wide range of movies—the elegant mystery *Laura* (1944), the feverish melodrama *Leave Her to Heaven* (1945), the high comedy *A Royal Scandal* (1945), the lavish Technicolor version of *The Three Musketeers* (1948), the film noir *While the City Sleeps* (1956), among so many—though he is rarely thought of as anyone but a master of fright. How many people remember that his career was practically bookended by two Bette Davis movies, *The Private Lives of Elizabeth and Essex* (1939) and *The Whales of August* (1987)? Or that he appeared in two hugely popular religious epics, *The Song of Bernadette* (1943) and *The Ten Commandments* (1956)?

A reminder of the titles most associated with the horrorful Price would have to include *House of Wax* (1953), *The Fly* (1958), and *The Tingler* (1959) from the '50s, followed by the best of his Edgar Allan Poe pictures, *House of Usher* (1960) and *Pit and the Pendulum* (1961) and *The Masque of the Red Death* (1964), of the '60s, and, finally, perhaps his campiest films, *The Abominable Dr. Phibes* (1971) and *Theater of Blood* (1973), from the '70s. His final big-screen appearance was fittingly as a mad-scientist type in Tim Burton's *Edward Scissorhands* (1990).

Price fans should seek him out in an unusual little sleeper called *The Baron of Arizona* (1950), which plays occasionally on TCM. It may be a "B" in budget, but it was directed by Sam Fuller and photographed by James Wong Howe. The title suggests a routine western, yet the film's plot (based on fact) is anything but ordinary. In one of his finer acting turns, Price is ideally cast as a master forger determined to take control of the territory of Arizona (not yet a state in 1872) through a series of elaborate machinations. He creates a phony heir and a phony Spanish land grant. The "heir" is a little girl who grows up to be Ellen Drew, with Price inventing her nobility and her fake claim (while Drew believes that she is everything she has been raised to be).

The film's standout section is when Price goes to Spain to alter the Spanish book of land grants, which is housed in a monastery. He becomes a monk and lives there for three years to accomplish his mission flawlessly. This carefully composed, highly suspenseful section is excellent, whereas the remainder of the movie is unable to sustain such a high level of tension and plausibility, including a weak, silly climax with an angry mob. Plus, things take a creepy turn when Price marries Drew, whom he has groomed since childhood. And, for some reason, she's madly in love with him!

If the film's quality is erratic, its star is secure, so smoothly deceitful, so casually soulless, despite being weakened by genuine love for Drew. He's much more attractive when he's confidently unrepentant. Price carries this mostly offbeat and compelling drama, a juicy and memorable little story.

Take this as your cue to check out not only *The Baron of Arizona* but some of the other things Price was up to when he wasn't trying to scare us to death.

Mr. Rattigan's Prince and Showgirl
June 6th, 2011

Before it became a vehicle for Marilyn Monroe, *The Prince and the Showgirl* began life as *The Sleeping Prince*, a 1953 London stage comedy by Terence Rattigan, starring Laurence Olivier and Vivien Leigh, later done on Broadway with Michael Redgrave and Barbara Bel Geddes. Mr. Rattigan adapted his play for the screen, with Olivier himself directing the film and recreating his starring role, now opposite Marilyn, with Olivier's then-wife Leigh deemed too old for the film version. Who ever could have imagined that Olivier and Monroe would be paired together? There has been so much written about the hell it was to make this movie, how Marilyn drove Larry mad, and how it ultimately didn't seem worth the trouble because the film was not successful critically or commercially.

Mr. Rattigan, who died at age 66 in 1977, would have turned 100 this week (on June 10), and, incidentally, Marilyn Monroe would have turned 85 last week. Rattigan may be best remembered for the overrated 1958 screen version of his play *Separate Tables*, which won David Niven (who's the best thing in it) the Best Actor Oscar. But the best screen version of a Rattigan play is undoubtedly *The Browning Version* (1951), with its outstanding performance from Michael Redgrave as an unhappy, unappreciated schoolteacher.

The surprise of *The Prince and the Showgirl* is how Marilyn Monroe walks away with it, making it a wondrous showcase for her abundant charms. Her acting is enchantingly spontaneous, while Olivier, clearly recreating what presumably worked so well on the stage, comes off as cartoonish, overemphatic, and all-around stagy. The set-up is the 1911 London coronation of George V (now best known as Colin Firth's daddy). Olivier plays the Prince Regent of Carpathia, formerly a Hungarian prince. His accent sounds phony, as if for a comedy sketch, and everything he does feels overly worked out and no longer (if ever) funny. Widowed, he's the father of the 16-year-old heir played by Jeremy Spenser, who seems a bit like the Prince of Siam here. (Spenser appeared with Vivien Leigh twice, first as a child in *Anna Karenina*, then, quite differently, as her stalker in *The Roman Spring of Mrs. Stone*.) Marilyn plays an American actress appearing in *The Coconut Girl*, though she's not the play's star. There's a midnight rendezvous at the Carpathian embassy for the two principal characters (though Marilyn thinks she's been invited to a party, not a seduction).

Marilyn may never have looked more beautiful than she does here. She's also effortlessly funny, adorably sunny and bubbly and positively radiant. The banal idea at the core of the plot is that Marilyn, in the course of three days, will bring love into this unhappy family, even repairing the father-son relationship. She's a smokin' hot Miss Fix-it. The film is overlong for something so slight, but it has rapturous color from cinematographer Jack Cardiff and it's a consistently pretty movie. However, I think we can blame Olivier for the lack of a necessary light touch (which Marilyn has in spades). It's all rather flimsy and unconvincing and not a fitting DVD to celebrate Rattigan's 100th (go with *The Browning Version* instead), and it's certainly not among the great Olivier's finest achievements, yet it remains the most forgotten and neglected of Marilyn's star performances. The picture isn't much but she's divine.

Ginger Peachy!
July 18th, 2011

Usually when I write these "Happy 100th" tributes, I focus on one of my subject's lesser-known gems, some movie I'm especially eager to talk about because I know that relatively few people have seen it. In the case of Ginger Rogers, who died at 83 in 1995 and who would have turned 100 this past weekend (July 16th), I'm going to revisit one of her more famous films, the sublime musical *Top Hat* (1935), the best of her ten pictures with Fred Astaire. Since Ginger was a quintessential example of a true triple-threat talent, I might have used this opportunity to remind you about *Primrose Path* (1940), which contains my favorite of Ginger's dramatic performances, or *Stage Door* (1937), *Bachelor Mother* (1939), and *The Major and the Minor* (1942), my three favorite comedies of hers. (Ginger was, it must be noted, the greatest wisecracker of all the leading ladies of the '30s and '40s.) However, I recently watched *Top Hat* again, just to see if it is really as good as we all remember. The verdict: it still truly is *that good,* a bona fide classic.

For sheer escapist splendor, of the 1930s variety, can *Top Hat* be beat? In fact it's so skillful that it's the rare musical comedy whose screenplay is funny and sharp enough to stand on its own, without the embellishments of songs and dances. Not that anyone, myself included, would ever want to test my theory, thus depriving us of some of the screen's greatest dance sequences and original songs. It was often the case with movie musicals that they were attached to irritatingly inane plots, which felt like the price you had to pay for the glory of the musical numbers. *Swing Time* (1936), the only other Astaire-Rogers picture that is frequently cited as their best, is, for me, one of those exquisite song-and-dance-fests whose plot is excruciatingly annoying. *Top Hat* and *Swing Time* are evenly matched musically and choreographically, but *Top Hat* is the hands-down winner as the overall better movie, as light and breezy as *Swing Time* is dumb and labored. I'd go so far as to call *Top Hat* one of the great screwball comedies of the '30s. As mistaken-identity plots go, this one is delightful, clever, plausibly sustained, and actually *funny.*

Astaire is at his most magically buoyant, always looking ready to soar into dance. He plays (you guessed it) an American dancing star about to open a show in London. Fred and Ginger have a great meet-cute scene when his dancing (to "No Strings") disturbs her sleep, leading to his "sandman" reprise. Along for the ride are Edward Everett Horton (Astaire's producer), Helen Broderick (Horton's wife), Eric Blore (Horton's valet), and Erik Rhodes (a fashion designer and Ginger's employer), each cast to type and each indelibly funny. The central misunderstanding has to do with Ginger thinking that Fred, with whom she is smitten, is married to her pal, Ms. Broderick, the Eve Arden of Astaire-Rogers land. When Broderick sees Mr. Rhodes kiss Mr. Horton (her husband) on both cheeks (in the Italian manner), she says to them, "Go right ahead boys, don't mind me." Then there's a great Irving Berlin score, a deliriously dazzling Art Deco version of Venice, and Ginger's chic Bernard Newman gowns. You even get a minor bit by a platinum-blond Lucille Ball, working for a hotel florist (and working her way up the RKO ladder).

As for Ginger, she exudes a fresh, all-American prettiness. Of course, she is a natural, easy comedienne, but she also astonishes with her versatility in the dances, from her playful coming together with Fred in "Isn't This a Lovely Day?" to the elegantly orgasmic "Cheek to Cheek" (with its feathery perfection) to the snappy giddiness of "The Piccolino."

"Heaven, I'm in heaven…" is an apt four-word review for the blissful *Top Hat*. For wit, glamour, and grace, you can't do better than Fred and Ginger, and for Fred and Ginger you can't do better than *Top Hat*.

Lucy, Bob, and the Facts of Life
August 3rd, 2011

While visiting friends on Fire Island this past weekend, I was tickled to see that one of the houses in Cherry Grove is named "623 East 68th Street." Devout *I Love Lucy* followers won't need to be told that this is a loving wink to the fictitious address of Lucy and Ricky Ricardo. How fitting to walk by this home in the week that marks the 100th anniversary of the birth of the incomparable Lucille Ball, born August 6th. Though she died at age 77 in 1989, few performing artists of the twentieth century share her rarefied level of immortality. She is, and will always be, America's most beloved comedienne.

I'd like to pay tribute to Lucy by bringing a bit more attention to one of her better but lesser-known big-screen vehicles, the best she ever made *after* the world had come to know her as Mrs. Ricardo. *The Facts of Life* (1960), directed by Melvin Frank and written by Mr. Frank and Norman Panama, is also the best of the four films that Lucy made with Bob Hope. The first two, *Sorrowful Jones* (1949) and *Fancy Pants* (1950), came pre-*I Love Lucy* (1951-57), at a time when it looked as though true stardom had eluded Lucy once and for all; the final one, *Critics' Choice*, came in 1963. Though *The Facts of Life* won five Oscar nominations (and won in the black-and-white costumes category), it isn't a movie that is much talked about today.

The fresh and funny premise here is that it can be damned hard to commit adultery, even when both parties are willing. Lucy is married to Don DeFore, Bob is married to Ruth Hussey. Can Lucy and Bob get their "affair" in motion, or will the challenging mechanics of arranging adultery simply wear them out? One of the pleasures of this grown-up picture is that it never feels like a Bob Hope movie or a Lucille Ball movie, just a strong middle-aged romantic comedy with two very good roles for two very fine comic actors. Both stars are excellent: easygoing, warm, honest, with their laughs arising effortlessly. In fact, it's a consistently relaxed film, relying more on charm and likability than on punchlines or shtick, which comes as a surprise considering the stars' reputations as treasured clowns.

The Facts of Life delivers more than expected, becoming an unusually smart and bittersweet comedy. Lucy is not Lucy Ricardo here, not by a long shot.

Pushing fifty, she is still a knockout, but the beauty of her performance comes in its softness, its yearning, its maturity. Yes, there are big laughs, notably a drive-in fiasco when the stars won't unlock their lips out of fear of being seen together, or when Bob drives all over town because he can't remember at which motel he deposited Lucy for their rendezvous.

The Facts of Life proved that zany Lucy could still be taken seriously as an actress, a subtle and intelligent player, a seasoned artist who had worked her way up from the chorus and was by now in a class by herself. As much as anyone, I love Lucy in the chocolate factory and stomping on grapes, but I also love the shrewd, knowing, and unexpectedly sensitive actress of films like *Dance, Girl, Dance* (1940), *The Dark Corner* (1946), and, yes, *The Facts of Life.*

The "Party Girl" Boys
August 7th, 2011

Sandwiching the great Lucille Ball's 100th birthday on August 6th are two other centenaries lost in the shuffle: actor Robert Taylor's on August 5th and director Nicholas Ray's on August 7th. (Taylor died at 57 in 1969; Ray died at 67 in 1979.) An ideal tribute to these two men would be to take a look at their joint venture *Party Girl* (1958), a cult film, but, unfortunately, I'm not part of the cult. Not one of Ray's ingenious subversions of a genre, like his one-of-a-kind western *Johnny Guitar* (1954), *Party Girl* is a glossy, shallow gangster movie, though Taylor's no-nonsense performance may be its most grounding asset. Or perhaps its vibrant color cinematography. Luscious Cyd Charisse, way out of her depths dramatically, plays the title role.

Johnny Guitar and *Rebel without a Cause* (1955) are probably Ray's two most enduring achievements, but if I had to pick a favorite among Ray's works I'd go with *The Lusty Men* (1952), his great rodeo picture, and, not coincidentally, one of the five westerns featured in my book *Screen Savers*. Chief among its many pleasures are the central performances from Robert Mitchum and Susan Hayward, terrific separately and pure dynamite together.

As for Robert Taylor, well, I'm often touting *Devil's Doorway* (1950) as his finest hour. (It's another of the five westerns discussed in *Screen Savers*.) So, let me take this opportunity to write about a film I've never written about before, a picture that came out at a perilous moment in Taylor's career. When he had departed from the screen to serve in WWII, he was one of the biggest male stars at MGM. Upon his return, his comeback vehicle, *Undercurrent* (1946), co-starring Katharine Hepburn and directed by Vincente Minnelli, was a real stinker, a soapy mystery that tried miserably to combine elements of *Rebecca* and *Suspicion.*

Taylor's stardom would not be fully restored until the one-two punch of *Quo Vadis* (1951) and *Ivanhoe* (1952), which means that his worthy *High Wall* (1947) was unfairly ignored. True, MGM was hardly the go-to studio for the emerging genre of film noir, and it's also true that *High Wall* seemed to be another Taylor picture trying to steal from Hitchcock (this time from *Spellbound*, rather than *Rebecca* or *Suspicion*). However, *High Wall* turned out exceedingly well and deserves attention it has never received.

Taylor gives one of his better performances as a man on the edge, a war veteran prone to blackouts. Accused of killing his cheating wife, and with all the evidence pointing to him, he can't believe that he's guilty. Audrey Totter is the psychiatrist who falls in love with Taylor, her patient, and she tries to help prove that he's no murderer. This superbly shot psycho-noir holds up far better dramatically than *Spellbound* does, offering an enticing mix of elements, including a memorable murder in an elevator shaft. (Coincidentally, *Ivy*, also from 1947, is another nifty thriller with an elevator-shaft death.) *High Wall* is a pleasurable, absorbing tangle of revenge, romance, psychiatry, insanity, etc. It was stylishly directed by Curtis Bernhardt, who also made the somewhat similar Joan Crawford vehicle, *Possessed,* that same year. Sure, it's somewhat far-fetched, and its climax is improbable, but *High Wall* is a high point of Robert Taylor's career.

VI. Five Birthdays and an Anniversary
screensaversmovies.com

Birthday "Bride"
March 31st, 2009

April 1st marks the 80th birthday of MGM songbird Jane Powell. Groomed by the studio in the mid-1940s to be a teen soprano in the Deanna Durbin mold, Powell scored a big success with *A Date with Judy* (1948). She was Fred Astaire's partner in *Royal Wedding* (1951), confidently holding her own on the dance floor alongside the master. (Despite their 30-year age difference, they were strangely plausible as brother and sister.) But it was *Seven Brides for Seven Brothers* (1954) that showed Powell off best, proving that she was a major movie-musical presence. Opposite Howard Keel, also at his best, and given some glorious tunes by Gene de Paul and Johnny Mercer, Powell was marvelous as Milly, the young woman who falls in love (with Keel) on sight. She marries him, only to find out that he was looking for someone to cook and clean for him and his six backwoods brothers. But she is more than a match for all seven of them!

The strength, warmth, and depth in Powell's performance set her apart from the manufactured emoting of her soprano rivals at MGM, Kathryn Grayson and Ann Blyth. If either of those ladies had played Milly, the character would have been arch and insufferable. The vigorous spunk in Powell's Milly feels authentic rather than cute. Her rendition of "Wonderful, Wonderful Day" is her vocal highlight, an uncontained expression of pure happiness, comparable to Julie Andrews' mountain-top outburst in the Alps. Powell's acting merited an Oscar nomination, to go with the film's Best Picture nod. *Seven Brides* is one of the screen's greatest movie musicals, enhanced by Stanley Donen's zesty direction, Michael Kidd's thrilling choreography, the irresistible ensemble of brides and brothers, handsome and rugged Keel, and, perhaps most of all, the gifted and altogether captivating Jane Powell. (You can read much more about *Seven Brides* and Powell in my book *Screen Savers*.) Happy Birthday, Milly!

Gigi's Gaston
June 16th, 2009

June 19th marks the 90th birthday of Louis Jourdan. I can't imagine that Jourdan has ever been anyone's favorite actor or biggest film-star crush, but I do think he was a better actor than most people realize. A later generation probably knows him only for his role in the James Bond franchise, memorably uttering the title character's name in *Octopussy* (1983). But his most famous and enduring role is as Gaston in the multi-Oscar-winning MGM musical *Gigi* (1958).

Despite its many assets, both musical and visual, *Gigi*, set in 1900 Paris, is a highly overrated work, though Jourdan's performance is just about impeccable. Gaston, heir to a sugar fortune, enjoys a playful relationship with the teenage Gigi (Leslie Caron), like that of a favorite uncle and his tomboy niece. Soon after seeing her in an evening gown, he wants to make her his courtesan. The film has taken a creepy turn from which it never recovers. Jourdan does, however, a nice job with the title tune, which has songwriters Lerner and Loewe stealing from themselves, turning Jourdan's soliloquy into a none-too-subtle rehash of their "I've Grown Accustomed to Her Face." In 1960, Jourdan was reteamed with *Gigi* co-star Maurice Chevalier in the horrifying *Can-Can,* a complete travesty in which Jourdan comes up smelling like a rose, light and charming amid the wreckage.

The Swan (1956) contains my favorite Jourdan performance, possibly his finest. A romantic comedy set among fictional European royalty in 1910, the film stars Grace Kelly as a princess, shortly before she became a real-life princess. Alec Guinness is her cousin, a crown prince in search of a bride. As Kelly's family pushes her and Guinness together, it soon becomes apparent that Kelly and Jourdan (as her brothers' lowly tutor) have fallen in love. This wide-screen treasure becomes a tingling love triangle, superbly acted by its trio of stars: Kelly has never been so warm and luminous; Guinness is a subtle and sublime comic master; and Jourdan surpassed himself in his display of sharp intelligence and intimate feeling. Directed by Charles Vidor, this underrated sparkler is one of the best American films of 1956, a witty fairy tale with overtones of bittersweet emotion.

Jourdan had been Hollywood's handsome new European of the late 1940s in *The Paradine Case* (1947), *Letter from an Unknown Woman* (1948), and *Madame Bovary* (1949), but he didn't get to do much "acting" until the '50s. Though the glossy soap *Three Coins in the Fountain* (1954) is an utter mediocrity, or worse, I rather like Jourdan's easygoing performance as a prince, despite his being foolish enough to bother romantically with the irritating Maggie McNamara. He also appeared in at least three camp classics: *Julie* (1956), in which he terrorized Doris Day; *The Best of Everything* (1959); and *The V.I.P.s* (1963), in a remarkably sexless love triangle, actually getting in between Elizabeth Taylor and Richard Burton!

Happy Birthday, Mr. Jourdan. I hope somebody somewhere is watching *The Swan* right now.

She Could (and Does) Go On Singing
June 25th, 2009

Earlier this week (June 22nd) marked the 40th anniversary of Judy Garland's death at age 47. She has been gone nearly as long as she lived, yet I guess such things don't much matter when you're immortal. I have written about the great Garland in two previous books. Her dazzling performance in *The Pirate* (1948) was one of my *100 Great Film Performances You Should Remember,* and *The Harvey Girls* (1946) became one of five original movie musicals that I wrote about in *Screen Savers,* with particular emphasis on Judy's marvelous work in the role that was the prototype—with its irresistibly funny mix of spunk and insecurity and repressed erotic longing—for her remaining vehicles at MGM. On this blog, I have already called *Everybody Sing* (1938) my favorite of her pre-*Oz* pictures, and no one needs any help from me in finding their way to *Meet Me in St. Louis* (1944) or *A Star Is Born* (1954). So, what other Garland moments should be recalled on this anniversary?

How about her gorgeous renditions of "But Not for Me" and "Embraceable You" in *Girl Crazy* (1943), or the poignancy she brought to "Friendly Star" in the underrated *Summer Stock* (1950)? All the concert scenes in *I Could Go on Singing* (1963) come as close as possible to capturing the excitement of being at "Judy at Carnegie Hall." Thanks to Garland's innate artistry, her vocal of "Look for the Silver Lining" is the hands-down highlight of the bloated *Till the Clouds Roll By* (1946). Similarly, she stops the enjoyably terrible *Ziegfeld Girl* (1941) dead in its tracks with the simplicity and perfection of her version of "I'm Always Chasing Rainbows," rendering her co-stars, an overacting Lana Turner and a zombified Hedy Lamarr, little more than mannequins beside her talent. And "How About You?" with Mickey Rooney, from *Babes on Broadway* (1941), may be the spirited duo's most charming and relaxed number of them all.

So, if this is a week to be reminded of Judy, as if we ever need a reminder, there is so very much to savor. Dig in.

Andy Hardy is 90!
September 17th, 2010

I want to take a moment to acknowledge the 90th birthday (on September 23rd) of Mickey Rooney, the perennial teenager of the Andy Hardy pictures and all those musicals with Judy Garland, colossal moneymakers for MGM in the late thirties and early forties. Though Rooney will always be linked with Garland as one of Hollywood's beloved teams, it is shocking to think that Rooney is headed toward living a life twice as long as the life lived by Garland, who died at 47 in 1969. They were never better together, or more eternally youthful, than when singing "How About You?" to each other in *Babes on Broadway* (1941).

No one has had a career like Rooney, from child star to teen superstar to has-been to comeback kid to has-been again to TV and Broadway star to all-around legend. He got a special juvenile Oscar in 1939, then an honorary one in 1983. Plus he got four nominations, two for Best Actor (for *Babes in Arms* in 1939, and *The Human Comedy* in 1943) and two for Best Supporting Actor (for *The Bold and the Brave* in 1956, and *The Black Stallion* in 1979). If that weren't enough, he was also briefly married to goddess Ava Gardner!

From his Puck in *A Midsummer Night's Dream* (1935) to his recent appearance in the hit comedy *Night at the Museum* (2006), Rooney is the essence of the showbiz trouper. He was the biggest star in the world in the early '40s, then utterly washed-up by the decade's end. But he waited out the lulls, taking any work he could get. He never really went away, too consumed with the love of performing ever to vanish for good.

He acted alongside Spencer Tracy in both of Tracy's Oscar-winning performances, in *Captains Courageous* (1937) and *Boys Town* (1938), and he gracefully took a top-billed backseat to Elizabeth Taylor in the wonderful *National Velvet* (1944). The Rodgers and Hart biopic *Words and Music* (1948) was a box-office success, but no one liked Rooney's Larry Hart, even though it wasn't his fault that censorship led to ruinous alterations in Hart's story. Instead of addressing Hart's homosexuality, the script turned his story into that of a man deeply unhappy about being *short*. Much later, he was the worst thing in *Breakfast at Tiffany's* (1961), as Audrey Hepburn's Japanese neighbor.

When I saw Rooney with Ann Miller in *Sugar Babies* on Broadway in 1980, it felt like a last-chance opportunity to see two of the great stars of MGM musicals. Who knew that thirty years later Rooney would still be going strong? That Andy Hardy fellow ended up having quite the life, didn't he?

Liza, Senior Citizen
March 13th, 2011

On March 12, Liza Minnelli turned 65, officially a senior citizen though perennially a Hollywood princess born during the Golden Age. She was ugly-duckling royalty who showed everyone that she could make a mark of her own (though never quite making us forget who her mother was). Liza's movie career has been a train wreck of sorts, mostly because there were few opportunities for musical stars in the 1970s and beyond. Thank goodness *Cabaret* (1972) came along, giving Liza her one bona fide screen classic and her richly merited Oscar as Best Actress. But it was in an earlier film that Liza proved she was a genuine actress, one who didn't have to be singing to hold our attention. *The Sterile Cuckoo* (1969) was directed by Alan J. Pakula, who had a knack for bringing out the best in major talents, not just Liza but also Jane Fonda *(Klute)* and Meryl Streep *(Sophie's Choice)*.

The Sterile Cuckoo is a simple, affecting, and nicely observed little drama of growing pains. As Pookie Adams, Liza is extraordinary. It's a remarkably self-assured performance, particularly from someone in her early twenties. Pookie is a lonely, strange, unloved and unpopular college freshman. She is also what used to be known as a kook, defiantly offbeat but also heartbreakingly vulnerable. Liza is vivid and alert—so focused and electric—as a child-woman trying to find her place in a world of, as she calls them, "weirdos." The character is also like a screwball-comedy heroine, not unlike Katharine Hepburn in *Bringing Up Baby* (1938), as she relentlessly pursues fellow freshman (at another school) Wendell Burton, barging into his life unstoppably, full of spunk and imagination. Open, unself-conscious Liza is able to make Pookie (and not Liza herself) pathetic and embarrassing, revealing the sad, scared girl underneath all her strenuous "show."

The movie is best remembered for her phenomenal phone-call scene (an unbroken five-and-a-half minute take), in which she senses that Burton is pulling away from her. Liza goes through what they used to call "the gamut of emotion," but it never feels self-indulgent; it's nakedly, purely emotional and honestly personal. Not since Shirley MacLaine in *Some Came Running* (1958), directed by Liza's dad, Vincente, had there been such an achingly moving portrait of romantic yearning from a sad-funny female. When Burton does break up with her, Liza (sitting in her car) never blinks. It's quite startling. The promise of Liza's perfectly judged performance was fulfilled only with *Cabaret* and some scenes in the mostly wrongheaded *New York, New York*

(1977). She got an Oscar nomination for *Cuckoo*, but Maggie Smith won for *The Prime of Miss Jean Brodie*. Despite Maggie and nominee Jane Fonda (for *They Shoot Horses, Don't They?*), I would have voted for Liza.

For the downside of Liza's movie career, there's *Lucky Lady* (1975) and *A Matter of Time* (1976), two painfully bad movies that I recently caught up with again after many years. With its worthless script, and confused direction from Stanley Donen (who wants both slapstick and blood), the 1930s-set *Lucky Lady* isn't fun or funny, even with both Burt Reynolds and Gene Hackman at Liza's side. Looking hideous as a strawberry blonde, Liza tries to be a tough broad in the Joan Blondell mold but comes off merely as shrill and unlikable. This tale of booze-running crooks tries for a *Butch Cassidy* kind of charm, but it has no charm of any kind.

A Matter of Time, disowned by everyone involved, is a depressing finish to Vincente Minnelli's career. It's like a chic after-school special, a treacly bit of whimsy that is never anything but empty, muddled, and confoundingly bad. Liza is an Italian hotel maid who befriends a hotel resident, a delusional and broke countess (Ingrid Bergman). Bergman gives Liza lessons in beauty and style and inspires her to be herself. As a waif, Liza pushes in her big scenes (as she didn't in *Cuckoo*) and generally overacts throughout, trying to wow us and perhaps save a dud, yet she sinks along with all else around her. Liza should have stuck with directors like Pakula and Bob Fosse, rather than Donen and Minnelli. Was she trying too hard to be Judy and work with the great old MGM directors? Ironically, this picture's theme is about being an original, not an imitation of anyone!

Revisit *The Sterile Cuckoo* and remember when Liza seemed to have an amazing movie career ahead of her.

Lili, Gigi, Gaby, Fanny...Leslie
May 31st, 2011

Dancing actress Leslie Caron will be turning 80 on July 1st, but I don't want to wait that long to say some nice things about her. I just finished reading her 2009 autobiography, *Thank Heaven*, one of the better star autobiographies of recent years, almost as marvelous as Julie Andrews' *Home*. Caron has already led many lives, making it seem astonishing that so very many things could have happened to one person. Born in France to a French father and an American mother (from Kansas), Caron grew up in the privileged world of her French grandparents, only to see that lifestyle vanish during the hardships and poverty of World War II. But she would soon become part of some amazing cultural moments of the twentieth century.

Caron was a standout dancer of France's post-war boom in classical ballet, then was whisked away by Gene Kelly to dance in the final glory days of the Hollywood musical. She left the movie capital to marry British director Peter Hall and, though she never acted for him, became by marriage the First Lady of the Royal Shakespeare Company. Caron moved gracefully from dancing roles to comic and dramatic roles, becoming, briefly, a major leading lady of 1960s cinema, not to mention Warren Beatty's girlfriend. It all came crashing down thanks to two unavoidable circumstances: her turning 35 in a business that continues to treat gifted women as disposable entities; and her identification with the old Hollywood while the new Hollywood of the late '60s was taking hold. She never regained her prominence but she managed to work with many illustrious, internationally renowned directors, including Rene Clair, Rene Clement, Nanni Loy, Francois Truffaut, James Ivory, Louis Malle, Lasse Hallstrom, and Ken Russell. So, there was much more to her than just working with Vincente Minnelli at MGM (not that that isn't mightily impressive). She even restored and renovated buildings that became a celebrated inn in France, owned and operated by her.

Caron is best remembered for her two Oscar-winning Best Picture Vincente Minnelli musicals, *An American in Paris* (1951) and *Gigi* (1958), though neither now seems deserving of such high praise. They both have exquisite moments but are also uneven, of considerably varying quality, while Caron remains enchanting, securely among the films' more consistent and enduring charms. She won a Best Actress Oscar nomination for her title role in *Lili* (1953), a surprise smash made without the budget or expectations of her Minnelli musicals. And Caron deserved her nomination. Like Judy Garland's Dorothy, Caron's Lili is a triumph of wondrous simplicity, expressed through a heartfelt immersion into a young woman's feelings and confusions.

Though *Lili* is a significant children's movie about an orphaned teenage girl who joins a carnival, it is also a movie about sexual awakening. Sweet, innocent Lili has trouble (for a while) connecting the carnival's beloved and sensitive puppets to the cold, forbidding man (Mel Ferrer) who operates and inhabits them. It's a musical with one song ("Hi Lili Hi Lili Hi Lo") and two dream ballets. Like *Seven Brides for Seven Brothers* in 1954, *Lili* was an unexpected critical and box-office darling in the ailing days of the MGM musical, and it's no wonder why audiences responded: it's magical, romantic, swift, and anchored by a deeply sympathetic and luminous Caron performance. As with *Oz*, you cannot overestimate the lead performance in explaining the film's reputation.

Caron belongs to the select club of women who danced on-screen with both Gene Kelly and Fred Astaire, with Kelly in *An American in Paris*, notably in the mostly stunning climactic ballet, and with Astaire in *Daddy Long Legs* (1955), irresistibly paired in the knockout "Sluefoot" number. Like Debbie Reynolds, she was able to remain a movie star after the demise of original musicals, but Caron found not just acceptance but recognition as a dramatic actress, specifically in *Fanny* (1961), a lovely film in which she is sensual and incandescent, and *The L-Shaped Room* (1963), for which she received her second Best Actress Oscar nomination, playing an unmarried and pregnant French girl who takes a flat in a London building filled with other misfits and outcasts. A nicely observed, small-scale drama, *L-Shaped Room* proved to anyone who still needed convincing that Leslie Caron, former ballerina and Astaire/Kelly partner, was indeed an accomplished, nuanced, and distinctive acting talent. Ballet's loss was the movies' gain, and let's hope that there are still a few more plum roles out there for her. Turning 80 cannot dim her singular beauty, warmth, and honesty.

VII. In Memoriam
screensaversmovies.com

Cyntillating Cyd Charisse
June 18th, 2008

In the summer of 1974, when I was thirteen, I saw *That's Entertainment!* thirteen times. One of the film's most entrancing clips is the "Dancing in the Dark" routine from *The Band Wagon* (1953). Danced exquisitely by Fred Astaire and Cyd Charisse, it begins as a nighttime stroll through Central Park, then effortlessly becomes one of the more romantic dance duets in screen history. We lost Ms. Charisse this week, and I can't let her passing go by without paying tribute to her. Of all Hollywood's great female dancing stars, Charisse is my favorite. She was sexy, powerful, beautiful, long-legged, and the greatest dancing vamp of all time (see *Singin' in the Rain* and the "Girl Hunt" ballet in *Band Wagon*).

Here are some lesser-known Charisse highlights to watch for: her sensational "Frankie and Johnny" number in *Meet Me in Las Vegas* (1956); a highly charged "Dance of Fury" with Ann Miller and Ricardo Montalban in the otherwise lousy *Kissing Bandit* (1948); and the rapturously sensual and exciting "One Alone" with James Mitchell in *Deep in My Heart* (1954), a case of a magnificent dance trapped in a terrible movie.

I met Ms. Charisse briefly in 1976 at the NYC premiere of *That's Entertainment Part 2*. She looked gorgeous in a green gown, and her hair was by now much lighter than it had been in her MGM days. I got her autograph and took a photo and she was warm and gracious. There she was, the woman who had brilliantly partnered both Astaire and Kelly. Yet she didn't need to be anybody's partner. One of her most glorious moments is the sequence in *Silk Stockings* (1957) in which she, through dance, makes the transition from severe comrade to silk-stockings-wearing goddess. It's a term thrown about too casually, but Charisse indeed was a screen goddess.

The Old Maid's Daughter
April 19th, 2009

On April 8th, Jane Bryan passed away at age 90. Bryan retired from the screen in 1940, but fans of Warner Brothers flicks of the late 1930s surely remember Bryan as an uncommonly talented ingenue, an actress who could be memorable in the kinds of roles that so often went unnoticed. She played featured parts in two of my favorite WB soaps, *Confession* (1937), in which she played Kay Francis' daughter, and *The Old Maid* (1939), in which she played Bette Davis' secret love child, growing up to believe that Davis is her severe aunt.

Confession is a *Madame X*-style melodrama, expertly served by director Joe May. It is one of Kay Francis' most accomplished pictures, stylish and affecting and great-looking (with Expressionist touches in the design). Francis moves from opera star to wife/mother to scandal/divorce (thanks to one drunken sexual indiscretion) to supporting herself in cheap cabaret. Basil Rathbone is the womanizing slime who ruins her and then goes after her daughter (Miss Bryan). There's a sublime final sequence, ending with Kay's walk to what appears to be an Art Deco prison.

The Old Maid begins as a Civil War-era love triangle, with Miriam Hopkins and George Brent alongside Bette Davis. Brent dies in the war, leaving the unwed Davis pregnant with his child, infuriating Hopkins (Davis' cousin as well as rival.) Davis' daughter, Jane Bryan, is raised by both Davis and Hopkins; she believes that she was a foundling. The delicious masochism is heightened by Davis' forced coldness, a tactic designed to keep Bryan from ever suspecting the truth. Bryan gives a colorful and feisty performance, and Davis is a marvel, at her peak (in the year of *Dark Victory* and *The Private Lives of Elizabeth and Essex*) and making dazzling transitions as she ages decades.

Though few movie watchers would be able to identify Jane Bryan, they would surely be able to say, "Who's that kid with all the talent?"

The "Red" and the "Black"
April 29th, 2009

On April 22, 2009, Englishman Jack Cardiff, one of the 20th-century's great cinematographers, died at the age of 94. He did extraordinarily beautiful work on such disparate films as *The African Queen* (1951), *The Prince and the Showgirl* (1957), and *Fanny* (1961), but he will be chiefly remembered for his work on two unforgettable color movies from the film-making team of Michael Powell and Emeric Pressburger, *Black Narcissus* (1947) and *The Red Shoes* (1948). (Cardiff also directed films, notably the much-praised but deficient 1960 adaptation of *Sons and Lovers*.)

The spellbinding *Black Narcissus* is, for me, the greatest of the Powell-Pressburger films, a hyper-real fever dream set in the Himalayas. Astoundingly, India was recreated on a soundstage. The film explores how "India" gets under the skin of five nuns, becoming the rare film of its time about female sexuality (with nuns no less!). The effect is that of a psychological pressure cooker, heightened by Cardiff's breathtaking use of color. (The nuns are housed in a palace that was formerly a harem facility.) In one of her first important roles, Deborah Kerr, as an Irish nun, gives a superbly controlled performance, severe and contained, though contrasted by her open vulnerability exposed in the Irish flashbacks. David Farrar is the sexy, rakish, half-dressed British male who, along with the heat and exotica, gets the nuns' blood racing. Kathleen Byron is electrifying as the nun who descends into lustful madness. Red lipstick has never been used more potently. Cardiff's work deservedly won the Oscar that year. (He also received an honorary Oscar in 2001.)

The Red Shoes is the most famous Powell-Pressburger film, specifically for its rapturously transporting 15-minute ballet sequence, a surreal explosion of color that is both outrageous and exquisite. The overall film can be melodramatic and kitschy, lacking the depths and fascinations of *Black Narcissus*, but it has the power to dazzle the imagination. Moira Shearer is radiant as the ballerina at the center of it all, with suave and imperious Anton Walbrook as the demanding impresario. The picture becomes a soapy love triangle, but it's one of the more inspiring films about the arts. The view may be deeply romanticized, but the impact is hypnotizing.

Both these films are ingenious in the way they use color to intensify the characters' emotions, while also overwhelming the audience in an abundance of sheer beauty. Thank you, Mr. Cardiff. They couldn't have done it without you.

A Man Called Richard
December 6th, 2009

This week's death of Irish-born movie star Richard Todd, at age 90, brings to mind what a fine film actor he was and how barely remembered he is in this country. He gave several memorable performances, from his poignant Oscar-nominated turn as the dying Scotsman soldier (of WWII) in

The Hasty Heart (1949), opposite Patricia Neal and Ronald Reagan, to what is perhaps his finest performance in *A Man Called Peter* (1955), as real-life minister Peter Marshall, another Scotsman, who became the chaplain of the U.S. Senate. Rarely has a "religious" performance been as stirring as Todd's. And he held his own opposite the formidable Bette Davis in *The Virgin Queen* (1955), which isn't as good as her *Private Lives of Elizabeth and Essex* (1939), nor is she as good *in* it, but Todd's Walter Raleigh is certainly as sexy as Errol Flynn's Earl of Essex and a darn sight better acted. Todd had already invited comparison with Flynn when he played Robin Hood in 1952 to the delight of a whole new generation. Then there's *Stage Fright* (1950).

Alfred Hitchcock's *Stage Fright* marked the end of the director's slump of the late forties, the years of *The Paradine Case, Rope,* and *Under Capricorn.* Though *Strangers on a Train* (1951) was the decisive turnaround in Hitchcock's career of the 1950s, a decade rife with masterpieces by the Master of Suspense, *Stage Fright* is often lost in the shuffle, featuring many sublime pleasures amid its noticeable lapses. Todd found himself between two major actresses, Marlene Dietrich (in one of her finest performances) and Jane Wyman (in one of her worst). This murder mystery, set in London, features delightful comic turns from Alastair Sim, Sybil Thorndike, and Joyce Grenfell, plus a deliciously nasty performance from the great Kay Walsh. Add Michael Wilding as the charming detective and Hitch's daughter, Patricia, as a girl named Chubby Bannister, and you have the makings of a first-class entertainment.

Todd plays the attractive young man who must keep us guessing. Is he a homicidal maniac or a victim? I'm not telling. Did he murder Dietrich's husband? Did *she*? Did someone else? It must be said that plausibility is not the picture's chief strength, yet it's thoroughly absorbing and enjoyable. The plot has shades of *All About Eve*, also from 1950, with Dietrich a glamorous stage star and Wyman an aspiring actress who worms her way into Dietrich's household. But Wyman is too old and too American for her role, which would have suited Jean Simmons perfectly. Dietrich, however, is stunning. She's elegant, worldly, cunning, and haughty. Plus she sings "The Laziest Gal in Town." No one stands a chance in her presence. Todd, with his good looks, intelligence, and talent, tries to give her a run for her money, alternately effective as both fine young man and possible menace.

Portrait of Jennifer
December 30th, 2009

Before 2009 ends, I want to acknowledge the passing of Jennifer Jones at the age of 90 on December 17th. She was never one of my favorite screen actresses, mostly because I usually feel that she is holding back, rarely free or spontaneous enough to give a truly great performance. She frequently lacks the depth that would have allowed her to forge greater emotional connections to her characters. She was, however, a major female star between 1943 and 1957, combining acclaim (one Oscar, five nominations) and popularity (starring in mega-hits like *Duel in the Sun* and *Love Is a Many-Splendored Thing*). My favorite Jennifer Jones pictures are *Portrait of Jennie* (1948), in which she is perfectly cast and positively incandescent, and *Carrie* (1952), though my affection for this William Wyler production has more to do with Laurence Olivier's astonishing performance than it does with Jones' presence.

Producer David O. Selznick (her second husband) was as committed to Jones' stardom as William Randolph Hearst had been to Marion Davies' career. The Selznick-Jones partnership also mirrored the personal/professional relationship between producer Irving Thalberg and wife Norma Shearer: Thalberg had been the force behind Shearer's first-lady-of-MGM status. If *Gone With the Wind* had come down the pike just five years later, there is no question that Selznick would have cast Jones as Scarlett O'Hara. (Though beautiful, sexy, and bewitching, Jones was no Vivien Leigh in the acting or personality departments.)

Jones won her Oscar for her first major film, *The Song of Bernadette* (1943), which holds up surprisingly well, thanks to its superb production values and impressive black-and-white photography, as well as Henry King's mostly restrained direction and an outstanding supporting cast led by the great Gladys Cooper (just as mean to Jones as she had been to Bette Davis in *Now, Voyager*). Despite too many holy choruses, the film is absorbing, even moving, and more complicated than expected, considering it's about the making of a saint. Yet Jones' acting is hardly award-worthy. She is well cast and properly subdued, transmitting an innocent radiance and a plausibly limited intelligence. However, it's a long movie and Jones is fairly one-note, tedious in her childlike sweetness and unspoiled nature. Of course, there's only so far you can go when playing a saint.

Bernadette was the start of her string of successes, followed by the WWII homefront saga *Since You Went Away* (1944), the amnesia romance *Love Letters* (1945), the charming comedy *Cluny Brown* (1946), and the torrid western *Duel in the Sun* (1946). But *Portrait of Jennie*, a major failure at the box office, is the one that stays with me, and the picture that shows Jones off best. Never before had she glowed with such magnetic star power or acted with such affecting sensitivity. *Jennie* is one of the forty films I write about in my book *Screen Savers*, and it remains one of my favorite love stories and fantasy films. Assisted by an expert Joseph Cotten, as the artist who paints her portrait, Jones ages beautifully, from youngster to teen to smoldering young woman. Hers is a mesmerizing transition from girlishness to sensuality. Cotten is the film's anchor and its central character, but Jones provides the magic, endowing the film with its considerable power to haunt. This exquisite time-travel movie offers no explanations, just the wonder of two fated souls colliding blissfully. *Jennie* was the fourth and final teaming of Jones and Cotten, after *Since You Went Away*, *Love Letters*, and *Duel in the Sun*, making them one of the more significant teams of the 1940s.

The Passing of Angel Face
January 24th, 2010

On Friday, we lost Jean Simmons, one of the more gifted and beautiful of screen actresses. She died at 80, just a week before her 81st birthday. Simmons is one of those stars who, no matter how famous or popular she became, always seemed underappreciated. She never won an Oscar, nominated for the award only twice, once at the very beginning of her movie career and once after her stardom was just about over. Where was the Academy when Simmons was delivering some of the best work in Hollywood in the years between 1952 and 1960? With her impressive body of work, she would have been an ideal choice for an honorary Oscar. But Oscar isn't known for his long-term memory.

In her years in the British film industry, beginning as a teenager, Simmons made several notable films, including *Great Expectations* (1946), *Black Narcissus* (1947), and *Hamlet* (1948). Though she made a lovely and fragile Ophelia opposite Laurence Olivier, and received her first Oscar nomination (as supporting actress) for this Best Picture winner, it was in the Dickens piece, David Lean's masterful adaptation, where she shone brightest. Her self-possessed Estella makes such a strong impression that the film never quite recovers once Valerie Hobson assumes the role in adulthood. Another treasure of Simmons' British period is the sleeper *So Long at the Fair* (1950), a terrific period thriller anchored by her relentless fortitude in solving the mystery of her brother's disappearance. With her raven hair and prominent eyes, Simmons often evoked Vivien Leigh, and she would have been eminently believable if she had ever been cast as Leigh's kid sister.

In Hollywood, Simmons starred opposite Robert Mitchum in *Angel Face* (1952), a knockout film noir from director Otto Preminger, a film in which she staked her claim as one of the essential femmes fatale of the genre. She is cool and complicated, emotionally disturbed in a frighteningly plausible way. It was *The Robe* (1953), Fox's CinemaScope sensation, that made her a box-office name. Despite the film's popularity, it is by no measure a good movie, though Simmons gives the film its only genuine emotion, in a role subservient to Richard Burton. As Elizabeth I in *Young Bess* (1953), alongside real-life husband Stewart Granger, Simmons is a commanding presence, as well as a bewitching redhead. In *The Actress* (1953), George Cukor's film of Ruth Gordon's early stagestruck days, Simmons is incandescent, consumed with her dream of going on the stage. She also gets to act with the great Spencer Tracy, and their father-daughter bond is a joy to behold.

Her two films with Marlon Brando, *Desiree* (1954) and *Guys and Dolls* (1955), were both enormous financial successes, if not first-rate movies. *Desiree* is nothing more than a soapy costume picture, even relegating Brando's Napoleon to the sidelines, but *Guys and Dolls*, though nowhere near as good as it could have been, showcased Simmons as a fearless musical-comedy actress, charmingly delivering "If I Were a Bell" with an infectious glee. *The Big Country* (1958), from director William Wyler, combined box-office muscle with all-around excellence, and Simmons, opposite Gregory Peck, continued to display effortless versatility. After all, here was this English rose perfectly at ease in a mega-western, as if she truly belonged there.

But the peak performance from Jean Simmons came in *Elmer Gantry* (1960), from writer-director Richard Brooks, the man who became Simmons' second husband. This Sinclair Lewis tale of religion, sex, and hucksterism won considerable praise (and Oscars) for Burt Lancaster (deservedly) and Shirley Jones (undeservedly), but Simmons is its magic ingredient. As a true-believing revival-meeting evangelist, she is full of surprises. She is a natural preacher, all aglow and truly inspired, but never holier-than-thou. Ambitious but worn out, strong but moody, she is also surprisingly sexual, not to mention honest and smart. In short, she is a real person, a multi-dimensional and genuinely soulful creation. Whereas Shirley Jones' laughably bad performance as a hooker is faux-sexy, Simmons wipes her off the screen with a palpable eroticism. The Academy's failure to nominate Simmons for *Elmer Gantry* goes down as one of that organization's supreme embarrassments, especially unforgivable in the year that Elizabeth Taylor was named Best Actress for *Butterfield 8*.

Simmons never again got an opportunity as good as *Elmer Gantry*. *The Grass Is Greener* (1961) is a disappointingly slight and unmemorable comedy, but it is worth mentioning because in this film Simmons manages to steal the show from the likes of Cary Grant, Deborah Kerr, and Robert Mitchum, with a witty high-style performance. She got that second Oscar nomination for another film directed by husband Brooks, *The Happy Ending* (1969), a shallow drama unworthy of Simmons' depths.

If she was somehow always in the shadow of other actresses, not just Vivien Leigh but also Deborah Kerr and Audrey Hepburn, may we now please give her her due. If you aren't already a Simmons admirer, then a triple bill of *Angel Face*, *The Actress*, and *Elmer Gantry* ought to do the trick.

James Mitchell, Screen Actor
February 1st, 2010

On the same day that we lost Jean Simmons, another screen performer died, someone who was much less of a household name than Simmons. James Mitchell passed away at 89, and his name might not be familiar even to those who watched him for decades on the daytime serial *All My Children*. To soap fans, he was simply Palmer Cortlandt, beginning in 1979. But Mitchell was a "name" to those of us who follow dance and Broadway and the movies. He had danced with American Ballet Theatre and was the first Harry Beaton in the original Broadway production of *Brigadoon* in 1947.

Mitchell was in Hollywood for the tail-end of the movie musical's golden age, and he did manage to appear in two films that most musical lovers have seen countless times. In the fabulous Fred Astaire classic *The Band Wagon* (1953), Mitchell plays a snooty choreographer, the mentor to ballerina Cyd Charisse. Unfortunately, he doesn't really get to dance here, merely rehearse with the two stars. In *Oklahoma!* Mitchell is Dream Curly, dancing Agnes DeMille's iconic choreography in her beautiful dream ballet. But Mitchell's finest musical moment on film comes in *Deep in My Heart* (1954), actually one of the worst of the MGM musicals, a biopic about Sigmund Romberg with a horrifying performance by José Ferrer (as Romberg). But the movie features a dance duet performed by Mitchell and Cyd Charisse, to the tune "One Alone" from *The Desert Song*. Probably Charisse's best romantic dance without either Astaire or Gene Kelly, it is a sexy, hypnotic, and physically demanding number and a real showcase for Mitchell's talent, presence, and dark handsomeness. The sequence should be a classic (and probably would be if not marooned in that awful movie).

When I finished writing my book *Screen Savers*, which covers forty under-rated movies of the 20th century, I noticed that Mitchell just happened to be in three of the films, not one of them a musical. Odder still was the fact that he didn't make many non-musical pictures. Mitchell plays disparate supporting roles in this trio, all from MGM. In *Border Incident* (1949), Anthony Mann's terrific docudrama noir, Mitchell is a Mexican farm worker (with a good Mexican accent), sharing a strong rapport with the film's star, Ricardo Montalban, who plays a Mexican undercover agent. Even better is Mann's western *Devil's Doorway* (1950), a deeply moving film containing the best performance Robert Taylor ever gave. Taylor plays an Indian, as does Mitchell, in a no-win situation with westward-moving homesteaders and anti-Indian land laws. The movie packs quite a punch and will someday, finally, be recognized as a classic.

The third Mitchell movie in *Screen Savers* is Jacques Tourneur's beautiful *Stars in My Crown* (1950), an honest heartwarmer about small-town American life in the latter part of the 19th century. The star is wonderful Joel McCrea at his best, simple and effortless and unerringly believable. He plays the plain-speaking parson, and Mitchell, in his best role, is the new doctor in town (son of the old doctor, who is soon to be deceased). For a while, Mitchell's character, a citified gentleman, doesn't want to be stuck in this nowhere burg. Good things happen (he finds love with schoolteacher Amanda Blake) and bad things happen (an outbreak of typhoid fever). At odds with McCrea's character for much of the film, Mitchell gives a remarkably fine performance. His conversion from stuck-up outsider to committed community member is vividly drawn and plausibly timed.

So, if you think of Mitchell only as that fellow lifting Dream Laurey, or sharing the small screen with Susan Lucci, then it's time to check out his black-and-white trio of outstanding dramas and give him his due as a solid big-screen actor.

With Sailors, a Show Boat, and Shakespeare
February 21st, 2010

Screen songbird Kathryn Grayson died last week at 88, further decreasing the number of stars who remain from the Golden Age of the MGM Musical. Though she never became a main player in the studio's celebrated Freed Unit (the maker of MGM's greatest musicals), Grayson was one of the key stars of the less prestigious musicals the studio churned out, produced more often by Joe Pasternak than the classier Arthur Freed. Grayson made three trips to the higher-tiered Freed Unit, making guest appearances in *Ziegfeld Follies* and *Till the Clouds Roll By*, both released in 1946, and then starring in the hugely profitable *Show Boat* (1951), the film for which Grayson is best remembered. But for most of her stardom, a solid decade between 1943 and 1953, Grayson starred in what might be called high-culture kitsch, slight musicals that were given a bit of classical heft by having Grayson trill an operatic aria or two. It never hurt that she had lovely raven-black hair, a girl-next-door prettiness, a teensy waist, and, oh yes, ample breasts.

Grayson made her screen debut in the typical fashion of many a young and attractive MGM hopeful: she was showcased opposite Mickey Rooney in an Andy Hardy picture, just as Lana Turner had done before her and as Esther Williams was about to do. Grayson graduated from *Andy Hardy's Private Secretary* (1941) to Abbott and Costello's *Rio Rita* (1942) and then got the full MGM push in the Technicolor A-list musical *Thousands Cheer* (1943), co-starring another relative newcomer, Gene Kelly, though the movie seems more intent on pushing Grayson than Kelly. Unfortunately, her side of the plot puts her in Shirley Temple territory, trying to reunite her separated parents. The only reason to recall *Thousands Cheer* is Lena Horne's sublime "Honeysuckle Rose," which has nothing to do with the nonsense surrounding it.

But the director, George Sidney, and both of his stars were reteamed on a little something called *Anchors Aweigh* (1945), which properly focuses more on Kelly than Grayson, and more on Kelly's teamwork with Frank Sinatra than on his romance with Grayson (who is cast here as a film extra hoping for her big break in the movies). Though Grayson perhaps has as much musical screen time as the fellas—who are irresistibly cast as sailors on leave—she can't quite compete with Kelly's innovative dance sequences or Sinatra's aching ballads. (But how many mortals could?) Ridiculously long at 139 minutes, *Anchors Aweigh* is trite and uneven yet sporadically magical and transporting. And it solidified Grayson as a top leading lady of the MGM musical, as well as the successor to the studio's recently retired (in 1942) soprano Jeanette MacDonald, whose superstardom Grayson never quite equaled, especially as the movie musical moved further away from operetta-type material.

If the 1940s kept Grayson busy on those two films with Kelly and three films with Sinatra (the other two being 1947's *It Happened in Brooklyn* and 1948's *The Kissing Bandit*), then the second half of her stardom allied her with two other male co-stars, two men who suited her more comfortably than the staggeringly gifted Gene and Frank.

That Midnight Kiss (1949) and *The Toast of New Orleans* (1950) were the two musicals that introduced tenor Mario Lanza to the screen, giving Grayson a handsome leading man with whom she could share operatic duets. But Grayson was clearly put in the secondary position, lending back-seat support to MGM's big push on Lanza's behalf. In *That Midnight Kiss*, it's Ethel Barrymore, as Grayson's grandmother, who steals the show (without moving a muscle, or singing a note). Though *The Toast of New Orleans* introduced "Be My Love," one of the songs most associated with Grayson, the film is one of her worst. (How did poor David Niven end up in this, playing second fiddle to both stars?) Though mired in excruciating happy-peasant comedy, the film did give the stars a shot at *Madame Butterfly* at the climax. Talk about a bizarre mix of high and low culture, which I guess might have been interpreted at the time as "something for everyone!"

The two roles for which Grayson is most remembered are two of the parts she played in her three vehicles with baritone Howard Keel, the leading man who suited her best of all. Their vocal renditions of "Make Believe" in *Show Boat* and "Wunderbar" in *Kiss Me Kate* (1953) are probably the two high points of her career. (*Anchors Aweigh* director George Sidney also directed *Show Boat* and *Kiss Me Kate*, making him the man who made Grayson's three most enduring musical pictures.) Grayson was far better suited to the ingenue simplicity of her Magnolia in *Show Boat* than she was to the more theatrically demanding and sophisticated requirements of playing stage star Lilli Vanessi in *Kiss Me Kate*, but she nonetheless became the Magnolia and Lilli that most of us grew up with. (In *Kate*, she is seen as both a blonde and a redhead but not as a brunette.) The middle teaming of Grayson and Keel is the thoroughly lackluster *Lovely to Look At* (1952).

Grayson and Keel were briefly the 1950s answer to Jeanette MacDonald and Nelson Eddy, just as Marge and Gower Champion were momentarily spoken of in the same breath as Fred Astaire and Ginger Rogers. Grayson's voice and personality never quite had the warmth of her fellow MGM soprano Jane Powell, nor did she have MacDonald's idol-of-millions level of popularity, but she made her contribution to the movie musical at a key moment in its history. It was a wunderbar decade for Grayson, and will I ever hear "Make Believe" without thinking first of her?

"You Ever Seen a Grown Man Naked?"
March 15th, 2010

T he above line, and "Joey, do you like movies about gladiators?" are the two best remembered sentences ever uttered on-screen by actor Peter Graves. These lines, spoken by pilot Graves to a boy in the beloved disaster-movie spoof *Airplane!* (1980), helped turn the middle-aged Graves into a deadpan comedy star after decades of firm-jawed leading-man status (admittedly of the second or third tier). With his cookie-cutter handsomeness and low-wattage personality, he was a natural for television stardom, which became his from 1967-1973 on *Mission: Impossible.* Later, he was the eminently comfortable host of A&E's *Biography* series, which lasted from 1994 to 2006. Graves passed away yesterday, four days before his 84th birthday, and I'd like to take a moment to remember his early big-screen career, before he became a small-screen staple, following in the footsteps of older brother James Arness.

Entering films in 1951, Graves got his big break in Billy Wilder's *Stalag 17* (1953), the WWII comedy-drama set in a German P.O.W. camp in 1944. The film is wildly uneven, juggling a very fine and suspenseful "informant" mystery with a lame "barracks" comedy, but it is ultimately satisfying, primarily because of William Holden's sly and altogether terrific Oscar-winning performance as the most cynical of the captured Americans. Holden cuts through the film's worst *Hogan's Heroes* aspects. Graves is among the incarcerated, and, in one of the better roles, shines in what becomes an unforgettable turn.

The Raid (1954) is one of my favorite overlooked movies, one of the war pictures I wrote about in my 2007 book *Screen Savers.* A Civil War film set primarily in Vermont, it's one of the best and most emotionally and morally complex movies about that conflict. Van Heflin stars as a Southerner who escapes, with six other Confederate officers, from a Union prison in 1864, soon plotting revenge on a small Northern town, part of their payback for the South's (and their own) losses. Arriving in Vermont as a Canadian businessman, Heflin ingratiates his way into the hearts of the locals, all the while scheming to rob the town and burn it to the ground. What Heflin didn't plan on was how attached he would become to the citizens, especially war widow Anne Bancroft and her 9-year-old son Tommy Rettig. Graves plays one of the other Southern officers in Heflin's band, part of the top-notch supporting cast gracing this outstanding war movie.

The finest film in which Graves ever appeared is *The Night of the Hunter* (1955), a magnificent and harrowing thriller, and the only film ever directed by the great Charles Laughton. Though Graves' role is small, it's the catalyst for the main action. Against a Depression-ravaged Midwest, Robert Mitchum gives a truly terrifying performance as a serial killer and "preacher," sharing a jail cell with Graves, a man awaiting execution for killing two men in a robbery. Only Graves' two young children know where he hid the $10,000 he stole, but Mitchum, arrested only for car theft, will soon make his way to Graves' widow, Shelley Winters, and the kiddies, bent on finding the money. In just a few scenes, Graves portrays a loving and decent man desperately led astray by unbearably difficult times. His is a memorable performance, helping to kick-start one of the great American masterpieces, featuring phenomenal performances not only from Mitchum, but also Winters and the legendary Lillian Gish.

But did Graves ever actually make a gladiator movie? Not that I can recall.

No Ordinary Face in the Crowd
August 13th, 2010

The loss of Patricia Neal (at 84) this week means that another great star actress of the twentieth century is gone. When Neal suffered those three severe strokes at age 39 in 1965, who would have guessed that she had more than half of her life ahead of her? Despite a life and career of enormous ups and shattering downs, Neal never was out of the spotlight for long, thanks to her rare combination of stunning yet highly individualized beauty and ever-deepening reserves of talent.

Her first phase in Hollywood, the Warner Brothers years, is now best remembered as the time of her great love affair with Gary Cooper, who was a quarter-century her senior. Their King Vidor picture, *The Fountainhead* (1949), has always been my choice for the greatest bad film ever made. Beyond terrible in many ways, it is nonetheless riveting, containing unforgettable visual sequences that are alternately campy/ridiculous and sublime/original. Though deeply pretentious and heavy-handed, how can you dismiss a movie in which Neal, as a frigid neurotic, lustily watches a sweaty Cooper in a rock quarry as he drills at about crotch level? Or, after he rapes her, when she tells him, a promising architect, "I wish I'd never seen…your building." The film ends with Neal ascending a never-ending building-site elevator to Cooper at the top, the effect being that she's riding the biggest phallus in movie history.

Neal fared better as the Canadian nurse in Burma in *The Hasty Heart* (1949) with Ronald Reagan and the wonderful Richard Todd, a moving, heartwarming post-war army-hospital drama in which a glowing Neal displays her smarts and sensitivity. In Michael Curtiz's *The Breaking Point* (1950), opposite the great John Garfield, Neal gives my favorite of her performances, as a high-class whore. She is not only slinky, bad-girl fun in the part, but she gives this familiar "tramp" type a penetrating depth and humanity. Plus, her chemistry with Garfield is electric. At Fox, she appeared in the sci-fi classic *The Day the Earth Stood Still* (1951), as a widowed secretary and mother who finds herself unforgettably involved with alien Michael Rennie and his robot Gort.

After years away from the screen, she returned for Elia Kazan's *A Face in the Crowd* (1957), a flop in its day but now a much-admired cautionary tale about television and its personalities, even if Kazan's touch isn't exactly light. It's Andy Griffith's movie, in which he dazzles and terrifies as a fireball hillbilly who becomes a national treasure (while morphing into a monster). Neal is his Dr. Frankenstein, who realizes she must destroy her out-of-control creation. The first half is pretty close to perfect, loose and airy in its Southern locations, and building dramatically quite beautifully. But the second half becomes preachy, obvious, hysterical, and smug. The film is a Capra tale in reverse, in which "Mr. Deeds" turns out to be the bad guy. But Neal shows an unapologetic sexuality with Griffith, able to suggest much more need and yearning than the censors would allow in 1957.

A problem with Neal's career is that she is not the main focus of any of her best films, second fiddle to the male stars. This continued into the 1960s, although in *Breakfast at Tiffany's* (1961) it was Audrey Hepburn who was the main attraction. Even so, who can forget Neal's illicit delight as a married woman sneaking around for trysts with "kept" stud George Peppard? Her best *Tiffany's* get-up is her black-cape coat and her red turban. Has anyone ever enjoyed the mechanics of infidelity more?

Neal won the Best Actress Oscar for her supporting performance in *Hud* (1963), a solid Paul Newman vehicle. Neal is superb as a sassy, easygoing, likable housekeeper, a barefooted divorcee who shares sexual tension with both Newman and his teen nephew Brandon de Wilde. She provides this contemporary western with humor, warmth, and authenticity, but it's simply not a lead performance.

From the high-fashion glamour of her *Fountainhead* and *Tiffany's* roles, to the unvarnished womanliness and sensuality of her *Face in the Crowd* and *Hud* performances, Neal was a gorgeously gifted star whose handful of fascinating movies should keep her in the public eye till the earth stands still.

Little Bonnie Blue Butler
September 3rd, 2010

O n Wednesday, Cammie King died at age 76. If the name doesn't ring a bell, it's because she's far better known as a character she played (rather than as an actress). At age 5, she appeared as the daughter of Clark Gable's Rhett Butler and Vivien Leigh's Scarlett O'Hara in *Gone With the Wind*, the little girl who dies when she falls off her pony. King was no wind-up child actress, the kind who already has a bag of tricks to sell, and so her acting as Bonnie is charmingly amateurish instead of cloying or showbizzy. There are few remaining surviving members of the cast of *Gone With the Wind*, most notably 94-year-old Olivia de Havilland, the film's glowing Melanie, and 89-year-old Ann Rutherford, Scarlett's baby sister Careen.

The most important thing about Cammie King's contribution to the film is the way in which Gable relates to her. In their few scenes together, Gable is so deeply loving, so gentle and openly affectionate, that it enriches Rhett Butler beyond our expectations, showing us the man underneath his cynicism, the man who surprises himself with his capacity for fatherhood and how it joyfully changes his life. His grieving over Bonnie is incredibly moving, and Rhett is never quite the same. After bringing him his happiest moments, she is the cause of his most enduring pain. Gable is superb in *Gone With the Wind*; it's a performance richly enhanced by those "Bonnie" scenes. So, although Cammie King showed no signs of budding acting talent, she is nonetheless partially responsible for one of the most beloved and admired performances in screen history. After all, another child actress may very well not have engendered the necessary emotional responses in Gable that Cammie King so obviously did. Little Miss King did her part in helping Gable sustain his tag as the King of Hollywood, connecting these two Kings for all time.

Tony Curtis and the Sweet Smell of Success
October 1st, 2010

T ony Curtis died this week at 85, and I can't say that he was ever one of my favorites, nor did I find him particularly good-looking. But he did have a very impressive run in the late 1950s, a trio of performances that got him out of his pretty-boy rut and proved he had genuine talent, even if he squandered much of that talent in rotten sex comedies in the 1960s. But in that little window between 1957 and 1959, he was a dark-haired golden boy.

I enjoy pointing him out to people in *Criss Cross* (1949), the terrific film noir in which he does nothing but partner Yvonne De Carlo on the dance floor (to a Latin beat). It was in *Sweet Smell of Success* (1957), playing Sidney Falco to Burt Lancaster's J. J. Hunsecker, that Curtis became an actor to watch. As a scrounging, hungry press agent, he is ideal, playing his role with an insatiable, relentless drive. The film is one of the key New York movies, maybe even *the* anti-New York movie, a down-and-dirty dazzler.

Curtis received his only Oscar nomination for *The Defiant Ones* (1958), as the racist convict handcuffed to fellow convict Sidney Poitier. The film has a great hook, with the stars unexpectedly on the run together, and the direction of Stanley Kramer is surprisingly restrained. Both stars are excellent, with Curtis (wearing a false nose) emotionally affecting and thoroughly committed to his role. Gorgeously shot, *The Defiant Ones* still packs a wallop.

But the most sublime achievement of Curtis' career is Billy Wilder's wondrous *Some Like It Hot* (1959), the endlessly blissful gender comedy, with Curtis in the triple-whammy role of womanizing saxophone player, refined lady musician, and Cary Grant-sounding millionaire. He's superb as all three, equal to Jack Lemmon's inspired comic skills and Marilyn Monroe's radiant funny-sad effects. If only he had made a few more comedies that aspired to the level of this classic, rather than all that '60s crap like *Sex and the Single Girl* and *Goodbye, Charlie!*

I'll leave you with an underrated Curtis performance in *The Outsider* (1961), as Ira Hayes, the Native-American marine who was one of the six men who hoisted the flag at Iwo Jima. Though it sounds like horrible casting, Curtis wisely underplays (and again wears a false nose). This is a surprisingly intelligent and thoughtful biopic, with a Curtis performance that should have been Oscar bait, though the film's financial failure put an end to any Oscar talk. Yet Curtis is remarkably open, moving from sweet and gentle to despairing, and into a life of hopeless alcoholism. He never acts with self-indulgence, remaining truthful and not even shying away from the gay undercurrents in the character.

A few more Curtis pictures like *The Outsider* would have been welcome. Oh well, "Nobody's perfect."

My Favorite Broadway Musical
November 3rd, 2010

Broadway composer Jerry Bock died on Wednesday morning at 81. Though he wrote the score, alongside the wonderful lyricist Sheldon Harnick, for the mega-smash *Fiddler on the Roof* (1964), neither Bock nor Harnick became household names outside of homes devoted to the musical theatre. No, it's not *Fiddler* that is my favorite Broadway musical, and its film version is hardly near the best of the movie musicals based on Broadway material. (In fact, the 1971 *Fiddler* film, though respectable, is unexciting and uninspired, which practically constitutes a rave when compared to most screen musicals of the '60s and '70s that were spawned from B'way.)

My favorite Broadway musical is the 1963 Bock-and-Harnick *She Loves Me*, which has a score that would have to be one of my desert-island picks. The songs, the book, the characters, and the plot radiate a consistency of charm, wit, and genuine warmth that, for my money, tops any other show. Maybe you can convince me that other shows are "greater" but you certainly couldn't make me believe that there's another one worthier of my affection. I was only a toddler when the original production opened in New York. It was later, when a BBC production played on PBS sometime in the late '70s, that I fell in love with the show. I went on to play the delivery boy, Arpad, in a 1983 summer-stock production and my solo, "Try Me," became my uptempo audition song for years to come.

The plot of *She Loves Me*, which began as a play titled *Parfumerie*, became known to moviegoers when it was filmed as *The Shop Around the Corner* (1940), directed by the great Ernst Lubitsch and starring James Stewart and Margaret Sullavan, and then later as the musical *In the Good Old Summertime* (1949), starring Judy Garland and Van Johnson. Lubitsch's film is a classic romantic comedy, as touching as it is funny and transporting, with considerably more emotional depth than most of the golden-age comedies that we love. The set-up is irresistible, with two co-workers who detest each other, not knowing that they are actually madly-in-love pen pals. Jimmy Stewart learns the truth first, and then sets out to make Ms. Sullavan fall for him, the man she is already in love with!

The Garland version is a pale remake, with two new ruinous subplots, yet it's also very unsatisfying as a musical, with a few songs thrown in rather than tailored to the story. (This is no "integrated" musical.) But Judy is her delightfully scrappy self, and she works nicely with Van Johnson. However, they needed a director more engaged and imaginative than Robert Z. Leonard.

And Judy's "Merry Christmas" ballad ain't no "Have Yourself a…" Yes, this story came around again as *You've Got Mail* (1998) with Tom Hanks and Meg Ryan, becoming the incontestably worst version thus far.

I'd say that *She Loves Me* surpasses Lubitsch's film as the greatest interpretation of this material, and it also restored the original parfumerie setting; Lubitsch set it in a leather-goods shop, and Garland and co. worked in a music store. There was a marvelous Broadway revival of *She Loves Me* in the 1990s, but do yourself a favor and listen to the original cast recording starring Barbara Cook. I was lucky enough to meet Sheldon Harnick and have the opportunity to tell him that *She Loves Me* is my favorite show. I never got to tell Jerry Bock, so this post will have to suffice as my way of saying thank you.

An Un-Oscared Woman
November 11th, 2010

With golden-age legends like Olivia de Havilland, Kirk Douglas, and Mickey Rooney still with us, it was a shock last week to learn that Jill Clayburgh, a star of the 1970s, had died at 66. Clayburgh's movie stardom was brief, less than a decade really, but she made her mark, becoming one of the key actresses of late '70s American film. Writer-director Paul Mazursky's *An Unmarried Woman* (1978) was something of a feminist landmark when it opened, and it retains much of its freshness. It is an unmelodramatic update of a '40s "woman's picture," a portrait of an Upper East Side wife who has it all until her husband (excellent Michael Murphy) leaves for a younger woman. It's a journey of self-discovery for her but not by choice. Clayburgh is outstanding, so open and consistently surprising, spinning emotionally through anger, hurt, fear, resentment, and some irrational behavior. And her inspired comic instincts and gutsy laugh lead to some great confrontations with the men in the movie.

Mazursky sustains a marvelously messy tone, a feeling of life being captured rather than staged. However, it must be said that Alan Bates is simply too good to be true—gorgeous, funny, smart, successful—as Clayburgh's new love. But the climactic choice had to be difficult so that we could feel the weight of Clayburgh choosing herself over a man, even this guy! It's a shame that she didn't win the Oscar because she deserved it more than the eventual winner: Jane Fonda in *Coming Home*.

The other key (and Oscar-nominated) performance of Clayburgh's brief reign can be seen in Alan J. Pakula's *Starting Over* (1979), one of the better romantic comedies of its decade, with a script by James L. Brooks. Essentially a Burt Reynolds vehicle, and a mighty good one, this is a serious-minded look at divorce, with Reynolds as the "unmarried man," moving forward with uncertainty and fear. Dumped by Candice Bergen, Reynolds "starts over" with Clayburgh. It may not be a top-notch film, but it's got sharp dialogue, good situations, and keen observations. The basic arc of the plot feels like an old '30s or '40s comedy, and the three stars give it the personality of an old-time movie-movie.

Cast superbly against type as a writer and teacher, Reynolds is without his cocky assurance as a man who is wounded and mild-mannered and intelligent. Too bad we didn't see more of this Reynolds in subsequent roles. Bergen is rather hilarious as a woman who uses her relationship with Reynolds as emotional fodder for her songwriting. (And she's a fabulously terrible singer.) Clayburgh is a nursery-school teacher, a lively and vulnerable presence. (She and Reynolds had already appeared together in 1977's *Semi-Tough*.) The love triangle sorts itself out happily if not especially believably. Clayburgh seemed poised to continue her career as a smart and quirky star comedienne, a modern-day Jean Arthur. It didn't quite work out that way, but Clayburgh was, for a spell, a major screen actress.

Blake Edwards (1922-2010)
December 17th, 2010

When I was a kid, Blake Edwards' elaborately zany farce *The Great Race* (1965) was one of my favorite movies, mostly because of Jack Lemmon's splendidly over-the-top renditions of two roles: the film's dastardly villain and its queeny prince. It's been a long time since I've seen this very long movie, so I wonder if it would still delight me in any comparable way, yet it occupies an affectionate place in my memory, of the time when I was falling in love with the movies.

Blake Edwards died at age 88 on Wednesday night, as famous for being Mr. Julie Andrews as he was for writing and directing movies since the 1950s. He acted small parts in movies in the 1940s, notably delivering a few lines as a soldier in the opening scene of *The Best Years of Our Lives* (1946). But it was the 1960s that put Edwards at the top of the movie profession, with a string of hits including *Breakfast at Tiffany's* (1961), *Days of Wine and Roses* (1962), and *The Pink Panther* (1964), the first film to feature Peter Sellers as Inspector Clouseau. I think the second Edwards-Sellers Clouseau film, *A Shot in the Dark* (1965), has many of the funniest and most inspired bits in the series, the kind that have you helplessly laughing out loud even if you're all alone in front of the television. A string of box-office flops followed, including *Darling Lili* (1970), his first picture to star Ms. Andrews. (They wed in 1969.)

I'd love to write a glowing tribute to Edwards but I don't love any of his movies. Oh, I love parts of many of them, but they are often undone by his excesses and his unsureness of tone. It's been too long since I've seen *"10"* (1979) or *Victor/Victoria* (1982) for me to comment on them now, though they gave me great pleasure when they came out. But recent viewings of other Edwards biggies warrant comment, and I wish I had nicer things to say about them.

The wildly uneven but also wildly enjoyable *Breakfast at Tiffany's* is about reinventing yourself. Audrey Hepburn may appear miscast as Holly Golightly, the former Lulu Mae Barnes, a Texas hillbilly and child bride, but she makes the character her own, enchantingly plausible as someone who recreated herself as a chic New Yorker even though she's still a lost soul in search of her real self. Hepburn is stylish and wittily comic but also quite touching and vulnerable, anchoring the film with her special radiance. Despite her beauty and extroverted poise, Hepburn never loses sight of Holly's underlying fear and insecurity. The film loses its way in the unconvincing romance that develops from the friendship between Hepburn and George Peppard, two characters who connect as fellow "tramps." There's no chemistry between the stars, all the way to the sentimentalized ending, mostly because the handsome but charmless Peppard is no fun at all. (Hepburn has a much stronger rapport with Buddy Ebsen as the husband she abandoned.) Edwards is at his best in the hilarious party in Hepburn's crowded apartment, and at his worst in all the excruciating scenes with Mickey Rooney mugging shamelessly as Mr. Yuniosohi. Still, it's a warm and funny movie, yet it wouldn't be a pop classic without Hepburn grounding all of the film's disparate elements.

Days of Wine and Roses is much less satisfying than *Tiffany's*. It's a decent alcoholism drama but nowhere near as ferociously potent as *The Lost Weekend* (1945) or *I'll Cry Tomorrow* (1955), the two previous decades' definitive takes on the subject. Directed in a mostly heavy-handed manner by Edwards, including his compulsive penchant for broad and odd comic touches, the film was praised for its star performances from Jack Lemmon and Lee Remick, neither of whom is at his/her best. Everybody's timing seems to be off. Set in the *Mad Men* world, the film offers two uninteresting characters, large gaps in the narrative, and a central love story not worth caring about. Lemmon appears to be begging for an Oscar the entire time. With its superficial set-up and thin psychology, this version is far inferior to the TV version that had starred Cliff Robertson and Piper Laurie, minus all of Edwards' so-called improvements.

It's a wonder that the Edwards-Andrews marriage lasted, considering that Edwards put the final nail in the coffin of Andrews' once-blazing movie career when they made *Darling Lili*. True, there would soon be no place for a star like Andrews in American movies of the '70s, and it's also true that it was *Star!* (1968) which first heralded the pending doom of her box-office prowess, but *Darling Lili* finished the job decisively (even though she's the only good thing about it). Edwards' intentions are mystifying here. If this WWI tale of an American fighter pilot (a lifeless Rock Hudson) and an English entertainer/spy (Andrews) is a spoof, then why is it so long and dull? If it's meant to be taken straight, then why did Edwards insert so much Clouseau-like slapstick into the proceedings? Nothing fits here, and what you get is a lavish dud, an empty spectacle with a colorless romance. Who wants to see a musical-comedy romance set in a fantasy WWI if it's going to be such a flabby, slow, and leaden ride? Despite her unlikely casting as a Mata Hari, Andrews enlivens the picture with her Henry Mancini–Johnny Mercer songs. But this is still the bomb that everyone thought it was in 1970.

Thank writer-director Edwards for many great moments in many unsatisfying movies. Let's face it, though: he wasn't exactly Preston Sturges.

Susannah York's Loss of Innocence
January 21st, 2011

English screen actress Susannah York died last week at age 72. She is best remembered as a star of the 1960s, playing the female lead in two Oscar-winning Best Picture period pieces: Tony Richardson's zesty comedy *Tom Jones* (1963), in which she's delightful as the spirited ingenue; and Fred Zinnemann's high-minded prestige picture *A Man for All Seasons* (1966), in which she's honest and impassioned (though the film was insanely overrated). York capped the decade with her only Oscar nomination (in the supporting category) in Sydney Pollack's grimly absorbing marathon-dance drama *They Shoot Horses, Don't They?* (1969), playing the fragile Jean Harlow wannabe who is systematically losing her mind; it's a striking performance (she lost the Oscar to Goldie Hawn in *Cactus Flower*). Good roles were few for screen actresses in the early 1970s, and York wasn't able to sustain her stardom the way Julie Christie did (thank you, Warren Beatty). However, whenever York worked (as in her brief appearance as Superman's mother in 1978) she was always a welcome sight, always lovely and fresh and intelligent.

One of her earliest films was Lewis Gilbert's offbeat and intriguing *Loss of Innocence* (1961), in which York, past twenty, plays sixteen. The film has a strange set-up: four young British siblings, on holiday in France to see famed battlefields, are staying at a chateau hotel while their mother, suddenly taken ill, has been hospitalized. Kenneth More, as a mysterious Englishman, takes a shine to the foursome. He is sleeping with Danielle Darrieux, the hotel owner, who has dumped her lesbian lover for him. Turns out that More is an international jewel thief.

The plot hinges on York's coming of age, realizing the sexual power she can wield with her beautiful face and body, soon posing a threat to Darrieux. The More-York union goes only as far as two kisses, but York turns vindictive once she feels that More prefers Darrieux. She contacts the police. *Loss of Innocence* is one of those movies, like *The Fallen Idol* (1948), in which young people tamper with things they don't fully understand, therefore causing great damage.

In an interesting grace note, York's brother (about ten or eleven) is first seen drawing female fashions, and then is later making doll-sized dresses. Nothing much is made of this, and it's rather fascinating and forward-looking to see a presumably gay child treated so matter-of-factly. The film itself has elegant clothes, as well as great color, scenery, and that chateau!

York is luminous as the child-woman at the center, innocent and naive yet brazen and spiteful. The film may be uneven and perhaps *too* oddball at times, but it's admirable and unusual, never more so than when young York holds the screen, declaring herself ready for the larger roles to come, those that will keep her in the memories of all serious moviegoers.

Eileen's Sister
February 13th, 2011

Thanks to four consecutive films made over a two-year period (1948-49), Betty Garrett became a bright light of the MGM musical: as love interest to Mickey Rooney in *Words and Music*; as part of the quartet (along with Esther Williams, Ricardo Montalban, and Red Skelton) that introduced the Oscar-winning "Baby, It's Cold Outside" in *Neptune's Daughter*; and, most indelibly, paired with Frank Sinatra twice, first in *Take Me Out to the Ball Game*, again with Esther Williams and also with Gene Kelly and Jules Munshin, and then reteaming with all three fellows (Gene, Jules, and Frank) in *On the Town*, with Ann Miller and Vera-Ellen making it a memorable sextet.

Garrett died at 91 on Saturday, February 12th. Let's just be grateful that she got to MGM when she did, in time to go "on the town" and "to the ball game." Her warm Broadway belt, easygoing likability, sparkling energy, and crackerjack comic timing made her every inch a first-rate musical-comedy performer. She'll always be remembered as Hildy, the lady cab driver who chases Sinatra through most of *On the Town,* eventually winning him. She delightfully harasses him to "Come Up to My Place."

Garrett was married to actor Larry Parks, the Oscar-nominated star of *The Jolson Story* (1946) whose career was destroyed by the '50s blacklist. She was away from Hollywood musicals until 1955 when she starred in a new version of *My Sister Eileen* (unrelated to the 1953 Broadway musical version titled *Wonderful Town*). Garrett played Ruth, created by Shirley Booth in the original play on Broadway in 1940, then portrayed by Rosalind Russell to Oscar-nominated effect in the 1942 film version and also in her Tony-winning performance in *Wonderful Town.* The 1942 film, though exceedingly popular, was overrated, both obvious and uninspired, exaggerated and forced. It's so damned ordinary.

I much prefer the barely known 1955 version with Garrett and, in the title role, Janet Leigh. The basic material is still conventional, as two sisters move to New York from Ohio to achieve their dreams, but this version feels pleasantly simple and unpretentious. Its appealing mildness can also be interpreted as blandness, and it does get mired in a '50s sense of virtue. With tunes by Jule Styne, the musical selections are primarily performed by a quartet of ex-MGM players, both Garrett and Leigh, plus Bob Fosse and Tommy Rall. (The fellas' dance-off in an alley is the film's one great moment.) Young Jack Lemmon is Garrett's love interest, not altogether at home in a musical but gamely forging ahead. See it for Garrett and her effortless grace, singing and dancing and making you laugh as if it were merely a lark. Which it very well might have been for someone as multi-talented as Betty Garrett.

Lumet's Long Journey
April 14th, 2011

Sidney Lumet, the epitome of the New York film director, died at 86 on April 9th. He had a remarkable career, hitting it big with *12 Angry Men* (1957), his first feature film, and ending his directorial career on a damn good note with *Before the Devil Knows You're Dead* (2007), exactly fifty years later! Not many directors have enjoyed such longevity, and it surely is lucky that he ended with a winner, especially considering his number of turkeys strewn among his classics.

For me, his masterwork is *Dog Day Afternoon* (1975), a perfect melding of action and character, depth and suspense, humor and tragedy. And, of course, set in New York City! Many would cite *Network* (1976) as his greatest film, but don't get me started on all the things I dislike about that movie, beginning with its smug, self-congratulatory tone and the fact that nearly every line of Paddy Chayefsky's dialogue sounds *so* "written," as if each character worked for days at perfecting (in advance) everything he or she was going to say. Guess I should do a separate blog piece someday on why *Network*, for all its impressive prescience on the future of our culture, is one of our most overrated classics.

I spent a good deal of time writing about Lumet in my book *Tennessee Williams and Company: His Essential Screen Actors* because Lumet directed two films based on plays by Williams. How interesting that he directed one of the best and one of the worst of the Williams films. Though a commercial and critical flop back in 1960, *The Fugitive Kind* (based on the play *Orpheus Descending*) is the most underrated of the Williams movies, a haunting black-and-white picture featuring two extraordinary performances from Anna Magnani and Joanne Woodward. (Unfortunately, Marlon Brando is the film's one major disappointment.) Ten years later, Lumet directed *The Last of the Mobile Hotshots*, based on Williams' *The Seven Descents of Myrtle*. It's what is known as a disaster, one of those utterly confounding efforts, a spectacularly bad movie. But I'll always be grateful to him for the beauty and artistry of *The Fugitive Kind*.

Lumet has the distinction of having directed what is a strong candidate for the American screen's greatest dramatic performance by a female: Katharine Hepburn as Mary Tyrone in *Long Day's Journey into Night* (1962). It was one of my selections (as was Magnani in *Fugitive Kind*) in my book *100 Great Film Performances You Should Remember But Probably Don't*. In Lumet's hands, Eugene O'Neill's greatest play got a superlative screen version, most notably in the magnificence of Hepburn's uncompromising—bravely ugly yet so unbearably moving—portrait of despair, one of the more complexly detailed breakdowns you'll ever see on-screen. As Mary succumbs to her morphine addiction, Hepburn makes lightning-speed transitions through her character's dark psyche, yet you don't miss a beat of the logic behind her mood swings, from forced gaiety and nervous chatter to defensive paranoia and venomous anger. One of our fastest-thinking actresses, Hepburn soars on a rush of conflicting emotions. Ravaged yet ferocious, delusional yet stingingly self-aware, girlish yet hardened, she is incomparable in one of the most daunting roles of the American theatre. Thank you, Mr. Lumet, for this piece of greatness, which proved you were as outstanding in New England as you were in New York.

Jackie Cooper, Survivor
May 5th, 2011

L ittle Jackie Cooper, frozen in time as the Depression era's favorite on-screen blond male moppet, died at age 88 on May 3rd. A survivor of childhood superstardom, he would go on to become a two-time Emmy Award-winning director of episodic television. And he still holds the record as the youngest Best Actor Oscar nominee of all time, for his title-role performance in Norman Taurog's *Skippy* (1931), which was soon followed by another mega-hit, King Vidor's *The Champ* (1931), which won Wallace Beery a Best Actor Oscar. (Cooper lost his Oscar to Lionel Barrymore in *A Free Soul*.) What those two films share, and what made audiences love them so much, was their unabashed sentimentality. Before Margaret O'Brien came along, Cooper was the king of the kiddie criers, wailing over pets or parents. He wasn't a particularly good actor, prone to excessive pouting and a forcing of those famous tears, but audiences clearly loved his combination of toughness and emotionality, of scrappiness and adorability. Most of his '30s vehicles are pretty hard to sit through today because they are so strenuously manipulative and so shamelessly sure of their effects. *The Champ* is a real weeper, kind of a male version of *Stella Dallas* (also directed by Vidor). Cooper reigned until Shirley Temple's emergence in 1934 and her dominance as the key child star of the latter half of the decade. Though Cooper prevailed in the pre-Code era, his films were mostly hokum (after all, he was a child), though *The Bowery* (1933), also with Beery, was pretty racy stuff for a kid to be running through.

Though you may remember him primarily, again with Beery, in *Treasure Island* (1934), I like Cooper best in Fritz Lang's *The Return of Frank James* (1940), a picture he made well after his box-office glory days. It's not that he suddenly became a nuanced and interesting young actor, but he did get rid of his bag of tricks, realizing quite sensibly that an 18-year-old couldn't get away with the self-conscious gimmicks of a seasoned 10-year-old. The film is a sequel to the very popular and highly entertaining *Jesse James* (1939), which starred Tyrone Power and Henry Fonda as the James brothers. With Power's Jesse killed off, the sequel focuses on Fonda's Frank and his mission of revenge on his brother's killers. The first picture, directed by Henry King, is conventional and superficial and utterly commercial-minded, whereas the sequel is a much more offbeat and stimulating movie, never feeling like a churned-out sequel (notably in its anti-racism and pro-feminism stances). Fonda has an incredibly powerful presence, able to be so quiet and contained without ever appearing dull or monotonous. His strong stoicism, impeccable honesty, and effortless ease draw us to him time and again, holding us with a firm yet unforced grip. Cooper plays his teen sidekick. The beauty of what Cooper does lies in what he doesn't do. Gone is his overemoting; gone is the pouting; gone is his obviousness. Cooper gives a simple, straightforward performance.

With its thrilling Technicolor, gorgeous riding scenes, plotting that rarely feels routine, and a screen debut from lovely Gene Tierney, *The Return of Frank James* is hardly remembered by anyone as a Jackie Cooper movie. But it should be. After all, he has a death scene and does *not* pull out all the stops. Maybe working with the masterfully restrained Fonda rubbed off on Cooper. So, if you're in the mood to revisit this childhood sensation, skip *Skippy* and the other usual suspects and familiarize yourself with Jackie Cooper, promising young teenager.

VIII. The Gold Rush
screensaversmovies.com

Sorry, Miss Scarlett
July 4th, 2008

Here's a really good Oscar-trivia question:
What's the first Oscar-winning performance to come from a color movie?

If your guess—and it would be perfectly logical—is either Vivien Leigh or Hattie McDaniel, both of whom won Oscars for 1939's *Gone With the Wind*, you'd be off by one year. The answer is Walter Brennan in the horse-racing saga *Kentucky*, certainly one of the most disposable movies ever to claim a major Oscar. This was Brennan's second of three Oscars in the supporting-actor category. (He won three of the first five awards in this category!) His first came for *Come and Get It* (1936), and his third (and the only one he deserved) was for *The Westerner* (1940).

In *Kentucky*, Brennan, in his mid-forties, plays an octogenarian, and he's clearly nowhere near that age. Brennan could be a wonderful actor, perhaps never better than in *My Darling Clementine* (1946), but in *Kentucky* his work consists of tediously cantankerous overacting, with lots of bellowing and head bobbing. (Looking like Colonel Sanders doesn't help.) This family-feud melodrama stars Loretta Young, lovely and gracious and relaxed, as Brennan's great niece. Why is she wearing such a dull hat at the Kentucky Derby climax? The picture is routine Americana hokum, but it will always be a Hollywood footnote as long as anyone gives a hoot about the Academy Awards.

The Curious Case of Oscar
February 19th, 2009

When I was in my teens in the 1970s, Oscar always seemed to pick the best movies and the best performances. Well, one of us has changed. Since 2000, only two Best Picture winners (*Chicago* and *The Departed*) were films I would have had on a year-end Ten Best list. I'm expecting Sunday to be an evening of disappointments, once again. Anyway, here's my two cents.

Slumdog Millionaire appears unbeatable (but then so did *Brokeback Mountain* not so long ago), and I think it will win because it flatters people into thinking that if they liked it, well, then they are sensitive to the poverty in Mumbai. Plus, the happy ending means that you never have to think about that poverty again! I thought it was a mildly effective movie, but it already feels like one of Oscar's "What were they thinking?" choices, which applies to about half of the movies they've picked in 80 years.

I disliked *The Reader,* mostly because I didn't believe a single moment of it. And isn't it borderline (or not so borderline) offensive to use the Holocaust as a plot twist? Despite being based on a novel, the whole thing feels like a high-concept gimmick pitched by a studio executive: "What if the 'Mrs. Robinson' character turned out to be a Nazi guard?!" It's a pretentious and empty movie. *Frost/Nixon* was certainly respectable, but Best Picture? It's a decent movie that has been wildly overrated because of its subject matter.

That leaves *Milk* and *The Curious Case of Benjamin Button,* the two movies in this category that I liked best. *Milk* is flawed by its dips into the cliches of most biopics, while *Benjamin Button* is diminished by the moments in which it reminds you of *Forrest Gump.* That said, *Milk* is vibrant and impassioned, and elevated by its phenomenal central performance by Sean Penn, and *Benjamin Button* is a lovely mood piece, a modern-day *Portrait of Jennie.* Tilda Swinton's scenes alone are enough to make this one of the year's more memorable movies. I still think that *Wall-E* is the year's only American masterwork, with its ingenious silent-film first half and its beautiful and surprising ending, a hopeful moment in which a numbed humanity bravely and eagerly chooses life over inertia. And any movie that could turn clips of the execrable *Hello, Dolly!* into something magical is something truly otherworldly!

If Sean Penn doesn't win, you'll hear me throwing my shoe like an Iraqi journalist. Mickey Rourke did a fine job in *The Wrestler,* a minor drama, but his work is not in a class with Penn's. Penn gave the performance of the year, showing us sides of himself that we've never seen before, while immersing himself completely into the character of Harvey Milk. Penn found reserves of charm and playful humor that knocked me out. If he loses, people (myself included) will be shouting "Homophobia!" at the Academy, the way we did when *Brokeback* inexplicably lost Best Picture to the slick and unconvincing *Crash*. There was no reasonable claim for *Crash*'s superiority; *Brokeback* lost because of its content. You actually had Academy members (yes, you Tony Curtis and Ernest Borgnine) bragging about *not* voting for *Brokeback,* as if they were protecting the sanctity of the industry! (Protecting it from quality?) Penn should win because he deserves it, and the flimsy excuse of Rourke's comeback (did we really miss him?) is no justification for awarding him the prize. It's going to look a lot like fear of the gays, yet again.

And where was Clint Eastwood's Best Actor nomination? His performance in *Gran Torino,* like John Wayne's in *True Grit,* is a summation of a legendary career, and, on those terms, it should have been acknowledged. I think *Gran Torino* is one of his better films, far better than the Oscar-endowed stinker *Million Dollar Baby* or the horror known as *Changeling.* America responded to *Gran Torino,* but why didn't the Academy? I wish Hollywood made more unabashedly commercial-minded dramas for adults like this one, or last year's *Michael Clayton,* but we rarely see them anymore.

I admire Kate Winslet but her role in *The Reader* was an enigma, a two-dimensional question mark. In *Doubt,* I felt like I was watching Meryl Streep give a good performance but never for a moment believed she was that woman. It felt like play-acting. Poor Ms. Jolie, having to play, over and over again, scenes in *Changeling* in which she had one tear streaming down her face. My pick would be Anne Hathaway. *Rachel Getting Married* was uneven, but Hathaway had a mix of bravado and vulnerability, similar to Liza Minnelli in *The Sterile Cuckoo,* that was exciting and smart.

If the Academy had given Heath Ledger an Oscar for *Brokeback,* as they should have, we wouldn't have to be dealing with the issue of a posthumous Oscar. He was fantastic as the Joker, but I'd be just as glad to see Robert Downey, Jr., or Josh Brolin win. Both were terrific. Philip Seymour Hoffman's nomination is absurd because he has a star part! And Michael Shannon, good actor though he obviously is, is playing a device not a character in *Revolutionary Road,* a miserable movie that belongs to my least favorite genre in the world: the suburbia-is-hell-for-*everyone* genre.

If Penelope Cruz loses, you will hear my other shoe being tossed. *Vicky Cristina Barcelona* caused me to utter seven words I never thought I'd ever hear myself say again: "I loved the new Woody Allen movie!" Cruz was sensational and she deserves the award.

I'm hopeful about Hugh Jackman as the host, but still have an overriding dread about the wrongs about to be made by Oscar. At this point, why do I care? If I had that answer, then maybe I, too, could win big on *Who Wants to Be a Millionaire?*

I Can't Complain
February 23rd, 2009

Though I still feel that *Slumdog Millionaire* is a wildly overrated movie, I can't say I was surprised by its big wins last night. Even so, eight Oscars seems excessive even for a popular favorite, certainly for a film as small in many ways as *Slumdog.* But I was so pleased by just about everything else that I was nearly shouting "Jai Ho!" myself! The deserved wins of Sean Penn and Penelope Cruz were sweet to behold. I may not have been a fan of *The Reader,* but it's a relief to know that the wonderful Winslet has finally gotten her Oscar. And the win for Ledger was a heartfelt tribute to the best screen actor of his generation. His Joker is truly one of the screen's great villains.

I should have guessed that the stinkeroo Hollywood-musical production number was the handiwork of hack Baz Luhrmann. Even with the extraordinary gifts of Hugh Jackman and Beyonce Knowles, Baz found a way to suffocate the stage and create tacky incoherence.

I was moved by the use of five previous winners to present each of the acting awards. Sophia Loren! Eva Marie Saint! It's true that this added considerable time to the overall show but it also provided the night with its most compelling moments. Isn't this exactly the kind of thing we watch the Oscars to see? *Yes!* Will this become the Oscar standard in presenting acting awards? It very well might. Cut the numbing montages and give us more of these emotional and surprising moments!

The lowest point last night was the botching of the dead-people montage. It's very simple: all that has to happen is that we see the faces of those who passed away. So, what did we get? Well, you had to squint to see the faces because the camera was rarely close enough, and rarely steady! Dreadful!!

And how about those clips of the Best Picture nominees mixed up with classics of the past? Again, incoherence! And please never sing "Jai Ho" and the *Wall-E* song *at the same time!*

But there were some wonderful speeches (from Penn, Cruz, Winslet, Lance Black) and charming, spontaneous moments, like Kate Winslet's father whistling so she could find him in the audience. And will we ever again see anyone balance an Oscar on his chin?

Not Since "Casablanca"
June 30th, 2009

Not since *Casablanca* won the Best Picture Oscar on March 2, 1944, a mere 65 years ago, has the Academy nominated ten films in its top category. Last week's announcement of Oscar's return to ten Best Picture contenders has aroused much discussion, which must have been the overall intention, actually getting people to talk about the telecast (aside from simply complaining about how hopelessly bad it is). I think this is just the kind of stunt that may be a shot in the arm for the tired old Oscars, something that isn't wearily familiar. The best moments of last February's Oscars were the surprising appearances of five former Oscar winners presenting each of the acting awards, a never-before brainstorm that worked beautifully. Perhaps next year's show will also be able to benefit from a novelty (at least for the TV-age Oscars), that of ten best-pic nominees. But won't that also bog the show down, with five more movies to pay attention to?

For those who think that ten nominees will pollute the system, all I can say is, "Are you kidding me?" The Oscars have only marginally been about rewarding the year's best. They were (and are) first and foremost a promotional device, and then a self-congratulatory means for the industry to decide each year how it would like to represent itself to the world (often as a vessel of high-minded values, sensitivities, and diversity). It would take a lot more than five additional nominees to alter the "integrity" of a glamorous party festooned with gold trinkets.

Many feel that this all stems from the omission of *The Dark Knight* from the most recent slate of Best Picture selections, since it was last year's one blockbuster which actually went into the race's run-up with some momentum. (I thought it was just about the most unpleasurable summer movie I have ever seen, aside from Heath Ledger's great performance, and was glad to see it snubbed.) But do people really choose not to watch the Oscars when something like *The Dark Knight* isn't included? You either are an Oscar watcher or you aren't. Anyway, the impulse behind the change is to include more movies seen by the general public, instead of making Oscar night a telethon for independent movies. But, seriously, when was the last time you thought to yourself, "Oh, if only they could nominate five *more* movies!" I usually can't come up with five. Yes, if this were 1939, a year in which they conceivably could have nominated 25 movies, or perhaps 1941, 1946, 1950, or 1962, but they don't make ten great movies a year nowadays and haven't for decades! So, what can we look forward to next year? Nominations for *Star Trek* and *The Hangover*? But is this really any more ludicrous than Best Picture of the Year going to *Forrest Gump, Crash, Titanic,* or *Million Dollar Baby*? And *Slumdog Millionaire* ain't exactly *On the Waterfront*. Is this really a process that can be "tainted"?

So, now we will have five decoy nominees sneaking in among the "real" nominees. Add five blockbusters, fine, but be careful you don't end up merely with five more movies nobody saw. Then what? On to 15?

Then came word that Best Song will only be awarded if there are any songs deemed good enough to warrant having nominees at all, making Best Song an occasional award. Why beat a dead horse? This award should have been dropped entirely somewhere around 1970. It was a category first instituted in 1934 when the Academy realized that Broadway's greatest composers were also doing great work in Hollywood, adding to the Great American Songbook, something that went on for the next twenty years or so. It was an award that stemmed from the phenomenal output of songs from original movie musicals, a genre that died by the end of the fifties. Yet the award crept on. Yes, there have been some great Oscar-winning tunes in the last forty years, just not enough of them to warrant a Best Song category at this late date. Put it out of its misery. And then we never have to hear another one of them sung on the telecast!!!

And what's this about presenting honorary Oscars in November? Movie legends will not be given their moment on the main broadcast? Can this be true? Is this to make room for those clips from the additional picture nominees?

Go ahead, Academy, do what you feel you must to give a dead awards show a jolt, even if the odds are heavily against next year's winner being another *Casablanca*.

Julie and Julia and Meryl and Oscar
August 26th, 2009

W ell it looks as though Meryl Streep is finally poised to bring home that elusive third Oscar she has come so close to getting in recent years (thanks to *The Devil Wears Prada* and *Doubt*). Oscar will arrive for a role and a performance worth the wait, one of Streep's all-time best. She doesn't look anything like Julia Child yet she makes you believe she *is* the physically formidable Child by the end of her first scene. *Julie and Julia* is a surprisingly effective and rather touching story of one woman's life (Julie) transformed by that of another (Julia).

More than anything else, I experienced this film as an expression of our capacity to be inspired by something outside of ourselves. As Julia Child finds her road to self-actualization, Julie Powell (Amy Adams) charts her own course, *inspired* by Child's life and work. It is a lovely thing to behold. The movie also happens to be a good film about good marriages, featuring not one but two husbands with egos healthy enough to allow them to do all they can to help their wives' dreams come true. Not since the Tracy-Hepburn *Pat and Mike* (1952) has there been such a prominent film about a male assisting a female in her quest to be all that she can be professionally.

To say that *Julie and Julia* is the best film directed by Nora Ephron sounds like a back-handed compliment because most of her previous work is so cloying and pandering and strenuously adorable. Much of the credit goes to Streep. Yes, she is very funny in her Child-ish intonations and offbeat line readings, but this is also a Streep who has rarely been seen as a personality this charmingly expansive. Through Child, Streep embodies the power of enthusiasm in our world, the power of joy in our dealings with others. Her appetite—for her husband (Stanley Tucci), for food, for cooking and the writing of her cookbook—is infectiously irresistible. But so is the happy passion she feels for her friends, her equally tall sister, and her beloved Paris. Streep turns Child into a tower of positive energy, but, like anyone, she has her disappointments and bouts of depression. Still, gleeful determination comes naturally to her.

Many have said that the Amy Adams scenes bring the film down, yet there really wouldn't be much of a movie without them. Instead of a rote biopic charting a life's events, *Julie and Julia* finds its context as Julie focuses her life around the example set before her by Julia. Adams is delightful as always, and Streep hovers over these scenes like a fairy godmother who can be seen only by her Cinderella. The cutting back and forth between the two stories is sometimes clumsy, and it can make the film seem overlong, but mostly it plays smoothly, even buoyantly, and any imperfections are worth the end result.

To appreciate just how great Streep can be, pay attention to the dramatic scene in which Julia receives a letter from her now-married sister, the contents of which lead to a moment in which Streep exquisitely balances genuine happiness with profound sadness, making this the most moving moment in the film. And it's all in the subtext. Streep doesn't have to say a word for us to know exactly what Julia is feeling. Get ready for Oscar number three, Meryl, the icing on the cake. Or should I say gateau?

Oscar Has Two Faces
September 21st, 2009

Last week it was announced that Lauren Bacall would be receiving an honorary Oscar. Whatever you think about the merits of such a gesture (more on that later), one thing is inarguable, the tacky and downright shameful decision to present this award not on the March 7th telecast, as would normally be the case, but at a Board of Governors dinner to be held on November 14th. There is already such a dearth of genuine excitement at Oscar ceremonies, and now the Academy is going out of its way to avoid a moment with the potential of being the broadcast's highlight.

Whatever your opinion of Bacall, she is the living-breathing connection to Humphrey Bogart, one of the true icons of film history, thus making the award something of a tribute to their enduring magic as an essential team for classic-film lovers. Since Bacall is still in good shape, this would be a unique opportunity for the whole world to hear her thoughts on Bogie and some of the other legends who touched her life and career, including Marilyn Monroe, Howard Hawks, and Vincente Minnelli. But Bacall has been relegated to the Siberia of November, allowing more time in March for incoherent montages and songs that will never be sung again. Thank you, governors.

With her lifetime-achievement award given on the sly, Bacall can feel honored and slighted at the same time. The other special-award honorees (John Calley, Gordon Willis, and Roger Corman) also deserve the respect associated with an on-air presentation, but in their cases you can at least understand (from a TV producer's slant) that, as behind-the-scenes people, they are mostly unknown to viewers. Of course, it would be wonderful to expose the home audience to the contributions of Calley, Willis, and Corman, but I guess that's too much to ask at this point. However, Bacall is a freaking movie star! And people watch the Oscars to see stars, and not just those of the twentysomething variety.

That said, let me now question the selection of Bacall for an honor denied to such extraordinary talents as Ida Lupino, Joel McCrea, Robert Mitchum, James Mason, William Powell, Irene Dunne, and Jean Arthur. True, just because Oscar made so many mistakes in the past is no reason to continue doing so, but before you get to Bacall shouldn't you be honoring Doris Day and Jean Simmons? Since honorary Oscars usually go to major talents, where in Bacall's filmography are any great performances? Her status as Bogie's Baby, as the gal who knew how to whistle, is secure, but what are her artistic accomplishments? Bacall has lasted in the industry by accepting character parts in movies for the last forty years or so, including *Harper* (1966), *Murder on the Orient Express* (1974), and her Oscar-nominated turn as Barbra Streisand's mother in *The Mirror Has Two Faces* (1996). She was considered a sentimental shoo-in that year, so is Oscar making up for that shocking loss? She was good in the movie, but she stuck out even more for being the only touch of class amid pure wreckage.

Aside from Bacall's four pictures with Bogie, featuring their classic exchanges, most notably in *To Have and Have Not* (1944) and *The Big Sleep* (1946), what can the Academy be honoring her for, aside from career longevity? John Huston's *Key Largo* (1948), her final film with Bogie, is a good movie but Bacall is its weakest link. Douglas Sirk's *Written on the Wind* (1956) is now considered a classic, but Bacall sleepwalks her way through most of it. And she wasn't really up to exploring the depths inherent in her lesbian role opposite Kirk Douglas in *Young Man with a Horn* (1950).

Bacall's main talent was as a light sophisticated comedienne, though she was hardly in the league of the great ladies of the screwball era. I'd say that her best performance is in *How to Marry a Millionaire* (1953), in which she is witty, sharp, and altogether polished. Her intelligence shines through, and she has a star's energy and presence. She continued in this vein in *Woman's World* (1954) and *Designing Woman* (1957), but neither showcased her as effectively as *Millionaire* had.

Whatever my reservations, I still want to see Bacall get her Oscar before a standing ovation at the Kodak Theatre. Come on, Academy, it's not too late to fix this situation and give an old-fashioned movie star an old-fashioned tribute. Think how pissed off Bogie would be to see his baby treated so shabbily.

Something Old, Something New at the Oscars
March 8th, 2010

I t was great to see Kathryn Bigelow accepting an Oscar as the first female to win as Best Director, and it brought me a sigh of relief to see Jeff Bridges finally take home a prize that could have (and should have) been his many times in the last 35 years. Though I was pulling for Meryl Streep and her elusive third Oscar, I thought Sandra Bullock's speech was the evening's highlight. However, every year we hear about how different and how retooled the Oscar show is going to be. Then we sit down and there it is, the same misjudged and overinflated marathon we watched the year before. A decision had been made, quite disrespectfully to my way of thinking, to hand out honorary Oscars in

November rather than on the main telecast, supposedly to save precious TV time. So, why then did we get a 15-minute tribute to John Hughes? I admit I was the wrong age for Hughes' films, which mean nothing to me, but did he really warrant the kind of treatment one expects when paying tribute to a Hitchcock or a Spielberg? I would much rather have seen Lauren Bacall get her Oscar "live." And where was 1949 Best Actor nominee Richard Todd in the "memoriam" reel? Are the 1980s now the height of Hollywood nostalgia?

And we still got the requisite pointless montage (on horror films) and the laughable dance piece. Whenever the telecast has tried to be a variety show, it has spelled disaster. This has been the case every single time I've watched the Oscars (and I've seen forty of them). It was dumb when they used to "dance" the costume nominees, and it was dumb last night, watching wonderful dancers interpret *The Hurt Locker*. Can you say "kitsch"?

As a concept, I like having five stars come out to talk about the nominees, but it did bring the show to a screeching halt. If the Best Actor and Actress presentations were separated by an hour or so, then it wouldn't feel so numbing. And did you notice how many presenters said "And the winner is...," rather than the kinder-gentler "And the Oscar goes to..."? Was this accidental? I'm fine with the use of "winner," which is more honest. Are we supposed to pretend that nobody won or lost? But the tackiest bit of the night was the orchestra launching into "I Am Woman" following Bigelow's speech. The Oscars have caught up to the 1970s!

Meryl Streep has been nominated in the Best Actress category thirteen times and won only once *(Sophie's Choice)*. Katharine Hepburn was nominated twelve times and won four Oscars. For all the praise and accolades heaped upon Streep, she is starting to seem overlooked, even ignored (at least each year at Oscar time). Yes, she also has three supporting nominations and one win in that category *(Kramer vs. Kramer)*, but Streep hasn't heard her name called out at the Oscars since 1983.

I actually had a better time last night than in most years, simply because I agreed with more of the choices than I usually do. The ten Best Picture nominees seemed to do what they were supposed to do, broadening Oscar's reach for the TV audience. And it surely was a blessing not to have full performances of the nominated songs. After all, the song category is the one hanging on by a thread in terms of relevance, so why give it more time than any other award? Now if we can just get Meryl that third Oscar, all will be right in the world, at least in the skewed, magical, and addictive world in which Oscar rules.

The 1947 Best Actress Oscar Race
October 25th, 2010

I suffered through all of *Mourning Becomes Electra* last night, wondering how in heck anyone could have thought that Rosalind Russell was the Oscar front-runner back in 1947. Her performance contains absolutely nothing to remind us why we love Roz. Never has she been so fidgety and effortful and pinched, clearly straining to prove herself a great tragedienne. Eugene O'Neill's pretentious claptrap, his Civil War-era version of Aeschylus, is overwrought in the extreme. This prestige project brought prestige to no one involved.

Raymond Massey plays Roz's father in *Electra* and he also appeared that year with one of her Oscar competitors, Joan Crawford, in *Possessed*, which is certainly a lot more fun than watching Roz improbably linked romantically with a boyish Kirk Douglas. *Possessed* is 1947's *Fatal Attraction*, with Crawford losing her mind after being rejected by Van Heflin. Things get worse after she marries widower Massey. Geraldine Brooks, as Massey's grown daughter, becomes Heflin's new (and much younger) girlfriend. It's no accident that the plot, a stepmother-stepdaughter love triangle, parallels the mother-daughter triangle in *Mildred Pierce* (1945), Crawford's smash hit for which she received an Oscar and career resurrection. Though *Possessed* is nearly undone by its 1940s-style psychobabble, it has at least two great sequences: a haunting opening in which Crawford wanders L.A. streets asking people for "David"; and a later Crawford hallucination in which she imagines doing away with her stepdaughter. Crawford gives a very proficient performance that stays entirely on the surface of things, reveling in the more melodramatic flourishes in the plot while conveying nothing in the way of subtext or inner torment. When it comes to emotion, she is the great indicator. So, there's no depth, but this surely is a great-looking Warner Brothers movie, moody and stylish and visually textured, thanks to director Curtis Bernhardt.

It was Loretta Young in *The Farmer's Daughter* who beat Joan and Roz for the Oscar that year, in what is still considered the biggest upset in Oscar history. Though hardly award-caliber, Young was certainly charming and skillful in a lightweight political comedy, and she was definitely more satisfying in her role than Joan and Roz were in theirs. If you include the two remaining nominees—Dorothy McGuire in *Gentleman's Agreement* and Susan Hayward in *Smash-Up*—I'd declare Hayward, in her alcoholic warm-up for *I'll Cry Tomorrow,* as the worthiest of the five contenders. However, I'd have gone with three un-nominated performances as the year's best from a lead actress: Deborah Kerr in *Black Narcissus,* Joan Fontaine in *Ivy,* and Ida Lupino in *Deep Valley.*

Random Oscar Thoughts
January 28th, 2011

Every year it gets a little bit harder to work up much enthusiasm for the Oscars, which is a surprise to me considering how much I used to look forward to this time of year. It's actually never been the same for me since *Crash* beat *Brokeback Mountain,* signifying a new marker in Oscar's closed-mindedness, cowardice, and bad taste. Anyway, here are a few random thoughts about this year's slate of nominations.

Are there really people in the world who think that Natalie Portman's tediously whiny performance in *Black Swan* is superior to Annette Bening's consummate work in *The Kids Are All Right*? Bening, a versatile actress who seems able to play anything, should waltz away with a long-overdue Oscar this year. However, I never dreamed that voters could actually prefer Sandra Bullock in *The Blind Side* to Meryl Streep in *Julie and Julia,* but they did! This bodes well for Portman.

Cinematographer Roger Deakins has received his ninth nomination this year for *True Grit.* He has never won before, and his work in *True Grit* is richly deserving. Come on, give Roger an Oscar!

The Best Song category has been an embarrassment for the last forty years. The only thing that might have made it fun this year would have been a "live" performance by Cher, singing that generic power ballad from *Burlesque.* But it didn't get nominated. Just put the category to rest already!!

Why the snub to Ben Affleck's *The Town*? No picture or screenplay nominations, only one for Jeremy Renner's excellent supporting work. I really liked Affleck's movie and would have liked seeing it in the top ten, replacing one of the three I liked least: *Black Swan, Inception*, and *The Fighter. Black Swan* is the only one of the ten best-pic nominees not to have a screenplay nomination, which is encouraging, as is the omission of Christopher Nolan *(Inception)* from the nominees for director.

Bummer that the lovely documentary short *Keep Dancing,* about Marge Champion and Donald Saddler, didn't make the cut in its category.

Nice to see Nicole Kidman redeeming herself with *Rabbit Hole* after too many years of horrifying movies, the worst being the Baz Luhrmann atrocity *Australia.*

Hailee Steinfeld has the leading role in *True Grit*, so nominate her as Best Actress, or give her a special juvenile Oscar like they used to in the old days. But Best Supporting Actress? It's as ridiculous now as it was when Tatum O'Neal won in that category for her mammoth-sized role in *Paper Moon* (1973).

Christian Bale and Melissa Leo will probably win in the supporting categories, not for "best" acting but for "most" acting, always doing ten things in a scene when four or five might have been marvelous. (Only Amy Adams really came through for me in that movie.) Bale and Leo should watch Jeff Bridges in *True Grit* for a lesson in how to play a larger-than-life character without self-consciousness; he immerses himself in his role without trying to smother the audience or beat them into submission.

Bravo to Colin Firth for being a deserved shoo-in for Best Actor. But, damn, that James Franco was terrific, too.

Guess I'm not quite as "over" the Oscars as I thought. More to come as Feb. 27 approaches.

Oscar...Is That You?
February 28th, 2011

I guess we've all helped to kill the Academy Awards. Now anyone can predict the winners with a reasonably high success rate. Just pick up any magazine or newspaper (on- or off-line) and someone is there to tell you who to pick in your Oscar pool. Everyone seems to know that the winner of the DGA will probably take home the Oscar. So, each year the show becomes more and more of an anti-climax, a series of foregone conclusions played out over a supposedly suspenseful three-hour-plus broadcast. And all the participants live in fear of mistakes, or, God forbid, spontaneity. The top designers tell the actresses what to wear, so there's little room for Oscar's outrageous fashions of the past. Plus, Joan Rivers and others have scared every star in town with the threat of being ridiculed by a "fashion police." Criticism of the bad-old production numbers now results in no-frills telecasts, yet we still must suffer through performances of never-to-be-heard-again nominated songs. Everything has become so safe, so predictable, so careful, so *dead*.

Remember when you first heard that James Franco was hosting? You probably thought, "What? That sounds awful. He's a talented actor but he's not a personality." Well, we were right, weren't we? The Franco we initially imagined was the Franco we got last night. Watching him with Anne Hathaway was like watching a high school's cutest jock and perkiest cheerleader host the big class assembly. We watched as the jock froze, thus making the cheerleader become even perkier, realizing that she was now hosting for two. I like both Franco and Hathaway very much, but this was not a good match-up. How cruel to bring Billy Crystal out there, just in case anyone needed reminding about how long ago it was when the Oscars were last considered "entertainment."

The only way the Oscars can become exciting again is if they precede the Golden Globes and the SAG awards (which ain't gonna happen). Poor Colin Firth! By Oscar night, how many acceptance speeches had he given? Such pressure to be witty over and over! Whatever excitement there is during awards season is ironically all drained away by Oscar night. It's as if the Oscars are now merely the final stop, the bland consensus of all the awards that come before it, arriving just about the time that most of us have stopped caring. When they got to the "In Memoriam" segment last night, didn't it feel like it was last year's reel? Again, this is because *every* awards show now has their own version of this moment. There's so little left for Oscar to call his own.

But, about last night:

Tom Hanks made an elaborate speech about connecting Best Art Direction and Cinematography to Best Picture, only to give the first award (for art direction) to non-pic-nominee *Alice in Wonderland*. So, never mind, Tom!

I hate it when the favorite (yes, you Melissa Leo) pretends to be shocked, and then gives the worst, sloppiest acceptance speech of the night.

If you want to include someone as old and legendary as Kirk Douglas, then don't leave him out there alone. Give him a younger co-presenter and please let the youngster call out the winner!

Ironic to see lovely Cate Blanchett present the costume-design Oscar while wearing the ugliest dress in the Kodak Theatre.

Isn't it in bad taste to have the montage of Best Pic nominees playing to a soundtrack of Colin Firth in *The King's Speech*? We already knew it was going to win, but did they have to rub it in the other nominees' faces?

Another Oscar Shake-Up
June 16th, 2011

The Motion Picture Academy announced new rules this week, part of their recent ongoing mission to shake things up on Oscar night and (most importantly) add several million television viewers. The big news is in the Best Picture category, in which *between* five and ten nominees will be allowed, based on a new merit system involving points and percentages a bit too boring to go into. The intention is to keep Oscar followers and the entire Hollywood publicity machine off-guard, supposedly elevating the interest of the already interested, while delivering much more suspense on the road to the announcement of the nominations. But won't the five Best Director nominees still tip us off to the five *real* Best Pic nominees, however many others make the cut? I do agree, though, that any additional element of suspense at this point in Oscar history is most welcome. And, as if anyone needed reminding, such changes reiterate that, hey, it's just a show, however nice it is when the right person or movie occasionally wins. I look forward to the wonderful contradictions, such as when a movie is nominated in the directing category but isn't nominated for Best Picture even when seven or eight movies make the Best Pic list.

In the 1931-32 year, *Grand Hotel* won among eight nominees. Then in 1934 and 1935 there were twelve (!) Best Pic nominees, a situation that obviously allowed for some undeserving selections, including *Flirtation Walk, Here Comes the Navy,* and *One Night of Love* (in 1934), and *Broadway Melody of 1936* (in, yes, 1935). Today it wouldn't be hard to pick twelve outstanding movies from either 1934 or 1935, though I shudder at the thought of trying to come up with twelve in, say, any of the last five years. Five choices seems best for the movie world in which we live; ten seems wildly optimistic (remember the inclusion of *The Blind Side*?). By the way, two Clark Gable movies took the top prize in '34 and '35, first *It Happened One Night*, still one of Oscar's best choices, and then *Mutiny on the Bounty.*

The Tony Awards are coming off their best show in memory, a real throwback to the glory days (the '70s and '80s) when it was hands-down year-after-year the best night of "live" television. Maybe Oscar should get Neil Patrick Harris and Hugh Jackman to co-host. Sign them up—two truly gifted triple threats, uncontrollably charming and witty—and then viewers won't care how many nominees there are in the Best Picture category.

IX. Modern Times
screensaversmovies.com

Pixar Is My Pick
November 16th, 2008

Though we have about six weeks of holiday releases to come, filled with what is known as Oscar bait, I'd have to say that, as of right now, my favorite American film of the year is Pixar's computer-animated *Wall-E* (released this week on DVD). *Wall-E* is set on a no longer habitable Earth, 700 years in the future, seemingly occupied by only Wall-E (a trash compactor) and his roach companion, plus all the detritus left behind by humans (now living on a starship). Wall-E is fascinated by all these artifacts of humanity, particularly his treasured VHS copy of *Hello, Dolly!* He may not have great taste in movies, but the songs in *Dolly*, with their sentimental sweetness, heighten the poignancy in Wall-E's non-human ache to feel and love as we do.

When the film moves to the starship, its satire of humanity, initially scalding, is ultimately replaced with a surprising generosity of spirit. Instead of finger-wagging at earthlings for their super-sized, shopping-mad passivity (and for hastening the planet's demise), *Wall-E* is a hopeful and forgiving work. Call it an optimistic cautionary tale. Lacking smart-aleck smugness and heavy-handed condescension, *Wall-E* swept me away. I'm not embarrassed to admit that it moved me to tears.

Mamma Meryl!
January 9th, 2009

Remember when movie musicals were vehicles for artists who could wow you with their singing and/or dancing skills? That would have been the age of Astaire and Garland and Kelly. Or remember the age of vocal dubbing, when non-musical stars got leads in adaptations of Broadway musicals? This was often an unfortunate era but it did result in some wonderful performances, such as Deborah Kerr's in *The King and I* (1956). Well, *Mamma Mia!* brings us a new era in movie musicals, one so appalling that no one could ever have predicted it. This travesty of a musical is an actual celebration of the inability to sing and dance, a proud display of flaunting it even when you ain't got it! It's the karaoke bar of movie musicals. Where once Fred Astaire elevated audiences with his ability to make us believe that such perfection was possible, *Mamma Mia!* demeans the genre, attempting to sell us the idea that even you at home can be *fabulous* just by putting on platform shoes, wearing a boa, and "empowering" yourself! Talent be damned!

I've had several discussions with highly intelligent and accomplished women who found this dreck inspiring. I believe them, though it's impossible for me to see what kind of inspiration can come from such all-around incompetence. Is enthusiasm really enough? How can anyone who respects the movie musical as an art form not be offended by this horror show? And what does Meryl Streep think, knowing that her biggest box-office smash is actually the worst thing she's ever done?

The script is inanely plotted, the filmmaking is amateurish, and the songs are lamely "integrated" into the action. All you get is a bad-taste spectacle that ceaselessly panders. It's the you-can-do-it-too musical, except that almost no one in the darn thing *can*! Streep, who *can* sing, laughs her way through the "book" scenes, half out of embarrassment it would appear.

It's hard to pick out the worst moments because the film is so consistently awful. The only aspect of it that comes off well is Greece. And when we get to the "curtain call" encores and the cast asks us if we want more, it's a terrifying, surreal moment. No one shouted out "Yes" when I saw it, but that didn't stop them!

Doesn't anyone remember that the plot is the same as in the old Gina Lollobrigida comedy *Buona Sera, Mrs. Campbell* (1968)? Compared to *Mamma Mia!*, Gina's picture looks like *Some Like It Hot*.

I guess when a picture celebrates badness it's only fitting that it be bad itself. The recent DVD release warns us that it contains musical numbers "not shown in theaters." One can only wonder what was deemed not good enough to make the final cut. If Pierce Brosnan's vocals made it in, and Christine Baranski's hideous number on the beach, and the grotesque duet between Julie Walters and Stellan Skarsgard, what could possibly have been deemed unworthy?

At the Golden Globes this Sunday, *Mamma Mia!* is nominated for Best Picture (Musical or Comedy). Bravo, Hollywood Foreign Press!

Beating a Dead Kangaroo
February 28th, 2009

March 3rd is the day that *Australia* premieres on DVD. This just gives the movie, one of 2008's worst, an opportunity to be panned all over again. Here goes! Baz Luhrmann's work has always been love-it-or-hate-it and I have always been defiantly in the hate-it camp. But even Baz sunk to new lows with this lavish piece of mindless kitsch. If he loves old Hollywood so much, then why does he try to recreate it without any taste or intelligence? Is it because he's incapable of the genuine emotions that made those Golden Age classics so beloved? Is that why he turns everything into cliches and camp and overblown melodrama? *Australia* is more insult than homage. The result is an overinflated bore, at the center of which is one of the limpest and most hollow of love stories.

Instead of acting her role as the owner of a cattle ranch, Nicole Kidman huffs and puffs her way through the movie. She is so thin that I couldn't help but notice her resemblance to a pencil. Poor Hugh Jackman, usually so appealing, makes a very unconvincing rugged he-man, a supposedly butch drover. There's no chemistry or heat between the stars, though Baz seems obsessed with Hugh, photographing his face and body as if no one could resist him. Yet has he ever seemed so sexless?

And no one directs "comedy" as badly as Baz. There are many scenes played here in the unfunny *Moulin Rouge!* style of mugging till it hurts. We get caricatures instead of characters and a tone of flamboyant idiocy. It's an epic of World War II Down Under, but it's all wrapping with nothing inside. If you want to see a movie that earned a title as large as *Australia,* then go see *The Sundowners* (1960), a great Australian-set film starring Robert Mitchum and Deborah Kerr, both at their peaks. This *Australia* is a cautionary tale, not with regard to its war-torn plot, but as a warning about what happens when a hack director gets an enormous budget.

Jungle Red Turned Beige
March 18th, 2009

Many people are now catching up with the DVD of last summer's remake of the 1939 comedy gem *The Women,* one of the odder choices of a classic to be remade for the 21st century. Despite being hilarious, marvelously acted, and incredibly stylish, *The Women* of 1939 has been criticized for its all-out bitchery in dramatizing female friendships. But, forgiving its politically incorrect content, the original film is actually a blazing celebration of women, specifically the great comedic talents of an illustrious cast. Without being subservient to any men, the all-female ensemble cast, under George Cukor's perceptive direction, lets loose with sublime performances, with even some of the bit players, like Virginia Grey, able to steal a scene or two. Then there's Rosalind Russell and Mary Boland, my two favorites, each giving one of the funnier performances ever committed to film.

Cut to 2008 and Diane English's misguided attempt to update the material into a cross between *Sex and the City* and a Lifetime self-esteem movie. Instead of matching the original's ferocious comic power, the remake becomes a soggy, condescending female-empowerment picture, and you don't believe a minute of it. If you went hoping to see a new generation astonish you with their comic inventiveness, what you got instead was a group of women mired in something pandering and unconvincing, kind of a muted (and far less terrible) *Mamma Mia!*

The original may have been more hair-pulling and eye-scratching, but it was also better at showing actual female camaraderie. Nothing about the new cast convinces you that they are friends, or would even know each other. Meg Ryan, in the Norma Shearer role, is still stuck with a case of the "cutes" and it's not aging well. The gifted Annette Bening is undone by her role's rehashing of Kim Cattrall mixed with Meryl in *Prada*. Bening is never the lovable horror that Roz Russell was; she's annoyingly "humanized." And non-actress Eva Mendes is a dim shadow where the Joan Crawford role is supposed to be. (Crawford, as gold-digging Crystal, gave what was probably her finest performance.) Poor Debra Messing is given the scene we never want to see again, the screaming woman giving birth! Only the older gals score here: Bette Midler, reduced to a cameo in the great Boland role; Candice Bergen, as Ryan's mother; and, best of all, Cloris Leachman, as Ryan's housekeeper. This trio locates some truth and genuine humor beneath the superficial gloss.

I'll take 1939's bitchy wit and fast-paced dialogue over 2008's limp and declawed uplift any day. If Cukor's film sparkled with jungle-red nail polish, then English's film is more like nail-polish remover.

Glorious "Basterds"

September 1st, 2009

Inglourious Basterds, set primarily in 1944 France, is certainly the best Quentin Tarantino film since 1994's *Pulp Fiction* and easily one of the best films of 2009. Tarantino is quite the showman and, more than anything else, *Basterds* is an epic entertainment, a voluptuously conceived and executed WWII movie brimming with suspense and humor and outrageous characters. Yes, it's violent, but I never had to avert my eyes (as I did at *The Wrestler* or *Pan's Labyrinth*), and it's so much more than its violent content. Tarantino has the confidence to build scenes leisurely but always assuredly, such as the great opening sequence of the Nazi colonel (Christoph Waltz) interrogating a French farmer about the Jews he is suspected of hiding.

The film has real juice, made with the kind of energy I associate with the WWII films Hollywood churned out during the war itself, films that were high in intrigue and adventure and determinedly short on serious analysis of what was actually going on in the war. Brad Pitt is a hoot as Aldo Raine (Tarantino's nod to actor Aldo Ray), the leader of the titular group, his own band of American Jewish soldiers on a mission to terrorize the Nazis, a variation of a dirty dozen. Pitt's broad comic turn perfectly captures Tarantino's spirit, and the actor is a joy to watch throughout, even though the film is stolen by Waltz's Nazi. There have been suave and dazzling villains throughout film history, like all those Nazis Conrad Veidt played during the war, but Waltz seizes his role with such actorly relish that he becomes the film's overnight sensation. He has a laughing scene in a theatre lobby, at the film's climax, that is absolutely brilliant, preceding a sequence in which he reminds us of the colonel's harrowing capacity for sub-human behavior.

Tarantino offers set pieces of a kind we associate with the Golden Age, combining the pictorial grandeur of David Lean, the color sense of Vincente Minnelli, some Hitchcockian tensions, and the generous excesses of C.B. De Mille. Tarantino designs sequences to knock you out, some of which, like the finale, keep finding ways to top themselves. One such scene is remarkably quiet, up to a point. It is a barroom game played between a suspicious Nazi and some Allied spies, and it's mesmerizingly fun to watch, incrementally moving toward its unavoidable outburst of violence.

A subplot about a secretly Jewish young woman (Melanie Laurent) running a Paris movie theatre (while plotting some exquisite revenge on those who killed her family) gains considerable emotional power as the film proceeds. It is a lovely touch to use a movie theatre and film itself as agents for good-guy forces, an extravagantly romanticized notion of art defeating evil. Laurent's relationship with the Nazi soldier-hero (turned movie star, like a German Audie Murphy) is a fascinating almost-romance that peaks in an unforgettable showdown of conflicting emotions and inevitable disaster. The way Tarantino makes all his plot threads converge is impressive, as is that slam-bang finale, as beautiful and haunting as it is combustible.

Basterds is scary and funny and vibrantly alive. Its emotional undercurrents prevent it from being dismissible as a show-offy spectacle. Michael Fassbender, too briefly seen, adds gravity and wit to the proceedings, cast as a British spy and film critic (who specializes in German cinema). And Diane Kruger is glamorous and sly as a German movie star working for the Allies, giving the film a dash of Dietrich.

It may not be a great film, but it has spectacular moments and sequences, distinctive humor, even poetry. Not to celebrate its achievements is to cut yourself off from the visceral pleasures of the movies. There isn't enough good work out there for us to ignore such a special motion picture.

A 5, 6, 7, 8...Nine
January 7th, 2010

I love Rob Marshall's film of *Chicago* (2002), but everything that went right with *Chicago* has gone sadly wrong with *Nine*, his film of the 1982 Broadway musical based on Fellini's screen masterpiece *8 1/2* (1963). *Chicago* was a triumph in concept, with all its musical numbers presented as expressions of Roxie Hart's imagination, and it was also a case of dream casting, with three stars (not known for their singing and dancing) doing a bang-up job in roles perfectly suited to their personalities. *Nine* is a movie in search of a concept; Marshall and his team never figured out *how* to make a movie of *Nine*. Almost all the numbers are done on the same half-dressed soundstage, a visual that gets old very fast and offers little illumination. And it doesn't even make sense, since not all the songs are coming from the perspective of Daniel Day-Lewis' Guido Contini, film director.

The original Broadway production soared on Tommy Tune's breathtaking stage pictures and ceaseless cleverness, and the recent inferior revival was salvaged by the considerable magnetism of Antonio Banderas. Which brings me to another reason why *Nine* fails: Daniel Day-Lewis. Even the critics who have hated this movie have been kind to its star. Day-Lewis is too highly regarded to get picked on, but it's only fair to report when he is bad, and he's bad in

Nine. He may be a great actor, but he lacks what a movie musical needs, a star personality. It's not that Guido is supposed to be a stud, but he does require the charisma to have so many women whirling through his life. Early reports that Javier Bardem was going to star as Guido were encouraging because Bardem has exactly what *Nine* needs. Without a star of that kind of vitality, a modern-day Marcello Mastroianni, the film has no center. Day-Lewis is a charmless shell here, and with a bad Italian accent.

Now to the bevy of women: Kate Hudson, as a reporter, is stuck with a new awful song ("Cinema Italiano") and the tackiest production number; Sophia Loren, as Guido's mama, wafts through like a legend, but it was hardly worth her trouble; Nicole Kidman is statuesque and toneless in her solo; Judi Dench at least has a dry humor as Guido's costume designer; Penelope Cruz can do no wrong lately, and she comes off as both delicious and touching as Guido's mistress. My favorite performance here is Marion Cotillard's as Guido's wife. Her ballad, "My Husband Makes Movies," is the only musical scene that offers anything personal or affecting. Amid much frenzy, Cotillard takes her time and delivers a lovely, intimate performance. For the most part, though, Marshall strands his illustrious band of talented ladies.

Chicago clicked with the public partially because it was so thematically fresh, expressing the lust for fame familiar to audiences in a world of reality-TV and a 24-hour news cycle. *Nine* comes off as nothing more than the whinings of a self-absorbed artist. Though I had been moved by the show in 1982 (I even saw it twice), and admire Fellini's film, this *Nine* seems so unnecessary, so useless and meandering. It may be relatively short but it feels interminably long. And has Italy ever been photographed this way, as if the sun never comes out?

I thought Rob Marshall was the guy we had been waiting for, someone to make a string of classy and dazzling movie musicals, but *Nine* makes it look as though he has already run out of inspiration.

A Not So Singular "Single Man"
January 14th, 2010

B elieve me, I hate to complain about the new gay-themed movie *A Single Man*, but I can't help it: I think I'm done with the sad-gay-man genre. I am more than ready for something *else*. I'm also tired of big gay-themed films that are period pieces. I want to see prominent film actors as gay characters in contemporary stories, and I wouldn't mind the occasional happy ending. I would at the very least like to see gay characters alive at the end of their movies. Is this really too much to ask in 2010?

The extraordinary *Brokeback Mountain* will, for many years to come, be the last word in the sad-gay-man genre, and nothing about *A Single Man* comes close to its impact. *Brokeback* is not only a great "gay" movie, but it gave the community a classic Hollywood love story to call its own, one to stand alongside the likes of *Casablanca* or *The Way We Were*. In the years since *Brokeback*, the biggest gay movie has been *Milk*, which did offer a strong and inspiring gay protagonist, but one who is martyred, in a film set in the '70s. It is important to have our stories told, our history acknowledged, and our heroes celebrated, but movies like *Milk* simply aren't enough anymore.

The recent gay films have contained some phenomenal performances, with Heath Ledger's Ennis Del Mar and Sean Penn's Harvey Milk two of the finest of the just-ended decade. Both can hold their place beside Peter Finch in the British *Sunday, Bloody Sunday* (1971), the first truly great performance in the sad-gay-man genre. Finch plays a successful doctor in the film, which still gets bonus points for being a contemporary drama about a gay life. One of the reasons so many gay men (including myself) love the little English film *Beautiful Thing* (1996), which I write about in my book *Screen Savers*, is that it turns the usual coming-out yarn into an exhilarating first-love story, leaving you on an emotional high, as well as a feeling of genuine empowerment.

Set in 1962 Los Angeles and featuring a British main character played by Colin Firth, *A Single Man* is awfully reminiscent of *Gods and Monsters* (1998), in which Ian McKellen plays aging gay film director James Whale. *A Single Man* is set five years after *Gods*, but they end up in roughly the same place, with the older gay Englishman finding himself in his home with a hot young male in nothing but a towel. McKellen and Firth are also both on the verge of suicide. In other words, I've seen *A Single Man* before, on many levels, another movie about a sad and gentle gay man suffering in silence. The 1964 Christopher Isherwood novel on which it is based was a groundbreaker in its matter-of-fact treatment of a gay life, but we're not in 1964 anymore.

A Single Man is actually not helped by Firth's fine performance. Firth has long been a master of minimalism and understatement, but this role plays too much to his strengths, actually depriving the performance of any surprises. If someone like Hugh Grant had played this character, a college professor, the film might have had more of a charge of the unexpected, rather than being merely another chance to admire Firth's clenched emotions and impeccable repression. His casting is simply too ideal. And I don't feel that director Tom Ford has added anything to the piece by injecting a *'night, Mother* device of

Firth's planned suicide, adding more melodrama than depth. I would much rather see the character continue to deal with his grief over the death of his longtime partner (Matthew Goode) than choose to opt out.

Am I too jaded to be wondering why Firth doesn't have sex with the gorgeous, intelligent, and sensitive Spanish hustler that he has already given money to? If you are planning to kill yourself later that evening, why not go out with a literal bang? Would that have made us take Firth's honorable angst less seriously? We know he still feels lust because of his earlier gaze on those shirtless athletes, so, again, why not? Equally confusing is the moment when Firth's best friend (Julianne Moore) refers to his great love as a "substitution," angering him only briefly. I'm sorry, but that comment—your best friend calling your 16-year gay relationship a substitution for a "normal" relationship—justifies grabbing one's coat and slamming the door. Again, his manners trump logic.

A Single Man has touching moments and is made with obvious care, and Firth's admirable performance will get him an Oscar nomination. But I imagined Firth's entire performance before I saw the movie, and I was dead-on. What I am ready for is the movie in which Firth and Hugh Grant get married, or the one in which George Clooney and Brad Pitt adopt kids together, or the drama about Sean Penn and Johnny Depp getting involved in the battle for marriage equality, or the triangular romantic comedy starring Ryan Reynolds, Ryan Gosling, and Jake Gyllenhaal. Please let's broaden the spectrum of what constitutes a gay-themed movie. Who will be man enough to take the next step?

85 Quizzes for Golden Age Movie Lovers

H ere's what you might call a delayed bonus round to my quiz book
And You Thought You Knew Classic Movies! (1999). The writing of
that book had been such all-consuming fun that I couldn't turn my
brain off simply because the book had gone to press. I continued to create
quizzes on and off for the next twelve years, mostly for my own pleasure since
I was never sure that there would be the right format in which to share them.

I present these 85 quizzes in the order in which I wrote them, rather than
categorizing them by topic. I hope this results in a pleasantly unpredictable
ride. If you recall my original book, you'll recognize new variations on former
quizzes. In some cases, I wanted to kick myself for thinking them up *after* the
first book had been published.

Again, they are predominantly matching quizzes, which is helpful when
guessing is involved. If the quizzes were easier, they wouldn't be as much fun
(at least that's what I tell myself). You'll find the answers immediately following the final quiz. If you've read all of this book's preceding text, you'll be in
much better shape to score well.

Quizzes

1. GET A NAME! Match the unusual (to say the least) character name to the actress who played her.

1. Vantine	a. Eva Marie Saint in *All Fall Down*
2. Keechie	b. Ethel Waters in *Pinky*
3. Fluff	c. Paula Prentiss in *Where the Boys Are*
4. Dicey	d. Bette Davis in *Kid Galahad*
5. Bijou	e. Cathy O'Donnell in *They Live By Night*
6. Tuggle	f. Marlene Dietrich in *Seven Sinners*
7. Echo	g. Carroll Baker in *Giant*
8. Zosh	h. Jean Harlow in *Red Dust*
9. Luz	i. Norma Shearer in *Smilin' Through*
10. Moonyeen	j. Eleanor Parker in *The Man with the Golden Arm*

2. And that goes for the fellas, too!

1. Bilge	a. Lionel Barrymore in *Captains Courageous*
2. Disko	b. Robert Young in *The Canterville Ghost*
3. Polo	c. John Wayne in *Angel and the Badman*
4. Berry Berry	d. Randolph Scott in *Follow the Fleet*
5. Cuffy	e. John Garfield in *Saturday's Children*
6. Rims	f. Mickey Rooney in *National Velvet*
7. Skid	g. Warren Beatty in *All Fall Down*
8. Quirt	h. Anthony Franciosa in *A Hatful of Rain*
9. Mi	i. Fred MacMurray in *Swing High, Swing Low*
10.Boake	j. Charlton Heston in *Ruby Gentry*

3. It surely must feel nice to get the vote of confidence that comes with an "Introducing..." credit announcing your arrival on the silver screen. Match the soon-to-be "name" to the film that officially launched him/her.

1. Maureen O'Hara	a. *The Romance of Rosy Ridge*
2. George Peppard	b. *Home in Indiana*
3. Janet Leigh	c. *Blonde Fever*
4. Faye Dunaway	d. *Dark City*
5. Patricia Neal	e. *The High Cost of Loving*
6. Jeanne Crain	f. *The Strange One*
7. Kim Novak	g. *John Loves Mary*
8. Gena Rowlands	h. *Jamaica Inn*
9. Gloria Grahame	i. *The Happening*
10. Charlton Heston	j. *Pushover*

4. Though your name is preceded by "Introducing," there's no guarantee of success, even if your debut film is a big one. Match the performer to the famous film that introduced him/her without resulting in stardom.

1. Susan Harrison	a. *The Bridge on the River Kwai*
2. Linda Harrison	b. *The Fortune Cookie*
3. Donna Anderson	c. *On the Beach*
4. Cathy O'Donnell	d. *The Garden of Allah*
5. Judi West	e. *The Best Years of Our Lives*
6. Hazel Brooks	f. *The Caine Mutiny*
7. Doe Avedon	g. *Sweet Smell of Success*
8. Tilly Losch	h. *Planet of the Apes*
9. Geoffrey Horne	i. *The High and the Mighty*
10. Robert Francis	j. *Body and Soul*

5. Preceding each famous film, I have listed the actress most associated with it. However, these actresses were not necessarily the stars of these films. Match each film to the actress who is the top-billed female in its opening credits.

1. Ginger Rogers in *Flying Down to Rio*   a. Janet Leigh

2. Luise Rainer in *The Great Ziegfeld*   b. Valerie Hobson

3. Angela Lansbury in *The Picture of Dorian Gray*   c. Bebe Daniels

4. Hedy Lamarr in *Algiers*   d. Signe Hasso

5. Ruby Keeler in *42nd Street*   e. Sigrid Gurie

6. Elizabeth Taylor in *Father of the Bride*   f. Joan Bennett

7. Peggy Lee in *Pete Kelly's Blues*   g. Donna Reed

8. Miyoshi Umeki in *Sayonara*   h. Myrna Loy

9. Shelley Winters in *A Double Life*   i. Dolores Del Rio

10. Elsa Lanchester in *Bride of Frankenstein*   j. Patricia Owens

6. Sometimes a mere title just isn't enough. Match each film title to its accompanying subtitle.

1. *Scarface* (1932)   a. *A Suitable Case for Treatment*

2. *Monsieur Verdoux*   b. *A Story of the London Fog*

3. *Susan Lenox*   c. *The Shame of a Nation*

4. *Kitty Foyle*   d. *A Song of Two Humans*

5. *Morgan*   e. *The Story of a Woman*

6. *Broken Blossoms*   f. *Her Fall and Rise*

7. *Dr. Strangelove*   g. *A Comedy of Murders*

8. *The Lodger* (1926)   h. *The Natural History of a Woman*

9. *Smash-Up*   i. *Or The Yellow Man and the Girl*

10. *Sunrise*   j. *Or How I Learned to Stop Worrying and Love the Bomb*

7. Match the star to the film for which he/she received an Oscar nomination in the supporting category.

1. Paulette Goddard	a. *Georgy Girl*
2. Maximilian Schell	b. *The Day of the Locust*
3. Joan Blondell	c. *Duel in the Sun*
4. James Mason	d. *The Bold and the Brave*
5. Anne Baxter	e. *The Blue Veil*
6. Burgess Meredith	f. *Judgment at Nuremburg*
7. Lillian Gish	g. *Julia*
8. Montgomery Clift	h. *So Proudly We Hail!*
9. Jennifer Jones	i. *Since You Went Away*
10. Mickey Rooney	j. *The Razor's Edge*

8. It's very amusing when identical character names appear in unrelated films. One of the performances on the right shares the previously existing—but in no way connected—character name of one of the performances on the left. Match them.

1. Clifton Webb as Robert Jordan in *Mister Scoutmaster*

a. Paul Newman in *The Towering Inferno*

2. Gene Kelly as Harry Palmer in *For Me and My Gal*

b. Charlton Heston in *Planet of the Apes*

3. William Demarest as Steve Martin in *The Jolson Story*

c. Spencer Tracy in *Inherit the Wind*

4. Jason Robards as Henry Drummond in *A Big Hand for the Little Lady*

d. James Stewart in *Thunder Bay*

5. Henry Fonda as Doug Roberts in *Mister Roberts*

e. Michael Caine in *The Ipcress File*

6. William Powell as John Prentice in *Evelyn Prentice*

f. Gene Kelly in *Cover Girl*

7. Joel McCrea as Johnny Jones in *Foreign Correspondent*

g. Gary Cooper in *For Whom the Bell Tolls*

8. John Hodiak as George Taylor in *Somewhere in the Night*

h. Alexander Scourby in *Affair in Trinidad*

9. Andy Devine as Danny McGuire in *A Star Is Born* (1937)

i. Ronald Reagan in *This Is the Army*

10. Gregory Ratoff as Max Fabian in *All About Eve*

j. Sidney Poitier in *Guess Who's Coming to Dinner*

9. Yes, we all know about Hitchcock and his blondes. What about his other female stars? Match the nonblonde actress to the Hitchcock film in which she appeared.

1. Jane Wyman	a. *Shadow of a Doubt*
2. Shirley MacLaine	b. *The Lady Vanishes*
3. Sylvia Sidney	c. *Sabotage*
4. Alida Valli	d. *Stage Fright*
5. Margaret Lockwood	e. *The Paradine Case*
6. Laraine Day	f. *The Trouble with Harry*
7. Ruth Roman	g. *Jamaica Inn*
8. Suzanne Pleshette	h. *Foreign Correspondent*
9. Maureen O'Hara	i. *Strangers on a Train*
10. Teresa Wright	j. *The Birds*

10. Match the performer to the two Hitchcock films in which he/she appeared.

1. Herbert Marshall	a. *Marnie; Family Plot*
2. Nigel Bruce	b. *Rope; Strangers on a Train*
3. Hume Cronyn	c. *To Catch a Thief; North by Northwest*
4. Vera Miles	d. *Shadow of a Doubt; Lifeboat*
5. Robert Cummings	e. *Rebecca; Suspicion*
6. Farley Granger	f. *The Wrong Man; Psycho*
7. Bruce Dern	g. *Jamaica Inn; The Paradine Case*
8. Michael Wilding	h. *Murder; Foreign Correspondent*
9. Charles Laughton	i. *Saboteur; Dial M for Murder*
10. Jessie Royce Landis	j. *Under Capricorn; Stage Fright*

11. Match the actress to the film in which she played a fictional movie star.

1. Esther Williams	a. *She's Back on Broadway*
2. Shirley MacLaine	b. *Silk Stockings*
3. Kim Novak	c. *My Geisha*
4. Joan Crawford	d. *Bombshell*
5. Ginger Rogers	e. *You're My Everything*
6. Janis Paige	f. *Dreamboat*
7. Jean Harlow	g. *The Ice Follies of 1939*
8. Virginia Mayo	h. *On an Island with You*
9. Leslie Caron	i. *The Legend of Lylah Clare*
10. Anne Baxter	j. *The Man Who Understood Women*

12. Match the actor to the film in which he played a boxer.

1. Anthony Quinn	a. *Kid Galahad* (1937)
2. Tony Curtis	b. *Right Cross*
3. John Garfield	c. *Requiem for a Heavyweight*
4. Wayne Morris	d. *City for Conquest*
5. Robert Ryan	e. *Flesh and Fury*
6. William Holden	f. *Body and Soul*
7. Douglas Fairbanks, Jr.	g. *Invitation to Happiness*
8. Ricardo Montalban	h. *The Set-Up*
9. James Cagney	i. *The Life of Jimmy Dolan*
10. Fred MacMurray	j. *Golden Boy*

13. Match the performer to the film in which he/she played a schoolteacher.

1. Jennifer Jones	a. *A Letter to Three Wives*
2. Charles Laughton	b. *Bigger than Life*
3. Shirley MacLaine	c. *Peyton Place*
4. Richard Kiley	d. *The Accused* (1949)
5. James Mason	e. *Two Loves*
6. Kirk Douglas	f. *These Three*
7. Mildred Dunnock	g. *This Land Is Mine*
8. Paul Henreid	h. *Goodbye, Mr. Chips* (1939)
9. Miriam Hopkins	i. *Good Morning, Miss Dove*
10. Loretta Young	j. *Blackboard Jungle*

14. Match the actress to the film in which she appeared with John Garfield.

1. Eleanor Parker	a. *We Were Strangers*
2. Shelley Winters	b. *Pride of the Marines*
3. Ida Lupino	c. *The Breaking Point*
4. Frances Farmer	d. *Gentleman's Agreement*
5. Hedy Lamarr	e. *The Sea Wolf*
6. Maureen O'Hara	f. *Tortilla Flat*
7. Jennifer Jones	g. *The Fallen Sparrow*
8. Patricia Neal	h. *He Ran All the Way*
9. Ann Sheridan	i. *Castle on the Hudson*
10. Dorothy McGuire	j. *Flowing Gold*

15. Match the actor to the film in which he appeared with John Wayne.

1. Lee Marvin	a. *The High and the Mighty*
2. Stewart Granger	b. *Reap the Wild Wind*
3. Ray Milland	c. *They Were Expendable*
4. Dean Martin	d. *Donovan's Reef*
5. Robert Montgomery	e. *Pittsburgh*
6. William Holden	f. *North to Alaska*
7. Robert Stack	g. *The Alamo*
8. Randolph Scott	h. *Flying Leathernecks*
9. Richard Widmark	i. *The Horse Soldiers*
10. Robert Ryan	j. *Rio Bravo*

16. Before Marilyn Monroe hit it big in 1953, she had been a busy support-ing player. Match each actress to the Monroe film in which she played a more significant role than Marilyn did.

1. Anne Baxter	a. *Clash by Night*
2. Claudette Colbert	b. *Monkey Business*
3. Barbara Stanwyck	c. *As Young As You Feel*
4. Constance Bennett	d. *Right Cross*
5. Ginger Rogers	e. *Let's Make It Legal*
6. June Haver	f. *Love Happy*
7. Vera-Ellen	g. *A Ticket to Tomahawk*
8. Marjorie Reynolds	h. *Love Nest*
9. Jean Hagen	i. *Hometown Story*
10. June Allyson	j. *The Asphalt Jungle*

17. Match the performer to the musical in which he/she danced with Fred Astaire. I've given Ginger and Cyd and Judy, among others, a rest.

1. George Murphy	a. *Holiday Inn*
2. Lucille Bremer	b. *Silk Stockings*
3. Joan Leslie	c. *Funny Face*
4. Betty Hutton	d. *Easter Parade*
5. Olga San Juan	e. *Broadway Melody of 1940*
6. Ann Miller	f. *Blue Skies*
7. Kay Thompson	g. *Let's Dance*
8. Paulette Goddard	h. *Second Chorus*
9. Janis Paige	i. *The Sky's the Limit*
10. Marjorie Reynolds	j. *Yolanda and the Thief*

18. Match the actress to the Frank Capra film in which she appeared.

1. Jane Wyman	a. *State of the Union*
2. Priscilla Lane	b. *Platinum Blonde*
3. Loretta Young	c. *Lost Horizon*
4. Ann Miller	d. *A Hole in the Head*
5. Jane Wyatt	e. *Arsenic and Old Lace*
6. Angela Lansbury	f. *You Can't Take It With You*
7. Eleanor Parker	g. *Pocketful of Miracles*
8. Hope Lange	h. *The Bitter Tea of General Yen*
9. Myrna Loy	i. *Broadway Bill*
10. Barbara Stanwyck	j. *Here Comes the Groom*

19. Match the actor to the film in which he appeared with Cary Grant.

1. John Garfield	a. *My Favorite Wife*
2. Melvyn Douglas	b. *Gunga Din*
3. José Ferrer	c. *Arsenic and Old Lace*
4. Victor McLaglen	d. *Crisis*
5. Ronald Colman	e. *The Pride and the Passion*
6. Fredric March	f. *The Eagle and the Hawk*
7. Randolph Scott	g. *Destination Tokyo*
8. Frank Sinatra	h. *The Grass Is Greener*
9. Raymond Massey	i. *The Talk of the Town*
10. Robert Mitchum	j. *Mr. Blandings Builds His Dream House*

20. Match the performer to the *two* versions of the same story in which he/ she appeared, sometimes in the same role, as when Clark Gable starred in both *Red Dust* (1932) and *Mogambo* (1953), and sometimes having aged into a different role, as when Jane Greer appeared in both *Out of the Past* (1947) and *Against All Odds* (1984).

1. Mickey Rooney	a. *Jesse James* (1939) *The True Story of Jesse James* (1957)
2. George Tobias	b. *Holiday* (1930) *Holiday* (1938)
3. Una Merkel	c. *The Major and the Minor* (1942) *You're Never Too Young* (1955)
4. Edward Everett Horton	d. *Ninotchka* (1939) *Silk Stockings* (1957)
5. Miriam Hopkins	e. *The Merry Widow* (1934) *The Merry Widow* (1952)
6. Alan Hale	f. *Kid Galahad* (1937) *The Wagons Roll at Night* (1941)
7. Humphrey Bogart	g. *These Three* (1936) *The Children's Hour* (1961)
8. John Carradine	h. *The Prisoner of Zenda* (1922) *The Prisoner of Zenda* (1952)
9. Diana Lynn	i. *Robin Hood* (1922) *The Adventures of Robin Hood* (1938)

10. Lewis Stone   j. *Ah, Wilderness!* (1935)
                               Summer Holiday (1948)

21. It's a hoot when an old movie features a character with a name that would later become famous as a *real person's name*. Match each of these characters to the actor who played him. These are really tough to get but worth including for their considerable amusement value.

1. Ed Harris	a. Richard Gaines in *Double Indemnity*
2. James Taylor	b. Mickey Rooney in *Strike Up the Band*
3. George Burns	c. Edward Arnold in *Mr. Smith Goes to Washington*
4. George Hamilton	d. J. Carrol Naish in *Frisco Jenny*
5. Edward Norton	e. Frank Albertson in *Ah, Wilderness!*
6. Dick Cheney	f. George Gobel in *The Birds and the Bees*
7. Arthur Miller	g. Tim Matheson in *Divorce American Style*
8. Mark Harmon	h. William Haines in *Tell It to the Marines*
9. Jimmy Connors	i. Wallace Beery in *The Bowery*
10. Chuck Connors	j. David Manners in *The Ruling Voice*

22. And the same goes for the ladies…

1. Helen Hunt	a. Irene Dunne in *Penny Serenade*
2. Jane Alexander	b. Loretta Young in *Midnight Mary*
3. Rita Wilson	c. Stefanie Powers in *Die! Die! My Darling!*
4. Pat Carroll	d. Margaret Sullavan in *Appointment for Love*
5. Carol King	e. Jean Parker in *Sequoia*
6. Julie Adams	f. Deborah Kerr in *The End of the Affair*
7. Toni Martin	g. Barbara Stanwyck in *You Belong to Me*
8. Sarah Miles	h. Barbara Stanwyck in *His Brother's Wife*
9. Mary Martin	i. Gladys Cooper in *The Bishop's Wife*
10. Mrs. George Hamilton	j. Joan Blondell in *Gold Diggers of 1933*

23. Match the vocalist to the film for which he/she provided the singing voice for the title tune.

1. Eydie Gorme	a. *Sunday in New York*
2. Mel Torme	b. *Until They Sail*
3. Perry Como	c. *Autumn Leaves*
4. Tony Bennett	d. *Gunfight at the O.K. Corral*
5. Vic Damone	e. *The Marriage-Go-Round*
6. Cher	f. *That Darn Cat*
7. Frankie Laine	g. *Somebody Up There Likes Me*
8. Ray Charles	h. *Alfie*
9. Nat "King" Cole	i. *Separate Tables*
10. Bobby Darin	j. *In the Heat of the Night*

24. Match the actress to the film in which she appeared with Robert Taylor.

1. Vivien Leigh	a. *Johnny Eager*
2. Arlene Dahl	b. *Ivanhoe*
3. Joan Crawford	c. *Waterloo Bridge*
4. Lana Turner	d. *Quo Vadis*
5. Eleanor Parker	e. *The Gorgeous Hussy*
6. Kay Kendall	f. *Rogue Cop*
7. Deborah Kerr	g. *Ambush*
8. Joan Fontaine	h. *Quentin Durward*
9. Ava Gardner	i. *Valley of the Kings*
10. Janet Leigh	j. *Knights of the Round Table*

25. Match the pair of female stars to the film in which they both appeared.

1. Jean Simmons/Deborah Kerr	a. *Ziegfeld Girl*
2. Deborah Kerr/Rita Hayworth	b. *Hold Back the Dawn*
3. Rita Hayworth/Olivia de Havilland	c. *Boom Town*
4. Olivia de Havilland/Paulette Goddard	d. *Reap the Wild Wind*
5. Paulette Goddard/Susan Hayward	e. *Dr. Jekyll and Mr. Hyde*
6. Susan Hayward/Ingrid Bergman	f. *Separate Tables*
7. Ingrid Bergman/Lana Turner	g. *The Strawberry Blonde*
8. Lana Turner/Hedy Lamarr	h. *The Grass Is Greener*
9. Hedy Lamarr/Claudette Colbert	i. *Under Two Flags*
10. Claudette Colbert/Rosalind Russell	j. *Adam Had Four Sons*

26. Match the song to the usually nonsinging star who sings it in a movie.

1. "It's Only a Paper Moon"	a. Ralph Bellamy in *The Awful Truth*
2. "Comin' Through the Rye"	b. Jason Robards in *A Thousand Clowns*
3. "The Varsity Drag"	c. Vivien Leigh in *A Streetcar Named Desire*
4. "Don't Sit Under the Apple Tree"	d. Peter O'Toole in *The Ruling Class*
5. "Yes Sir, That's My Baby"	e. Lillian Gish in *Duel in the Sun*
6. "Home on the Range"	f. Ava Gardner in *Mogambo*
7. "Aura Lee"	g. Robert Mitchum in *Heaven Knows, Mr. Allison*
8. "My Darling Clementine"	h. Bette Davis in *Beyond the Forest*
9. "Chicago"	i. Frances Farmer in *Come and Get It*
10. "Beautiful Dreamer"	j. Robert Walker and Jennifer Jones in *Since You Went Away*

27. Match the pet to the film in which it appears.

1. Emma (a snake)	a. *The Awful Truth*
2. George (a dog)	b. *The Fallen Idol*
3. Mr. Smith (a dog)	c. *Courage of Lassie*
4. Pywacket (a cat)	d. *Friendly Persuasion*
5. MacGregor (a snake)	e. *Bringing Up Baby*
6. Samantha (a goose)	f. *The Man Who Laughs*
7. Bill (a dog)	g. *The Lady Eve*
8. Homo (a wolf)	h. *I Remember Mama*
9. Gertrude (a duck)	i. *Journey to the Center of the Earth*
10. Uncle Elizabeth (a cat)	j. *Bell, Book and Candle*

28. Match the 30s/40s star to the 60s/70s film in which he/she is a supporting player.

1. Walter Pidgeon	a. *The Towering Inferno*
2. Charles Laughton	b. *Barefoot in the Park*
3. Charles Boyer	c. *Grease*
4. Ray Milland	d. *Spartacus*
5. Chester Morris	e. *Love Story*
6. Joan Blondell	f. *The Great White Hope*
7. Constance Bennett	g. *Madame X*
8. Jennifer Jones	h. *Heaven Can Wait*
9. Martha Scott	i. *Funny Girl*
10. James Mason	j. *The Turning Point*

29. Match the Oscar-winning performance to a previous collaboration between the performer and his/her Oscar-providing director.

1. Donna Reed in Fred Zinnemann's *From Here to Eternity*	a. *The Little Foxes*
2. James Cagney in Michael Curtiz's *Yankee Doodle Dandy*	b. *The Major and the Minor*
3. Olivia de Havilland in Mitchell Leisen's *To Each His Own*	c. *Boomerang!*
4. Gary Cooper in Howard Hawks' *Sergeant York*	d. *Jimmy the Gent*
5. Judy Holliday in George Cukor's *Born Yesterday*	e. *Eyes in the Night*
6. Thomas Mitchell in John Ford's *Stagecoach*	f. *The Hurricane*
7. Ray Milland in Billy Wilder's *The Lost Weekend*	g. *Today We Live*
8. Julie Christie in John Schlesinger's *Darling*	h. *Adam's Rib*
9. Karl Malden in Elia Kazan's *A Streetcar Named Desire*	i. *Hold Back the Dawn*
10. Teresa Wright in William Wyler's *Mrs. Miniver*	j. *Billy Liar*

30. Match the actress to the film in which she played a nightmare mother.

1. Gladys Cooper	a. *Marnie*
2. Gladys George	b. *Peyton Place*
3. Katina Paxinou	c. *Now, Voyager*
4. Kate Reid	d. *Mourning Becomes Electra*
5. Madame Konstantin	e. *He Ran All the Way*
6. Geraldine Fitzgerald	f. *Notorious*
7. Erin O'Brien-Moore	g. *I'll Cry Tomorrow*
8. Louise Latham	h. *All Fall Down*
9. Angela Lansbury	i. *This Property Is Condemned*
10. Jo Van Fleet	j. *Ten North Frederick*

31. Match the food-related event to the film in which it appears.

1. A woman's attempt at domesticity results in   a. *All About Eve*
a waffle-iron disaster.

2. A woman calmly tips a plate of ravioli onto   b. *Guess Who's Coming*
her ex-lover's lap.   *to Dinner*

3. A woman's soufflé doesn't rise because she   c. *Giant*
forgets to turn on the oven.

4. A trio goes out for oysters weekly in search   d. *Sabrina*
of a pearl.

5. A man teaches a woman the right way to   e. *Designing Woman*
dunk a donut.

6. Thanksgiving is ruined when three kids   f. *Woman of the Year*
realize they knew the turkey personally.

7. The gun with which a man threatens a   g. *Cover Girl*
couple turns out to be made of licorice.

8. A man mistakes mustard for cream as he   h. *It Happened One*
slathers his plate of strawberries.   *Night*

9. A woman looks at her enemy and then mur-   i. *Adam's Rib*
derously bites into a scallion.

10. A man is disappointed by his drive-in res-   j. *The Great Dictator*
taurant's Fresh Oregon Boysenberry sherbet.

32. Match the drink-related event to the film in which it appears.

1. A woman dips a potato chip into her champagne.   a. *Notorious*

2. A woman ends her engagement by dropping   b. *The Seven Year Itch*
her ring into her fiancé's drink.

3. A woman stirs her cocktail with her hat pin.   c. *Gone With the Wind*

4. A man brings his wife a glass of milk (which   d. *The Grass Is Greener*
may be poisoned).

5. A woman's face is scalded when a man flings   e. *Hail the Conquering*
hot coffee at her.   *Hero*

6. A woman gargles with cologne to conceal   f. *Hold Back the Dawn*
that she's been drinking.

7. A woman is appalled to learn that an Upson   g. *The Big Heat*
daiquiri is made with honey.

8. A woman is systematically being poisoned by the coffee she is served.

h. *Suspicion*

9. A woman uses champagne to seal an envelope.

i. *How to Marry a Millionaire*

10. A woman knows she has a fever whenever rum smells like a carnation.

j. *Auntie Mame*

33. Match the pair of male stars to the film in which they both appeared.

1. Charlton Heston/Gary Cooper
2. Gary Cooper/Burt Lancaster
3. Burt Lancaster/Clark Gable
4. Clark Gable/Victor Mature
5. Victor Mature/Richard Widmark
6. Richard Widmark/James Stewart
7. James Stewart/Spencer Tracy
8. Spencer Tracy/Van Johnson
9. Van Johnson/Fred MacMurray
10. Fred MacMurray/Errol Flynn

a. *Plymouth Adventure*
b. *Kiss of Death*
c. *The Caine Mutiny*
d. *Vera Cruz*
e. *Malaya*
f. *Dive Bomber*
g. *The Wreck of the Mary Deare*
h. *Two Rode Together*
i. *Betrayed*
j. *Run Silent, Run Deep*

34. Match the actress to the film in which she appeared with Edward G. Robinson.

1. Susan Hayward
2. Joan Bennett
3. Bette Davis
4. Loretta Young
5. Marlene Dietrich
6. Paulette Goddard
7. Ann Sothern
8. Joan Blondell
9. Ida Lupino
10. Miriam Hopkins

a. *Brother Orchid*
b. *The Stranger*
c. *House of Strangers*
d. *Bullets or Ballots*
e. *Manpower*
f. *Kid Galahad*
g. *Scarlet Street*
h. *Barbary Coast*
i. *Vice Squad*
j. *The Sea Wolf*

35. Even after the Production Code "cleaned up" the movies, Hollywood still managed to keep "the oldest profession" alive, although sometimes such characters had to be referred to as "hostesses" or "escorts." Even so, it's not hard to figure out what they do. Match the actress to the film in which she played a prostitute or a madam.

1. Joan Bennett		a. *Gone With the Wind*
2. Gladys George		b. *Roughshod*
3. Vivien Leigh		c. *Dead End*
4. Gloria Grahame		d. *Flamingo Road*
5. Claire Trevor		e. *The Breaking Point*
6. Ona Munson		f. *Waterloo Bridge*
7. Paulette Goddard		g. *Man Hunt*
8. Mary Astor		h. *Marked Woman*
9. Patricia Neal		i. *Act of Violence*
10. Bette Davis		j. *Vice Squad*

36. Match the movie star to the film in which she played a stage actress.

1. Rosalind Russell		a. *Forever Female*
2. Ginger Rogers		b. *Everybody Sing*
3. Gloria Swanson		c. *Scaramouche*
4. Sophia Loren		d. *The Velvet Touch*
5. Kay Francis		e. *Heller in Pink Tights*
6. Bette Davis		f. *Father Takes a Wife*
7. Eleanor Parker		g. *It's Love I'm After*
8. Maureen O'Hara		h. *I Found Stella Parish*
9. Billie Burke		i. *To Be or Not to Be*
10. Carole Lombard		j. *Sentimental Journey*

37. For each film, pick the one cast member who received an Oscar nomination for his/her performance in this movie.

1. *The Maltese Falcon*
   a. Mary Astor
   b. Humphrey Bogart
   c. Peter Lorre
   d. Sydney Greenstreet

2. *Lost Horizon*
   a. Margo
   b. H. B. Warner
   c. Sam Jaffe
   d. Ronald Colman

3. *The Asphalt Jungle*
   a. Sam Jaffe
   b. Jean Hagen
   c. Louis Calhern
   d. Sterling Hayden

4. *Singin' in the Rain*
   a. Gene Kelly
   b. Donald O'Connor
   c. Jean Hagen
   d. Cyd Charisse

5. *Some Like It Hot*
   a. Tony Curtis
   b. Jack Lemmon
   c. Marilyn Monroe
   d. Joe E. Brown

6. *Notorious*
   a. Cary Grant
   b. Ingrid Bergman
   c. Claude Rains
   d. Louis Calhern

7. *You Can't Take It With You*
   a. Spring Byington
   b. Lionel Barrymore
   c. Jean Arthur
   d. Edward Arnold

8. *Anna and the King of Siam*
   a. Irene Dunne
   b. Rex Harrison
   c. Lee J. Cobb
   d. Gale Sondergaard

9. *Bus Stop*
   a. Marilyn Monroe
   b. Don Murray
   c. Arthur O'Connell
   d. Hope Lange

10. *The Quiet Man*
    a. John Wayne
    b. Maureen O'Hara
    c. Victor McLaglen
    d. Barry Fitzgerald

38. Pick the film for which each star received his/her only Oscar nomination.

1. Eve Arden   a. *Stage Door*   b. *Anatomy of a Murder*
c. *Mildred Pierce*   d. *The Dark at the Top of the Stairs*

2. Richard Widmark   a. *Kiss of Death*   b. *Hell and High Water*
c. *Madigan*   d. *Judgment at Nuremburg*

3. Gene Tierney   a. *Laura*   b. *Leave Her to Heaven*
c. *The Razor's Edge*   d. *The Ghost and Mrs. Muir*

4. Lew Ayres   a. *Holiday*   b. *All Quiet on the Western Front*
c. *Johnny Belinda*   d. *Advise and Consent*

5. Robert Ryan   a. *The Set-Up*   b. *Bad Day at Black Rock*
c. *Crossfire*   d. *The Wild Bunch*

6. Miriam Hopkins   a. *These Three*   b. *Becky Sharp*
c. *The Heiress*   d. *Dr. Jekyll and Mr. Hyde*

7. Laurence Harvey   a. *Darling*   b. *The Manchurian Candidate*
c. *Room at the Top*   d. *Summer and Smoke*

8. Ethel Waters   a. *Pinky*   b. *The Member of the Wedding*
c. *Cabin in the Sky*   d. *The Sound and the Fury*

9. Debbie Reynolds   a. *The Catered Affair*   b. *How the West Was Won*
c. *Mother*   d. *The Unsinkable Molly Brown*

10. Doris Day   a. *Pillow Talk*   b. *The Man Who Knew Too Much*
c. *Calamity Jane*   d. *Love Me or Leave Me*

39. For each composer, pick the tune of his that won a Best Song Oscar.

1. Harry Warren   a. "That's Amore"   b. "I Only Have Eyes for You"
c. "The More I See You"   d. "Lullaby of Broadway"

2. Jerome Kern   a. "A Fine Romance"   b. "The Way You Look
c. "Lovely to Look At"   Tonight"
d. "Long Ago and Far Away"

3. Harold Arlen   a. "Over the Rainbow"   b. "The Man That Got Away"
c. "That Old Black   d. "One for My Baby"
Magic"

4. Irving Berlin   a. "Cheek to Cheek"   b. "A Couple of Swells"
c. "White Christmas"   d. "This Year's Kisses"

5. Frank Loesser   a. "Baby, It's Cold   b. "I Wish I Didn't Love You
Outside"   So"
c. "Thumbelina"   d. "Anywhere I Wander"

6. Richard Rodgers   a. "Lover"   b. "It Might as Well Be
c. "Isn't It Romantic?"   Spring"
d. "It's Easy to Remember"

7. Frederick Loewe   a. "I Remember It   b. "Thank Heaven for Little
Well"   Girls"
c. "Gigi"   d. "Say a Prayer for Me
Tonight"

8. Jule Styne   a. "It's Magic"   b. "I Fall in Love Too Easily"
c. "Time After Time"   d. "Three Coins in the
Fountain"

9. Henry Mancini   a. "Charade"   b. "Days of Wine and Roses"
c. "Dear Heart"   d. "Bachelor in Paradise"

10. Burt Bacharach   a. "The Look of Love"   b. "What's New, Pussycat?"
c. "Alfie"   d. "Raindrops Keep Fallin'
on My Head"

40. Pick the un-nominated performance for each of these three-time Oscar losers.

1. Natalie Wood   a. *West Side Story*   b. *Splendor in the Grass*
c. *Rebel Without a Cause*   d. *Love with the Proper Stranger*

2. Kirk Douglas   a. *Champion*   b. *The Bad and the Beautiful*
c. *Spartacus*   d. *Lust for Life*

3. Gloria Swanson   a. *The Trespasser*   b. *The Loves of Sunya*
c. *Sadie Thompson*   d. *Sunset Boulevard*

4. Charles Bickford   a. *Johnny Belinda*   b. *The Farmer's Daughter*
c. *The Song of Bernadette*   d. *Days of Wine and Roses*

5. Angela Lansbury   a. *Gaslight*   b. *The Picture of Dorian Gray*
c. *The Long, Hot Summer*   d. *The Manchurian Candidate*

6. William Powell   a. *The Thin Man*   b. *The Great Ziegfeld*
c. *My Man Godfrey*   d. *Life with Father*

7. Gladys Cooper   a. *Now, Voyager*   b. *The Song of Bernadette*
c. *My Fair Lady*   d. *Separate Tables*

8. Clifton Webb   a. *The Razor's Edge*   b. *Three Coins in the Fountain*
c. *Laura*   d. *Sitting Pretty*

9. Eleanor Parker   a. *The Sound of Music*   b. *Detective Story*
c. *Caged*   d. *Interrupted Melody*

10. James Mason   a. *Georgy Girl*   b. *The Verdict*
c. *Lolita*   d. *A Star Is Born*

41. Pick the un-nominated performance for each of these three-time Oscar nominees. They are all winners in this group, and the films for which they won their awards are in boldface (consider this a hint, narrowing each field to three possibilities).

1. James Cagney
   a. *White Heat*
   c. ***Yankee Doodle Dandy***
   b. *Love Me or Leave Me*
   d. *Angels with Dirty Faces*

2. Joan Fontaine
   a. *Rebecca*
   c. *The Constant Nymph*
   b. ***Suspicion***
   d. *Jane Eyre*

3. William Holden
   a. ***Stalag 17***
   c. *Picnic*
   b. *Sunset Boulevard*
   d. *Network*

4. Joan Crawford
   a. *Sudden Fear*
   c. *Possessed* (1947)
   b. ***Mildred Pierce***
   d. *Humoresque*

5. Rod Steiger
   a. *On the Waterfront*
   c. *The Pawnbroker*
   b. *Doctor Zhivago*
   d. ***In the Heat of the Night***

6. Celeste Holm
   a. *All About Eve*
   c. ***Gentleman's Agreement***
   b. *The Snake Pit*
   d. *Come to the Stable*

7. Claire Trevor
   a. *Stagecoach*
   c. *Dead End*
   b. *The High and the Mighty*
   d. ***Key Largo***

8. Claudette Colbert
   a. ***It Happened One Night***
   c. *The Egg and I*
   b. *Private Worlds*
   d. *Since You Went Away*

9. Wendy Hiller
   a. *Pygmalion*
   c. *Sons and Lovers*
   b. ***Separate Tables***
   d. *A Man for All Seasons*

10. Charles Laughton
    a. *Mutiny on the Bounty*
    c. ***The Private Life of Henry VIII***
    b. *The Hunchback of Notre Dame*
    d. *Witness for the Prosecution*

42. Match the actor to the film in which he appeared with Joan Crawford.

1. John Wayne	a. *Mannequin*
2. Gary Cooper	b. *Reunion in France*
3. Walter Huston	c. *A Woman's Face*
4. William Powell	d. *Possessed* (1931)
5. Melvyn Douglas	e. *Possessed* (1947)
6. Dana Andrews	f. *The Last of Mrs. Cheyney*
7. Clark Gable	g. *Today We Live*
8. Spencer Tracy	h. *Susan and God*
9. Van Heflin	i. *Rain*
10. Fredric March	j. *Daisy Kenyon*

43. Match the actor to the film in which he appeared with Marlene Dietrich.

1. Charles Boyer	a. *Blonde Venus*
2. Ray Milland	b. *Kismet*
3. Gary Cooper	c. *The Garden of Allah*
4. John Lund	d. *Rancho Notorious*
5. Ronald Colman	e. *Desire*
6. Cary Grant	f. *Seven Sinners*
7. Arthur Kennedy	g. *Stage Fright*
8. Richard Todd	h. *A Foreign Affair*
9. Victor McLaglen	i. *Dishonored*
10. John Wayne	j. *Golden Earrings*

44. Match each multi-nominated star to the film for which he/she was **not** nominated for an Oscar.

1. Barbara Stanwyck   a. *Stella Dallas*   b. *The Lady Eve*
                          c. *Ball of Fire*   d. *Sorry, Wrong Number*

2. James Stewart   **a.** *Harvey*   b. *It's a Wonderful Life*
                   c. *Vertigo*   d. *Anatomy of a Murder*

3. Rosalind Russell   a. *His Girl Friday*   b. *My Sister Eileen*
                     c. *Sister Kenny*   d. *Auntie Mame*

4. Laurence Olivier   a. *Rebecca*   b. *Wuthering Heights*
                     c. *Sleuth*   d. *Pride and Prejudice*

5. Deborah Kerr   a. *The King and I*   b. *An Affair to Remember*
                 c. *Separate Tables*   d. *The Sundowners*

6. Spencer Tracy   a. *San Francisco*   b. *Bad Day at Black Rock*
                  c. *Adam's Rib*   d. *Father of the Bride*

7. Ingrid Bergman   a. *Notorious*   b. *The Bells of St. Mary's*
                  c. *Joan of Arc*   d. *For Whom the Bell Tolls*

8. Gregory Peck   a. *The Yearling*   b. *The Keys of the Kingdom*
                 c. *Roman Holiday*   d. *Twelve O'Clock High*

9. Thelma Ritter   a. *All About Eve*   b. *With a Song in My Heart*
                 c. *Pillow Talk*   d. *Rear Window*

10. Gary Cooper   a. *Ball of Fire*   b. *Mr. Deeds Goes to Town*
                c. *The Pride of the*   d. *For Whom the Bell Tolls*
                     Yankees

45. The following stars are all two-time Oscar nominees in the acting categories. Under their names are the films for which they won their Oscars. Pick the film that brought each his/her *other* nomination.

1. Rex Harrison
(*My Fair Lady*)
   a. *Cleopatra*
   c. *Doctor Dolittle*
   b. *Anna and the King of Siam*
   d. *The Ghost and Mrs. Muir*

2. Grace Kelly
(*The Country Girl*)
   a. *High Noon*
   c. *Mogambo*
   b. *Rear Window*
   d. *Dial M for Murder*

3. Sidney Poitier
(*Lilies of the Field*)
   a. *Blackboard Jungle*
   c. *The Defiant Ones*
   b. *In the Heat of the Night*
   d. *A Raisin in the Sun*

4. Loretta Young
(*The Farmer's Daughter*)
   a. *Ramona*
   c. *The Bishop's Wife*
   b. *Come to the Stable*
   d. *Rachel and the Stranger*

5. Wallace Beery
(*The Champ*)
   a. *Viva Villa!*
   c. *Dinner at Eight*
   b. *The Big House*
   d. *Treasure Island*

6. Patricia Neal
(*Hud*)
   a. *The Fountainhead*
   c. *The Hasty Heart*
   b. *A Face in the Crowd*
   d. *The Subject Was Roses*

7. Henry Fonda
(*On Golden Pond*)
   a. *The Lady Eve*
   c. *Mister Roberts*
   b. *The Grapes of Wrath*
   d. *12 Angry Men*

8. Marie Dressler
(*Min and Bill*)
   a. *Emma*
   c. *Anna Christie*
   b. *Dinner at Eight*
   d. *Let Us Be Gay*

9. John Wayne
(*True Grit*)
   a. *Red River*
   c. *The Searchers*
   b. *She Wore a Yellow Ribbon*
   d. *Sands of Iwo Jima*

10. Robert Donat
(*Goodbye Mr. Chips*)
   a. *The 39 Steps*
   c. *The Citadel*
   b. *The Inn of the Sixth Happiness*
   d. *The Ghost Goes West*

46. Match the actor to the film in which he appeared with Greta Garbo.

1. George Brent   a. *Anna Christie*

2. Melvyn Douglas   b. *Anna Karenina*

3. Ramon Novarro   c. *The Painted Veil*

4. Charles Boyer   d. *The Kiss*

5. Robert Montgomery   e. *Ninotchka*

6. Clark Gable   f. *Mata Hari*

7. Charles Bickford   g. *Inspiration*

8. Fredric March   h. *Queen Christina*

9. Lew Ayres   i. *Susan Lenox: Her Fall and Rise*

10. John Gilbert   j. *Conquest*

47. Match the film to the state in which it is primarily set.

1. *Anatomy of a Murder*   a. New Hampshire

2. *The Trouble with Harry*   b. New Jersey

3. *Friendly Persuasion*   c. Michigan

4. *The Petrified Forest*   d. Louisiana

5. *Our Town*   e. Rhode Island

6. *The Cincinnati Kid*   f. California

7. *Ace in the Hole*   g. New Mexico

8. *The Birds*   h. Arizona

9. *High Society*   i. Indiana

10. *Cheaper by the Dozen* (1950)   j. Vermont

48. Match the film to the description of an earlier, unrelated film with the exact same title.

1. *Top Gun* (1986)	a. 1938 Charles Bickford drama
2. *Million Dollar Baby* (2004)	b. 1936 James Stewart drama
3. *The Verdict* (1982)	c. 1948 Roddy McDowall animal picture
4. *Speed* (1994)	d. 1946 Sydney Greenstreet drama
5. *Gangs of New York* (2002)	e. 1937 Roland Young drama
6. *Iron Man* (2008)	f. 1941 Ronald Reagan comedy
7. *Dressed to Kill* (1980)	g. 1955 Sterling Hayden western
8. *Rocky* (1976)	h. 1931 Lew Ayres drama
9. *Gypsy* (1962)	i. 1934 Constance Bennett comedy
10. *Moulin Rouge* (1952)	j. 1946 Basil Rathbone mystery

49. Match the performer to the film in which he/she played an alcoholic. Can you believe that I managed not to include Ray Milland and Susan Hayward?

1. Van Johnson	a. *Come Fill the Cup*
2. Walter Huston	b. *Beloved Infidel*
3. Jean Simmons	c. *Come Back, Little Sheba*
4. Joan Fontaine	d. *The Bottom of the Bottle*
5. Tony Curtis	e. *The People Against O'Hara*
6. Errol Flynn	f. *The Happy Ending*
7. James Cagney	g. *The Wet Parade*
8. Spencer Tracy	h. *The Outsider*
9. Gregory Peck	i. *The Roots of Heaven*
10. Burt Lancaster	j. *Something to Live For*

50. For each pair of similarly titled films, can you identify which is which?

1. *That Certain Feeling*   a. A 1956 Bob Hope comedy

2. *That Uncertain Feeling*   b. A 1941 Merle Oberon comedy

3. *G-Men*   a. A 1947 Dennis O'Keefe film noir

4. *T-Men*   b. A 1935 James Cagney drama

5. *Torch Song*   a. A 1953 Joan Crawford musical drama

6. *Torch Singer*   b. A 1933 Claudette Colbert drama

7. *Three Wise Girls*   a. A 1936 Deanna Durbin musical comedy

8. *Three Smart Girls*   b. A 1932 Jean Harlow melodrama

9. *Two Girls and a Sailor*   a. A 1944 June Allyson musical

10. *Three Sailors and a Girl*   b. A 1953 Jane Powell musical

51. Match the actress to the film in which she played a princess.

1. Virginia Mayo   a. *The Prisoner of Zenda* (1937)

2. Angela Lansbury   b. *The Prisoner of Zenda* (1952)

3. Grace Kelly   c. *Thirty-Day Princess*

4. Deborah Kerr   d. *The Swan*

5. Olivia de Havilland   e. *Love Me Tonight*

6. Madeleine Carroll   f. *The Court Jester*

7. Miriam Hopkins   g. *Princess O'Rourke*

8. Maureen O'Hara   h. *The Princess and the Pirate*

9. Jeanette MacDonald   i. *Bagdad*

10. Sylvia Sidney   j. *The Smiling Lieutenant*

52. Okay, you've seen *Gone With the Wind* countless times. You are thoroughly familiar with its secondary characters, but have you ever learned the names of those who portrayed them? Match each performer to the *GWTW* role he/she played.

1. Rand Brooks   a. Belle Watling

2. Laura Hope Crews   b. Brent Tarleton

3. Carroll Nye   c. Bonnie Blue Butler

4. Ona Munson   d. Big Sam

5. Everett Brown   e. India Wilkes

6. Cammie King   f. Dr. Meade

7. Fred Crane   g. Mrs. O'Hara

8. Alicia Rhett   h. Frank Kennedy

9. Harry Davenport   i. Aunt Pittypat

10. Barbara O'Neil   j. Charles Hamilton

53. Dead or alive?

1. Who is dead at the end of *The Guns of Navarone*?
   - a. Anthony Quinn
   - b. Gregory Peck
   - c. David Niven
   - d. James Darren

2. Who is alive at the end of *The Alamo*?
   - a. Frankie Avalon
   - b. John Wayne
   - c. Laurence Harvey
   - d. Richard Widmark

3. Who is dead at the end of *Grand Hotel*?
   - a. Lionel Barrymore
   - b. John Barrymore
   - c. Greta Garbo
   - d. Wallace Beery

4. Who is alive at the end of *The Bridge on the River Kwai*?
   - a. Alec Guinness
   - b. Sessue Hayakawa
   - c. Jack Hawkins
   - d. William Holden

5. Who is dead at the end of *Battleground*?
   - a. Van Johnson
   - b. Ricardo Montalban
   - c. George Murphy
   - d. John Hodiak

6. Who is alive at the end of *Hush...Hush, Sweet Charlotte?*

   a. Bette Davis   b. Olivia de Havilland
   c. Mary Astor   d. Agnes Moorehead

7. Who is dead at the end of *Little Women?*

   a. Joan Bennett   b. Katharine Hepburn
   c. Jean Parker   d. Frances Dee

8. Who is alive at the end of *And Then There Were None?*

   a. Judith Anderson   b. Walter Huston
   c. Roland Young   d. Louis Hayward

9. Who is dead at the end of *Dinner at Eight?*

   a. John Barrymore   b. Lionel Barrymore
   c. Marie Dressler   d. Wallace Beery

10. Who is alive at the end of *Beau Geste?*

   a. Gary Cooper   b. Brian Donlevy
   c. Robert Preston   d. Ray Milland

54. Match the character to the film in which he/she is much talked about but never actually appears. (In some instances this is because the character is dead.)

1. Barney Quill   a. *Gaslight*

2. Al Magarulian   b. *Mr. Skeffington*

3. Komoko   c. *Lifeboat*

4. Buck Winston   d. *The Shop Around the Corner*

5. Sean Regan   e. *Bad Day at Black Rock*

6. Janie Clarkson   f. *The Big Sleep*

7. Alice Alquist   g. *The Women*

8. Emma Matuschek   h. *Anatomy of a Murder*

9. George Kaplan   i. *The Bad Seed*

10. Bessie Denker   j. *North by Northwest*

55. Match the performer to the film in which he/she is the narrator.

1. Walter Pidgeon	a. *The Red Badge of Courage*
2. Lionel Barrymore	b. *How the West Was Won*
3. Anne Baxter	c. *The Picture of Dorian Gray*
4. Spencer Tracy	d. *Quo Vadis*
5. Louis Jourdan	e. *Dragon Seed*
6. James Whitmore	f. *Irma la Douce*
7. Kim Stanley	g. *Mother Wore Tights*
8. Orson Welles	h. *The Vikings*
9. George Burns	i. *To Kill a Mockingbird*
10. Cedric Hardwicke	j. *The Solid Gold Cadillac*

56. One of the films on the left is seen on television in one of the films on the right. Match them.

1. *Rebecca*	a. *Midnight Cowboy*
2. *Harvey*	b. *Cocoon*
3. *Spellbound*	c. *Goodfellas*
4. *The Quiet Man*	d. *Lovers and Other Strangers*
5. *The Gay Divorcee*	e. *Close Encounters of the Third Kind*
6. *Dark Victory*	f. *Five Easy Pieces*
7. *The Jazz Singer* (1927)	g. *Desperately Seeking Susan*
8. *The Ten Commandments*	h. *The Departed*
9. *The Informer*	i. *Field of Dreams*
10. *You Can't Take It With You*	j. *E.T.*

57. Match the film to the fictional land in which it is primarily set, or from which an important character comes.

1. *The Great Dictator*	a. Marshovia
2. *Duck Soup*	b. Lichtenburg
3. *The Student Prince*	c. Morovia
4. *Call Me Madam*	d. Tomainia
5. *Cinderfella*	e. Carpathia
6. *Million Dollar Legs* (1932)	f. Freedonia
7. *The Merry Widow* (1934)	g. Romanza
8. *Rosalie*	h. Flausenthurm
9. *The Prince and the Showgirl*	i. Karlsburg
10. *The Smiling Lieutenant*	j. Klopstokia

58. Once again, for each pair of similarly titled films, can you identify which is which?

1. *Remember the Day*	a. A 1941 Claudette Colbert drama
2. *Remember the Night*	b. A 1940 Barbara Stanwyck drama
3. *His Kind of Woman*	a. A 1959 Sophia Loren drama
4. *That Kind of Woman*	b. A 1951 Jane Russell drama
5. *Three Faces West*	a. A 1948 Joel McCrea western
6. *Four Faces West*	b. A 1940 John Wayne drama
7. *Star!*	a. A 1968 Julie Andrews musical
8. *The Star*	b. A 1952 Bette Davis drama
9. *John and Mary*	a. A 1969 Mia Farrow drama
10. *John Loves Mary*	b. A 1949 Patricia Neal comedy

59. Match the performance to the accent the actor adopted (sometimes atrociously) for his role.

1. John Wayne in *The Long Voyage Home*   a. Mexican

2. Spencer Tracy in *Captains Courageous*   b. Australian

3. Edward G. Robinson in *House of Strangers*   c. Portuguese

4. Humphrey Bogart in *Virginia City*   d. French

5. Marlon Brando in *Sayonara*   e. American Southern

6. James Mason in *The Desert Rats*   f. Indian (from India)

7. Robert Mitchum in *The Sundowners*   g. Italian

8. Peter Sellers in *The Millionairess*   h. Swedish

9. Frank Sinatra in *The Pride and the Passion*   i. German

10. Cornel Wilde in *The Greatest Show On Earth*   j. Spanish

60. Match the titular characters to the pair who played them.

1. *The Major and the Minor*   a. Robert Walker and June Allyson
2. *The Cowboy and the Lady*   b. Dick Powell and June Allyson
3. *The Farmer Takes a Wife*   c. Gary Cooper and Merle Oberon
4. *The Sailor Takes a Wife*   d. Robert Young and Ruth Hussey
5. *The Doctor Takes a Wife*   e. Henry Fonda and Janet Gaynor
6. *He Married His Wife*   f. Robert Montgomery and Carole Lombard

7. *Rich Man, Poor Girl*   g. Ray Milland and Ginger Rogers
8. *The Reformer and the Redhead*   h. Ray Milland and Loretta Young
9. *The Devil and Miss Jones*   i. Joel McCrea and Nancy Kelly
10. *Mr. and Mrs. Smith*   j. Charles Coburn and Jean Arthur

61. Match the actor to the film in which he appeared with Sophia Loren.

1. William Holden	a. *The Pride and the Passion*
2. Alan Ladd	b. *El Cid*
3. John Wayne	c. *Legend of the Lost*
4. Gregory Peck	d. *The Key*
5. Paul Newman	e. *The Black Orchid*
6. Charlton Heston	f. *Boy on a Dolphin*
7. Cary Grant	g. *Arabesque*
8. Anthony Quinn	h. *It Started in Naples*
9. Marlon Brando	i. *A Countess from Hong Kong*
10. Clark Gable	j. *Lady L*

62. Match the actor to the Oscar-winning Best Picture in which he starred.

1. Mark Lester	a. *Wings*
2. Gary Merrill	b. *The Broadway Melody*
3. Clive Brook	c. *Cimarron*
4. Richard Beymer	d. *Cavalcade*
5. Broderick Crawford	e. *All the King's Men*
6. Charles King	f. *All About Eve*
7. Richard Arlen	g. *West Side Story*
8. Ben Cross	h. *Oliver!*
9. John Lone	i. *Chariots of Fire*
10. Richard Dix	j. *The Last Emperor*

63. Match the pair of actresses to the film in which they had a knockdown brawl.

1. Susan Hayward/Marsha Hunt   a. *Here Comes the Groom*

2. Susan Hayward/Eleanor Todd   b. *Destry Rides Again*

3. Susan Hayward/Patty Duke   c. *The Women*

4. Ann Miller/Dolores Gray   d. *Valley of the Dolls*

5. Joan Bennett/Vivian Blaine   e. *Colorado Territory*

6. Jane Wyman/Alexis Smith   f. *Ladies They Talk About*

7. Barbara Stanwyck/Dorothy Burgess   g. *The Lusty Men*

8. Rosalind Russell/Paulette Goddard   h. *The Opposite Sex*

9. Marlene Dietrich/Una Merkel   i. *Nob Hill*

10. Dorothy Malone/Virginia Mayo   j. *Smash-Up: The Story of a Woman*

64. Match the actor to the real-life sports star he played.

1. Glenn Ford   a. boxer Jim Corbett in *Gentleman Jim*

2. Ronald Reagan   b. boxer Rocky Graziano in *Somebody up there Likes Me*

3. James Stewart   c. decathlete Jim Thorpe in *Jim Thorpe—All American*

4. Dan Dailey   d. golfer Ben Hogan in *Follow the Sun*

5. Anthony Perkins   e. baseball player Babe Ruth in *The Babe Ruth Story*

6. Burt Lancaster   f. baseball player Monty Stratton in *The Stratton Story*

7. Errol Flynn   g. baseball player Jimmy Piersall in *Fear Strikes Out*

8. Gary Cooper   h. baseball player Lou Gehrig in *The Pride of the Yankees*

9. Paul Newman   i. baseball player Dizzy Dean in *The Pride of St. Louis*

10. William Bendix   j. baseball player Grover Cleveland Alexander in *The Winning Team*

65. Match the film to the unusual way in which its opening credits are presented.

1. *Mildred Pierce*	a. On a mailbox
2. *Maytime*	b. In finger paint
3. *Life with Father*	c. On tree trunks; also written in apple blossoms
4. *Auntie Mame*	d. Washing up on the beach
5. *Carefree*	e. On wooden slats on a signpost
6. *Summer Stock*	f. Through a kaleidoscope
7. *Desk Set*	g. Through a viewfinder
8. *My Darling Clementine*	h. Dragged through the sky by a Goodyear blimp
9. *Gunga Din*	i. On a computer printout
10. *A Hole in the Head*	j. Beat out on a gong

66. Match the actress to the film in which she appeared with Charles Boyer.

1. Katharine Hepburn	a. *Back Street* (1941)
2. Olivia de Havilland	b. *All This, and Heaven Too*
3. Joan Fontaine	c. *Break of Hearts*
4. Margaret Sullavan	d. *History Is Made at Night*
5. Jean Arthur	e. *The Constant Nymph*
6. Jessica Tandy	f. *Tovarich*
7. Bette Davis	g. *Cluny Brown*
8. Jennifer Jones	h. *Love Affair*
9. Claudette Colbert	i. *A Woman's Vengeance*
10. Irene Dunne	j. *Hold Back the Dawn*

67. Match the film on the left to the fictional book on the right that is written by a character in the film.

1. *Sitting Pretty*	a. *The Deep Well*
2. *Breakfast at Tiffany's*	b. *The Lost Generation*
3. *Little Women* (1949)	c. *Hummingbird Hill*
4. *Auntie Mame*	d. *The Lone Rider of Santa Fe*
5. *The Snows of Kilimanjaro*	e. *Demagogue in Denim*
6. *The Third Man*	f. *Nine Lives*
7. *Leave Her to Heaven*	g. *The Parched Garden*
8. *The Best Man*	h. *The Pirate Cove*
9. *A Face in the Crowd*	i. *My Beth*
10. *The Dark Angel*	j. *Enemy Around Us*

68. Match the actress to the film in which she appeared with Gary Cooper.

1. Jean Arthur	a. *Sergeant York*
2. Patricia Neal	b. *They Came to Cordura*
3. Dorothy McGuire	c. *The General Died at Dawn*
4. Rita Hayworth	d. *The Plainsman*
5. Paulette Goddard	e. *Beau Geste*
6. Joan Leslie	f. *Friendly Persuasion*
7. Claudette Colbert	g. *Bluebeard's Eighth Wife*
8. Ann Sheridan	h. *Unconquered*
9. Madeleine Carroll	i. *Good Sam*
10. Susan Hayward	j. *Bright Leaf*

69. Match the Oscar-winning performance and its co-star to the film that reteamed the two stars in the hope of lightning striking twice.

1. Loretta Young in *The Farmer's Daughter*, co-starring Joseph Cotten

a. *Design for Living*

2. Yul Brynner in *The King and I*, co-starring Deborah Kerr

b. *Tugboat Annie*

3. Grace Kelly in *The Country Girl*, co-starring Bing Crosby

c. *The Journey*

4. Fredric March in *Dr. Jekyll and Mr. Hyde*, co-starring Miriam Hopkins

d. *Flamingo Road*

5. Ingrid Bergman in *Gaslight*, co-starring Charles Boyer

e. *Boom Town*

6. Marie Dressler in *Min and Bill*, co-starring Wallace Beery

f. *Half Angel*

7. Joan Crawford in *Mildred Pierce*, co-starring Zachary Scott

g. *Let's Do It Again*

8. Ray Milland in *The Lost Weekend*, co-starring Jane Wyman

h. *High Society*

9. Ginger Rogers in *Kitty Foyle*, co-starring Dennis Morgan

i. *Arch of Triumph*

10. Clark Gable and Claudette Colbert in *It Happened One Night* (both won Oscars)

j. *Perfect Strangers*

70. Match the actor to the film in which he appeared with Bette Davis during her pre-*Of Human Bondage* (1934) dues-paying period.

1. James Cagney   a. *The Cabin in the Cotton*

2. George Brent   b. *The Big Shakedown*

3. Warren William   c. *The Rich Are Always with Us*

4. Richard Barthelmess   d. *The Working Man*

5. Spencer Tracy   e. *Bureau of Missing Persons*

6. George Arliss   f. *The Dark Horse*

7. Gene Raymond   g. *Fashions of 1934*

8. Pat O'Brien   h. *Jimmy the Gent*

9. William Powell   i. *Ex-Lady*

10. Charles Farrell   j. *20,000 Years in Sing Sing*

71. Many actors (including Bogart, Fonda, and Tracy) worked with both Bette Davis and Katharine Hepburn. Match each actor to the pair of films in which he appeared, the first alongside Davis, the second alongside Hepburn.

1. Paul Henreid a. *The Little Foxes*
 A Woman Rebels

2. Douglas Fairbanks, Jr. b. *Dangerous*
 Quality Street

3. Herbert Marshall c. *Juarez*
 Sylvia Scarlett

4. Cecil Kellaway d. *Parachute Jumper*
 Morning Glory

5. Brian Aherne e. *Pocketful of Miracles*
 Holiday

6. Barry Fitzgerald f. *Watch on the Rhine*
 Little Women

7. Franchot Tone g. *The Catered Affair*
 Bringing up Baby

8. Edward Everett Horton h. *The Girl from 10th Avenue*
 Christopher Strong

9. Colin Clive i. *Deception*
 Song of Love

10. Paul Lukas j. *Hush...Hush, Sweet Charlotte*
 Guess Who's Coming to Dinner

72. Match the masculine character name to the actress who played her.

1. Marvin a. Olivia de Havilland in *In This Our Life*
2. Quentin b. Jean Arthur in *The Whole Town's Talking*
3. Gregg c. Joanne Woodward in *The Sound and the Fury*
4. Wally d. Claudette Colbert in *Without Reservations*
5. Bill e. Janet Leigh in *Living It Up*
6. Roy f. Eve Arden in *Goodbye, My Fancy*
7. Teddy g. Hedy Lamarr in *H.M. Pulham, Esq.*
8. Hank h. Suzy Parker in *The Best of Everything*
9. Woody i. Bessie Love in *The Broadway Melody*
10. Christopher j. Carolyn Jones in *Invasion of the Body Snatchers*

73. And, yet again, for each pair of similarly titled films, identify which is which.

1. Yes, My Darling Daughter   a. A 1961 Juliet Mills comedy

2. No, My Darling Daughter   b. A 1939 Priscilla Lane comedy

3. One Foot in Heaven   a. A 1960 Alan Ladd western

4. One Foot in Hell   b. A 1941 Fredric March drama

5. She Had to Say Yes   a. A 1933 Loretta Young pre-Code picture

6. She Couldn't Say No   b. A 1954 Jean Simmons comedy

7. Road to Singapore   a. A 1931 William Powell drama

8. The Road to Singapore   b. A 1940 Hope and Crosby comedy

9. Decision at Sundown   a. A 1957 Randolph Scott western

10. Decision Before Dawn   b. A 1951 Richard Basehart war movie

74. Match the performer to the kind of professional or amateur musician he/she played on-screen.

1. Paul Newman in *Paris Blues*   a. cellist

2. Henry Fonda in *The Wrong Man*   b. drummer

3. Richard Burton in *Look Back in Anger*   c. bass fiddler

4. Mary Astor in *The Great Lie*   d. pianist

5. Cary Grant in *The Bishop's Wife*   e. violinist

6. Celeste Holm in *The Tender Trap*   f. trombonist

7. Gary Cooper in *Mr. Deeds Goes to Town*   g. harpist

8. Audrey Hepburn in *Love in the Afternoon*   h. saxophonist

9. Frank Sinatra in *The Man with the Golden Arm*   i. trumpeter

10. Robert Montgomery in *Here Comes Mr. Jordan*   j. tuba player

75. Match the film to the date and place in which it begins.

1. *Captain Blood*	a. "South America 1901"
2. *East of Eden*	b. "Edinburgh 1880"
3. *Anastasia*	c. "Edinburgh 1932"
4. *Splendor in the Grass*	d. "New York 1883"
5. *Journey to the Center of the Earth*	e. "Paris 1928"
6. *The Naked Jungle*	f. "Africa 1897"
7. *The Prime of Miss Jean Brodie*	g. "1917 Monterey"
8. *Life with Father*	h. "1928 Southeast Kansas"
9. *King Solomon's Mines*	i. "Portsmouth, England, 1787"
10. *Mutiny on the Bounty* (1935)	j. "England—1685"

76. Match the actor to the film for which his hair was blonded.

1. Robert Shaw	a. *Cleopatra* (1963)
2. Anthony Quinn	b. *Bullfighter and the Lady*
3. Laurence Harvey	c. *Christopher Columbus*
4. Roddy McDowall	d. *Sabrina* (1954)
5. William Holden	e. *The Running Man*
6. Marlon Brando	f. *The Young Lions*
7. Robert Stack	g. *From Russia with Love*
8. Stephen Boyd	h. *Warlock*
9. Laurence Olivier	i. *The Fall of the Roman Empire*
10. Fredric March	j. *Hamlet* (1948)

77. Match the performer to the film in which he/she played a physician.

1. Robert Donat		a. *People Will Talk*
2. Gary Cooper		b. *The Citadel*
3. James Garner		c. *The Nun's Story*
4. Anne Bancroft		d. *The Last Angry Man*
5. Charlton Heston		e. *7 Women*
6. Cary Grant		f. *The Story of Dr. Wassell*
7. Peter Finch		g. *The Thrill of It All*
8. June Allyson		h. *The Girl in White*
9. Paul Muni		i. *Love Is a Many-Splendored Thing*
10. Jennifer Jones		j. *Bad for Each Other*

78. Match the performer to the film in which he/she played a psychiatrist, psychologist, analyst, or therapist.

1. Claudette Colbert		a. *The Mark*
2. David Niven		b. *The Snake Pit*
3. Rod Steiger		c. *The Cobweb*
4. Lew Ayres		d. *Private Worlds*
5. Richard Conte		e. *The Three Faces of Eve*
6. Richard Widmark		f. *Oh, Men! Oh, Women!*
7. Rosalind Russell		g. *Whirlpool* (1949)
8. Lee J. Cobb		h. *The Dark Mirror*
9. Leo Genn		i. *Lady in the Dark*
10. Barry Sullivan		j. *She Wouldn't Say Yes*

79. Match the fictional movie studio to the film in which it appears.

1. Monumental Pictures   a. *The Bad and the Beautiful*

2. Esoteric Pictures   b. *The Big Knife*

3. Galaxy Pictures, Inc.   c. *The Carpetbaggers*

4. Oliver Niles Studio   d. *A Star Is Born* (1954)

5. Norman Studio   e. *Singin' in the Rain*

6. Hoff-Federated   f. *The Oscar*

7. Monarch Films   g. *Never Give a Sucker an Even Break*

8. Swan   h. *The Star*

9. Shields Pictures, Inc.   i. *Bombshell*

10. Morrison Studios   j. *Inside Daisy Clover*

80. Match each star to his/her posthumously released film.

1. Kay Kendall   a. *Saratoga*

2. Walter Huston   b. *The Misfits*

3. Robert Donat   c. *The Inn of the Sixth Happiness*

4. Jean Harlow   d. *Big Jack*

5. John Hodiak   e. *My Son John*

6. Clark Gable   f. *The Furies*

7. Wallace Beery   g. *Once More, With Feeling!*

8. Ralph Richardson   h. *On the Threshold of Space*

9. Edward G. Robinson   i. *Greystoke*

10. Robert Walker   j. *Soylent Green*

81. Match each star to the film he/she began but was unable to complete because of illness, death, or the extended shutdown of the movie, OR was fired because of unprofessional behavior or an unsatisfactory performance.

1. Vivien Leigh	a. *Kiss Me Stupid*
2. Tyrone Power	b. *The Yearling*
3. Frank Morgan	c. *Forever Amber*
4. Buddy Ebsen	d. *Elephant Walk*
5. Vera Zorina	e. *Solomon and Sheba*
6. Spencer Tracy	f. *Annie Get Your Gun*
7. Peter Sellers	g. *Hush...Hush, Sweet Charlotte*
8. Marilyn Monroe	h. *Something's Got to Give*
9. Peggy Cummins	i. *For Whom the Bell Tolls*
10. Joan Crawford	j. *The Wizard of Oz*

82. For each film, which cast member played the title role?

1. *Test Pilot:* Clark Gable OR Spencer Tracy?

2. *Libeled Lady:* Jean Harlow OR Myrna Loy?

3. *The Old Maid:* Bette Davis OR Miriam Hopkins?

4. *My Darling Clementine:* Linda Darnell OR Cathy Downs?

5. *The Lady Vanishes:* May Whitty OR Margaret Lockwood?

6. *A Date with Judy:* Elizabeth Taylor OR Jane Powell?

7. *Cat Ballou:* Jane Fonda OR Lee Marvin?

8. *Roberta:* Irene Dunne OR Helen Westley?

9. *Becket:* Peter O'Toole OR Richard Burton?

10. *Mister 880:* Burt Lancaster OR Edmund Gwenn?

83. Match the star to the director who helmed his/her screen debut.

1. Marlon Brando	a. Alfred Hitchcock
2. Lauren Bacall	b. Rouben Mamoulian
3. William Holden	c. George Cukor
4. Ann-Margret	d. Howard Hawks
5. Burt Lancaster	e. Lewis Milestone
6. Shirley MacLaine	f. Frank Capra
7. Kirk Douglas	g. William Wyler
8. Jack Lemmon	h. Fred Zinnemann
9. Barbra Streisand	i. John Ford
10. Spencer Tracy	j. Robert Siodmak

84. Match the film or Shakespearean play on the left to its westernized remake, sometimes loosely, sometimes unofficially, but unmistakably.

1. *Captains Courageous*	a. *Colorado Territory*
2. *The Asphalt Jungle*	b. *Broken Lance*
3. *Rashomon*	c. *Jubal*
4. *Yojimbo*	d. *Cattle Drive*
5. *The Seven Samurai*	e. *The Outrage*
6. *High Sierra*	f. *Barricade* (1950)
7. *House of Strangers*	g. *The Badlanders*
8. *The Sea Wolf*	h. *Yellow Sky*
9. *The Tempest*	i. *The Magnificent Seven*
10. *Othello*	j. *A Fistful of Dollars*

85. Match the play or musical on the left to the film in which it is being rehearsed and/or performed.

1. *Footsteps on the Ceiling*	a. *Hangover Square*
2. *A Gentleman's Gentleman*	b. *The Prince and the Showgirl*
3. *Femme Trouble*	c. *Valley of the Dolls*
4. *Tempest and Sunshine*	d. *Show Boat* (1951)
5. *Gay Love*	e. *Flirtation Walk*
6. *Hit the Sky*	f. *Torch Song*
7. *Evening with Jenny*	g. *All About Eve*
8. *The Coconut Girl*	h. *White Christmas*
9. *The Golden Bough*	i. *A Double Life*
10. *Playing Around*	j. *Morning Glory*

The Answers

1.	2.	3.	4.*	5.
1-H	1-D	1-H	1-G	1-I
2-E	2-A	2-F	2-H	2-H
3-D	3-H	3-A	3-C	3-G
4-B	4-G	4-I	4-E	4-E
5-F	5-B	5-G	5-B	5-C
6-C	6-E	6-B	6-J	6-F
7-A	7-I	7-J	7-I	7-A
8-J	8-C	8-E	8-D	8-J
9-G	9-F	9-C	9-A	9-D
10-I	10-J	10-D	10-F	10-B

*Note: Robert Francis died at age 25.

6.	7.**	8.	9.	10.
1-C	1-H	1-G	1-D	1-H
2-G	2-G	2-E	2-F	2-E
3-F	3-E	3-D	3-C	3-D
4-H	4-A	4-C	4-E	4-F
5-A	5-J	5-A	5-B	5-I
6-I	6-B	6-J	6-H	6-B
7-J	7-C	7-I	7-I	7-A
8-B	8-F	8-B	8-J	8-J
9-E	9-I	9-F	9-G	9-G
10-D	10-D	10-H	10-A	10-C

**Note: Only Baxter's performance won. Schell got a lead Oscar for
Judgment at Nuremburg.

11.	12.	13.	14.	15.
1-H	1-C	1-I	1-B	1-D
2-C	2-E	2-G	2-H	2-F
3-I	3-F	3-E	3-E	3-B
4-G	4-A	4-J	4-J	4-J
5-F	5-H	5-B	5-F	5-C
6-B	6-J	6-A	6-G	6-I
7-D	7-I	7-C	7-A	7-A
8-A	8-B	8-H	8-C	8-E
9-J	9-D	9-F	9-I	9-G
10-E	10-G	10-D	10-D	10-H

16.	17.	18.	19.	20.***
1-G	1-E	1-J	1-G	1-J
2-E	2-J	2-E	2-J	2-D
3-A	3-I	3-B	3-D	3-E
4-C	4-G	4-F	4-B	4-B
5-B	5-F	5-C	5-I	5-G
6-H	6-D	6-A	6-F	6-I
7-F	7-C	7-D	7-A	7-F
8-I	8-H	8-G	8-E	8-A
9-J	9-B	9-I	9-C	9-C
10-D	10-A	10-H	10-H	10-H

***Note: Horton and Hale repeated their original roles.

21.	22.	23.	24.	25.
1-D	1-G	1-B	1-C	1-H
2-C	2-D	2-A	2-G	2-F
3-H	3-H	3-G	3-E	3-G
4-F	4-C	4-E	4-A	4-B
5-A	5-J	5-I	5-I	5-D
6-J	6-A	6-H	6-H	6-J
7-E	7-E	7-D	7-D	7-E
8-G	8-F	8-J	8-B	8-A
9-B	9-B	9-C	9-J	9-C
10-I	10-I	10-F	10-F	10-I

26.	27.	28.	29.	30.
1-C	1-G	1-I	1-E	1-C
2-F	2-E	2-D	2-D	2-E
3-D	3-A	3-B	3-I	3-D
4-G	4-J	4-E	4-G	4-I
5-B	5-B	5-F	5-H	5-F
6-A	6-D	6-C	6-F	6-J
7-I	7-C	7-G	7-B	7-B
8-J	8-F	8-A	8-J	8-A
9-H	9-I	9-J	9-C	9-H
10-E	10-H	10-H	10-A	10-G

31.	32.	33.	34.	35.
1-F (Katharine Hepburn)	1-B (Marilyn Monroe)	1-G	1-C	1-G
2-E (Dolores Gray)	2-E (Ella Raines)	2-D	2-G	2-D
3-D (Audrey Hepburn)	3-D (Jean Simmons)	3-J	3-F	3-F
4-G (Kelly, Hayworth, Silvers)	4-H (Cary Grant)	4-I	4-B	4-B
5-H (Clark Gable)	5-G (Gloria Grahame)	5-B	5-E	5-C
6-C	6-C (Vivien Leigh)	6-H	6-I	6-A
7-I (Spencer Tracy)	7-J (Rosalind Russell)	7-E	7-A	7-J
8-J (Charlie Chaplin)	8-A (Ingrid Bergman)	8-A	8-D	8-I
9-A (Bette Davis)	9-F (Paulette Goddard)	9-C	9-J	9-E
10-B (Spencer Tracy)	10-I (Betty Grable)	10-F	10-H	10-H

36.	37.	38.	39.	40.
1-D	1-D	1-C	1-D	1-A
2-A	2-B	2-A	2-B	2-C
3-F	3-A	3-B	3-A	3-B
4-E	4-C	4-C	4-C	4-D
5-H	5-B	5-C	5-A	5-C
6-G	6-C	6-B	6-B	6-B
7-C	7-A	7-C	7-C	7-D
8-J	8-D	8-A	8-D	8-B
9-B	9-B	9-D	9-B	9-A
10-I	10-C	10-A	10-D	10-C

41.	42.	43.	44.	45.
1-A	1-B	1-C	1-B	1-A
2-D	2-G	2-J	2-C	2-C
3-C	3-I	3-E	3-A	3-C
4-D	4-F	4-H	4-D	4-B
5-B	5-C	5-B	5-B	5-B
6-B	6-J	6-A	6-C	6-D
7-A	7-D	7-D	7-A	7-B
8-C	8-A	8-G	8-C	8-A
9-C	9-E	9-I	9-D	9-D
10-B	10-H	10-F	10-A	10-C

46.	47.	48.	49.	50.
1-C	1-C	1-G	1-D	1-A
2-E	2-J	2-F	2-G	2-B
3-F	3-I	3-D	3-F	3-B
4-J	4-H	4-B	4-J	4-A
5-G	5-A	5-A	5-H	5-A
6-I	6-D	6-H	6-I	6-B
7-A	7-G	7-J	7-A	7-B
8-B	8-F	8-C	8-E	8-A
9-D	9-E	9-E	9-B	9-A
10-H	10-B	10-I	10-C	10-B

51.	52.	53.	54.	55.
1-H	1-J	1-D	1-H (the dead guy)	1-D
2-F	2-I	2-A	2-C (William Bendix's rival)	2-E
3-D	3-H	3-B	3-E (the dead guy)	3-G
4-B	4-A	4-C	4-G (Mary Boland's new husband)	4-B
5-G	5-D	5-B	5-F (the guy everyone's looking for)	5-F
6-A	6-C	6-A	6-B (Bette Davis' friend)	6-A
7-J	7-B	7-C	7-A (Ingrid Bergman's dead aunt)	7-I
8-I	8-E	8-D	8-D (Frank Morgan's wife)	8-H
9-E	9-F	9-A	9-J (Cary Grant is mistaken for him)	9-J
10-C	10-G	10-D	10-I (Nancy Kelly's killer mother)	10-C

56.	57.	58.	59.	60.
1-G	1-D	1-A	1-H	1-G
2-I	2-F	2-B	2-C	2-C
3-D	3-I	3-B	3-G	3-E
4-J	4-B	4-A	4-A	4-A
5-B	5-C	5-B	5-E	5-H
6-A	6-J	6-A	6-I	6-I
7-C	7-A	7-A	7-B	7-D
8-E	8-G	8-B	8-F	8-B
9-H	9-E	9-A	9-J	9-J
10-F	10-H	10-B	10-D	10-F

61.	62.	63.	64.	65.
1-D	1-H	1-J	1-D	1-D
2-F	2-F	2-G	2-J	2-C
3-C	3-D	3-D	3-F	3-G
4-G	4-G	4-H	4-I	4-F
5-J	5-E	5-I	5-G	5-B
6-B	6-B	6-A	6-C	6-A
7-A	7-A	7-F	7-A	7-I
8-E	8-I	8-C	8-H	8-E
9-I	9-J	9-B	9-B	9-J
10-H	10-C	10-E	10-E	10-H

66.	67.	68.	69.	70.
1-C	1-C (Clifton Webb)	1-D	1-F	1-H
2-J	2-F (George Peppard)	2-J	2-C	2-C
3-E	3-I (June Allyson)	3-F	3-H	3-F
4-A	4-G (Robin Hughes)	4-B	4-A	4-A
5-D	5-B (Gregory Peck)	5-H	5-I	5-J
6-I	6-D (Joseph Cotten)	6-A	6-B	6-D
7-B	7-A (Cornel Wilde)	7-G	7-D	7-I
8-G	8-J (Cliff Robertson)	8-I	8-G	8-E
9-F	9-E (Walter Matthau)	9-C	9-J	9-G
10-H	10-H (Fredric March)	10-E	10-E	10-B

71.	72.	73.	74.	75.
1-I	1-G	1-B	1-F	1-J
2-D	2-C	2-A	2-C	2-G
3-A	3-H	3-B	3-I	3-E
4-J	4-E	4-A	4-D	4-H
5-C	5-B	5-A	5-G	5-B
6-G	6-A	6-B	6-E	6-A
7-B	7-J	7-B	7-J	7-C
8-E	8-I	8-A	8-A	8-D
9-H	9-F	9-A	9-B	9-F
10-F	10-D	10-B	10-H	10-I

76.	77.	78.	79.	80.
1-G	1-B	1-D	1-E	1-G
2-H	2-F	2-F	2-G	2-F
3-E	3-G	3-A	3-F	3-C
4-A	4-E	4-H	4-D	4-A
5-D	5-J	5-G	5-C	5-H
6-F	6-A	6-C	6-B	6-B
7-B	7-C	7-J	7-I	7-D
8-I	8-H	8-E	8-J	8-I
9-J	9-D	9-B	9-A	9-J
10-C	10-I	10-I	10-H	10-E

81.	82.	83.	84.	85.
1-D (illness)	1-CG	1-H *(The Men)*	1-D	1-G
2-E (death)	2-ML	2-D *(To Have and Have Not)*	2-G	2-I
3-F (death)	3-BD	3-B *(Golden Boy)*	3-E	3-E
4-J (illness)	4-CD	4-F *(Pocketful of Miracles)*	4-J	4-D
5-I (inadequacy)	5-MW	5-J *(The Killers)*	5-I	5-A
6-B (shutdown)	6-JP	6-A *(The Trouble with Harry)*	6-A	6-C
7-A (illness)	7-JF	7-E *(The Strange Love of Martha Ivers)*	7-B	7-F
8-H (unprofessionalism)	8-HW	8-C *(It Should Happen to You)*	8-F	8-B
9-C (inadequacy)	9-RB	9-G *(Funny Girl)*	9-H	9-J
10-G (illness)	10-EG	10-I *(Up the River)*	10-C	10-H

OTHER BOOKS BY JOHN DILEO
from Hansen Publishing Group

Screen Savers: 40 Remarkable Movies Awaiting Rediscovery

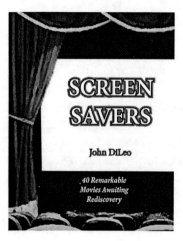

Spanning titles and eras from *The Student Prince in Old Heidelberg* (1927) to *Three Kings* (1999), **Screen Savers: 40 Remarkable Movies Awaiting Rediscovery** by John DiLeo is not the typical collection of nostalgia-minded movie reviews. DiLeo provides such detailed analyses and enlightening critiques that readers will finish the book eager to view all of the forty films featured in his third and latest book. Moviegoers of all persuasions will discover fresh spins on the careers of famous stars and new insights into the screen's essential genres.

Paperback $24.95 • ISBN 978-1-60182-654-1 • 360 pages
eBook $9.95 • available for the Kindle, the Nook, and the iPad

Tennessee Williams and Company: His Essential Screen Actors

Tennessee Williams and Company: His Essential Screen Actors takes a critical look at eleven actors and their roles, bonded by their sustained artistic and professional association with Tennessee Williams, specifically the success, and sometimes failure, of their interpretations of his characters for the screen. The results include some of the more remarkable performances in movie history, from Marlon Brando and Vivien Leigh in *A Streetcar Named Desire* to Anna Magnani in *The Rose Tattoo* and Geraldine Page in *Sweet Bird of Youth*.

Paperback $25.95 • ISBN 978-1-60182-423-3 • 214 pages
eBook $9.95 • available for the Kindle, the Nook, and the iPad

About the Author

Photograph: Lynne Bookey

John DiLeo's first book was *And You Thought You Knew Classic Movies!* (St. Martin's, 1999), hailed by Pauline Kael as "the smartest movie quiz book I've ever seen." His second book was *100 Great Film Performances You Should Remember—But Probably Don't* (Limelight Editions, 2002), which Adolph Green called "a valuable and touching work." TCM host Robert Osborne said, in the *Hollywood Reporter,* that the book "delightfully throws the spotlight on some remarkable film work," and the *Washington Post's* reaction was, "Not only is this helpful criticism, but *100 Great Film Performances* can serve as balm for anyone who has ever been disgruntled by the Academy's choices on Oscar night." Turner Classic Movies devoted a night of prime-time programming to films featured in John's third book, *Screen Savers: 40 Remarkable Movies Awaiting Rediscovery* (Hansen Publishing Group, 2007). His fourth film book, *Tennessee Williams and Company: His Essential Screen Actors* (Hansen Publishing Group, 2010), led to his presentations and panels at the Tennessee Williams festivals in Provincetown and New Orleans. Essays by him appear in two anthologies, *City Secrets Movies: The Ultimate Insider's Guide* (2009) and *City Secrets Books: The Essential Insider's Guide* (2009). John has been a contributing book reviewer for the *Washington Post* and currently writes DVD and film-book reviews for multiple publications. He frequently hosts classic-film series, appears on radio programs, lectures on cruise ships, conducts film-history seminars, and has been an annual participant in the Black Bear Film Festival (Milford, PA) where he interviewed Farley Granger (2005), Arlene Dahl (2006), and Marge Champion (2010) on the festival's stage. His website is johndileo.com and his blog is screensaversmovies.com. Born in 1961 in Brooklyn, John was raised on Long Island and graduated from Ithaca College in 1982 with a B.F.A. After 27 years together, he married partner Earl McCarroll in 2009 in MA.